THE WAY OF
THE NEW WORLD
The Black Novel in America

". . . We want a Black Poem, And a Black World.
Let the world be a Black poem . . ."

We'll become owners of the   New World
the   New World
will run it as unowners
for
we will live in it too
& will want to be remembered
as   realpeople.

Don L. Lee

THE
WAY OF THE
NEW WORLD

The Black Novel in America

———◆———

Addison Gayle, Jr.

ANCHOR PRESS/DOUBLEDAY
GARDEN CITY, NEW YORK
1975

Grateful acknowledgment is made for the use of the following material: Poem by Imamu Baraka. Reprinted from *An Anthology of Afro-American Writing*, edited by Leroi Jones and Larry Neal, by permission of Mr. Baraka's agent and Larry Neal.
Poem by Don L. Lee. Reprinted by permission of the publisher, Broadside Press.

Library of Congress Cataloging in Publication Data

Gayle, Addison, 1932–
    The way of the new world.

    Bibliography: p. 325
    1. American fiction—Negro authors—History and criticism.   2. Negroes in literature.   I. Title.
PS374.N4G3   813′.03
ISBN 0-385-04103-9
Library of Congress Catalog Card Number 74–9449

In Memoriam: For *David Llorens*

CONTENTS

INTRODUCTION

Questions concerning the function of literature and the role of the artist in society are as old as the dialogues of Plato. Yet such questions received little consideration from the African-American writer until the twentieth century. Early black writers, forced into daily combat with an almost completely closed society, believed that the function of literature and the role of the artist were similar: Literature was an instrument to be used in warfare against an oppressive society; it was, also, the medium that allowed the black writer to serve as interpreter between the Black and white society. The dual roles—that of the writer as combatant and that of literature as a weapon in the struggle for human freedom—have received condemnation over the years from critics, black and white, and led to accusations such as those forwarded by Allen Tate that the black writer has been limited "to a provincial mediocrity in which feelings about one's difficulties become more important than [literature] itself."[1]

Most African-American critics have been less dogmatic and more analytical than Tate. If the function of literature is to deal with the conditions under which men live—to analyze the effects of a hostile environment upon the human personality, then the proper label for such works, according to some critics, is "sociology." This attempt to define literature by pointing out what it is not has led Ralph Ellison to argue that "People who want to write sociology should not write a novel."[2] Literature, pure artifact, is thus stripped of all save metaphors, myths, images, and symbols, and presented to us without substance or body, dazzling us not with the concreteness of message, but with the magic of words: ". . . If a moral or perception is needed," writes Ellison, "let them [the readers] supply their own. For me, of course, the narrative is the meaning."

Not surprisingly, the white critics have preferred Ellison's pronunciations to those of Tate, for black literature has presented obstacles difficult to overcome. If there is no such dichotomy as Ellison proposes—between sociology and literature—the white critic faces a serious dilemma. The literary artifact must be viewed as something more than form, something more than mechanical construct, which, concerned with the social, economic, and political ideas of the times, mandates the kind of exploration suggested by B. Traven. In a little recognized comment upon his own work, Traven admits that he cannot write about people, places, or things, of which he has little intimacy or direct knowledge: "I must have seen the things, landscapes, and persons, myself, before I can bring them to life in my works. . . . It is necessary for me to have been afraid almost to madness before I can describe terror; I must myself suffer all sadness and heartache before I can visit suffering on the figures which I have called into life."[3]

Despite the differing functions between literature and criticism, Traven's remarks retain their import for both. The critic, the cultivator of the soil in which the best ideas might be nurtured, like the novelist, must possess a pervasive grasp of his subject, must know the landscape, the valleys, hedges, highways, and byways of the human soul. Only such knowledge enables him to evaluate the works of others. Unless one is to view literary criticism as an exact science, James Baldwin's comments in this respect have meaning for writer and critic alike, for one writes out of one thing only, his own experiences.

Ellison, on the other hand, argues that one writes out of other books—a view, which, if correct, defines literature as pure artifact and literary criticism as exact science. This definition gained modern import from the writings of the Agrarian critics of the nineteen twenties and thirties, who sought to establish rules for literary criticism which conformed to criterion established by an intellectual elite, designed to satisfy those for whom literature as history and sociology demanded too great a commitment to the world of practical experience. Those critics, whose chief nourishment has been "other books," turned from Baldwin to Ellison and received a much needed reprieve. For to evaluate the literary artifacts of black people from Phillis Wheatley to Don L. Lee entails little more than knowledge of the rudimentary aspects of literary criticism; to evaluate the black novel, for example, requires only such technical knowledge as that concerning plot, language, setting, and conflict.

These are the major elements in the new criticism forwarded by the Agrarian critics, and their modern-day followers have failed to recognize their limitations. The Agrarian critics did their best work in poetry, a genre which more readily lends itself to verbal gymnastics. In evaluating drama and the novel, the critics failed miserably, due to the complexity of the experiences which these two genres contained—experiences which supersede the form that contains them. Such genres are not autotelic, reach outside of themselves, feed upon the tensions in a universe alive with joy, despair, passivity, and rebellion; one where man, mammoth no longer, pits his feeble strength against the forces of his society, wanders from the planet Earth to the solar system in a never-ending quest to attain that which the followers of the Agrarians would deny him—the knowledge of human existence and purpose.

To define literature in terms of pure artifact, therefore, to evaluate it by methods applicable to science and technology, would make of every novel, poem, or play a hodgepodge of gibberish and would reduce each writer to the stature of a player in the witches' chorus in *Macbeth,* who, securely nestled upon his own tower of Babel, cackles ceaselessly, in tongues unintelligible to those who hold no magic key. Not autotelic, the novel, like its sister genres, depends upon the creative genius of the author, which, heightened by political, social, and historical factors, depicts the experiences of man and, reaching beyond form and structure, communicates with men everywhere. The novel is the one genre which attempts in dramatic and narrative form to answer the questions, What are we? and What is it all about?

These are social questions. They comprise such an essential part of the makeup of the novel that the evaluation of such novels requires an understanding of the social, political, and historical forces which produced them. What, asks Ellison, do we know of Sophocles' wounds? The answer is nothing. Yet to know of Sophocles' wounds might shed new light on *Oedipus Rex.* We know something of the wounds of Dostoevsky, Kafka, and Richard Wright, and as a result their works take on added significance.

Individual wounds are one thing. What does one make of racial wounds, those that make of one black man a black everyman, that hold meaning for each member of the race, that allow each black man, when confronted with injustice enacted against another, to avow that there, but for the grace of some God, go I. What does one make of such wounds buried, covertly or overtly, within the literary format? "I snuck the racial thing in," remarks Frank Yerby. What formula will enable the critic to evaluate literature replete with the effects of such wounds? One turns in answer to the real meaning of Traven's remarks, for to understand madness is to be a bit mad, to understand the Jewish experience, the Russian experience, the Chinese experience, is to be Jewish, Russian, and Chinese. No white man, argues Claude McKay, could have written my books. The message is clear: To evaluate the life and culture of black people, it is necessary that one live the black experience in a world where substance is more important than form, where the social takes precedence over the aesthetic, where each act, gesture, and movement is political, and where continual rebellion separates the insane from the sane, the robot from the revolutionary.

The history of Africans in America is one of rebellion and revolution, and the novelist who finds meaning in their survival upon this continent must be cognizant of the social, political, and historical milieu from which the necessity for rebellion springs. This is truer for the critic, who remains the final adjudicator. If he is to adequately separate truth from distortion, to pass judgment upon those who seek to create and recreate the artifacts of the racial past, he must be aware of those forces that have produced a distinctive history and a distinctive culture.

Ignoring their own history and culture, the early black writers attempted to create a literature patterned upon that of whites. With the possible exception of Martin Delany, the world of the early novelists—William Wells Brown, Frank Webb, and Francis Ellen Watkins—and that of the poets—Phillis Wheatley, Jupiter Hammon, and George Moses Horton—was modeled upon that of such Anglo-Saxons as Pope, Carlyle, Mills, and Byron. They were—Webb excepted—abolitionists, who, in fighting the cause of emancipation, adopted almost in total the mannerisms, language, and world view of their white allies. Influences from masters and abolitionist allies pushed the writers toward romanticism at a time when it was becoming the plaything of adolescents and led them to believe, that is, in the eventual assimilation of white and black cultures.

As a result they did not attempt to recreate legends of the past, create symbols, images, and metaphors anew, nor provide literary vehicles by which men, out of the marrow of suffering, might be redeemed in myth if not in actuality; instead, they either accepted the propaganda of their detractors or burned their talents into ashes in attempts to refute them. They became the first proponents of the assimilation philosophy and helped to transform the Gabriel Prossers, Sojourner Truths, and Frederick Douglasses into Uncle Toms, Mingoes, and Aunt Sues. The courageous men and women who set examples for Blacks yet unborn, by stealing away from slavery, murdering masters and overseers, and committing untold acts of rebellion against the slave system, find little recognition in their poems and novels.

Yet, these writers were black men and women, and in their breasts, if sometimes only feebly, also dwelled the hell-fire of revolt. How then does one account for the failure of their works, for their commitment to the romantic dream, for their inability to come to grips with the fundamental realities of the society in which they lived? The answer is that they were firsts—those who came to maturity in the early decades of the republic. For them, the period between 1800 and 1865 was one in which slavery presented the major conundrum, a solution to which was viewed as a solution to the over-all problem between Blacks and whites. They knew no world other than that divided through sectional strife, centered around the conflict of slavery, and America, at that period of time, appeared as innocent to them, as it would later to such men as Henry James and Van Wyck Brooks.

America was a nation yet to be born and, despite slavery, the romantic belief was shared equally among the early writers that once slavery had ended, a better world would be erected upon the debris of the old. One finds this sense of innocence in the speeches of Douglass between 1863–65, in the poetry of Wheatley, the novels of Brown and Webb. For these writers, the new frontier lay beyond the boundaries erected by slavery; the new world was to be born on the seventh day of emancipation, the second coming ushered in by the last rifle shot fired in the "irrepressible conflict." Upon such a romantic foundation they constructed literature doomed to extinction in the years following Appomattox, and it is not surprising that during the fateful years of Reconstruction no major work is produced among them. Having failed to interpret American reality, they were jolted by the fact that the demise of slavery did not produce the new society, that the black man's condition was not appreciably altered. The America seen through the eyes of Thomas Jefferson, Henry David Thoreau, Ralph Waldo Emerson, and Walt Whitman was one which neither they nor their progeny were ever to know.

This failure to understand the country in which they lived produced an unfounded reservoir of hope and faith in America and its people that pervades the black novel from 1853 to 1962. The American dream, as set forth in legal documents, might become real if only certain blemishes upon the body politic were eradicated. Few questioned the thesis that the blemishes were part of the society's character and being, that the legal documents were the creations of men— Jefferson and Washington—for example, themselves corrupted by the issue of prejudice and racism. Failure to realize such facts led black people and black writers alike to visualize a world to be after the apocalpyse—a theme which pervades African-American literature.

Each period—slavery, Reconstruction, early and late twentieth century—has its version of the apocalypse, each its Rubicon which must be forded, crossed, before the period of universal brotherhood, not to mention true creativity, is possible. One apocalypse gives way to another; one Rubicon is but a tributary stream, flowing, merging eventually with the other. The demise of slavery produced segregation and discrimination; the legal ending of segregation and discrimination produced economic and social problems of a magnitude as great as that of slavery and legal segregation. The first writers, therefore, were pioneers, foraging in the literary underbrush, believing always that reality was not what existed at the moment. They were literary visionaries: Brown, Delany, and Webb of one sort; Charles Chesnutt, Paul Laurence Dunbar, and Sutton Griggs of another. Each maintained a common belief and faith that America, after periods of overwhelming darkness, would lift the veil and eternal sunshine would prevail.

We do not know at what point this thesis first came under serious questioning. Martin Delany in *The Condition, Elevation, Emigration and Destiny of the Colored People of the United States* (1852) evidenced cynicism concerning American ideals and pretensions, some of which pervades his novel, *Blake; or the Huts of America* (1859). After two full-length novels designed to change the thinking of white men in regard to their treatment of Blacks, Charles Chesnutt evidences a sense of hopelessness in his final novel, *The Colonel's Dream* (1905). Paul Laurence Dunbar, more optimistic in fiction than in poetry, nevertheless, interjects a note of foreboding and despair in his final novel, *The Sport of the Gods* (1902). Serious, sustained questioning of American ideals by a sizable number of black writers does not occur until the late twentieth century, after the Supreme Court decision in Brown versus Board of Education, Topeka, Kansas (1954), the freedom riders, the crusades of Martin Luther King, Jr., and the rebellions in New York, California, Illinois, and Michigan. Re-examination, however, begins during the Harlem Renaissance, when black writers achieved success in the novel genre, both in terms of technical progress and readership acceptance.

This re-examination, never completed, was spurred in part by the Garvey movement, in part by the Pan-Africanism of W. E. B. Du Bois, and in part by a growing intellectual class, differing in educational attainments from their counterparts in the nineteenth century. William Wells Brown, Frederick Douglass, Jupiter Hammon, and Frank Webb were educated in the university of hard knocks; Alain Locke and W. E. B. Du Bois were educated at Harvard, Langston Hughes at Columbia, and James Weldon Johnson at Atlanta and Columbia. There was, in addition, the factor of time. The second coming was overdue by one hundred years—a long time had elapsed between the nineteen twenties, the beginning of the Renaissance years, and the day in 1865 when Douglass, with a group of well-wishers, awaited news of the issuance of the Emancipation Proclamation. The dream, in short, had been too long deferred. The "Great Migration," which by 1920 resembled a small-scaled avalanche, was important in bringing about re-examination of the perceptions held by Blacks in regard to society, and the exodus of men, women, and children from the South had a profound effect upon black literature in general and the novel in particular. Unlike some of their more prosperous brothers, those who came north, following the great migration, were driven from their homes as a result of attacks by mobs, economic exploitation, and execution without benefit of trial by judge and jury. Langston Hughes sums up their hopes and disappointments in *The Dream Deferred:* "I've seen them come dark wondering/wide-eyed/dreaming out of Penn Station/. . . The gates open—but there are bars/at each gate."

The North failed to provide a locale and social climate much different from that of the region which they had fled. Many, as a result, soon came to surrender the American dream, to despair of ever witnessing a second coming upon these shores, and in protest and disillusionment, swelled the ranks of the new prophets—Marcus Garvey, Father Divine, and Bishop Grace. Their new-found disillusionment created new difficulties for the novelist. The yardstick of measurement by which change is recorded must, in the final analysis, be those for whom the system has not worked at all. Yet to accept these as the criterion of measurement is to suggest that the system cannot work, that the world envisioned by the earlier black writers and intellectuals was impossible of being brought into being.

The intellectuals of the Renaissance period attempted to deal with this difficulty by reverting to romanticism. They argued that the problem was not that American society could not work for Blacks, but only that it had not been sorely tested. Resentful of the dilemma proposed in the persons of the unlettered, primarily dark and poor migrants from the South, they sought to buttress their contention by postulating a questionable thesis structured upon the theory of the blessed and the damned. Initiated early in the novel, *The Garies and Their Friends,* this thesis suggested that the denominator man was more important than the numerator Black, that the society envisioned in the Constitution was possible of attainment by those who equaled their white counterparts in terms of culture and material acquisition.

The theory divided black men along lines first devised by ingenious slaveholders, and the result of the schism accounts for much of the tension between black intellectuals and the black middle class in the nineteen seventies. Reacting, in part, against the division, Langston Hughes in "The Negro Artist and the Racial Mountain" struck a proletarian note in 1925: "But then there are the low-down folks, the so-called common element, and they are the majority—may the Lord be praised." These common folk, distinguished by their unashamed adoration for such black artifacts as the spirituals and the blues, were those who had either survived the exodus themselves or children of those who had survived. In their refusal to follow the assimilationist route, they were, for the artist, those upon whom a viable literature might be founded, for they held "their own individuality in the face of American standardization."[4]

"The Negro Artist and the Racial Mountain" is among the more significant critical documents written during the Renaissance years. Hughes suggested that the black writer confront the problem posed by a loss of faith in American society, not by creating divisions, but by rewriting the formula that defined the function and objectives of African-American literature. Return to William Wells Brown and Jupiter Hammon and the function of writer and work alike remain unchanged by most of their early twentieth-century counterparts: Literature is a weapon in the quest for black freedom, and the author is the interpreter of the ways of black folk to white folk. Hughes paid scant attention to the first supposition but sought to restructure the second. Empathizing with the new migrants to a degree impossible for most writers of the period, and knowing that their disillusionment had sunk deep indeed, he dreamed of a literature to describe accurately their hopes, fears, and anxieties, one to truthfully depict their experiences. He knew, contrary to Richard Wright's suppositions some forty years hence, that black people did not understand the meaning of their lives, were not cognizant of the rich cultural and historical milieu from whence they came, and that the black writer should waste little time and energy in directing his works to audiences composed of whites and the black middle class.

Thus, despite his difficulty in living up to his own prescriptions, Hughes demanded more important objectives from the black writer than had been demanded previously. The role of ambassador to the white world was to be exchanged by that of teacher to the black. The advocate for racial justice and democracy was to become the Lycurgus to the black masses; the entertainer to whites and the black middle class was to become the analyzer and explicator of African-American culture here and abroad. Not surprisingly, therefore, Jean Toomer, caroling softly, journeys back to the southland, the first home away from home, though despairingly, Countee Cullen broaches the question, "What is Africa to me?" Rudolph Fisher and Claude McKay look with critical eyes upon a Harlem struggling to be born; Arna

Bontemps views the history of Haiti and America; Langston Hughes describes, in fiction, the ways of white folks.

Yet, literature directed toward explicating the lives of "the low-down folk" held dangers which the Renaissance men could not foresee. To deal truthfully with the history, culture, and sociology of the black masses is to deal openly with anger and resentment expressed in unabashed terms. To accurately analyze the life-style of the poor and embittered Blacks who followed Marcus Garvey and Sufi Abdul, the writer had to attack the false premise upon which the middle class and the romantics had structured their cosmology. From the vantage point of the migrants, America was desperately in need of revolution, and the writer who sought to function as their amanuensis would have to record this desire for violent change. That *Native Son* (1940) is the most celebrated novel of the post-Renaissance years evidences the black writer's disregard of the dangers inherent in accepting a new function for the black writer.

Native Son remains the most controversial book written by an African-American. Attacks upon the novel and its author have ranged from the hysterical utterances of Communists, to the bemused, bewildered comments of white liberal critics, and to the apologia of such black writers as James Baldwin and Ralph Ellison. The black and white critics—the Communists excluded—have this in common: an unbending faith in the American dream and an assumption that, despite the failure of Americans to live up to the ideals of justice and equality, hope should still spring eternally in the breast of the African-American. *Native Son* is not a novel for the hopeful or the faithful, but one which results from the inability of men to fulfill the tenets of their own tables of the law. It was written during a period of history wherein mass murder symbolized the moral depravity of Western man. It was written at a time when the incarceration of men of different skin color, ideas, and religion was the rule, in Europe and America as well. It is a novel which illuminates the reality of its time.

It succeeds, also, on a much more fundamental level, undoing the work of black novelists heretofore, pointing out the dangerous consequences of romanticism and unlimited faith in an America of the future, and calling for a total restructuring of the society along egalitarian lines. It mandates that black people forsake abstractionism and dedicate themselves to the possible. It avers that if Bigger Thomas, black everyman, is to be saved, he will not be saved in an integrated country in which each man walks the path of justice, equality, and brotherhood. Such postulates were difficult for the ideological descendants of Frederick Douglass to embrace. To accept Wright's thesis in total means to forego the attempt to achieve the integrated society. It means, moreover, that Blacks who seek a sense of their own self-worth must dedicate themselves either to nihilism or revolution. For the most part, the black writer walked the ambivalent line between Wright's postulates and those adhered to by Douglass' ideological kinsmen, despite Wright's own insistence that if the African-American writer was to serve as a "purposeful agent" of his people, he would have to create those values by which they were "to live and die."

Yet, Wright and his followers, Chester Himes, William Gardner Smith, and Ann Petry, were the first black literary iconoclasts, modern-day Zarathustras, determined to bury the old dead god and his ideas. By nineteen-sixty they had succeeded in changing the course of the African-American novel, moving it in the direction that the younger writers of the Renaissance had wanted it to go. After Richard Wright, the novel of outright assimilationism and romanticism no longer appealed to a black reading audience. The novel that functioned as a vehicle for allaying the fears of whites and Blacks of some affluence was now the novel which depicted unadorned truth. When Chester Himes, writing of the hatred which each black man feels for his white countryman, assumed that much the same hatred forms part of the psychic makeup of the black writer as well and suggested that the real question for the writer was "How much does this hatred affect the Negro's personality?" he was signaling the end of the age of ambiguity and ushering in the age of truth—the age of the new black writer.

Before such a new writer could emerge, there were old plants to be plowed under; confrontations with old ideas and theories were necessary. Men who wage warfare with words must be conscious of the meaning of their existence. It is this that Richard Wright might have said to such detractors as James Baldwin, this that Langston Hughes might have said to the black bourgeois writers and their representatives who opposed him in the nineteen twenties—that to confront reality was to step outside of the realm of hate and fear, to posit a world far different from that vouchsafed by the Americans. The first step toward transforming reality is to admit the reality that exists at the moment. For only when black men have moved beyond romanticism and acknowledged the Bigger Thomas in their character, then and only then can the novelist truthfully explicate the world of black folks. It is this, in part, that the writers of the seventies have accomplished. They are indebted to Baldwin and Ellison in the same sense that the former are indebted to Attaway, Wright, and Himes, who in turn are indebted to the younger writers of the Renaissance. For the most part, each contributed to the steady eroding of the romanticism and futile faith which plagued their predecessors; each managed to purge himself of the hatred which consumed the works of many of the most talented of black writers. Acknowledging the existence of the Bigger Thomas living constantly in his skull, the black writer was capable of seeing newer visions, of moving back into the past, of coming to grips with the terrors and joys of those for whom visions of the river Jordan in days gone by were as bold, stark, and immediate as a newborn day.

In short, he embarked upon a new direction, and in so doing, repudiated the idea that the novel should be a vehicle for protest. He moved beyond the example of Richard Wright, seeing, more clearly than Du Bois, that the problem of the twentieth century centered upon power, not race. In the quest for power, the protest novel is a useless vehicle and the author who addresses himself to the power broker in obsequious, piteous pleadings and cajolings emphasizes his powerlessness. "I do not," wrote Richard Wright, "write for black people, but for whites," because whites know nothing of the problems confronting Blacks, whereas Blacks do. Read differently, the statement suggests that whites have the power to determine the destiny not only of the country, but of Blacks as well. The events of the nineteen sixties, however, evidence the fact that the white majority no longer has such frightening power.

On a hot summer night in 1965, the borough of Manhattan erupted in violence. Led by the young and the more defiant, men, women, and children took to the streets to articulate their grievances in terms almost too realistic for the printed page. Past and present merged as Molotov cocktails symbolized centuries of hostility transmitted from one generation to another. Before the decade of vengeance and redemption was over, Watts, Hough, Detroit, and Chicago had added their names to a period of American history different from any that had preceded it. In the ashes and rubble of the major urban centers of America, the black power revolt had its genesis, and "the Black Aesthetic," its cultural and literary arm, was an outgrowth of the same historical events.

Had the rebellions of the sixties not taken place, black literature in general, and the African-American novel in particular, may not have continued along the road paved by the younger members of the Renaissance, might have veered sharply from the path prescribed by Wright and his followers into art for art's sake, abstractionism, or surrealism. The baptism by fire and blood produced the catharsis, violent in nature, that gave birth to a new literary Renaissance.

Traditional plots in the black novel, situations, and character became anachronistic. Form, as defined by the Europeans beginning with Cervantes, refined by Henry Fielding and Tobias Smollet, and brought forward as an accomplished instrument by Jane Austen, James Joyce, and Marcel Proust, was no longer the form which the serious black novelist deemed necessary of emulation. The Blacks who came north in the early part of the twentieth century had undergone almost complete alteration, recognized and transformed the Bigger Thomases in their skulls, and arrived at a sense of political and social awareness which mandated new literary forms. The novels of the early writers, based upon the Euro-American tradition in form and content, became obsolete; such novels as *Invisible Man* hailed for formalistic innovation were more important in terms of content and message. (For many of the younger writers, Ellison's novel, in terms of form, was a refinement of the genre handed to the Western world by Cervantes.)

These younger writers were now able to divine the real forces at work in the society, to understand the power that dominated the lives of black people in ways that Wright could hardly imagine. The symbol of the twentieth century, wrote Wright, is the man on the corner with a machine gun, and Imamu Baraka asks, "Will the machine gunner please step forward?" At long last, form and structure were recognized as little more than cousins to content, and the black novelist, machine gunner in the cause of mankind, prepared to move forward in the most monumental undertaking of the twentieth century—the task of redefining the definitions, creating new myths, symbols, and images, articulating new values, and recording the progression of a great people from social and political awareness to consciousness of their historical importance as a people and as a nation within a nation—a task which demanded, in the words of poet Don L. Lee, that black people walk the way of the New World.

I

PARADIGMS OF
THE EARLY PAST

In the beginning was the word, and it was the word that proved the greatest obstacle for the black writer. Words, to be sure, may be used as weapons; they are, however, the property of protagonist and antagonist alike and, like an unfaithful woman, capable of serving two masters simultaneously. By 1853, the year of publication of *Clotel, or the President's Daughter,* the first novel written by a black man of American descent, the word, in the skillful hands of American propagandists, performed tasks comparable to those performed by leg irons, patrollers, overseers, and other paraphernalia of the institution of slavery. The word, or rather a conglomeration of words, preceded the "twenty neegars" who disembarked in Jamestown, Virginia, in 1614, and by the time of the Civil War had helped to change chattel slavery into mental slavery by convincing black men, as well as white, that African-Americans, representing only three fifths of complete human beings, had no rights which white men need respect. The prevailing sentiment of the time was stated by John Saffrin of Massachusetts, who evaluated "The Negroes character":

> Cowardly and cruel are those blacks innate
> Prone to Revenge, Imp of Inveterate hate,
> He that exasperates them; soon espies
> Mischief and Murder in their eyes.

Libidinous, Deceitful, False and Rude,
The spume issue of ingratitude.[1]

Whether the vehicle for the dissemination of such images was poetry,
prose, or fiction, the word was used to distort truth to an alarming
and dangerous degree. In part, this was due to the inability of the black
writer to retaliate in kind, to use the weapons of the oppressor in his
own defense. Stripped of his language, the symbols, images, and
metaphors which had sustained him in the faraway home, he was
forced, like a man come naked into the world, to measure himself by
yardsticks fashioned by others and to face the wilderness without the
most elemental of defenses—the capacity to utilize language to define
his own experiences. This task was entrusted to men of such varying
temperaments and professions as Thomas Jefferson, Cotton Mather,
John Saffrin, Albert Taylor Bledsoe, John C. Calhoun, and Abraham
Lincoln—men whose sentiments are more or less summed up in the
words of Samuel Sewall: "[There is] such a disparity in their Conditions, Colour, & Hair, that they can never embody with us and grow
into orderly Families, to the Peopling of the land; but still remain in
our Body Politick as a kind of extravasate Blood."[2]

Sewall, America's first white liberal, is early pinned upon the horns
of the dilemma which would impale his counterparts in coming years.
He desired release of the black Josephs from bondage on the one hand,
while, on the other, he desired equally to prevent them from exercising
the functions of human beings. He lived and wrote during the early
colonial period when liberalism was respectable, when agitation for
the demise of slavery was not uncommon. In but a few years, the
"peculiar institution" would begin to die of its own accord in the cities
and states along the eastern seaboard, and, even in the South, it would
cling precariously upon the precipice of extinction. This was nearly one
hundred years before Eli Whitney and the cotton gin, the instrument
bequeathed to the slaveholder as a rationale for continuing what
Thomas Nelson Page, peering from the rubble of the Civil War years,
later eulogized as the sweetest, purest life that ever existed.

Technology and language joined hands in the undertaking to control
black people by manipulation of words. The economic miracle, wrought
by the invention of the cotton gin, made more necessary the importa-
tion of slaves. More important, it mandated institutionalization of a
language system that would serve the twin purpose of rationaliz-
ing slavery and binding the slave mentally to the slavocracy. Techno-
crat, theologian, slave master, and man of letters joined in constructing
a cosmology that, in explaining the ways of God to man, served to com-

plete the task of robbing black people of their identity and making them totally dependent upon others for pictures of themselves.

It was necessary to justify slavery anew, and here, theologian, literary figure, and college president proved equal to the task. President William Drew of William and Mary College, writing in 1832, compared Blacks to animals, asserting an "order of nature" as justification for his charge that superior beings should not only control, but also "dispose of those who are inferior." More direct and to the point, John Burgess, Dean of Columbia University, reverted to a curious interpretation of natural law to justify the enslavement of an inferior race by a superior race and defined black men as those who had never subjected passion to reason, nor "created any civilization of any kind." Commenting upon the necessity for such sentiments, Milton Cantor has observed, "To treat the Negro brutally, it was necessary to find him less than a man; to find him a beast, a thing without a soul to lose. The goal was attainable, since the Negro was *sui generis* from the outset—different in color, language, religion, and appearance."[3] The usage of language to justify slavery was no more important, however, than its usage to convince the black man of his inferiority.

Go to John P. Kennedy, author of *Swallow Barn,* the first fruit of the Plantation school of literature, for the image of the happy, feeble-minded darky who inhabited the plantations of old. Read Kennedy and understand why those who tilled the soil from sun up til sundown, who suffered unbelievable acts of deprivation and abuse, maintained their simple-minded faith in God and white men. Go to Kennedy and we know why each plantation in fiction, as well as fact, was peopled with Aunties, Uncles, and Mammies, minstrel bands, and doting, obsequious slaves. Not content with merely enslaving black men, the Americans undertook the task of stripping him of all semblance of humanity and, like Kennedy, applying the word as skillfully as the surgeon might apply the scalpel, attempted to reduce the man to the status of child.

How quickly black people were seduced by the image makers can be seen in the works of two of the earliest writers, poets Phillis Wheatley and Jupiter Hammon. Wheatley, born in Senegal and purchased at a young age, achieved distinction as a poet in America and abroad. Hammon, slave of a New York family, is better known for his essay "An Address to the Negroes in the State of New York" (1787) than for his poetry. They are the first black writers to accept the images and symbols of degradation passed down from the South's most intellectual lights and the first to speak with a sensibility finely tuned by close approximation to their oppressors: "O come you pious youth!"

wrote Hammon in 1760, "Adore/The Wisdom of thy God/In bringing thee from distant shore/To learn his holy word." Wheatley with similar sentiments and almost the same terminology celebrates a like event: "Father of Mercy! T'was thy gracious hand/Brought me in safety from those dark abodes."

The pattern, established during the days of slavery, is revealed with clarity in the works of Daniel Webster Davis, educator and minister, writing in 1897, after the end of Reconstruction. That the pattern remains intact from Hammon to Davis is evidence of the success of America's first makers of images. "E'en in our slavery," Davis looks back, "we can trace the kindly hand of God/That took us from our sunny land and from our native sod/Where, clad in nature's simplest garb, man roamed a savage wild/Untamed his passions; half a man and half a savage child."[4] The magnitude of the problem confronting the black writer in the attempt to regain control over his images, symbols, and metaphors is revealed more explicitly in another poem attributed to Davis entitled *Common Sense:* "The time am ripe to take account/of whut we'se gwine t' do—/Is we a-aimin' to bus out/An' git us shot clean thu?/Or is we a'ter peaceful ways/Eroun de cabin do/To joy de white man's blessin/Fur now an' ebermo?"[5]

To Prospero's rationale, "I have taught you language," Caliban's reply was taunting and direct: "Better to curse you with." For black writers, given the example of Wheatley, Hammon, and Davis, the language of the oppressor was the vehicle for assimilating into white society the instrument which allowed one to "joy de white man's blessin." Push this sentiment to its logical conclusion and the desire is nothing less than to become the white man. Here, the truth of the philosopher Frantz Fanon is evidenced over one hundred years before his birth: The colonized yearns to become the colonizer, the slave, to become the master. Stripped of his own cultural identity, the black writer in the main succumbed to a system of language designed to prove that the black man was "half a man and half a savage child."

From Sewall's *The Selling of Joseph* (1700) to Thomas Nelson Page's *In Ole Virginia* (1897), the message remained the same: Be like us and approach humanity. The echo resounded from Hammon to Davis: Be like them and enjoy their blessings. The simile was sharp and clear, and the meaning behind it formed the foundation upon which a race literature would be built, became the *élan vital* propelling numbers of black writers through American letters, became the unifying theme in too many African-American novels. To be like them was the objective, "them" the mirror which reflected all images, "them" the oracle which handed down the indictum to anxious ears, "Touch me and I will make you as white as snow." To be like "them" meant assimilation on a scale heretofore undreamed of, and in practical, realistic terms, few Blacks could accomplish this feat by the route prescribed by the Narrator in Chesnutt's volume of short stories, *The Wife of His Youth* (1899): intermarriage between mulattoes, quadroons, and octoroons until, through the process, "whiter and whiter every generation," black people eventually disappeared. For the overwhelming majority, those not light in complexion, this formula offered little redress. Thus, in time, a passage toward assimilationism must be found through foliage less thick, the romantic dream must give way to means, if not goals, more pragmatic.

Romanticism remains, however, an incurable disease. Having fallen sway to the master manipulators of the word, having, in fact, accepted their own inferiority, the black middle class, from that day to this, has been forced to move simultaneously on two planes—the romantic and pragmatic. It erased the word Black from its vocabulary; replaced it with "people," "human beings," "Negroes," and "American Negro," evidencing to all that there is, indeed, a great deal in a name. Martin Delany might shout to the rafters, thunder forth in magazine articles and from speakers' rostrums, "I thank God for making me a black man," but his words had little effect upon those who dreamed the impossible dream, who desired the unattainable. The black middle class demanded a literature which pointed out ways in which they might become like their oppressors, and Delany was anathema to them. Their first champion was William Wells Brown (1815–84), escaped slave, abolitionist, and exemplar of the Booker Washington thesis, one hundred years before the incident in Atlanta. Though acknowledged as the first black novelist, he is regarded also as the first black playwright, having written *The Escape* in 1858, and among the first historians, contributing in this genre, *The Negro in the American Revolution*. His contribution to the genre of the novel was limited to three versions of *Clotel, or the President's Daughter*.

Brown may be immediately dismissed as a novelist of style, one who observed people well enough to portray them without reliance upon old stereotypes. In neither version of the novel, *Clotel,* does he improve in technical efficiency, is he capable of singularity of plot, organizational unity, or apt characterization. Like his successor, Sutton Griggs, his novels are marked by nothing so much as structural chaos. This chaos bears resemblance to the chaotic life of an ex-slave, one of little organization, where people and incidents too often assume the guise of the grotesque. Brown, the ex-slave, was forced to learn of man on the run, to live a disorganized existence; it is not surprising that being forced to come by ideas secondhand, secondhand ideas proliferate in his works.

To speak of him as the great borrower is not to defame him, nor to denigrate his accomplishment, though one of the most important factors in his work is his ability to borrow from whatever source he deemed necessary. From the eighteenth-century neoclassicists, he borrowed diction; from the nineteenth-century English and American Romantics, he borrowed sentimentality and a sense of the Gothic. The nuances of plot he borrowed from American history. What he did not borrow, what he came upon firsthand, was his belief in the perfectability of man, a belief that led him to conclude, with Copernicus, that man was the center of the universe.

Because Brown accepted, all too readily, many of the romantic aspirations of the black middle class, he was incapable of moving The Novel in the right direction. Given the events following publication of Harriet Beecher Stowe's *Uncle Tom's Cabin* two years before *Clotel,* something more was needed from the black writer than iteration of the white man's inhumanity to black men. As a result of Mrs. Stowe's halfhearted attack upon the institution of slavery, the southern propagandists carried their verbal warfare against Blacks to new heights. Proficient in language, such men as Albert Taylor Bledsoe and George Fitzhugh moved to replace the image of the black man as feeble-minded child, as depicted in *Uncle Tom's Cabin.* To cast aspersion upon Uncle Tom, the meek-mannered, mild, brainless man-child, southern writers resurrected the portrait of the "brute Negro," born not of woman but of animal, whose capacity for murder, rapine, and destruction was mitigated by the stern tutelage of benevolent masters. With the "irrepressible conflict" only four years in the future, the propaganda machinery of southern intellectuals was directed at men in the North.

Yet the propaganda was based, as always, upon the purported inhumanity of Blacks; hence what the times demanded of black writers were works whose primary objective was the destruction of those images and symbols which black people had accepted. Protest, of course, was necessary. Black abolitionists like Douglass, Henry Highland Garnet, Harriet Tubman, and Brown himself, mounted the platform almost daily; yet to point out the evils of the institution of slavery without counteracting southern propaganda meant to leave the major front of the war unprotected. At a crucial time for black people, when the novelist should have been engaged in redefining definitions, in moving to rebut both Mrs. Stowe and her detractors, Brown is found lacking. His solution to the problem of images is to offer counterimages, more appealing to whites and the black middle class than to those on the slave plantation who bore the brunt of the Southerners' attacks. *Clotel,* the octoroon heroine of his novel, is no less a romantic image than that concocted by the imagination of Mrs. Stowe and Grayson. The only difference is that the former was acceptable to many Blacks while the latter was acceptable only to whites. Thus after Brown's pen falls silent in 1874, the black novelist must reap the fruit of the bitter harvest which he helped to plant, must turn to confront a world constructed along lines which he did not oppose, must do battle with a society in which Blacks join whites as the major upholders of Anglo-Saxon values. He is not to be censured because he was a poor novelist, because he did not match his white contemporaries in mastery of the fictional form. Censure must be leveled against him for his failure, as a black novelist, to undertake the war against the American imagists. The struggle for man's freedom begins with the mind and Brown's inability to recognize this fact was his major drawback as a novelist.

The pattern in each of the four versions of *Clotel, or the President's Daughter* is the same throughout. Borrowing extensively from readings and common gossip of the day, Brown wove his many-plotted novel around the rumored amours between Thomas Jefferson and his slaves. Sexual relationships between Jefferson and his housekeeper, Currer, result in the illegitimate birth of two daughters, Clotel and Althesa. When Jefferson tires of his mistress, the family is broken up. Currer and Althesa are sold to a slave speculator, and Clotel to a "young gentleman of Richmond," Horatio Green. Althesa is the luckier of the three. Sold to a kind master, James Crawford, she later meets and marries a Vermont doctor, Henry Morton. Her new condition enables her to send agents to purchase Currer; however, Brown, pinpointing the cruelty of some masters as opposed to others, has the owner refuse the sale. Currer dies of scarlet fever.

Clotel is the tragic heroine. She is purchased as a mistress because of her beauty. In union with her owner-lover, Horatio, an ambitious man, she gives birth to a child, Mary. However, when the possibility of wealth, influence, and a political career mandate that he relinquish Clotel for marriage to the daughter of a wealthy man, he acquiesces. He acquiesces also, when his new wife insists that the beautiful quadroon be placed on the auction block. Sold once again into slavery and forced to leave her daughter behind, the maternal instinct brings about Clotel's undoing. She escapes from her new owner, returns to her former home to rescue her child, is discovered, recaptured, and transported to Washington, to await passage into the deep South. In maneuvering Clotel to Washington and having her escape yet another time, Brown's symbolism, upon describing her eventual suicide, is all too obvious. With her pursuers at her heels and in sight of the White House, Clotel "vaults over the railings of the bridge" and disappears forever "beneath the waves of the [Potomac] river."

The second version of *Clotel* was published serially in the weekly *Anglo-African,* from December 1860 to March 1861, under the title, *Miralda: or, the Beautiful Quadroon.* A third version, *Clotelle: A Tale of the Southern States* was published in 1864, and the final version, *Clotelle: Or, the Colored Heroine. A Tale of the Southern States* was published in 1867. The story line developed in the first version is maintained through three revisions, although changes in names and some incidents, and alterations in plot, distinguish *Miralda* and the final version from the other two. Of the four, *Clotel: Or, the Colored Heroine* has undergone the most severe alteration.

Basically, the plot remains the same as in *Clotel, or the President's Daughter,* though an anonymous senator becomes the surrogate for Jefferson. The roles once held by Currer, Clotel, and Althesa are held by Agnes, Isabella, and Marion. For Clotel, a new role has been created. Her old role has been passed on to Isabella, who, discarded by her master-lover, ends her life in the waters of the Potomac. Clotel, now the daughter of Isabella, escapes both the fate of the Clotel of old and that of her new mother. After numerous experiences, which include slavery, escape, and slavery again, from which she is liberated by a French officer, she marries and sojourns in India. After the death of her husband, she travels to England and here meets and effectuates a union with Jerome, a former slave. Widowed once again, she returns to America during the Civil War, serves as a spy for the Union forces, and later, after the war, opens a school for freedmen in the South.

Brown recognized no dichotomy between propaganda and art. Living in an age of tumult and chaos, he would have championed the argument that art must be instrumental in liberating the people. This objective, prevalent in each version of his novel, depicts him as the moral propagandist. Any device that damages the institution of slavery —sentimentality, melodrama, contrived plots, or stolen phrases—is to be used by the writer. In this regard, sexual license granted the owner and his family over black women are singled out for special concern. For Brown, illegitimacy, the result of the ravaging of black women, which leads to the breakup of the familial structure, is the foundation of corruption inherent in the institution of slavery. Arguing Sewall's point in *The Selling of Joseph,* with more factual evidence than the former author possessed, Brown notes that the Pharaohs are in reality selling their own children. To give this thesis validity, therefore, he peoples his novel with those like Clotel, who "was not darker than other white children."

She inhabits what might be called the world in between, one populated by octoroons, quadroons, and mulattoes, and, at least in the final version of the novel, is allowed to escape the fate of the outcast—the total isolation assigned the mulatto in fiction by whites—and evidences her ability to move freely between the white and black worlds by marriage to first a white man, then a Black. Her life ends in philanthropy, her "trials and tribulations" rewarded by service to others. For those freed Blacks, now beginning to constitute the hierarchy based upon color, she is a heroine, who for all practical purposes has the skin color, morals, and ethical values of white people. To call Brown the first novelist of the black bourgeoisie is not too far wrong; despite the apologia of his biographer, each version of *Clotel* singles him out as the conscious or unconscious propagator of assimilationism. Given her choice of several worlds in the novel, Clotel retained a more than casual affinity for the white.

She was one at this juncture with the black bourgeoisie, a small class composed mostly of mulattoes, quadroons, and octoroons, men and women, often the bastard children of whites, who, in some cases, educated them, emancipated them, and enabled them to assume positions of leadership among African-Americans. More often than not, their struggle was waged in the interest of class and caste rather than against the evils of slavery. In time, they would become almost a separate nation within a nation, straddlers, like Clotel, between two worlds, having more in affinity with the white than with the Black. They would claim the values, morals, images, and symbols of whites, wherever possible, as their own. Having secured some form of recognition from whites, they would turn upon those for whom assimilationism by means of skin color was impossible.

They came in time to believe that they were a special species of Blacks, whose ingenuity and intellect, rather than accident of birth, enabled them to prosper, whose similarity to whites in facial features, skin color, and mannerisms was a badge to be worn with honor. Clotel and Jerome (black artisan, whom Clotel marries) were touchstones of reality for them, for both validated their theories of superior and inferior people—superiority determined by proximity to the skin color of whites. Certainly not all mulattoes fell sway to such ideas—Frederick Douglass did not, neither, one supposes, did Brown himself. However, far too many did, and in so doing sustained the argument of the Americans that man's worth was determined by the amount of melanin in his skin.

In one sense, it is wrong to accuse Brown of providing the rationale for such ideas, wrong to label him the first important ideologue of the assimilationist philosophy. He was more abolitionist than novelist, more warrior than theoretician. By the time he had completed the first version of his novel in England, the propaganda which he later championed was already widespread among Blacks. Moreover, no individual can be held responsible for that folly which caused some Blacks to believe that one shade closer to the color of white men transformed them into different human beings. Brown is the first black protest novelist, and as such he waged war in support of the cause of manumission; for this act he is to be applauded.

Yet he leaves the major ground untilled, shies away from the equally important battle to be waged in behalf of the right of a people to define themselves. In so doing, he sets an ominous precedent for writers to come. To understand the ideas and attitudes expressed in *Clotel* is to begin to understand as well why the cause of Black Nationalism is set back almost two hundred years, why assimilationism after the Civil War becomes the major objective of the black bourgeoisie, why the black writer dedicates himself to spurious theories of art for art's sake and literature which evidences little more than his educational attainments.

The first novel by a black writer, written on behalf of black people and directed toward whites, *Clotel* is designed to solve the problem of differences between the races by pointing out that in essentials no differences exist. If this is so, then the images, symbols, and metaphors constructed by whites are common property, belonging equally as much to black and white Americans; cultural experiences and history, too, are merely part of the American matrix, copyright being held by each and every citizen. Cultural and intellectual differences existed to be sure; yet, such existed not between race and race but between various members (white and black lower classes) within each race. The war, therefore, was to be fought not so much against the imagists, as against laws and rule which procluded Blacks from assuming their rightful positions as American citizens—an act, which, in the view of this pioneer novelist, meant to surrender all claim to a distinct history or culture.

"Season it as you will," writes Saunders Redding, "the thought that the Negro is different from other Americans is still unpalatable to most Negroes. Nevertheless, the Negro is different. An iron ring of historical circumstances has made him so." Few Blacks have been comfortable with this assertion, and even Redding sought to qualify it: "But the difference is of little depth." Such qualification, or the necessity for it, points up the refusal of many Blacks to accept their differences from white Americans. No such rationale, however, has operated to keep them from admitting, and ofttimes boasting of, their differences from other Blacks. "Let the criminal and viscious elements of the race," wrote Booker Washington, "have, at all times, our most severe condemnation. Let a strict line be drawn between the virtuous and the criminal."[6]

The refusal to acknowledge differences between themselves and whites, and to extol them in the case of one another, meant that the black middle class and most black intellectuals by the end of the nineteenth century had come close to the position of Wheatley and Hammon, had surrendered the right of self-definition to others. Despite the fact that whites regarded them as a different species of human being, many professed their allegiance for America and chanted daily hymns to the American deities of status and respectability. Whatever differences there were could all be wiped away through the process of assimilation. When Brown in his novel depicted Blacks in white face, he helped to substantiate the growing desire for integration and assimilation, though his proscriptions were too narrow in scope. Those who might assimilate via the mulatto route were too few in number. Those who did not possess light skins or Caucasian features outnumbered the Clotels and Jeromes almost five to one, and, for these, the process whiter and whiter every generation was inoperative. To make assimilationism a goal within reach of every black man, irrespective of color, criteria based upon other than skin color was necessary. The age of Booker T. Washington was some years in the future; but Frank Webb, of whom little is known, like William Wells Brown, was alive and well in England.

His first and only novel, *The Garies and Their Friends,* was published in England in 1857 and reprinted in America for the first time in 1969. The first novel to address itself to the postulates of Booker T. Washington, it explicates the future leader's program more articulately than he did himself. Read Washington thirty-seven years later and discover how the middle class *should* live; read Webb and discover how they lived in the nineteenth century. In terms of structure, character development, and theme, it is the finest production by a black writer between 1853 and 1900, the publication date of Charles Chesnutt's *The House Behind the Cedars.*

For nuances of plot, Webb borrowed from the English novelists, from Samuel Richardson and Henry Fielding. The result is a novel of multiple plots, in which the major story line is too often obscured. His strong sense of the Gothic led him to impose suspense and mystery upon the major conflict—that between Walters and Stevens. The story line, therefore, is not only obscured but lost, to all but the most discerning reader. Though his characters, for the most part, represent a departure from those of most antislavery fiction, they are so encumbered with English traditions in diction, manners, and actions that they resemble puppets maneuvered upon the literary stage by a talented master.

Three distinct plots are discernible in the novel: the experiences of an interracial couple in the North, the hardships undergone by a middle-class-black family, and the conflict between Blacks and whites, symbolized in the characters of Walters, black, and Stevens, white. The initial plot centers upon Clarence Garie, slaveowner, his black concubine, Emily, and their two children, Clarence and Emily. Though Garie remains wedded to the southern ideal regarding slavery—"he had never had a scruple respecting the ownership of slaves"—he is depicted as a kind master, who deals fairly with Blacks and whites alike. Upon purchasing Emily for a very high price, he became so enamored with the young beauty that he stepped outside of southern custom—making her wife in everything but name. The common-law marriage produced two children, neither of whom showed traces of their African origin.

Emily, however, is uncomfortable with common-law status. Through polite, constant cajolings, frequently pointing out southern law in regard to the children (the children of slaves took the status of the mother: In the event of the death of Garie, Clarence and Emily would have to surrender their freedom), Mrs. Garie persuades her husband to leave the southern plantation and travel north. The wife's connections with a Philadelphia family, the Ellises, enable the two to consummate their journey with little difficulty. Thus, Webb shifts the setting of his novel from south to north and forces the reader to explore the comparison between two families, one all Black, the other interracial.

Webb's hostility toward interracial liaisons, however, renders a just comparison impossible. His concern in this pioneer novel is with the black family as a workable, functioning unit, and the plight of the Garies a non-black family, is foreordained in the opening pages. The Ellis family, husband, Ellis; wife, Mrs. Ellis; daughters, Esther and Caddy; and son, Charles, who is the favorite of the author. The hardworking father, a semiskilled mechanic, is representative of the middle-class husband. Through strict obedience to the Protestant ethic—hard work, thrift, and diligence—he has risen to a position of eminence accorded few freedmen in the North. His role as head of a middle-class-family unit is complemented by the other members of the family. The wife is dutiful, loyal, and obedient—a good mother and housekeeper. The daughters are strong-willed and inclined toward the domestic. The son, everyboy, is mischievous, prankish, goodhearted, and strong of will and character.

For all his attainments, however, Ellis is but a shadow image of the black middle-class male. Neither wealthy nor cultured, he has moved as far as possible toward equality with whites. The goal, however, has not been reached. He has been unable to accumulate capital, to display the ruthlessness and determination of the capitalist; an acceptable man, he is not, however, an exceptional one. The latter description is applicable to Mr. Walters, a self-made man, not only equal to whites, but to most of them, superior. His presence in the novel unifies the various plots, centers attention upon his personality and accomplishments, so that the novel resembles nothing so much as the *Poor Richard's Almanack* of the black middle class.

Self-will and pragmatism are the mainstays of Walters' character. He realizes the immense advantages offered to whites as opposed to Blacks in his native land, knows that despite his many accomplishments were he white, they would be magnified tenfold. "When I look around me and see what I have made myself in spite of circumstances," he argues, "and think what I might have been with the same heart and brain beneathe a fairer skin, I am almost tempted to curse the destiny that made me what I am."[7] Yet Walters, the pragmatist, knows well the vicissitude of the world in which he lives, realizes that the mark of a man depends primarily upon how he performs against other men, that to be an American is to accept one's drawbacks and to make the best of them, to confront one's antagonists honestly and fearlessly: ". . . with all I have endured, and yet endure from day to day, I esteem myself happy in comparison with that man, who, mingling in the society of whites, is at the same time aware that he has African blood in his veins and is liable at any moment to be ignominiously hurled from his position by the discovery of his origin."[8] Assimilation by means of material acquisition is preferable to assimilationism based upon pigmentation.

The two family heads are casualties of a race riot engineered by Stevens, a bigoted attorney, enemy of both Walters and Garie. The Southerner is murdered as planned, when his home is attacked by the mob. Ellis, on his way to warn the Garies of impending danger, is, himself, attacked by the mob and incapacitated. Severe beatings and lacerations render him, for the remainder of the novel, little more than a vegetable. The removal of the heads of the respective families enables Webb to focus attention upon their offspring. His main concern is with the male members of the families, one mulatto, the other Black. As each attempts to assimilate into society, Webb is able to dramatize two different approaches to American acceptability. The central conflict of the novel, that between Walters and Stevens, therefore assumes less importance than the comparison between Clarence Garie and Charles Ellis. Clarence attempts to validate his humanity by moving into the white race, Charles by emulating the accomplishment of Mr. Walters.

Through ambition and hard work, Charles emerges into middle-class respectability; Kinch, his friend, inherits a large sum of money. Clarence, on the other hand, having chosen to pass for white, is revealed as a dissimulator, loses his white fiancée and dies in hopelessness and despair. In two comments upon the families of Charles and Kinch, Webb reveals his sentiments toward those who emulate the Walters of the world and points out the rewards which follow as a result. On Kinch and Caddy: "When last heard from they had a little girl, Cadd, the very image of its mother—a wonderful girl, who, instead of buying candy and cake with her six pence as other children did, gravely invested them in miniature wash-boards and dust brooms, and was saving up her money to purchase a tiny stove with a full set of cooking utensils." On Charles and Emily after returning from a two-year voyage in Europe: "They were unremitting in their attention to father and mother Ellis, who lived to good old age, surrounded by their children and grandchildren."

The primary concern of Frank Webb in *The Garies* is not the institution of slavery, but the plight of freedmen in the North. Discrimination against them in restaurants, polling booths, and schools appears to affront Webb's sensibility more than acts of cruelty committed against those in bondage. Not with the slaves, therefore, lies the sympathy of this middle-class novelist, but with those who, through hard work and initiative, seek to travel light-years from their brothers. The racial unity espoused in the works of Martin Delany, voiced in the speeches of Henry Highland Garnet, and embodied in the aborted revolts of Vesey and Turner is revealed by Webb to be little more than the romantic hopes of foolish men. For the black pragmatist, individuality must take preference over racial unity; he who runs alone, runs surer and swifter.

"Why," asks Eldridge Cleaver, in 1968, "is there dancing in the slave quarters?" If the question, historical in nature, is to make sense in the twentieth century, we must have some idea of what it meant in the nineteenth. To accept the theology implicit in *The Garies and Their Friends* is to ask what malicious fate gave the race its Douglasses, Walkers, Truths, Veseys, and Turners? Why those who risked their lives in order to free other men alongside those who operated only in

terms of individual gratification? "No slave," adds Cleaver, "should die
a natural death," but what of the descendants of slaves? What should
be their fate? See them in the fiction of Frank Webb and they have re-
nounced their heritage, avowed by example that the African values of
old—those which stress man's commitment to man, instead of material
things—are no longer applicable in a world based upon the Darwinian
ethic. They have discovered ways of maintaining a precarious existence
upon American shores, have learned to enjoy the white man's blessings
by striving to equal him in mastery over men and things. One with
white America, they discovered a transcendental value in the scriptures
of the Protestant ethic and moved to cement the bond between
themselves and others, while furthering the distance between themselves
and those in bondage.

Webb is only their historian, the chronicler, recording the events of
the day. We learn from his efforts that at the very moment when men
cowered in terror of the slaveowner, other slaves, but a little removed,
danced in secure quarters. We learn at what time in history the dream
of racial unity died within the breasts of a people, at what time men
began to seek ways of becoming like others by emulating their worst,
instead of best, characteristics. In the pages of *The Garies and Their
Friends* not only is the present foreshadowed but also dire forebodings
of events yet to come.

New archetypal characters appear in *The Garies and Their Friends,*
for Webb is intent upon constructing images to counteract those of the
southern propagandists. Few novels until the nineteen seventies will
be complete without at least one of these types—the black middle-
class striver, the self-made black capitalist, the dutiful, loyal wife, or
the unprincipled white villain. Mr. Walters emerges as the predominant
character and what he symbolizes will hold meaning for black novelists from this time onward. A man of culture and attainment, having
modeled himself upon the white paradigm, he is the middle-class
ideal come full bloom, the anti-image not only to Uncle Tom but to
Clotel as well. He has learned that one need not sing the songs of his
forefathers in a strange land; that, instead, prudence and pragmatism
mandate that the song be surrendered, that a new one be learned, and
that a commitment to individualism means to forego the past altogether, to look with assured eyes upon a materialistic future. Webb's
idea of assimilationism, as opposed to that of Brown, demanded, at
least, that men struggle and sacrifice. At this point, it is a marked
improvement.

What effect the trend toward assimilationism had upon the men on
the firing line between 1859 and 1865 is difficult to discern. Brown

and Webb articulated the sentiments of a number of Blacks, and were the champions of life-styles, which many, slave and free, had begun to emulate. It is known that Douglass complained about Blacks who, enjoying some aspect of freedom in the North, refused to take part in or contribute to the abolitionist struggle, and the trend toward caste discrimination among Blacks was prevalent long before Delany publicly attacked such practices during Reconstruction. There were, however, a small number of Blacks who remained adamant against assimilationism, men like Robert Purvis, shipbuilder, architect of the "Back to Africa Movement" long before Marcus Garvey. Henry Highland Garnet, zealously extolling the actions of Vesey and Turner from the abolitionist rostrums, urged revolution and asked aloud, Why is there dancing in the slave quarters?

That others championed a movement outside that depicted in the fiction of Brown and Webb is evidenced by the Negro National Convention of 1854. The debate between the participants was furious and vociferous, as delegates lined up on the side of colonization, assimilationism, or nationalism. Garnet and Delany were among the proponents of nationalism; their chief adversary was Frederick Douglass. It is due, mainly to Douglass, this giant of a black man, that the assimilationist ideal enters the arena of politics. A paradox to those who knew him, he was more integrationist than assimilationist, dedicated not to denigrating racial culture but to achieving freedom and equality. Not an advocate of the thesis "whiter and whiter every generation," nor a subscriber to black individualism, he argued that the black minority could not liberate other Blacks through their own endeavors. Unwilling to surrender the racial, historical, and cultural artifacts, he, like Du Bois, implored the black "talented tenth" to render the old myths of Anglo-Saxon cultural superiority untenable.

His autobiography, *The Life and Times of Frederick Douglass,* published in final form in 1881, is a singular literary event, depicting both the pragmatist and the man dedicated to his people. Read the narrative of this escaped slave become counselor to Presidents, leader of his people during the terrible period of the holocaust, and he can be forgiven his naive optimism, his belief that an America yet to be born would honor the commitments enunciated in its own doctrine of the laws. The last chapters of the autobiography, however, remain unwritten, for the heartbreak of the man of faith, who watches the undoing of years of struggle and sacrifice by callous, uncaring men, is difficult to describe through the autobiographical form.

Still, he fought the major battles of his day, refused to dance with others in the slave quarters. Not withstanding this, he is not at all times too far from Frank Webb, not convinced that ultimately the system will not work for Blacks. His break with the Garrisonians—prompted by his association with Wendell Phillips—led him to conclude that the Constitution, the moral edifice upon which the nation rested, was a reliable document for effective change, one to which the aggrieved might turn for redress. He could not conceive of it as an effective document only for men of power, could not understand that the war waged by black men was not against the Constitution but against those who defined its terms and enforced its provisions, based upon their own definitions.

In all of this, in his optimism, in his belief in the commitment of the country to righting national wrongs, in his faith in integration, he differed from his friend, fellow journalist, and abolitionist, Martin Robison Delany, of whom he writes: "I thank God for making me a man; Martin thanks God for making him a black man." The differences between them are many—and more pointed than the faith of one in the government and the disdain of the other for it. Yet, Delany (1812–85) was closer to Douglass than to any other man of the age, with the possible exception of the revolutionary minister, Henry Highland Garnet. A descendant of African royalty, born to a free mother and a slave father, throughout his lifetime he was a doctor, newspaper editor, major in the Union Army, and politician.

To most of his age, and to its leading men, black and white, he is a paradox; nevertheless, he is the major antithesis—philosophically, ideologically, and literarily—to men who hold the views of Brown and Webb. This is so despite the fact that in certain passages in *The Condition, Elevation, Emigration and Destiny of the Colored People of the United States* (1852), he is more Booker Washington than even Frank Webb; despite too, that in later years he served as a major in Lincoln's segregated army, supported the corrupt Democratic machine of South Carolina's Wade Hampton, and accepted the designation of that state's Republican party as its candidate for lieutenant governor. Yet his understanding of the central problems confronting his people and his fierce racial pride make him the most important African-American novelist in the nineteenth century. For despite his lapses in later years, the best years of his youth were given over to his race, the best, most productive years, when, almost alone, he set about to redefine the definitions, to offer his own evaluation of what it meant to be a black man in the United States.

His first book, *The Condition,* a political treatise, is the most important prose work of the nineteenth century by a black writer, surpassed only by David Walker's *Appeals* (1829) and the autobiographies of

Frederick Douglass. Though he possessed neither the eschatological vision of Walker nor the fluency of style which marks Douglass' later works, he is the first to cover the varying elements of black nationalism as they have become known in the twentieth century. The twenty-three chapters comprise a compendium of thought upon many topics: the condition of Blacks in America, the achievement of black men and women, an analysis of the American Colonization Society, and the Immigration of Blacks to distant shores. In the opening chapter he argues universality of condition between slave and freedman: "Reduced to abject slavery is not enough, the very thought of which should awaken every sensibility of our common nature; but those of their descendants who are freemen even in the non-slaveholding states occupy the very same position politically, religiously, civilly and socially (with but few exceptions) as the bondman occupies in the slave States."[9]

Attention is directed to the central problem of the age, that which, beginning here in the early days of the American nation, has survived the centuries—the assumption by white men that they are capable of objectively interpreting the historical and cultural artifacts of African-Americans: "The colored people are not yet known, even to their most professed friends among the white Americans; for the reason, that politicians, religionists, colonizationists, and abolitionists, have each and all, at different times, presumed to *think* for, *dictate,* and *know* better what suited colored people than they knew for themselves; and consequently, there has been no other knowledge of them obtained, than that which has been obtained through these mediums. Their history—past, present, and future—has been written by them, who, for reasons well known . . . are not their representatives, and, therefore, do not properly nor fairly present their wants and claims among their fellows."[10]

Not surprisingly, the book received little notice in either the black or the white press, for the central theme demanded that black men think for themselves and move forthrightly, in unison, to destroy the myths created by those who knew nothing of the black experience. Like Douglass, Delany was firm in his conviction that "the man who has *suffered the wrong* is the man to *demand redress*—the man *struck* is the man to cry out— We must be our own representatives and advocates."[11] Only men of such stature, those capable of thinking for themselves and believing in unity of race and purpose, are able to understand the historical forces arrayed against them and move forthrightly in the cause of liberation. It is no accident of history that men from Caesar to present-day Americans have considered those who think long and hard about their conditions to be dangerous men.

Such men, and many are named throughout the book, do not want to become like the Americans, realize that like other national and racial groups, black people constitute "a nation within a nation," and that "A child born under oppression has all the elements of servility in its constitution; who, when born under favorable circumstances, has to the contrary, all the elements of freedom and independence of feeling." Realize these truths and understand why black men from that time to this have dreamed of erecting the new Canaan, far from American shores.

Chapter by chapter, *The Condition, Elevation, Emigration and Destiny of the Colored People of the United States* reveals the mind of a courageous man, who flinches neither from raising his voice against the detractors in his own race nor against those, professed friend or foe, whose actions and pronouncements denigrate his people. Delany is willing to address himself to the conditions under which black people live honestly and forthrightly; yet, he refuses to think of the race in terms of such categories as class and caste. He realizes the great diversity of color and stratification within the group—blacks, mulattoes, poor people, middle class, house slaves and field slaves—yet he knows that what is necessary to ensure liberation for all is unity, perseverance, diligence, and determination to learn skills useful in serving the black community now in its infancy: ". . . We desire accomplishments, but they must be useful."

After a people have acquired skills, the exodus to another continent might be undertaken, and they and their offspring might become rulers of their own lands and create not only the nation-state, but a nation in which such terms as justice, freedom, and morality can be defined anew, a place in which the term "man" is earned only after passage through the dark night of existential struggle. Such a nation would produce the moral state and serve as an example for the rest of the world. This message fell upon deaf ears. Delany became little more than another casualty of historians and academicians who remained oblivious not only of his works, but of his existence, until the Black Power revolt of the nineteen sixties focused interest upon the black past. With the exception of Douglass, he is the first black intellectual, more of a thinker than either Webb or Brown, equally as pragmatic as Douglass, able like Walker to hold the romantic vision, to postulate the existence of the promised land. When he turned his hand toward fiction he left a document as important and impelling as the prose work. Of greater importance, however, *Blake; or the Huts of America* (1859) provides a sharp contrast to, and departure from, the works of Brown and Webb.

It is a sprawling, cumbersome book, the first picaresque novel by a black writer. Held together more by the actions of its central character than by any single thread connecting one plot to another, we learn much about Henry Blake, through narration and from the character himself. Born in Cuba, christened Carolus Henrico Blacus, at the age of seventeen, he leaves on a ship bound for the West Coast of Africa. The ship turns out to be a "slaver" and Blake finds himself in a difficult position. He is numbered as one among slaves, destined to sail, not back to Cuba, but to America, there to be sold with the ship's other cargo into bondage: "The last cargo was taken to Key West, where Franks [Colonel Franks] was waiting, when final settlement of the affairs resulted in my being taken to the United States, and held there as a slave. . . ."[12]

On Franks's plantation, Blacus marries Maggie, mulatto daughter of the slaveowner, and assumes the name Henry Holland, one of the three aliases used throughout the novel. The sale of Maggie by Franks provides the conflict around which Delany structures two distinct plots. The purchasers, Judge and Mrs. John Ballard, employ Maggie as a maidservant, and she accompanies them to Cuba. Enraged by the betrayal of his master, Blake engineers his escape and dedicates himself to fomenting revolution among others: His search for his wife takes him back to Cuba, where, in league with the poet, Placido, he lays the groundwork for revolution in his South American country.

Part One deals with the exploits of the enraged Holland. After his escape from bondage, the search for his wife leads him along the route once traveled by the author himself, into Arkansas, Louisiana, and Texas. At each way station, he brings the message of revolution! "Clasping each other by the hand, standing in a band together, as a [pledge] of their union and fidelity to each other, Harry said, 'I now impart to you the secret; it is this: I have laid a scheme and matured a plan for a general insurrection of the slaves in every state, and the successful overthrow of slavery.' "[13] Deliverance of the word consumes much of the action of Part One. After Holland rescues the slaves of his former master during a raid on the old plantation, the keynote of the novel is suggested in his parting remarks, made after leading the group to freedom in Canada ". . . Nothing can separate you; your strength depending upon your remaining together." The discovery that his wife has been taken to Cuba propels the black revolutionary back to his native land, where, in Part Two, he attempts her rescue and joins in an attempt to destroy white rule in the Spanish colony.

Blake; or the Huts of America remains a fragment, and this is partly responsible for the implausible plot sequences and the over-all episodic quality. Despite these flaws, however, and despite inept characterization and stilted dialogue, the novel is the most important by an African-American before Sutton Griggs's *Imperium in Imperio,* published in 1902. More so than the number of tracts, poems, and books rushed into rebuttal against Mrs. Stowe's portrait of Uncle Tom, *Blake* is a more telling attack upon the former author's caricature. In contradiction to the pious Tom, whose character is, in part, defined by his obsession with Christianity, Blake has contempt for this white man's religion: ". . . I'm not only losing but I have altogether lost my faith in the religion of my oppressors. As they are our religious teachers, my estimate of the thing they give is no greater than it is for those who give it."[14]

Unlike Tom, he understands the true meaning of Christianity, knows that the scripture forces black men to submit to arbitrary authority, demands obedience in the name of a higher power—white. Therefore, he argued for a black religion to serve the interests of the slave as a white religion served that of the master. Nor was he, like Tom, ignorant of the enormous debt owed him by the master: "I have . . . taken by littles some of the earnings due me for more than eighteen years' service to this man Franks, which at the low rate of two hundred dollars a year would amount to sixteen hundred dollars more than I secured, exclusive of the interest, which would have more than supplied my clothing, to say nothing of the injury done me by degrading me as a slave. 'Steal' indeed: I would that when I had an opportunity, I had taken fifty thousand instead of two."[15] Not only is he the first black counterimage to Uncle Tom in literature, but he serves a similar function in relation to the mulattoes. What is most important about Blake is not that he is courageous, brave, and determined, but that he is "a black—pure Negro—handsome, manly, and intelligent. . . ."

The first black revolutionary character in black fiction, he symbolizes black bravery and courage and gives the lie to white writers, historians, and politicians alike, who equated Blacks with the thousands of fictional aunties, uncles, and Sambos concocted to rationalize the practice of slavery. Attack Mrs. Stowe for her portrait of Blacks as many did, still whites were more comfortable with the Toms than the Blakes, did not want to know that black history offered more examples of the latter than the former. For the Blakes of America were angry men, who, deprived of liberty, began by striking out as a result of personal maltreatment and discovered later that no such treatment was peculiar only to them, that others awaited the coming hour of revolt, danced not the dance of joy but the dance of war. *Such men were legion: Cinque, on the ship Amistad, angry, hostile, rebellious, leading men in revolt, knowing before Lord Byron, that he who would be free must himself strike the first blow; Denmark Vesey of the state of South Carolina, having seen the lash fall upon the naked black bodies of men, women, and children, gathering arms and men, planning to usher in the day of rebellion; Gabriel Prosser, recruiting an army from among the wretched of the earth, selecting only those whose bitterness equaled his own, moving to achieve the liberation of a people; Nat Turner, the most celebrated of black revolutionaries, moved by the words of the Calvinist God, knowing intuitively that in a land ruled by the sword, slaves must utilize the weapons of war, teaching his gospel of defiance and revolution, moving forward in rebellion to a certain Armageddon; Shields Green, one of five black followers of old John Brown, standing on that next to fateful day of the raid at Harpers Ferry, staring into the eyes of the great Douglass, his mind transgressing past and present, remembering the horrors he had witnessed, black men hung by the neck, women and children branded and maimed for life, families destroyed, separated; remembered and turning from Douglass, speaking those words which stand as monuments of black strength and bravery, "I guess I'll go with the old man."*

Such are the images of black men suggested by *Blake; or the Huts of America,* and it is not surprising that publication in novel form does not occur until the twentieth century. Those who published the poetry of Wheatley and Hammon and the novels of Brown and Webb were not anxious to publish the exploits of a black revolutionary, not willing to publish a work which went so far toward destroying negative symbols and images of black men. For what, at this propitious moment in history, would such a book avail? In 1858, while Delany labored over the final pages of *Blake,* even the most ambivalent Southerner knew that war was but a short distance away, that the nullification policies of John C. Calhoun could not endure, that somewhere in this century the decision would be made as to whether America would be all slave or all free.

If war came—and that it must come was inevitable—what would confront black people in its aftermath? What specters of the past would still haunt the country? What would be the fate of those who, heretofore, had danced the dance of joy in the slave quarters? The proposition all slave was intolerable to such Blacks as Douglass, Garnet, and Delany. Had Douglass not already sanctioned guerrilla warfare? The proposition all free placed great responsibilities upon North and South, demanded that men find an answer to the question, What is to be done with the Blacks, those unassimilatable elements, whose very existence was a reminder of the most bestial chapter in the book of Euro-American man?

What is to be done with them? Delany's plan was untenable. Black men, united, working in the interests of their own race, could not be tolerated. Yet, Blacks are not, in the words of Samuel Sewall, to be welcomed into the body politic, not in the words of Jefferson and Lincoln, assimilatable within the society. Neither are they free to unite, to produce a new nation from among their ever-increasing numbers. The answer to the question was one with which sane men agreed, though none voiced it aloud; do nothing, allow the present course of action to continue and, in the event of emancipation, move with increasing vigor to codify the existing metaphors, symbols, and images, and accentuate the divisions between one Black and another. If the proposition—all free—is accepted, institute quasi slavery.

Blake; or the Huts of America is the only novel in the nineteenth century which addresses itself to such problems. Racial unity instead of racial division, rebellion instead of passive resistance, nationalism instead of assimilation—these are the alternatives left men with no bargaining position on matters concerning their own fate. Come what may, Delany averred, freedom won by our own hands, or freedom gained at the expense of war, the job of black resurrection will have just begun. New men, imbued with the determination and faith of old, must begin the task of rebuilding racial unity and debrainwashing a people of the propaganda that argued their inferiority. Like *The Condition, Blake,* a merging of several disciplines—literature, sociology, and history—was written to accomplish these ends.

Yet, the novel had minimal impact upon the black thinkers of the age, who were, in most cases, men of mulatto background, who had sanctioned racial division in the past. Delany's attacks upon the group did not help. Have they not, he thundered from magazine article and public rostrum alike, accepted the thesis that the drop of white blood in their veins differentiates them from their fellows? Were they not the major vehicle for dissemination of corrupt images and symbols concerning black men in general? Had they not made their own peace with the Euro-Americans? The attacks were justifiable. Due to the colorphobia inflicting Blacks and whites, mulattoes were in positions to profit from racial division. Their major roles would be played upon the stages of coming centuries, when, usurping the mantle of leadership of the race, they would do almost as much to ensure quasi slavery based upon the word, as much to validate the false symbols, images, and metaphors as Joel Chandler Harris, Thomas Dixon, and

Thomas Nelson Page. To such men, *Blake* and its author were anathema—both preached racial unity when the survival of such men depended upon racial division.

Delany emerges, therefore, as a man alone, and almost alone, this doctor, pamphleteer, editor, and novelist warred against the controllers of language. Never content to allow white men the right to interpret the ways of black men, he fought the war of the mind, knowing, long before the birth of Don L. Lee and Carolyn Gerald, that to control the image was not only to be where the action was but also to determine the fate of a people. He is the first black novelist to attempt the debunking of the phenomenological world constructed by those who forced their own language system upon Africans, the first writer to argue that Blacks were more African than American.

Compare *Blake* with *Clotel* and *The Garies and Their Friends* and we know where the black novelist might have gone, are aware of the tradition that might have been. Had Henry Blake become the symbol of black men instead of Mr. Walters, Bigger Thomas and his cousins would not have been necessary. *Native Son* is most important as a novel and Bigger Thomas relevant as a character because each succeeds in cleansing black fiction of such mainstays as Clotel and Walters. The inability of the black novelist to build upon the foundation laid down by Delany meant that no viable literary tradition was possible until after *Native Son*. And yet, it is in the former, not the latter novel, that the characters, themes, and ideas to which the African-American writer must return are to be found. Move to the novelists of the twentieth century—to John A. Williams, Ernest Gaines, and John Killens, and note the distance traveled from Richard Wright—back two centuries to arrive at the position of Martin Delany.

II

THE SOULS OF BLACK FOLK

By the time the guns fell silent at Appomattox in 1865, the total production of novels by black Americans was three. Of these, one, *The Garies,* was published only in England, the other, *Blake,* only in magazine format. No censure is due the authors for not having written more novels. Though little is known of Frank Webb, both Brown and Delany were men constantly on the run, engaged, until the ends of their lives, in such pursuits as abolitionism, temperance, and politics. Nor are Blacks to be faulted for not regarding fiction as a serious art form. Those who achieved an education devoted themselves to an art form (oratory) more relevant to the lives of the people, more easily grasped by laymen and educated men alike, and more important in the struggle for black liberation. Oratory was mastered by such artists as Frederick Douglass and Sojourner Truth, and their proficiency with the form made the period between 1830 and 1895 more noted as "a period of spoken literature of protest" than for the writing of fiction.

Yet black men had begun to write novels, and the demand that this art form, too, be enlisted in the struggle for liberation is one which few of the pioneers would not have accepted. Each conceived of the novel as a vehicle for protest in written, instead of oral, form and though their protest against slavery is to be commended, the coming years will point out the consequences of their failure to wage war simultaneously on more than one front. That there was only one Martin Delany in the period, and this one seldom read, meant that sentiments, ideas, and beliefs contrary to those of others never received an honest hearing. How disastrous this was for Blacks, writer and layman alike, can be seen in the case of Mrs. Frances Ellen Watkins Harper (1825–1911). Better known for poetry than prose, the writer, who asked for ". . . no monument proud and high/To arrest the gaze of the passer-by/All that my yearning spirit craves/Is bury me not in a land of slaves," believed that the function of the novel was to "awaken in the hearts of our countrymen a stronger sense of justice and a more Christlike humanity."[1]

Go to her one novel, *Iola Leroy, or Shadows Uplifted* (1892), thirty-four years after *Blake,* and the ideas espoused by Delany are almost non-existent, those held dear by Brown and Webb, extolled. Of her doctor character, she writes pointedly: "The blood of a proud aristocratic ancestry was flowing through his veins, and generations of blood admixture had effaced all traces of his negro lineage." What is most important about this continuation, in fictional form, of the assimilationist theory is that after emancipation, through an unprecedented push for education, via the freedmen's schools and private and church colleges, Blacks were ready for fiction far different in terms of content. If any literary genre was to gain their support, the novel had a clear advantage if only for the reason that reading and writing novels evidenced educational attainment. Far more important, however, was the fact that freedom, ushered in by the Emancipation Proclamation, was threatened anew, almost from the moment the Proclamation was issued. The creation of the Freedmen's Bureau and the passage of the thirteenth, fourteenth, and fifteenth amendments were designed only to free men physically. Freedom in a total sense, however, which is to say mentally, was possible only when a race was certain of its own worth and conscious of its own identity.

There were those determined to deny both—certainty of worth and identity—and to continue mental bondage. Building upon the foundation established by their predecessors in the eighteenth century—those whose control of language had produced a number of disparate images, symbols, and metaphors of black men, each attesting to his inhumanity and inferiority—their successors were intent upon utilizing language to a greater extent. The men of the preceding century—the Graysons, Helperns, Jeffersons, and Fitzhughs—were concerned primarily with justifying the institution of slavery. Their successors, on the other hand, were intent upon proving that Blacks, now free of chains and leg irons, were undeserving of the status of citizenship, or recognition as human beings.

The results of their endeavors are stultifying to the modern mind. Never before in the history of civilization have men bent their energies more toward denigrating a race of people; no other century, save the nineteenth, witnessed the purposive attempt of a nation to transform a people into images of its own fantasy. The century that midwived the theories of Darwin and Marx also gave birth to those of Thomas Nelson Page, Thomas Dixon, and Joel Chandler Harris. The former were dedicated to the evolution of man and society, the latter to the destruction of a race, by codifying in fiction, such images of black men as the "contented slave, entertaining and docile ward until misled by radical agitators when he became a dangerous beast."[2]

Mention the terms "contented slave," "entertaining child," and "docile ward," and Joel Chandler Harris (1848–1908) and Uncle Remus come readily to mind. Harris, considered something of a rebel in his youth, began work as a printer before establishing himself as a leading member of the Plantation school of writers. On a slave plantation, he meets George Terril, destined for immortality as Uncle Remus. Far more important to the national mind, than the value of the Remus tales as folklore, was the symbol of Remus, kind, mellow-cheeked black man, attired in workday clothes, entertaining the sons and daughters of his white masters. Were he merely an entertainer, as symbol he may not have survived the test of time. But Remus is the racial Socrates as well—he who must serve the wishes of masters intent upon mental enslavement: ". . . Put a spellin-book in a nigger's han's," he avers in one of his many homilies, "en right den en dar' you loozes a plow-hand. Whats a nigger gwineter 'larn outen books? I kin take a bar'l stave an fling mo sense inter a nigger in one minnit dan all de schoolhouses betwixt dis en de state er Midgigin. . . ."[3]

Thus begins the tradition of the entertainer as spokesman for the people. Here too is an image with which many Blacks will become familiar, who will walk the classrooms of the nation as boldly as did little black Sambo, helping render invisible the images of the thoughtful, scowling Douglass, the tempestuous Remond, or the angry Garnet. Chandler is not his creator, only his publicist. Call him docile child, contented slave, or darky entertainer, he is the old minstrel Negro, born upon the stage and into the national arena in 1830, when "T. D. Rice first jumped Jim Crow in the theatres along the Ohio River." "Apparently immortal," writes Sterling Brown, "this stereotype was to involve in its perpetuation such famous actors as

Joseph Jefferson and David Belasco . . . to mean affluence for a
Jewish comedian of whom only one gesture was asked: that he sink
upon one knee, extend his white-gloved hands, and cry out,
'Mammy.' "[4]

Al Jolson and Uncle Remus notwithstanding, the darky entertainer
was necessary to the national mind, so much so that had there been no
Harris and no George Terril, he would have been invented. Yet
Harris knew well the demands of the times: he knew that literature
served the national interest, that the mere publicity given to such
denigrating images suggested authenticity. Preferring the portrait of
Uncle Remus, even to that of Uncle Tom, white people rushed to
embrace him in the attempt to eradicate guilt for the sins of the
fathers on the one hand and, on the other, to maintain belief in the
myth that Blacks were far from being either bitter or rebellious.
Battered by the armed forces of repression—the Ku Klux Klan, the
White Knights of the Camelia, and the Citizens' Guard—left to defend
themselves against superior fire power, in order to forestall extinction
as a race, many Blacks assumed the guise of the darky entertainer,
became Uncle Remus transformed from image to flesh. "If the Negro
knew anything," writes Redding, "he knew that laughter was his instrument now as it had been under the lash, the broiling sun, and the
threats of being sold down the river. He pursued the Gods of servile
laughter as another race might pursue the God of war. He sang his
gay nonsense music, the laughing, desperate music of heartbreak. He
made jokes and turned them upon himself. He became a minstrel, a
buffoon."[5]

Yet guilt among whites was not so easily assuaged, the black man's
ability to mask his true feelings, not quite adequate. So extensive was
white paranoia that even Uncle Remus, the minstrel man, could not
be completely trusted. The white-gloved hands, waved so obsequi-
ously, might contain a dagger; the dance of joy might be, in reality,
the dance of death. Under the tattered old coat, Remus—mellow
complexion, wide grin and all—might harbor a musket, might have
visions of emulating Nat Turner. The minstrel man was necessary,
the darky entertainer essential to any plan involving emasculation.
He remained, however, an uncertain quality, and in the case of Blacks,
the white South wanted nothing less than certainty.

Certainty was to be had by resurrecting the images of the past, by
engendering nostalgia for yesteryear, by returning to a time when the
black man was as contented and happy as a docile child, to that
time, now gone forever, "wey down souf befo de war." To remember
the lines from Kennedy's *Swallow Barn* is to indicate the symbol the

South wished to recall, the image it was determined to codify: "No tribe of people has ever passed from barbarism to civilization whose . . . progress has been more secure from harm, more genial to their character, or better supplied with mild and beneficent guardian-ship, adapted to the actual state of their intellectual feebleness, than the Negroes of *Swallow Barn*."[6] To such an area of supposed peace and tranquillity, to the time of magnolia blossoms and peach trees, to happy banjo-strumming darkies, the new champions of the plantation tradition seek to return, to ask with white people, North and South, "Aunt Phebe, Uncle Tom, Black Mammy, Uncle Gus, Aunt Jonas, Uncle Isom, and all the rest—who shall speak all your virtues or enshrine your simple faith and fidelity?"[7]

The task was not impossible. Thomas Nelson Page (1833–1922) was ready to enshrine in fiction, if not the faith and fidelity of the above-named characters, at least the progeny of his own fanciful imagination. The Virginia-born Page was among the most popular of ante-bellum writers and a leading apologist for the "old regime" based upon caste and class. With the exception of some of the admitted stereotypes of the short works of Paul Laurence Dunbar, no black characters in American fiction surpass Page's in terms of docility, loyalty, stupidity, and subservience. Uncle Billy of *In Ole Virginia* fame (1887) testifies to the good old days before carpetbaggers and black legislators: "Oh! Nuttin warn' too good for niggers dem times; an de little niggers wuz running roun' right 'stracted . . . Dis nigger ain nuver gwine forgit it."[8] Page was determined in addition that the nation would not forget. His theme varies little from short story to novel to essay. In each there is the comparison between then and now. The contrast between the glories before emancipation and the perdition into which the nation sinks afterward, intermingled always with appropriate comments upon the simplicity and childishness of Blacks, coupled with hints of the *Götterdämmerung* yet to come: ". . . the Negro race does not possess, in any development which he has yet attained, the elements of character, the essential qualifications to conduct a government, even for himself, and . . . if the reins of government be intrusted to his unaided hands, he will fling reason to the winds and drive to ruin."[9]

The attack, here leveled against the emancipated slaves, was cham-pioned by Southerners and Northerners alike. Not only did the freed-men remain a problem in the house that Calhoun built, but they constituted problems for the whole nation. To Southerners like Harris, Page, and Dixon, they were granted privileges which many white men did not have. The vote, taken from some white men, was granted to Blacks; the Freedmen's Bureau was erected in their behalf; colleges and schools were begun to educate them. Poor whites, who had never owned slaves, viewed such with envy and hostility. Having fought a war to prevent secession, having reluctantly made emancipation a feature of that war, the North unhappy with the growing number of Blacks in its own midst, out of motives stemming far more from guilt than opportunism, embraced the mythology of southern chivalry, accepted the images of kindly masters and docile slaves. Dreams of the glories of the past, for Northerners and Southerners alike, mandated plans to reduce the African-American to the status of docile child.

Politicians in both regions gave form and content to such plans. True to his campaign promise, President Garfield Hayes withdrew federal troops from the South in 1877 and helped initiate the series of events which led Henry Grady to conclude in 1889 that "the Negro as a political force has dropped out of serious consideration." He had dropped out, or had been dropped out, of serious consideration in every area of American life: ". . . By 1885 most Southern states had laws requiring separate schools. With the adoption of the new constitutions, the states firmly established the color line by the most stringent segregation of the races and in 1896 the Supreme Court upheld segregation in its 'separate but equal' doctrine set forth in Plessy *vs.* Ferguson."[10]

These events were not precipitated by Page. In his writings, however, he lent them support by depicting Blacks as docile children, prone to acts of irrationality and rebellion, when not under the stern hand of benevolent masters. Equally popular, north and south, his images of black people helped to establish criteria by which Blacks were evaluated for years to come. Insisting that freedom had merely transformed the African-American into a ward of the state and thus begun the progression from child to beast, he argued that evolution must be halted, the process to reverse the changes brought about by the events of 1865 must be the duty, no, the obligation of the man of fiction. His views were sanctioned by whites north and south, and as a result, he gained a national constituency. In the early years of the twentieth century, the well-oiled machinery of white supremacy was determined to control the fate of a race of people; to accomplish this end, the black man as contented slave and docile child was more important than the black man as darky entertainer.

The image of the black man as child was important, to be sure; yet events were occurring which justified the creation of yet another image. Thousands of Blacks fell victim to the attempt by whites to re-establish

social and political hegemony over the South. In the program to invalidate the work of the Reconstruction legislatures, to make null and
void the language of the fourteenth and fifteenth amendments, and to
return the South to the ownership of its former ruling classes, mass
murder and other atrocities were daily fare of the defenseless freedman.
And here, of course, the conflict emerges. For if, indeed, the black man
was little more than darky entertainer and docile child, what justified
the outrageous attacks upon him? What rationale could suffice for un-
leashing hordes of vigilantes, intent upon committing racial genocide,
upon such a people?

The answer lay in discovery of yet another image: one which not
only depicted Blacks as inferiors but also justified the excesses of
white nationalism. In *The Southerner's Problem,* Page laid the
groundwork in the eventuality that such an image might be necessary,
without surrendering his fondness for the old: ". . . the old-time Negroes
were industrious, saving, and when not misled, well-behaved, kindly,
respectful, and self-respecting . . . the 'new issue' for the most part,
are lazy, thriftless, intemperate, indolent, dishonest, and without the
most rudimentary elements of morality. . . . Universally, they report
a general depravity and retrogression of the Negroes at large in sections
in which they are left to themselves, closely resembling a reversion to
barbarism."[11]

He was too kindly a man to do justice to such an image, too enamored
of his own creations: The new century needed a Negrophobe of the
highest order, one who would not shrink from the task at hand—to
justify brutality against black people. No candidate for this job had
better credentials than Thomas Dixon, chronicler of the Ku Klux Klan.
Like Page, Dixon was a much-read and well-respected novelist—his
novel, *The Clansman,* which became the controversial motion picture,
Birth of a Nation, reveals him as more of a Negrophobe than his contemporary. Read his two major works, *The Leopard's Spots: A Romance of the White Man's Burden* (1902) and *The Clansman: An
Historical Romance of the Ku Klux Klan* (1905), and the direction
of the campaign is revealed. The darky entertainer and the docile
child pale into insignificance alongside the "brute Negro" who, out of
lust and hatred, presents a clear and present danger to the purity and
sanctity of white womanhood and civilized America as well. The
transformation of the onetime loyal, docile creature has been wrought
by education, political power, and the relaxing of the bonds of social
intercourse between the races. To understand the extent of Dixon's
departure from the images conceived by Harris and Page, examine the
chapter headings of *The Leopard's Spots:* "The Black Peril," "The Un-

spoken Terror," "A Thousand-Legged Beast," "The Hunt for the Animal."

In graphic terms, though in involuted prose, Dixon presents the twentieth-century version of the African-American, sometimes contrasting him with that of the nineteenth. In reality, the darky entertainer is a demented animal; the docile child, a mutant upon the genus Homo sapiens; the contented slave now "transformed by the exigency of war from a chattel to be bought and sold into a possible beast to be feared and guarded."[12]

The literature of Harris, Page, and Dixon point out that what is at stake in the post-Reconstruction era is not only political, social, and economical control of the South but the institution of quasi slavery to replace chattel slavery and the emasculation of a people through utilizing the power of the written word. Certainly these were not the only practitioners of the art of literary propaganda; they were only the most well known, and the images of black men found in their works were accepted all too often as realistic portraits by their white audiences. Theirs was a literature, more honest in intent than that of their emulators in the coming years, designed to ensure the superiority of one race over another. They bequeathed to the twentieth century a group of images, gave them publicity and status not forthcoming in the preceding centuries, and helped Americans to gain surcease from guilt and, in many cases, fear. In creating the "brute Negro," they began the rationale for the systematic execution of black men by white men from that day to this. In all this, they served all too well the interests of white nationalism.

In the program to make sacrosanct negative images of black men, the manipulators of language lacked the active collusion of black men themselves. Not even the assimilationists were comfortable with stereotypes which included all black men under the same labels. Despite an occasional poem by Daniel Webster Davis, few Blacks were ready to accept such definitions of their race. Nor were a great many willing to accept evaluation from others: "We looks to see how the white man votes," a black farmer told an astonished Booker T. Washington, "and then we votes the other way." If the propaganda was to be effective, therefore, tacit acceptance by African-Americans was necessary. To deprive Blacks of manhood, disenfranchise them, reinstitute the Black Codes, without serious injury to white conscience, the nation needed a black man willing, at least, to sanction the roles of "darky" entertainer and docile child (no black man, for obvious reasons, was willing to think of himself as a beast). One who would adhere to the thesis that Blacks, ranked along the scale from child to man, were closer to the child. One who, in the area of truth, was egotistical enough to believe that he had found the only possible one.

Booker Taliaferro Washington (1856–1915) was that man. The autobiography *Up from Slavery* (1902), written with the aid of his chief lieutenant, J. Emmett Scott, is the thesaurus to which whites turned to substantiate their beliefs concerning black inferiority. Though such was often forthcoming, in other respects the autobiography is misleading. After the first section, it is difficult to ascertain truth from fiction, to distinguish actuality from fantasy, objective reportage from egotistical bombast. The first section, however, is quite believable. In depicting the author's early years, it validates courage and determination. Having neither name nor status, recently freed by the Emancipation Proclamation and forced away from the plantation, the only home he had ever known, to travel over two hundred miles to join a black stepfather, who had, undoubtedly, little affection for this mulatto offspring of a white man, Washington began life as he often advised his race to do, from the ground up.

The desire for education was early aroused. While working in a West Virginia coal mine, he studied at the feet of a black teacher, hired to service the children of the neighborhood. In the mines, he first heard of Hampton Institute, a vocational school designed for black freedmen, in Hampton, Virginia. After winning his mother's consent, he set forth with little money, and no educational background, to seek enrollment in a school of higher learning. He made his way, on foot most of the time, from town to town. Sometimes he slept under porches; when hunger became unbearable, he worked at odd jobs; he endured inclement weather and racial hostility. Upon reaching the objective of his travels, he was presented with the supreme test, that determined to gauge his determination: "After some hours had passed, the head teacher said to me: 'The adjoining recitation-room needs sweeping. Take the broom and sweep it.' "[13]

Here was the singular event in the life of Washington; upon his success in sweeping clean a recitation room lay the destiny of the race. Because of his performance here, the history of black folk from 1895 to 1972 will be vastly changed, the work of Douglass, Garnet, and Delany undone, the lives of a number of black men, Monroe Trotter, Thomas Fortune, and W. E. B. Du Bois, altered considerably. Imagine the future leader, broom in hand, sweeping the floor "three times" and dusting "it four," he stands revealed as the embodiment of work and progress, the metaphor of the doctrine of perseverance under great odds, which he later exemplifies. As the reader is forced, through identification, to merge himself into the narrative, sweeping and dusting the floor with the author, awaiting the return of the stern school-marm, he shares something of Washington's anxiety, is relieved when, after an examination that would have pleased a drill sergeant, the teacher announces with satisfaction: "I guess you will do to enter this institution."

Though full reward for this accomplishment lay many years in the future, this was Washington's finest hour. From this moment in time one might trace the path of his life, watch him overcome adversity with the same resolve as previously: graduation from the institute, a trip back to West Virginia, where he serves a stint as a teacher, a re-turn to Hampton Institute to become housefather to "a group of wild Indians," and finally the summons to become principal of Tuskegee In-stitute, a job for a man of self-assurance and determination. Though the institution was little more than a third-rate elementary school, pos-sessing neither students nor buildings, Washington industriously set forth to procure both. The little shanty and church in which he held his first classes soon disappeared, and in twenty years, his success in build-ing the institution alone justified the name "Wizard" bestowed upon him by his well-wishers: "At the present time the institution owns twenty-three hundred acres of land, one thousand of which are under cultivation each year, entirely by student labor. There are upon the grounds, counting large and small, sixty-six buildings. . . . The value of our property is now over $700,000. If we add to this our endowment fund . . . the value of the total prospect is $1,700,000."[14]

These twenty years—during which Tuskegee moves from poverty to affluence—comprise the age of Booker T. Washington. It is one almost completely dominated by this onetime housefather to Indians, who, to much of the country, seemed to be playing the same role in relationship to Blacks. The age, like Tuskegee, is a tribute to the man; it is a testi-monial to the doctrine of progress-through-struggle that he symbolized. Time and time again, the zeal and tenacity displayed in sweeping the recitation floor are duplicated as he rises to leadership of his race. The friendships that he made with such wealthy men as Collis P. Huntington and Andrew Carnegie were based upon persistence: "The first time I ever saw . . . Collis P. Huntington, he gave me two dollars for our school," he relates with pride. "The last time . . . he gave me fifty thousand. . . ."

His major contributions in the area of race, however, remain his educational and racial policies set down in Atlanta in 1895. The road to Atlanta was paved with numerous other speeches, south and north, the most important, given at The International Meeting of Christian Workers held in Atlanta, Georgia, in 1893. Though the speech lasted only five minutes, his call for industrial education and racial conservatism earned a constituency among Southerners that would serve him well in later years. More important, a group of Atlanta citizens, who had attended the conference in 1893, summoned him to Washington in the spring of 1895: ". . . for the purpose of appearing before a committee of congress in the interest of securing government help for the Exposition." The speech he delivered before "about twenty-five of the most influential men of Georgia" made him one of the leading candidates to represent African-Americans at the Atlanta Exposition.

On the eve of his entrance upon the platform at Atlanta, however, the reader steps back from *Up from Slavery*. There is no longer wonderment and surprise at the incidents which make up Washington's mature life. Those who have followed him through the first pages begin to sense, at this point in the book, that there are few surprises left. Certainly there are no incidents as thrilling or as suspenseful as that which gained him entrance to Hampton Institute. From this moment in the autobiography, as he recounts the steps which led him to Atlanta, the book appears contrived, events seem manipulated in such a way as to prove his infallibility, to foster the argument that the real Booker T. Washington was not full blown, long before Atlanta.

When he writes of his indecisiveness on the eve of the Atlanta address, the reader knows full well that even as this historical moment approaches, Washington is the second coming of the stereotype, whose advent was foretold in the works of Harris, Page, and Dixon. That he is but the reincarnation of the uncles, aunties, and mammies of yesteryear—the purveyor of sweetness and light, the image of the contented darky become flesh and blood. This observation is not due only to what he said at Atlanta. Most of what he said there was repetition: "As we have proved our loyalty to you in the past, in nursing your children, watching by the sick-bed of your mothers and fathers, and often following them with tear-dimmed eyes to their graves, so in the future, in our humble way, we shall stand by you with a devotion no foreigner can approach, ready to lay down our lives, if need be, in defence of yours. . . . In all things that are purely social, we can be as separate as the fingers. . . ."[15]

More important, the images he evoked of black people in his writings and his speeches, complement those of the Plantation school of writers "I know . . . of all the Negroes weaknesses, that only a few centuries ago they went into slavery in this country pagans, that they came out Christians; they went into slavery as so much property, they came out American citizens; they went into slavery without a language, they came out speaking the proud Anglo-Saxon tongue. . . . It is with an ignorant race as it is with a child; it craves at first the superficial, the ornamental signs of progress rather than the reality. The ignorant race is tempted to jump, at one bound, to the position that it has required years of hard struggle for others to reach."[16]

The housefather has returned to lecture his flock on the virtues of cleanliness, the dangers of a liberal education, the rewards to be gained by building a better mousetrap than one's neighbor. Like all leaders, he sometimes despairs of the success of his undertaking—"The work to be done in order to lift these people seemed almost beyond accomplishing. . . ." He is determined, however, against opposition, mainly from Blacks, to make his race respectable in the eyes of white men. To many like Thomas Nelson Page, he succeeded. After reading *Up from Slavery,* Page deemed him ". . . the wisest, sanest man of color in the country, and who has, perhaps, done more than any other to carry out the ideas that the Southern well-wishers of his race believe to be the soundest and most promising of good results."[17]

White America, in almost unanimous agreement, raised Washington to the status of a Lycurgus, invested him with power and prestige unknown to any Black before or since. He strode, mammothlike, the stage of the late nineteenth-early twentieth century, the embodiment of the stereotypes of old symbolizing "the conversion of the minstrel Negro into a cornfield Negro, who was still a minstrel, still, for all his labor and sweat, a buffoon."[18] What the white controllers of language could not do—demand that Blacks live up to the definitions imposed upon them—Washington did for over twenty years, by uttering his homilies on almost every conceivable topic. On the Back-to-Africa Movement: ". . . there is no such place in Africa for him [Blacks] to go where his condition would be improved." On the inferiority of Blacks: ". . . it may be some time before the Negro race as a whole can stand comparison with the white man in all respects." On the black man as martyr: ". . . This race has been placed here that the white man might have a great opportunity of lifting himself by lifting it up." On black salvation: "If we make ourselves intelligent, industrious, economical, and virtuous, of value to the community in which we live, we can, and will, work out our salvation right here in the South."

Opposition to Washington and his program was not long in coming. As early as 1901, Harvard-educated Monroe Trotter and his associate George Forbes founded *The Guardian,* primarily to contradict the policies of Washington. Ida Wells Barnet, Harry C. Smith, and Sutton Griggs openly opposed the Tuskegean from the outset, and muted opposition came from Paul Laurence Dunbar and Charles Chesnutt. In the main, the opposition was ineffectual. Washington was little more than the creation of white America, who "had raised this man up because he espoused a policy which was intended to keep the Negro docile and dumb in regard to civil, social, and political rights and privileges. Having raised him to power, it was in white America's interest to keep him there." To do battle with the principle and the surrogate required a man of intellect, creativity, and unflinching devotion to principle. Such a man was born five years after the Civil War in Great Barrington, Massachusetts, and though not early opposed to Washington or his program, in time he realized that "the policies of the Negro's greatest leader" were mere echoes of those of the past, leading to the training "of black boys and girls forever to be hewers of wood and drawers of water for the cowardly people who seek to shackle our minds as they shackled our hands yesterday."[19]

The life of William Edward Burghardt Du Bois (1868–1963) seems more fitting for the genre of fiction than biography. His first full-length biography, published in 1968, unlike that of Washington's, is not embellished with the dramatic tension that forces identification from the reader. There is too much strength of intellect in his character, much like that which the modern mind has come to expect from its intellectual heroes since Henry Adams. The first of the titanic leaders born after the Civil War, his early years of maturation in Massachusetts, though not without mishap, are not highlighted by a sense of existential attempt and failure. Thus, his autobiography—especially those episodes which deal with his youth—lacks a sense of mystery or an element of surprise. Though, in terms of personality, he is a difficult man to grasp, furtive, easily misunderstood, one knows that all adversity which he confronts will be mastered. A way will be found to send him to college, first Fisk and later Harvard University. When he applies for a Slater Fund Fellowship to enable him to study abroad, though he is initially rebuffed, we know that eventually he will succeed in persuading ex-President Hayes to reverse his almost solitary decision. We know too that once abroad, he will do well at the University of Berlin, later return to America to receive a doctorate from Harvard, and move to replace his "hitherto egocentric world by a world centering and whirling about my race in America."

The assurance of his prose style, its unapologetic manner, that almost arrogant phraseology with which he describes his relationship to people and events, convinces us that his autobiography is a sincere document, that he is a man too arrogant and too self-assured to lie. Despite all of this, there is in *The Autobiography of W. E. B. Du Bois* (1968) a belief in his people, a surety that "If somewhere in this whirl and chaos of things there dwells eternal Good, pitiful, yet, masterful, then anon in his own good time America shall rend the veil and the prisoned shall go free."[20] This belief took hold during the days at Fisk in those summer months when he forewent summer recess to teach among the people of Tennessee. Years later, his work as a major spokesman of his people just begun, on returning to Tennessee, he mused upon the fate of those friends of old: ". . . How shall man measure progress there where the dark-faced Josie lies? How many heartfuls of sorrow shall balance a bushel of wheat? How hard a thing is life to the lowly, and yet how human and real: And all this life and love and strife and failure—is it the twilight of nightfall or the flush of some faint-dawning day?"

Such musings pinpoint the twin characteristics of the man: the brooding intellectual, whose massive ego prevents him from losing all sense of optimism, and the creative man, believing always that the human spirit must survive. Together with Washington he represents the twin dichotomy of the black soul—that between the creative and the mechanical, between chance and determinism. As a major factor in the life of Washington, chance is negated after the first year as principle of Tuskegee Institute; from the moment he concludes the Atlanta Exposition address, his life is as determined as Aristotle's acorn. Chance, however, plays a major role in the life of Du Bois, despite the fact that we know, intuitively, that he will overcome all adversity. Therefore, we receive a truer portrait from his autobiography, than from Washington's, though his was written long after the author had somewhat retired from battle, long after the major antagonists had disappeared from the scene.

For a clearer picture of the man and his thoughts, one must turn to his classic, to those fugitive pieces written at the height of battle. *The Souls of Black Folk* (1902) is the first major attempt by a black writer, since Delany, to wrest control of the images, metaphors, and symbols of Blacks from the southern propagandists, by analyzing the central dilemma of black life. The black man is gifted with "second sight" in America, a land "which yields him no true self-consciousness"; which only allows him to see himself through the "revelation of the white world." This double consciousness, this continual viewing of one's image as reflected in the mirror-eyes of the other, of measuring one's soul by the tape of a world that looks on in amused contempt and pity, leads to ambivalence! "One ever feels his two-ness—an American, a Negro; two souls, two thoughts, two unreconciled strivings; two warring ideals in one dark body, whose dogged strength alone keeps it from being torn asunder."

The major problem confronting Blacks, as he saw it, was the need to serve two masters, to be both Blacks and Americans in a society that demanded that one be surrendered and the other granted only on its own terms. This strife is historical; this longing to attain self-consciousness, which Du Bois, like Douglass, equated with manhood, is the psychic malady of black men which forms so much of an ambivalent history, marked by the desire to retain manhood, while merging "his double self into a better and truer self: In this merging he wishes neither of the older selves to be lost. He would not Africanize America, for America has too much to teach the world and Africa. He would not bleach his Negro soul in a flood of white Americanism, for he knows that Negro blood has a message for the world."[21]

It is a conflict of universal import and forms the major thesis of what Du Bois calls "the three streams of thinking" in the twentieth century. One, the product of idealism in America and abroad, calls for a commitment to satisfying human wants. This ideal demands a common unity, one pulling nearer not only "the earth" but all men, "black, yellow, and white." The second thought is that of the men of the "older South" who believe that God created the Negro as "a clownish, simple creature, at times lovable within its limitations. . . ."[22] And last, there is what he calls "the darker thought," the thought of the things themselves, the confused, half-conscious mutter of men who are black and whitened crying "Liberty, Freedom, Opportunity—vouchsafe to us, O boastful world, the chance of living men."[23]

There is, in the pages of this remarkable book, not chauvinistic breast-beating, not solely criticism of Washington's program, not even unmitigated anger and rage, but instead a belief in a common humanity, in the ideal that men might create a better world. The man who emerges from its pages is one troubled by the burdens of the age, seeking some middle ground between extremists of right and left. One gathers from his early speeches and from parts of *The Souls of Black Folk* that he would have liked rapprochement with Washington, and one senses that this failure plagues him throughout his life as he moves closer, in many aspects, toward elements of Washington's program. Yet, in *The Souls of Black Folk,* he is the "loyal opposition," not unduly harsh to this man created as leader of his people by white America, noting in the essay "On Mr. Booker T. Washington and Others" the tremendous debt which the race owed Washington in light of his achievements.

To measure his accomplishments in light of those of the Tuskegean in terms of material progress for the race is to admit that he was a failure, that in terms of practical programs, of solutions to the problems of education and employment, housing, and political disenfranchisement, he had little new to offer. His accomplishments must be measured, therefore, by other yardsticks, those which more accurately gauge his impact as symbol upon the men of his time and ours. If Washington personified Uncle Remus, the minstrel man, done over in twentieth-century garb, Du Bois personified the courageous, determined man, the humanist, concerned more with the problems of men than things, more with changing the human condition than accepting its limitations. Kelly Miller, who traced Du Bois' lineage back to Frederick Douglass, knew that both men were cut from the same cloth—were men of principle and unfaltering devotion to black liberation.

The choice for the novelist was clear cut: Du Bois or Washington; one man symbolizing positive images, the other, negative ones. Almost to the man, the major novelists of the period chose to accept, in fiction at least, if not the image symbolized in the works and actions of Washington, at least his philosophy, making of their characters replicas of the middle-class heroes of Frank Webb. As symbol and image, Du Bois was to go the way of Delany; *The Souls of Black Folk* to be regarded as little more than the intellectual ravings of a jealous and bitter man. Eschewing principle, therefore, black novelists ofttimes accepted the worst stereotypes of the Plantation school of writers, adhered to definitions constructed by the race's most severe critics. They will leave a body of literature, at times both entertaining and exciting. In light of Du Bois' masterpiece, however, it is a literature to be amended by future writers. In the battle for control of images, only two black novelists from 1901 to 1920 would mount the barricade.

Paul Laurence Dunbar (1872–1906), the first major black novelist to fictionalize the arguments of Harris and Page, was not one of them. A prolific writer, the first to achieve distinction in three genres—poetry, short fiction, and the novel—he is better known as a poet than a writer of fiction. Of his four novels, only one, *The Sport of the Gods,* deals specifically with Blacks, though each draws upon aspects of his own life experiences. Themes based upon freedom as opposed to restraint, the individual as opposed to the group, preference for the small town over the city, and the influence of fate/destiny in man's achievements occur in each work. Each, in addition, is encumbered with the faulty naturalistic machinery of Émile Zola, Frank Norris, and Stephen Crane by an author uncertain of the ramifications of the term. *The Uncalled* (1898) and *The Sport of the Gods* (1902) are proof positive of this assertion.

The Uncalled, a novel dealing exclusively with white characters, was written while Dunbar sojourned in England, and was first published in serial form in *Lippincott's Magazine.* The plot, set in a small, religious town, Dexter, Ohio, centers around Freddie Brent. The conflict is pronounced in the opening pages of the novel. Freddie's mother, Margaret, deserted by her husband—an alcoholic—lies near death. The townspeople are concerned about the fate of the soon-to-be orphan. Who will adopt him in light of the background of his family and in spite of their own strongly held Calvinist beliefs that ". . . with that owdacious father o' his before him . . . blood's bound to tell, an' with sich blood as he's got in him . . . I don't know what he'll come to. . . ."[24]

Reader and townspeople alike are surprised when, after the death of Margaret, Hester Prime, the town spinster, offers to adopt the boy. ". . . I want you all to understand that it ain't a matter of pleasure or desire with me; it's dooty. Ef I see a chance to save a soul from perdition an' don't take it, I am responsible, myself, to the Lord for that soul." The spinster provides one pole of the conflict confronting Freddie. She is symbolic of the religious and social bigotry of the town itself. Through her, the conflict between himself and his familial background is somewhat abated. Under Hester's tutelage, he succeeds in high school and, due to her insistence, prepares for the ministry. He graduates at the top of his class, is engaged to the daughter of the town minister, and in line to inherit the church pulpit of Dexter. Still, he is cognizant of the major war in which he is engaged: "I am fighting old Tom Brent now, and I must conquer him."

In the other war, that against the spinster and the town, Freddie has one ally, Eliphalet Hodges, who after years of perseverance persuades the spinster to become his wife. Taking sides with the young man, he lectures wife and town alike: "Its funny to me . . . how it is that Christians know so much more about the devil's ways than they do about the Lord's. They're allus asayin' 'the Lord moves in a mysterious way,' but they kin allus put their fingers on the devil." With Hodges' support, Freddie achieves success, though revolt smolders within him: "However else one may feel," he writes to a friend, "one must be fair to the ambitions of others, even though one is the mere material that is heated and beaten into form on the anvil of another's will. But I am ripe for revolt. The devil is in me—a restrained quiet, well-appearing devil, but all the more terrible for that."

The devil of revolt soon surfaces. Shortly after assuming pastorship of the town church, Freddie is importuned by the ex-pastor, his future father-in-law, to condemn a young woman who had mothered a child out of wedlock. The minister refuses and initiates the chain of events which lead to the novel's swift conclusion. He resigns his pastorship, breaks his engagement, leaves Dexter, and settles in Cincinnati. Through contrived incident, he is brought face to face with the specter of old—his father. The meeting takes place when Freddie attends a temperance meeting. The star repenter is a man known as the "California Pilgrim." Faced with the reality of approaching death, the Pilgrim vows to return to the town from which he came (Dexter) to make amends for his sins. The congregation, moved by the suffricant's tale, takes up a collection to allow Brent to return to Dexter.

Freddie is filled with consternation and bitterness. He is angered, initially, because his father, in returning to Dexter, will increase the opprobrium attached to the Brent name. Days later, however, when Freddie receives a letter informing him that his father lay near death, bitterness turns to compassion. He rushes to his father's side and accepts his deathbed confession. After the funeral, the past behind him, he leaves Dexter for the final time. Sometime later, after marriage and a new career, he writes in a letter to Hodges: "My life has been very full here of late, it is true, but not so full as to exclude you and good Aunt Hester. I feel I am growing. I can take full breaths here. I couldn't in Dexter; the air was too rarefied by religion."[25]

The Uncalled, a novel of personal protest, is the first of its kind by an important black writer. Webb, Brown, and Delany fashioned the novel of protest into an instrument of war on behalf of black people, in general. Dunbar, however, set aside from others of his race, though constantly reminded of his racial background by public and critics alike, sought not general, but individual, salvation. The philosophy is dramatized in the character of Freddie Brent who, though he "had long seen the futility of blind indignation against the unseen forces which impelled him forward in a heated path," nevertheless, survives in unnaturalistic fashion, asserts his natural inclinations, manages to achieve an individual salvation, and proves the truth of the theory of the survival of the fittest.

The life of Dunbar bears comparison. In the lexicon of the southern imagists, here was a young man destined to remain an elevator operator. The obstacles standing in his way—bigotry, ignorance, and oppression—stand also in the way of Freddie Brent. Like his fictional surrogate, Dunbar overcame them all. He made his way in nineteenth-century America against tremendous odds. Yet, so effective was the propaganda that he was unable to recognize the immensity of his accomplishment, unable to shake free of the old stereotypes and images permeating society and much of his poetry and short fiction. The ramifications of this conflict have been pointed out by Saunders Redding: "The story of a Negro boy living through Dunbar's experiences would not win credence. Negroes simply could not have certain emotional and spiritual things happen to them. So, in the novel . . . Dunbar characterized himself as Frederick Brent, a white youth. . . . He did not say that he was looking at white characters from a colored point of view. He simply assumed inherent emotional, intellectual, and spiritual identity with his characters."[26]

Dunbar not only identified with whites emotionally, intellectually, and spiritually; all too often he sanctioned their evaluation of Blacks. Though this tendency is most apparent in the short stories and poetry, it is discernible in at least two of his novels, *The Fanatics* and *The Sport of the Gods*.

The Fanatics (1901), the first of Dunbar's novels in which a black character is awarded a major role, is best characterized as distorted history disguised as fiction. The Civil War is the background against which to examine the actions and thoughts of the families of Union sympathizer, Bradford Walters, and Confederate sympathizer, Stephen Van Doren. The conflict between the patriarchs is paralleled by that between the Union forces and the townspeople and, to a lesser extent, between Blacks and whites. Town and family are divided as a result of the war; but its major repercussions are felt by the offspring of Walters and Van Doren. Robert, Van Doren's son, joins the Confederate Army at the outbreak of hostilities. Walters demands that his daughter sever the engagement between the two. Mary rebels. "She loved Bob, not his politics. What had she to do with those black men down there in the South? It was none of her business." Mary's view of "those black men down there" is shared by the town. Despite strong sentiment toward the Union, once escaping Blacks attempt to settle in the town, liberal and conservative forces join hands: "For the time being, all party lines fell away, and all the people were united in one cause— resistance of the black horde." Such attitudes symbolize the fanaticism of family and town alike. Van Doren and Walters are equally fanatical on the question of war and the treatment of black men. The key statement of the novel is sounded by Nannie, wife of Walters' son, a soldier in the Confederate Army: "Everyone is mad, you and I and all of us. When shall we come to our senses?" A return to sanity is possible after the two families are reconciled with one another. Walters loses his hostility for his friend and neighbor after his son is killed in the war and gives his blessings to the union between Mary and Robert. The Van Doren-Walters reconciliation serves as a model for the opposing elements in the town. Only the Blacks, whose entrance into the town had sparked a race riot, remain unreconciled with the townspeople.

The Fanatics evidences how completely Dunbar has adopted the images created by Harris and Page. A novel dealing with the Civil War would be incomplete without a black character. Numerous models were available for the black writer: the men of Colonel Robert Shaw's all-black army unit; Major Martin Delany; Union spy, Harriet Tubman; even the author's father and foster father, both of whom fought on the side of the Union during the war. Dunbar, however, creates the character of Nigger Ed, who is loyal, obedient, and subservient, and who "has a picturesque knack for lying." The plan of the novel was to depict Ed moving from town drunkard and buffoon to respectability and equality with others of the town: "There were women," Dunbar relates at the end of the novel, "who begged him [Ed] to come in and talk to them about their sons who had been left on some Southern field, wives who wanted to hear over again the last words of their loved ones." For performing such tasks Ed is made a ward of the town: ". . . they gave him a place for life and everything he wanted. . . ."

Measured against Van Doren, Walters, and their sons, Ed is an inferior being with the mentality of a child. For a black writer to adopt such a view of his character was an act of tacit agreement with his audience that said, in effect, there are those of us who know that many Blacks are, indeed, little more than docile wards and feeble-minded children. These are lower-class Blacks, of whom the Nigger Eds, Aunt Sophies, and Mammie Porgies (from Dunbar's short fiction) are representative. They differ from us to a greater degree than we differ from you. This admission from the race's most famous writer, like the model presented by Booker T. Washington, was instrumental in validating and proliferating the images of black men which have permeated nineteenth- and twentieth-century literature.

Four years before his death, Dunbar published *The Sport of the Gods* (1902), the only one of his novels which deals specifically with black people. The opening lines of the novel evidence his intention to move away from previous stereotypes, from the stock characters of the Plantation Tradition: "Fiction has said so much in regret of the old days when there were plantations and overseers and masters and slaves that it was good to come upon such a household as Berry Hamilton's, if for no other reason than that it afforded a relief from the monotony of tiresome iteration."

The main concern of the novel is the Hamilton family. Berry, Fannie, Kit, and Joe—husband, wife, daughter, and son respectively—symbolize "the New Negro" born after Reconstruction. No longer slaves, the family maintains a cabin on the estate of Maurice Oakley, for whom Berry has been a trusted butler for over twenty years. Though freed by the Emancipation Proclamation, he had refused to leave the South, his "beloved section," but instead had worked diligently in order to rise with the regions "rehabilitated fortunes." His wife works as housekeeper for the Oakleys, and his son works as a barber for the white townspeople. The Hamiltons, self-made members of the black middle class, achieve status through hard work and frugality and flaunt their achievements among less fortunate Blacks: "What the less fortunate Negroes of the community said of them and their off-spring is not really worthwhile. Envy has a sharp tongue, and when has not the aristocrat been the target for the plebian's sneers?"[27] The family's social rating is certified by the husband's position as treasurer in a black social club, The Tribe of Benjamin. His estimation of his own importance is summed up in the statement: "Its de popah thing fu' a man what waits on quality to have quality mannuhs an' to waih quality clothes."

Tragedy, however, strikes the Hamilton family. Francis Oakley, half-brother to Maurice, a man "always trembling on the verge of a great success without quite plunging into it," steals money from himself given him by his brother. A playboy, living abroad in Paris and constantly in need of money, Francis intends to pocket both the original sum and the replacement. The crime is attributed to the loyal servant of twenty years, and his employer has no difficulty in believing in his guilt: ". . . the Negroes are becoming less faithful and less contented, and more's the pity, a great deal more ambitious. . . ."[28] Circumstantial evidence points toward Hamilton as the thief and, as a result, he is arrested and remanded to jail and his family is evicted from the estate.

Demoralization, degeneracy, and crime await the Hamilton family up North. Fannie is tricked into marriage with a brutal man; Kit enters upon a career as a show girl; Joe, after becoming a dandy of sorts, murders his sweetheart. After a reporter proves his innocence, Berry, released from jail, travels to New York to find his family in ruins. The drunken-brawl murder of Fannie's new husband makes possible reunion between former husband and wife. Minus the children, the two return to the estate they were forced to leave. Maurice is dead of a heart attack and a guilty conscience, occasioned after discovering, and then covering up, evidence of Berry's innocence. His wife, however, welcomes the returning couple in true plantation tradition style: "[she] . . . heard of their coming, and with her own hands reopened and refurnished the little cottage in the yard for them. There the white-haired woman begged them to spend the rest of their days in peace and comfort."

Dunbar is the first African-American to capitalize upon the purported sensationalism of black life. In time, a more condescending, if not more talented, writer, Carl Van Vechten, looking through the pages of *The Sport of the Gods,* will write the sensational exposé par excellence, creating symbols, myths, and images more welcomed by the nation than those bequeathed it by the imagists of Dunbar's era. Like the more experienced naturalists, Zola, Dreiser, and Wright, Dunbar sought only to move his characters from one region to another and to record the effects of a new environment upon them. His people, unlike those of Van Vechten who inhabit the "lowly world of Harlem night life," are not natural-born subhumans. They are men and women transformed by urban life, so much so that they become a special class of people, living upon others and taking pride in idleness and poverty. There are representatives in each black community: "Some play the races a few months of the year; others, quite as intermittently, gamble at 'shoe-string politics,' and waver from party to party. . . . But mostly they are like lilies of the field."[29]

Such sentiments are designed to appeal to a white audience. Without the care and guidance of white people, suggests Dunbar, Blacks can only travel the route of ruin and degeneracy. No matter how oppressive conditions in the South, there, the black man is healthier—physically, mentally, and morally. The choice between north and south may be the choice between questionable freedom and semislavery, but Dunbar urges his black readers to opt for semislavery, despite the fact that determinism is more operative in the South than in the North. The choice for Hamilton in the South is not complex: live always under the guidance and control of benevolent despotism. For Joe, in the North, the choices are complex, personal ones. The disaster which overtakes him in New York is of his own making, more attributable to the exercise of free will, than to the mythology of environmental determinism. Away from whites, he is thrown upon himself, given the opportunity to grow, to succeed, or fail.

He is a failure in the fiction of Dunbar, primarily because the author is unable to believe in equality between Blacks and whites, incapable of believing that black survival was not dependent upon white patronage and benevolence. True to his own middle-class bias, he can only view his lower-class characters with the contempt of one who imagined himself as a white man in black face. To him, and to his white contemporaries alike, black people were little more than the sport of the gods. Wards of the society, their fate lay not in their hands, but in those of others; their freedom is to be parceled out in shares as others see fit. Such is the fate of those, like Joe and Kit, who are incapable of dealing with adversity alone.

Of the three major black novelists between 1900 and 1920, Dunbar is least able to regard black people as other than the stereotypes and images created in the minds of Euro-Americans. At this point, he was one with Booker T. Washington, believing also that most Blacks were minstrels, still, for all their new-found freedom, feeble-minded children lost without the parental guidance of the master race. Dunbar's reputation, nevertheless, is salvaged by the fact that other novelists, more confused about black humanity than he, will attempt in more sophisticated fashion to build upon his example.

This is not altogether true of his contemporary, Charles Waddell Chesnutt (1858–1932). The mulatto schoolteacher and law clerk, turned writer of fiction, dealt with the stereotypes of the time in some of his short fiction; for the most part, however, he created foils to the stereotypes of Page, Harris, and Dixon. The narrator in *The Conjure Woman* (1899), Uncle Julius McAdoo, is a fictional contradiction, an answer even to Harris's Uncle Remus. Julius fulfills the role of the darky entertainer, amusing the Yankees come South with humorous tales of ante-bellum times. This first dissimulating Black in African-American fiction performs this role, however, in order to secure personal gain for himself and his relatives. In each of the seven stories, he is revealed as being more akin to the "darky trickster" of the African literary tradition than the stereotype of the "darky entertainer." In his second volume of short stories, *The Wife of His Youth and Other Stories of the Color Line* (1899), Chesnutt steps back from full endorsement of the stereotypes of the literature of his white contemporaries. One of these, that of the "tragic mulatto," has its genesis in the nineteenth century and was promulgated in the fiction of Harris, Page, and Dixon alike. Mythology held that the mulatto possessing a mixture of the blood of both races was a hybrid creature, whose character traits were determined by the dominant strain of blood. Blacks and whites held different ideas concerning genetic dominance. Evidence of a minimal amount of white blood meant for Blacks that the mulatto was closer to the Anglo-Saxon than his darker brothers. For whites, the mulatto was a freak of nature; admixture of white blood, dominated by the black, caused them to veer toward criminality, deception, and arrogance; they resembled nothing so much as players in a theater of the damned.

Chesnutt's view of the mulatto was twofold. There were, admittedly, such people as depicted in the works of white writers—arrogant, deceitful, and pretentious—who set themselves off as a race apart. Yet, there were others who were not damned because of an admixture of blood, but rather because of the oppressive nature of the society in which they lived. This dual view led him to counteract the southern imagists on the one hand, on the other, closer to the world envisioned by Brown and Webb—closer, that is, to arguing anew the values of assimilationism based upon caste and class. "The races," he argued, "will be quite as effectively amalgamated by lightening the Negroes as they would be by darkening the whites."[30] The major objective of his fiction, therefore, is to plead the case of the mulatto before his white audience, to seek not so much to create new images, but to counteract those prevalent in the literature of his day, to sanction the divisions to which Dunbar and Washington adhered. *The House Behind the Cedars* (1900) is his first attempt in long fiction to achieve this task.

Initially entitled *Rena Walden,* the novel was designed as a character study of the heroine—Rena Walden. In commenting upon the mulatto characters found in the fiction of Albion Tourgée, Chesnutt differentiates between his and those of his white contemporaries: "In the fiction of Judge Tourgée, cultivated white Negroes are always bewailing their fate and cursing the drop of black blood which 'taints'— I hate the word, it implies corruption—their otherwise pure race."[31] Rena Walden, though a cultivated "white Negro," is "a young woman fighting for love and opportunity against the ranked forces of society, against immemorial tradition, against pride of family and of race."[32] The plan for the novel, based upon the distinction between Rena Walden and her contemporaries in the fiction of the day, was ingenious.

Take an illegitimate child, offspring of "a wealthy cultured white man" and a "free colored woman," who "in Louisiana or the West Indies . . . would have been called a quadroon or more loosely a creole; in North Carolina where fine distinctions were not the rule in matters of color, she was sufficiently differentiated when described as a bright mulatto." Upon this family arrangement build a plausible plot. At the behest of her brother John, Rena is encouraged to "pass" into the white race. She adopts a new name, Rena Warwick, is educated by her brother who, having passed previously, has achieved status and success. The mulatto becomes engaged to George Tryon, scion of a respectable southern family.

Upon receiving a telegram informing her of the illness of her mother, Rena returns to the home of her birth. A few days later, Tryon arrives in town on family business; through chance he discovers her presence and after an investigation into her parentage finds out that she is not white but Black. In light of the discovery, Chesnutt editorializes, attacks the argument that black blood leads to corruption: "Had they [Rena and John] possessed the sneaking, cringing, treacherous character traditionally ascribed to people of mixed blood—the character which the blessed institutions of a free slave-holding republic had been well adapted to foster among them; had they been selfish enough to sacrifice to their ambition the mother who gave them birth, society would have been placated or hum-bugged, and the voyage of their life might have been one of unbroken smoothness."[33] A strong moral sense, coupled with devotion to her mother, prevented Rena from taking precautions against discovery by Tryon. Far from being deceptive, she had attempted on occasion to inform him of her true racial status. In Chesnutt's view that she tried to disclose the facts, that she did not undertake strenuous precautions against discovery, leads her to undergo the fate of the "tragic mulatto."

Rejected by Tryon, she receives a position as a schoolmistress to black students and becomes the target of Jeff Wain, a mulatto. Wain measures up to the mulatto image prevalent in white fiction, and Rena's appraisal of him equals the author's: "Her clear eye, when once set to take Wain's measure, soon fathomed his shallow, selfish soul, and detected, or at least divined, behind his mask of good nature a lurking brutality which filled her with vague distrust. . . ." Wain is joined in his pursuit of Rena by Tryon. The latter, having surrendered all ideas of marriage, desires the mulatto as a mistress. Her opposition to the intentions of both Wain and Tryon enables Chesnutt to drive home the major thesis of the novel: the mental breakdown later sustained by Rena, and her death thereof, occurs not because of immorality on her part, but instead because she is morally superior to those for whom purity of blood is indicative of human worth. Her guiding principle is purity of sex—not purity of race—and when she dies in the arms of black Frank, a committed, though secret, lover, her death is attributable in part to the fact that she remained true to her womanhood, that she opposed the ethics of a society wherein values of the color line are more highly regarded than those founded upon virtue and morality.

Though Rena Walden is the central character of the novel, Molly Walden, her mother, is important in any understanding of the color-phobia among Blacks, persisting still, in this, the early part of the twentieth century. Unlike her daughter, she glorifies in her caste position, though she is not fair enough to pass for white. Happiness, along with prestige and status, are found in her role as a mulatto and her select membership in the "blue-veined society," a group composed of Blacks so fair that the blood in their veins is clearly visible through their skin. Molly is representative of those Blacks, who use pigmentation as a means of carving a special niche for themselves, who seek status based upon nothing more tangible than proximity, in terms of color, to whites. Lacking education, competence, and strength of character, her only sense of herself as a human being comes from the knowledge that though "she was not the rose, she had at least been near the rose."

Chesnutt remains sympathetic to the class of which Molly is an apt representative. Such people, he knows, are counterfeit human beings living lives of fantasy, yet the fault, in part, is attributable to the society in which they live. Unable to achieve the impossible—to become white—they were forced to construct their own world, in an attempt to distinguish themselves from oppressed Blacks. They resembled nothing so much as Pied Pipers, following the lead of the black mythologists who, true to the ethic of Social Darwinism, postulated the thesis that man in mutated form represented an improvement, culturally and morally, over the old species. Not yet so stately as the rose, the Molly Waldens were grateful for their near approximation.

The House Behind the Cedars is sentimental, overly propagandistic and badly plotted. Nevertheless, as the first novel by an African-American to deal with the ramifications of caste upon whites and Blacks, it is an important novel. Chesnutt's personal views are suspect; yet, he maintains a certain objectivity in his treatment of his characters. Each receives a certain amount of sympathy, even Wain, arrogant, pompous, unprincipled, and immoral, is proven to be no more than an adequate metaphor for the society which created him. Chesnutt's plea in his first novel, unlike that of Dunbar in *The Sport of the Gods,* is that fate can and must be altered. Change the society and "the tragic mulatto" will have no reason for existence, a nation torn by questions of color and caste no necessity for being. If the fall of Rome be attributable to corruption and decadence, the fall of America will be attributable to tradition erected upon the disseradatum of color and caste. *The House Behind the Cedars* is a protest novel, one designed to rouse the conscience of those who determine the actions of men and events.

The Marrow of Tradition, Chesnutt's second novel, appeared in 1901. Dixon's *The Leopard's Spots: A Romance of the White Man's Burden* (1865–1900) appeared one year later, and the attitude of both men toward their subject matter bears comparison. Both centered their attention upon the changing African-American, upon the transformation undergone since the days of slavery. *The Leopard's Spots* argued as its main thesis that change for Blacks was no change at all despite manumission and attempts at reconstruction, they remained inferior beings, still hewers of wood and drawers of water. For Dixon the images from preslavery days remained outstanding. Chesnutt accepted Dixon's argument in the main. Real-life examples could be found of the images and stereotypes of which Dixon was so enamored. To be sure, Blacks existed who were true to the image of "hat-in-hand servitors, uncles, aunties, and mammies." Yet Chesnutt protested accepting these as metaphors of the race. They were non-representative, specific examples of types, not general paradigms of an entire race. Having envisioned the New Negro before his birth was announced in the nineteen twenties, in contrasting Blacks of pre-slavery times with those of the Reconstruction years, he averred that the New Negro differed markedly from the old.

His assumptions on this score led him to set objectives for himself in his second novel, difficult of attainment. In an attempt to contrast Blacks before and during the Reconstruction years, he chose to analyze the social structure of a small town, Wilmington, South Carolina, scene of a race riot in 1898, and to use the town as a metaphor for the entire South during the period of Reconstruction. In *The House Behind the Cedars,* he had sought to analyze the character of Rena Walden; in his second novel, the attempt to analyze an entire community means that he must deal with too many disparate elements and individuals. The result is a badly plotted, loosely organized novel, lacking central focus. The novel is replete with conflicts. There is romantic entanglement dramatized in the quest of two young men for the hand of a woman whose guardian is one of the town's leading men; there is murder and suspense, involving the framing of a black man for a crime committed by a white. Three of the town's most powerful men engage in activities designed to disenfranchise African-Americans and an attempt is made to steal the rightful inheritance of the mulatto wife of the town's leading Black. Finally, there is the vendetta which rages between the town's two extremists—the militant angry Black, Josh Green, and the onetime slave trader, now prosperous politician, Ed McBane.

A full-scale novel might have been structured around either of these conflicts. Thrown together in the same novel they cause confusion and disorganization, bringing to mind *The Garies and Their Friends.* For Webb's novel, beset with similar difficulties, succeeded better in presenting important portraits of individuals than a comprehensive analysis of a society in transition. *The Marrow of Tradition* succeeds on much the same level. Its strength lies in the contrast between old and new images of black men. Chesnutt, in this single novel, presents the stereotype and its opposite side by side, and thus, for the first time in a black novel, balance in terms of black images is achieved.

His treatment of white characters makes the point equally as well as his treatment of black ones. Knowing that the Euro-Americans do not constitute a homogeneous grouping, he depicts a wide range of characters: the onetime overseer and slave tender, George McBane; Major

Carteret, representing the old aristocracy rising to power during Reconstruction; Delamere, kindly old ex-slave master; and young Ellis, white liberal. The animosity between white man and white man is shown in Chesnutt's discussion of the attitudes of Carteret and his associates to McBane, one which places the white man on almost equal plane with the Black. McBane, who affronted the aristocratic sensibilities of Carteret because of crudeness and vulgarity, was ". . . a product of the democratic idea operating upon the poor white man, the descendant of the indentured bondservant and the socially unfit." For a man of Carteret's standing, to rub shoulders with "an illiterate and vulgar white man of no ancestry" was surpassed only by having similar contact with Blacks.

The aristocracy is as divided upon the subjects of Blacks as they are upon other things. The elder Delamere, depicted by Chesnutt as "an old-fashioned gentleman whose ideals not even slavery had been able to spoil . . ." is not only favorable to black enterprise but also takes an interest in "their [Blacks] achievement." This attitude is dramatized in the old man's relationship to his black ward, Sandy Campbell. Mrs. Ochiltree, a wealthy old dowager, is murdered by Delamere's son Tom, who is in need of money to pay off gambling debts. Tom, who committed the murder disguised as a Negro, wore the costume belonging to Campbell. Delamere, however, refuses to accept the fact of Campbell's guilt, and when forced to choose between loyalty to his son and devotion to truth and justice, chooses the latter. He is not, however, romanticized by Chesnutt. His perceptions of Blacks are distorted by tradition. His dogmatic assertion of his ward's innocence rests upon the belief that ". . . My Negroes . . . were well raised and well behaved."[34]

Ellis, "son of a whig and non-slaveholder," displays the ambivalence concerning black men peculiar to liberals from that day to this. Favorably disposed toward Blacks, he is unable to adhere to his own principles, hold fast to his own convictions. The race riot which results from the machinations of Carteret and McBane force Ellis to reveal his true character: "In his heart he could not defend the deeds of this day. The petty annoyances which the whites had felt at the spectacle of a few Negroes in office; the not unnatural resentment of a proud people at what had seemed to them a presumptuous freedom of speech and lack of deference on the part of their inferiors—these things, which he knew were to be made the excuse for overturning the city government, he realized full well were no sort of justification for the wholesale murder or other horrors which might well ensue before the day was done. He could not approve the acts of his own people; neither could he, to a Negro, condemn them. Hence, he was silent."[35]

Chesnutt is equally successful in dramatizing differences among black people. There were, in actuality, he readily admits, such characters as Pip, Nigger Jim, Aunt Mamie, and Uncle Tom, yet there were others whose views ranged in political and social matters from ultra-conservative to strident militant. He paid obeisance to the stereotypes of old in the characterizations of Mammy Jane and her nephew, Jerry. Jane's actions and attitudes make her an apt metaphor for the "loyal darky." Listen to her comments to a young nurse, hired to help care for the Carteret child: "Look a here gal . . . I wants you ter understan' dat you got ter take good keer er dis chile; fer I nussed his mammy dere, an his gran'manny befo' im, and you is got a priv'lege dat mos lackly you don' 'preciate. I wants you to 'member, in yo incomins and outgoins, dat I got my eye on you, and am gwine ter see dat you does yo wo'k right."

The major contrast between one black character and another, however, is dramatized in the roles of the militant, Josh Green, and the conservative, Adam Miller. Green, representative of the lower classes, is the first such character in African-American fiction, and despite a sympathetic portrayal, Chesnutt is not always comfortable with the image. Men like Green, potential anarchists, are warnings of the Götterdämmerung to come if no *modus vivendi* can be worked out between the Adam Millers and the Major Carterets. Green and McBane symbolize the poles of white-black anarchy in the novel, and their conflict mirrors that between the forces of radicalism and conservatism in the town. Unable to portray Green as a race patriot, therefore, Chesnutt attributes his militancy, in part, to anger engendered by the murder of his father at the hands of the Ku Klux Klan, led by McBane: ". . . he wuz boss, he wuz de head man, an tol' de res w'at ter do. . . ." Green is prepared to ". . . die a vi'lent death in a quarrel wid a wite man. . . ."

Green and McBane represent the forces of irreconciliation pronounced in the town of Wellington. Centuries of antagonism between Blacks and whites have resulted in a vendetta between the two. This vendetta is the marrow of tradition, and if tradition continues unchanged, the smoldering fires of mistrust, hatred, and discontent will explode in conflagration marked by violence. Having created the characters of McBane and Green, Chesnutt moves beyond the optimism of his contemporaries, of Dunbar and Griggs, and envisions the world in terms of the coming apocalypse. He is, however, more moralist than cynic, though unable to maintain the moral vision throughout the novel. The apocalypse need not come. The tradition that produced Green and McBane is the tradition that also produced Adam Miller and the older Delamere. Miller serves the author in this respect as a *deus ex machina,* one, who, in the best of the Washington tradition, having survived adversity, can walk the hot coals of contention, overcoming antagonism with strength and intelligence.

He is the offspring of industrious stock. His father, an ex-slave, purchased his own freedom and achieved prosperity as a tradesman. He educated his son, who becomes a renowned man of medicine, a doctor respected everywhere except in his own town, in the best universities of America and Europe. Like Clotel, Miller is mulatto, and like Mr. Walters, ambitious and capable. But above all, though he is proud of his Anglo-Saxon heritage, he has no ambitions to enter the white race. He is closer in this respect to the characters of the novels of Jessie Fauset than to those of James Weldon Johnson or those in Chesnutt's *The House Behind the Cedars.* He is the image of the new man, representative of a special group of black men, those more fortunate in terms of education and material accomplishments than others. He is well-equipped for the role of race missionary and upon him falls the duty of uplifting his people. As a doctor, he attempts to do this by improving the health care of Blacks in the town.

He is, however, no egalitarian, and an important facet of his character is revealed in his evaluation of lower-class Blacks. He finds them at times to be good-natured, free and uninhibited, when not under the scrutinizing eyes of whites, a people capable of atavistic, sensual pleasure. On the other hand ". . . personally, and apart from the mere matter of racial sympathy, these people were just as offensive to him as to the whites. . . ." In such areas as public transportation, Miller welcomes classifications leading to barriers: "Surely if a classification of passengers on trains was at all desirable, it might be made upon some more logical and considerate basis than a mere arbitrary, tactless, and, by the very nature of things, brutal drawing of a color line."

Thus Chesnutt's argument for fair treatment of his major character is not that he is a black man, but a special kind of black man. The rebuffs which he suffers simply points out the severity of oppression, highlighting the adherence to tradition. When asked by a fellow doctor to observe an operation to be performed upon the daughter of the Major, Miller is refused. Discovered in the seating compartment of a train with the same companion, he is made to move to the dirty, smelly quarters reserved for Blacks. His wife, half-sister to the wife of Carteret, is cheated out of her inheritance, and his son is a victim of the race riot. Despite all of this, he remains a man of reason and compassion, a striking contradiction to Josh Green, the saving grace for Blacks and whites alike, metaphor of a special group within the American body politic, deserving of better treatment than other members of the race.

Chesnutt's attempt to drive home this point, however, weakens the character of Miller, making him, in the final analysis, not a special man, but one who has more in common with saints than with men. The attempt to prove Miller's dedication to peace and love rings hollow and false during the events which transpire after the race riot. Miller's own son is murdered by the rioters; he, himself, is badly mishandled. The hospital he had built is reduced to rubble. Many members of his class, personal friends, either lose their lives or flee their homes and property. Despite this, when called upon to save the life of the son of Carteret, the prime force behind the riot, Miller does so, though not without rendering a moral verdict: "There Major Carteret . . . there lies a specimen of your handiwork: There lies my only child, laid low by a stray bullet in this riot which you and your paper have fomented: struck down as much by your hand as though you had held the weapon with which his life was taken."

The contrast between Green and Miller is pronounced. A white man caused the death of Miller's son, even as a white man caused the death of Green's father. Chesnutt, however, because of his own middle-class bias, has little difficulty in unveiling the anger, unmasking the hatred, and ascribing motives of revenge to his lower-class character. Such characteristics must not be a part of the makeup of special men, for it is this that separates them from the lower class; they are capable of forgiveness and love in face of the most blatant provocation. Thus, Miller saves the life of the son of the man responsible for the murder of his own, while Josh Green violently murders the object of his hatred, Ed McBane.

Middle-class bias aside, Chesnutt is forced to face the reality of the weakness of Miller's position. Non-violence and turn the other cheek were philosophies incapable of producing change in the early part of the twentieth century. Factual evidence was not difficult to come by: There were such riots as that which took place at Wilmington, North Carolina (1899), upon which the novel was based; there was the successful disenfranchisement of Blacks; there were the resurgent lawlessness and indiscriminate violence of the Ku Klux Klan. These facts combine to make Miller's advocacy of the politics of peace and harmony appear forced and ludicrous: "Try as we may to build up the race in the essentials of good citizenship and win the good opinion of the best people, some black scoundrel comes along, and by a single criminal act . . . neutralizes the effect of a year's work." When compared to the sentiments expressed by McBane, those shared by the majority of the whites in the town, Miller's remarks are not only ludicrous but ironic as well: "Burn the nigger. . . . We seem to have the right nigger, but whether we have or not, burn a nigger. . . . The example would be all the more powerful if we got the wrong one. It would serve notice on the niggers that we shall hold the whole race responsible for the misdeeds of each individual."

Though favorably disposed toward Miller, in Green, Chesnutt has come closest to creating the image of the New Negro. Green, the revolutionary, is closer than the conservative Miller to twentieth-century man, more representative of those imbued with concern for improvement of the human condition. Anger and bitterness, at first derived from personal treatment, soon become a creative force, one which seeks to limit oppression by utilizing the tools of the oppressor. Violence becomes, for Green, a cathartic force; it is the barrier to man's ambitions enacted at the expense of others, the hour hand upon the clock of human endurance which the oppressor must not push forward. Compare the sentiments of Green on the night of the riot with those previously stated by Miller, and Green, despite Chesnutt, is the image of modern black man: "De w'ite folks are killin de niggers, an' we an' gwine ter stan' up an' be shot down like dogs. Deres two niggers in dis town ter eve'y w'ite man, an' ef we've got ter be kilt, we'll take some w'ite folks long wid us. . . ."[36]

Still Miller's is the last word, his sentiments those with which the black middle class finds accord, those championed by black men from that day to this: "My advice is not heroic, but I think it is wise. In this riot we are placed as we should be in a war; we have no territory, no base of supplies, no organization, no outside sympathy—we stand in the position of a race, in a case like this, without money and without friends. Our time will come,—the time when we can command respect for our rights, but it is not yet in sight. Give it up boys, and wait. Good may come of this, after all."[37] The black middle class has always opted for *supposed* wisdom instead of heroism.

By focusing upon situations and events, and presenting contrasts between one character and another, Chesnutt, in *The Marrow of Tradition* and *The House Behind the Cedars,* attempted to analyze the social consequences of heritage and history upon the individual. The new naturalism was still in its infancy, yet Chesnutt had already moved beyond its major premise, that the environment in which men live directs and controls their lives. There were, for him, factors equally as important—history and tradition; these were less difficult to confront and to change. Both novels, therefore, are historical, in the sense that the characters of each are always in conflict with the past. When he looked at the American society through the eyes of a black novelist, Chesnutt saw men engaged in a futile battle to alter the course of history and tradition. His conclusions, in the main, are not encouraging. Society and environment are conducive to change. Tradition, due to human failure, is not. Man's inability, therefore, to free himself from tradition and to learn from history were major factors in his inability to produce the humane social order. Like Du Bois, Chesnutt demanded that his age leap across the barriers erected by history and tradition, and by burying the old gods of irrelevance—hatred, prejudice, enmity— move forward to create a better world.

He is at one and the same time pessimist and optimist; and yet, despite this, he is more idealistic than his contemporaries. His horizons are higher, his belief in the ability of men and institutions to change, stronger than that of Washington, who appeared more cynic than believer, or than that of Dunbar, who held few such beliefs in regard to either men or institutions. Unlike Delany, Chesnutt cannot foresee a new world ushered in upon the shoulders of revolution, yet in his better moments, he might pray for a society in which the "talented tenth," having dramatized by example the true worth of black men, might bring about substantive change in the black condition. He believed that the human condition might be changed if the negative values derived from old traditions were destroyed. Without such fundamental changes, the future was bleak for Black and white alike. Despite technical deficiences, *The Marrow of Tradition* is Chesnutt's best effort in long fiction. Unlike Dunbar, he did not shirk from warfare with the imagists, did not agree totally to the proposition that the stock characters of the Plantation school of literature were adequate representatives of a people who had survived numerous holocausts throughout their history. He was inhibited by time and age from developing a sensibility that bordered upon egalitarianism; he could not truthfully adhere to the democratic ideal. As aristocratic in intention as his white contemporaries, like Webb and Brown he did not oppose categorization, sought not the destruction of class stratification, but only those based upon race and caste. His portrait of Adam Miller, like that of Josh Green, will transcend the ages—Green, no less than Blake, doomed to oblivion until the nineteen seventies. Yet, the very manifestation of the Greens in the modern era, their resurgence in life and literature after the tumultuous sixties, says something about the clarity of Chesnutt's vision concerning the future. His major thesis from one novel to another is that the failure to confront history and tradition means to make obsolete such representative black men as Adam Miller. That Richard Wright, forty years later, would conclude that such circumstances mandated the creation of Bigger Thomas, cast in the mold of Josh Green, is already to speak of the Adam Millers, in fiction, if not in fact, as relics of a bygone era.

III

THE NEW NEGRO

Dunbar died in 1906, having published his last novel, *The Sport of the Gods,* four years earlier. Though Chesnutt lived until 1932, he published his last novel, *The Colonel's Dream,* in 1905. In the war against the imagists, Dunbar scarcely entered the fray at all, while Chesnutt did so in limited fashion in *The Marrow of Tradition.* Neither was successful, however, in stemming the tide of acceptance, north and south, by Blacks as well as whites, of the images popularized by Harris, Page, and Dixon. This was due, in part, to the fact that neither saw this task as the function of the novel, and though Chesnutt unwillingly used the novel for such ends, his books were not widely read in the black communities. This meant that such new images as represented by Josh Green were unavailable to Blacks except those of the middle class, that in those cases where positive images were created, only whites had unlimited access to the material. The war was doubly difficult to wage in a country where Blacks had no control over the media of propaganda and where the novelist found himself in daily competition against the tabloid, more quickly and easily read than a long work of fiction.

As offensive as most tabloids were to the masses of Blacks, they were apt to be of more importance, to be valued more highly than novels, and the writers accorded greater status than poets or writers of fiction. Part of Dunbar's fame (and pain) can be attributed to the fact that in writing poetry, let alone novels, he was considered something of a freak, a mutant upon the genus Homo sapiens. Knowing little of Brown, Webb, or Delany, the African-American was apt to be as astonished as whites at the fact that one of his number was capable of writing a novel. Like other artifacts which attested to one's mastery of culture, books were not deemed the prerogative of the sons and daughters of darky entertainers, docile children, and brute Negroes. Thus the problem of acceptance and distribution of material plagued the early novelists to an extent that made them almost unknown—Dunbar remains an exception—among all but a few Americans, black or white.

This problem, however, did not daunt the determination of the Baptist minister, Sutton E. Griggs (1872–1930). One of the early opponents of Washington, he was the first black writer to establish his own publishing company. He solved the problem of distribution by selling his books in the black community and, as a result, as Hugh Gloster points out, he was more widely read among African-Americans than his contemporaries. Unlike Dunbar and Chesnutt, he was not indebted to white patronage: Dunbar owed much of his success and fame to William Dean Howells; Chestnutt owed much of his to Richard Gilder, editor of *Century* magazine. Such patronage assured the novelist a place in posterity and meant that his works would receive some publicity; on the other hand, however, it imposed censorship upon him that made it almost impossible for him to be candid with his audience. Exercising control over his material, Griggs was immune to censorship and more prone to honesty than his fellow novelists.

Very little recognition has been accorded him, though he is perhaps the most important black novelist since Martin Delany. To read Griggs is to be propelled light-years into the future, bypassing the era of the Harlem Renaissance, the years of the Richard Wright rebellion, the years of reaction by such writers as Baldwin and Ellison, to arrive, finally, in the modern era. His contribution to the genre is not, to be sure, in terms of style, technique, or innovation in form; in each of these areas he is inferior to both Chesnutt and Dunbar. In fact, his approach to the mechanics of the novel was one of laissez-faire, and one comes away with the impression that form for this novelist was merely the vehicle for the discussion of ideas, one that served too often as an impediment to more serious undertakings. No, the black writer would learn nothing from Griggs in terms of technical construction of the novel. He is a novelist of ideas, and it is here that his strength lay. Look to him in 1889 and already the age of Marcus Garvey has arrived, the internecine warfare between Blacks of differing skin color becomes more intensified, the effects of class stratification and the headlong rush of men to negate their own cultural artifacts displayed in argumentative prose reminiscent of the nineteen fifties and beyond.

When Robert Bone, author of *The Negro Novel in America* (1958), argues that Griggs is an impostor, that he is not the forerunner of the New Negro, that his militant Black Nationalism was a façade beneath which he hid his accommodationist philosophy, he is not to be taken seriously. For an understanding of Black Nationalism, not surprisingly, Bone consulted his own imagination.* Griggs, on the other hand, through association with black people, knew firsthand the conflict facing the Black Nationalist, born on American soil and lacking land, the major element of a nationalist philosophy. Whether Griggs is nationalist or assimilationist must be determined by reading his novels; the question cannot be answered by accepting the words of a white critic, prone to view Black Nationalism and assimilationism from his own limited perspective. In each of his five novels, Griggs objectively presents side by side the viewpoints of radical and conservative alike. Attention is focused more upon debate than upon personalities, more upon advancing ideas than championing any particular one. His first novel, *Imperium in Imperio* (1889), evidences his desire to present a many-sided debate, to focus attention upon the two major ideas in African-American thought and history—nationalism and assimilationism.

The novel centers around the experiences of its two major characters, Belton Piedmont and Bernard Belgrave. Both men represent parallel, yet contradictory, positions on the question of black survival in America. Piedmont, poor and dark in complexion, represents "the spirit of conservatism in the Negro race." Belgrave, mulatto son of an interracial marriage, represents the spirit of intractable militancy. The story is told through the narration of a onetime member of the "Imperium," and the first episodes in the novel deal with the education of the two central characters. Educational attainment is difficult for Piedmont. Lack of funds, discrimination, and a background of poverty are impediments. However, in Booker T. Washington fashion, he overcomes each and upon graduation from college becomes president of an all-black college. Aided by his white father's money and influence, Belgrave, on the other hand, has no difficulty in completing his education and becoming a lawyer of such stature that he argues a case before the Supreme Court.

By presenting the educational ambitions and attainments of his two

* Bone's hackneyed evaluation of Black Nationalism may be found in his study, *The Negro Novel in America*, pp. 6, 7, and contrasted with W. E. B. Du Bois' approach to the subject in the essay, "The Conservation of Races" (Washington, D.C., The American Negro Academy), 1897, pp. 5–15.

central characters, Griggs evidences his belief that education is indispensable in confronting the problems of race. So important is this belief that it forms the working thesis of the novel and is dramatized in the creation of the Imperium, an organization which maintains as its objective ". . . to unite all Negroes in a body to do that which the whimpering government childishly but truthfully says it cannot do." Such an organization can be successful only to the extent that it is manned by educated men. This thesis, presented three years before Du Bois reached similar conclusions in *The Souls of Black Folk,* is the key to achieving success in the war against the imagists. Look again at the novels of Dunbar and Chesnutt and, in the one case, education remains the primary possession of whites—in none of Dunbar's novels does an educated Black appear—and in Chesnutt, education is technical, leading to the creation of doctors, lawyers, and newspapermen. Missing are the thinkers, those capable of dealing in abstractions, of molding language into implements of warfare designed to create a new language system.

In *Imperium in Imperio,* characters appear, whose education has been designed to produce thinkers, creative men instead of pragmatists, who for the first time achieve eminence in an African-American novel. Griggs knows full well that such men represent a danger not only to the status quo, but even more so to white propagandists: Once men begin to think for themselves, the era of acceptance of other men's definitions and terminology is at an end. Both Piedmont and Belgrave are thinking men. They are also activists, who view education as the means of bringing about revolution. With these qualifications the two men become important in the formation of the new organization, and, after careful interrogation, Belgrave is chosen as its first president.

Though Piedmont and Belgrave are archetypes of the intellectual rebels of black fiction found in the seventies, they are of less importance to Sutton Griggs than the idea of the Imperium itself. The idea is unique, and to understand the distinction between the Imperium and similar secret societies among Blacks demands an understanding of the makeup and character of those which had grown in number since the Civil War. Such organizations—lodges, fraternities, and orders—were composed of middle-class Blacks like Jerome, Ellis, and Berry Hamilton, characters in the Fiction of Brown, Webb, and Dunbar respectively, men with low-status occupations, and here and there, members of the black professional class. Most of the organizations were, and remain, carbon copies of those of whites. Most were, and are, vehicles for the aspirations, statuswise, of the black middle class. Those devoted exclusively to the liberation of black people lay many years in the future and not until Marcus Garvey, in 1916, will an attempt be made to establish an organization resembling that of the Imperium.

The Imperium, unlike the civil rights organizations of a later period, was an organization with membership limited exclusively to Blacks. Moreover, it represented a government in exile. Here, all Blacks were to bring their grievances; here all differences within the race were to be adjudicated. Blacks were no longer to fight each other "before prejudiced courts." In addition to a judiciary, the Imperium boasted its own army, enlisted every available citizen, elected a congress, "one member for every fifty thousand citizens," and modeled a constitution, "except in a few important particulars," upon that of the United States. The organization, having lain dormant for many years, performing its work in secret, surfaces after a fatal attack upon a black postmaster, an Imperium member, by a white mob. The Imperium is called into session to ". . . consider what shall be our attitude, immediate and future, to this Anglo-Saxon race." The president, in convening the assemblage, is more direct: "Let us . . . decide what shall be the relations that shall henceforth exist between us and the Anglo-Saxon race of the United States of America."

A bill of particulars is drawn up against the American Government. On such topics as the industrial situation, education, civil rights, and justice in the courts, Piedmont's indictments draw accolades from the assembled body. His summary is aimed at government and individual white citizen alike: "The monarchical trait seems not to have left their blood. They have apparently chosen our race as an empire, and each Anglo-Saxon regards himself as a petty king. . . . Our kings, the Anglo-Saxons, speak for us, their slaves." The Imperium is admonished ". . . at all hazards [to], strike a blow for freedom. If it calls for a Thermopylae, be free. If it calls for a Valley Forge, be free. If contending for our rights, given unto us by God, causes us to be slain, let us perish on the field of battle. . . ."

After the bill of particulars are presented, three major ideas predominate the discussion. The assimilationist idea is argued by one speaker: "As long as we remain here as a separate and distinct race we shall continue to be oppressed. We must lose our identity. I, therefore, urge that we abandon the idea of becoming anything noteworthy as a separate and distinct race and send the word forth that we amalgamate." Emigration to the African Congo "met with much favor"; however, because the speaker did "not make clear the practicability of his scheme," it was not considered. The proposal accorded the greatest applause, that which brings the Imperium to its feet in unison, is the proposal for war: "Whereas the history of our treatment by the Anglo-Saxon race is but the history of oppression, and whereas, our patient endurance of evil has not served to decrease this cruelty, but seems rather to increase it; and whereas, the ballot box, the means of peaceful revolution is denied us, therefore: *Be it Resolved* that the hour for wreaking vengeance for our multiplied wrongs has come. *Resolved* secondly: That we at once proceed to war for the purpose of accomplishing the end just named, and for the further purpose of obtaining all our rights due us as men."

This proposal precipitates the conflict between Piedmont and Belgrave, reveals the former as the man of conservative mien, the latter as the radical. "Allow me to note this great fact"—Piedmont assumes the rostrum in rebuttal—"that by enslavement in America the Negro has come into possession of the great English language. . . . Nor must we ever forget that it was the Anglo-Saxon who snatched from our idolatrous grasp the deaf images to which we prayed, and the Anglo-Saxon who pointed us to the lamb of God that takes away the sins of the world." Piedmont's objective is to prevent the Imperium from adopting a platform of all-out war. To accomplish these ends, he argues that the good which derived from being an American citizen offsets the evil, and that rather than declare war, the Imperium should accept a compromise resolution, one which allows the Anglo-Saxons time to address remaining grievances. He argues, therefore, that the Imperium spend four years in an attempt to "impress the Anglo-Saxon that he has a New Negro on his hands" and that the nation must surrender its hegemony over his life and destiny. If this approach fails, if after four years, Blacks have not secured the rights and privileges due them as citizens, then the members of the Imperium should abandon their homes, emigrate in a body to the state of Texas, and secure "possession of the State government." This accomplished, the group might proceed to work out its ". . . destiny as a separate and distinct race in the United States of America."[1]

Piedmont, to be sure, is an improvement over the characters offered in the novels of Webb, Dunbar, and Chesnutt; yet, he falls far short of being a black revolutionary. He is more symbolic of the black men who dominate the affairs of African-Americans in the coming years, those able to compromise militancy in the interests of a spurious patriotism. He is an assimilationist who believes, above all, that the solution to racial conflict is possible when black men approach the norms established by whites. Were he the final definition of twentieth-century black man, offered by Griggs, he would still be the "New Negro"—a marked improvement over the offerings of black writers in the past. Concomitantly, however, he is but another image which black writers will have to demolish, another definition of man to be erased from the black mind. Though imbued with a social consciousness and committed to the welfare of his people, he remains wedded to the value system of the Anglo-Saxons, believes that Euro-American civilization constitutes the zenith of man's accomplishments, that the black man's fidelity must be first to the Christian God, second, to the white nation, and third, to black people. He is to be numbered among those who have forgotten the holocaust, who have said to their sons and daughters that as bad as slavery might have been, it provided us with benefits, enabled us to live among the Americans, and gave us an opportunity to partake of Euro-American civilization.

Despite Griggs's own bias and intentions, Belgrave, not Piedmont, is destined to fulfill the role of the New Negro. As depicted by Griggs, he symbolizes the mulatto class, is descended from Clotel, Molly Walden, and Jeff Wain. Because of his parentage, special privileges are accorded him, and in comparison with Piedmont, he receives adulation and praise from society and teacher alike: "Belton [Piedmont] was singled out by the teacher as a special object on which he might expend his spleen. . . . But toward Bernard none of this evil spirit was manifested. . . . To the one he was all kindness; while to the other he was cruel to the extreme." Conversely, however, it is these privileges, granted as a result of his complexion, that Belgrave rebels against. Interracial liaisons become his main target, and though one may follow Griggs and charge self-hatred as motivation, still, Belgrave accepts the dying command of his fiancée, devotes his life to war against the illicit union which produced him. "Study the question of the intermingling of the races." If miscegenation "is causing the destruction of the race, then you must devote your energy to bring about separation of the races, and if this cannot be achieved on American shores, then lead our people forth from this accursed land."[2]

Once again, like Blake and Josh Green, a hero emerges, who is thrust into the role because of personal acts of injustice, and as a result, moves to embrace the cause of justice for all. Upon ascending to the presidency of the Imperium, Belgrave is reminiscent of mulatto heroes of the stature of Frederick Douglass, those who knew that the war against injustice was the first priority. His program, offered in substitution for Piedmont's, is based upon revolution: "Quietly purchase all Texas land contiguous to states and territories of the Union. Build small commonplace huts on these lands and place rapid fire disappearing guns in fortifications dug beneath them. . . . We will demand the surrender of Texas and Louisiana to the Imperium. Texas, we will retain. Louisiana, we will cede to our foreign allies for their aid. Thus will the Negro have an empire of his own, fertile in soil, capable of sustaining a population of fifty million people.[3] I know the Anglo-Saxon race," he adds in rebuttal to his proposal. "He will never admit you to equality with him. I am fully determined on my course of action and will persevere."

With Piedmont dead and the Imperium, under Belgrave, moving toward war with the United States, Griggs, with the aid of a deus ex machina, brings his novel to a denouement. The plans adopted by the Imperium are revealed to the government. Though the fate of the organization is not told, the two options, as the narrator-informer Berl Trout informs the audience, are that the Imperium will be either "broken up or watched." The betrayal, as Trout himself calls it, however, was motivated by love of liberty and justice, and Griggs, speaking through his narrator, warns his readers that if you destroy one device, love of liberty will cause men to construct others even "more powerful." "When," he asks, "will all races and classes of men learn that men made in the image of God will not be the slaves of another image?"

Despite internal contradictions, faulty structure, inept characterization, and stilted dialogue, *Imperium in Imperio* is the first novel by a black writer to attempt to coalesce the predominant ideas of black Americans at the time. The struggle for the supremacy of the ideas of assimilationism or nationalism is symbolized in the persons of Piedmont and Belgrave, and the questions they pose have ramifications far beyond the nineteenth century: Is it possible for a people to work out their destiny under the hostile rule of another people? Should members of a minority assimilate with the majority or seek physical separation? *Imperium in Imperio* provides no answers to these questions. It is almost alone, however, in the nineteenth century in bringing them to the fore, and Griggs is singular in presenting both sides of the argument with objectivity if not always with clarity.

The novel is transitional, representing a bridge between the fiction of outright accommodation and that of questioning militancy. The questions asked are to be answered by a later generation, and Griggs's greatest accomplishment in this novel, outside of providing paradigms for the "New Negro," was to provide a framework upon which later novelists might build. Moreover, he bequeathed to those who would follow a legacy of inquisitiveness, a questioning born out of a determination to accept nothing as fact without close examination. Label his plan "fantastic" if one will. Yet but a few years and over one million people will believe in the viability and necessity of an organization similar to the Imperium—The Universal Negro Improvement Association. The value of *Imperium,* over all, lay in the relevancy and immediacy with which it speaks to the modern black sensibility.

The Hindered Hand (1905), Griggs's fourth novel, ranks with *Imperium in Imperio* as one of the major contributions to black fiction before the Renaissance years. This evaluation has little to do with form and structure, character delineation, or dialogue. The faults in these areas are even more outstanding than they were in his previous novels. Plots are so numerous that no central one emerges; language is as stilted as that in the former works. Lacking even an elementary knowledge of the usage of time, Griggs moves his characters from one continent to another, in and out of incidents, with little attention to coherence or organization. The book, however, is the only work of the period between Delany and Chesnutt to directly answer the charges made by Thomas Dixon. And Griggs is the first novelist since Delany to unequivocally engage in the war for control of images. In *Imperium* and *Overshadowed* (1901), his second novel, he had waged a caustic battle, matching propaganda for propaganda. He was more concerned in these works with presenting alternatives to the images created by Page and his followers—Blacks of unquestionable virtue, superior educational attainments, and more than average intellect. This is true also, to an extent, in his fourth novel; yet, here he surpasses his previous efforts. In direct reference to Dixon's *The Leopard's Spots,* Griggs, speaking through Ensal, his major character, pinpoints the major dilemma facing Blacks in the centuries-old war: "Ensal thought of the odds against the Negro in this literary battle: how the Southern white people, being more extensive purchasers of books than Negroes, would have the natural bias of the great publishing agencies on their side; how the Northern white people, resident in the South, for social and business reasons, might hesitate to father books not in keeping with the prevailing sentiment of Southern white people; how the residents of the North, who assayed to write in defense of the Negro, were laughed out of school as mere theorists ignorant of actual conditions; and finally, how that a lack of leisure and the absence of general culture handicapped the Negro in fighting his battle in this species of warfare."

The major objective of *The Hindered Hand* is to serve as an offering in this war. For this reason, characters and situations alike are used by the author to do battle with his antagonists—the southern propagandists. If Dixon and others defined the black man as a degenerate, Griggs represented him, in the persons of Earl Bluefield and Ensal Ellwood, as the black man having reached the apex of civilization. If the argument was made that the desire of black everyman was for a white woman, Griggs counterattacked by offering evidence of the destruction wrought upon the race as a result of miscegenation, caused by the actions of white men. If Dixon insisted that Blacks achieve status as Americans, accept their designations as wards of the state, Griggs countered by advocating immigration; if the Southerners remained enamored of past images—the black man as darky entertainer and contented child—Griggs depicted, in Earl, the image of the militant Black.

Thus the conflict in the novel mirrors the larger conflict between Griggs and the southern writers. The Southerners enunciated the conditions under which America would tolerate the "inferior element" in its midst; Griggs's objective, in rebuttal, was to enunciate the terms upon which black men were willing to live and die in America. However, conclusive response from Blacks depended upon resolution of the conflict between the militant and conservative elements of the race. Ensal Ellwood and his friend Earl Bluefield ". . . represent two types in the Negro race, the conservative and the radical. They both stood for the ultimate recognition of the rights of the Negro as an American citizen, but their methods were opposite." Like Piedmont, his literary ancestor, Ensal favors moral suasion, believing that ". . . acceptance of slavery on the part of the Negro in preference to extermination was evidence of adaptability to conditions that assured the presence of the Negro on the earth in the final windup of things. . . ." In a plan addressed "To the People of the United States," Ensal points out the relationship between politics and race, arguing that the government must move out of the business of repression, cease obstructing the desire of a faithful people to become one with other Americans.

Earl is the literary descendant of Bernard Belgrave. A militant, who continually chides the race for its lack of aggressiveness, he opts for violence over non-violence: "In Almaville here I have a picked band of five hundred men who are not afraid to die. Tonight we shall creep upon yonder hill and take charge of the state capital. . . . When called upon to surrender, we shall issue forth our grievances as a race and demand that they be righted. . . . We shall not surrender. Each of us has solemnly sworn not to come out of the affair alive, even if we have to commit suicide." Having presented the two ideologies along with plans of action, Griggs puts forward an evaluation, charting a middle ground between the two. Both ideologies and programs are necessary; yet, any plan that evolves must "be the output of brains, rather than veins."

The plan offered by the mother of the heroine, Tiara Merlow, however, is unacceptable, though it will find favor in another form, in 1972, with the publication of John A. Williams' *Captain Blackman*. Putting the assimilationist ideal, "whiter and whiter every generation," into practical use, Tiara's mother hoped to create a class of mulattoes, who by infiltrating the white race, would take over control of the political apparatus: "My mother's ancestors," relates Tiara, "made a practice of intermarrying with mulattoes, until in her case, all traces of Negro blood, so far as personal appearance was concerned, had disappeared." The plan was to create a race of mixed bloods ". . . who could pass for white." This group, maintaining "unswerving devotion" to the Negro race, once having secured all power in the nation, would "shake the Southern system to its foundation." None of the plans for the salvation of the race bear fruition. Those of Tiara's mother are laid bare by the daughter in a court of law. Ensal, after a fight with Earl and misconceptions regarding his fiancée, emigrates to Africa, returning at the end of the novel to discover that Earl has adopted a more conservative stance, has embarked upon a program to induce the national government to make the issue of repression a national question to be adjudicated in open referendum by the American people.

The Hindered Hand is one man's attempt to combat the malicious propaganda of his time, to wage war in defense of the right of his people to define themselves. He does not move all the way, does not call for total evaluation of American values. Like William Wells Brown, Griggs is essentially a moralist, his philosophy geared toward faith and belief in the nobility of man. Thus he wavers between conservatism and radicalism, between revolution as symbolized by Bluefield and passive action as symbolized in the person of Ensal. If forced to choose, there is little doubt, in this novel or the others, that his choice would have weighed heavily upon the side of men like Ensal and Piedmont, would have chosen conservatism over militancy. Yet he was too honest a man to sublimate his anger, too outraged by the events since emancipation to adopt a policy of outright accommodation. *The Hindered Hand,* therefore, is another novel that sounds a warning to white America; yet, equally as important, it is a novel which tries to clarify the central dilemma confronting black people at the turn of the century. For torn between faith in American principles, yet distrustful of those charged with upholding them, where did hope lie for the race? "The overwhelmingly predominant sentiment of the American Negroes," Griggs concludes *The Hindered Hand,* "is to fight out their battles on these shores." Given the tremendous odds against them, however, what success was possible?

At this point, Griggs moves away from the pessimism evidenced in *Overshadowed,* takes a stance similar to that of thinking black men of his age. The decision was to return to the American battlefield, to wage war against the imagists, to attempt to free men by making them conscious of their identity, history, and culture. To do this was to move toward constructing the great society upon American shores. In his last novel, *Pointing the Way,* Griggs makes this the central theme, evidences a conciliatory posture missing from the former novels. Convinced that he had christened the New Negro in his previous works, and that he had brought into the open debates centering upon race relations as they affected whites and Blacks, and having, for pragmatic reasons, leaned toward conservatism, he moved in his final novel to point out the way in which both races, through political co-operation, might bring about the new society.

The last novel, *Pointing the Way,* ranks below *Imperium in Imperio, The Hindered Hand,* and *Overshadowed,* but above the third novel, *Unfettered.* Though the old doubts raised in the previous works of black-white co-operation are present in this latter novel, Griggs evidences uncharacteristic optimism, chooses the path of hope instead of outright despair. Looking back upon the period in which he lived, and considering his own achievements, it is not difficult to understand why. Despite conditions in the latter part of the nineteenth century—race riots, disenfranchisement, legalized discrimination, there was considerable activity and movement among black people. By focusing debate upon the questions of conservatism and radicalism, the Washington-Du Bois controversy forced black intellectuals into the arena of ideas. Once the debate gained in intensity, they were forced to question the nature of society itself, to view the holocaust as other than an unfortunate, even, benevolent occurrence, to look for the deeper implications of its meaning.

At some point they were forced to ask if it might not be re-enacted and engulf them also, despite the barrier they maintained between themselves and the less fortunate. Thus the idea of individualism began to recede, and the idea of racial unity gained ascendancy. This shift by some members of the black middle class was pragmatic in nature. Theirs was acceptance of the fact that the Adam Millers were no freer from oppression than the Josh Greens. In addition, as education became widespread, many Blacks became aware of the debilitating effects of racial stereotypes and of the dangers that resulted when the race was defined by its adversaries. They realized the awesome power exercised by those who controlled the system of language: "The historical and literary libels," wrote novelist J. W. Grant, in 1909, "the minstrel show, the 'ragtime' music and advertising designs have, at all times, held the Negro up to contemptuous gaze, and pictured him as a fawning fool."[4] If then, black men wanted ". . . the truths of [their] history, thralldom, persecution, degradation, ostracism, and success and triumphs over [their] enemies told, [they] must tell it."[5]

In this area lies the major contribution of Sutton Griggs. Unwilling to accept the images and definitions handed down through the years, he attempted to create new ones based upon his own knowledge of the great diversity within the race. Thus none of his black men, unlike some in the novels of Dunbar and Chesnutt, are without dignity; none either clownish or brutal. He saw the race as being comprised of conservatives and radicals, and he was cognizant of the growing class of educated black men and women who had tired of the old definitions and, though not willing to accept completely the programs of either Du Bois or Washington, were no less intent upon finding new ways to wage the old struggle.

Such insights make him the prophet of the New Negro. The themes he enunciated and the images of black men and women he created people the novels of the twentieth century. The success he realized in unfettering the minds of thousands of black readers was not his alone. Of all the novelists since Delany, Griggs is more closely allied to the nineteenth-century writer in terms of spirit and vision. Both would have agreed that a new image must emerge from the ashes of the old, and this image, becoming flesh, then body, must devote his talents and energies to the liberation of African-Americans as a whole.

This idea, which orginated as far back as Delany, received explication in Du Bois' concept of the "talented tenth"—those individuals within the race, more gifted than others, who were to exercise their talents in bringing about changes that would benefit less fortunate Blacks. The idea finds its way into Du Bois' novel, *The Quest of the Silver Fleece* (1911). The best novel, technically conceived, between *The Garies and Their Friends* and *The Autobiography of an Ex-Coloured Man,* it is the first *Bildungsroman* in African-American literature. Tracing the lives of its two major characters, Bles and Zora, from childhood to adulthood, the action shifts from the South to the North, and back to the South again. Here the novel might be compared with Dunbar's *The Sport of the Gods,* in which a similar shifting of the action of the story and the major characters takes place. The difference between the two, however, is pointed up by the events which proceed the return south of the characters of each work. In *The Sport of the Gods,* Joe and his wife return to the paternalism and benevolence of the wife of their former employer. In Du Bois' work, however, Bles and Zora return to wage war against the cotton barons, who in controlling the economy of the region control the lives of the people as well.

The central metaphor of the novel is cotton, and its influence is measured by the power it symbolizes for southern landowners and "Yankee capitalists" and the serfdom it represents for Blacks and poor whites. Wielding the reins of power are John Taylor, shrewd northern manipulator and the blue-blooded southern aristocrat, Colonel St. John Cresswell. In order to acquire more power and money, a combination is formed between northern capital, represented by Taylor, and southern influence, represented by Cresswell. The two men are determined to defraud the small landholder and planter of their crops. Such an undertaking involves national politics, the manipulation of elections, north and south: ". . . but look here," Taylor remonstrates, "we've got the stock so placed that nothing short of a popular upheaval can send any child-labor bill through Congress in six years. . . . Same thing applies to the tariff. The last bill ran ten years. The present bill will last longer . . . especially if Smith is in the Senate."[6]

Like a giant octopus, cotton, the silver fleece, controls the lives of black men at present as completely as it did in the days of bondage: "When cotton rose, the tenants had already sold their cotton; when cotton fell, the landlords squeezed the rations and lowered wages. So it was that the bewildered black serf dawdled in listless inability to understand." There is a marked continuity between yesterday and today, symbolized by the permanence of things—the existence of slavery in new form. The old feudal system of master and slave, with accompanying evils—miscegenation, brutality, and exploitation—has been passed down from one Cresswell to another and become so central an element to the slavocracy that its roots run as deep as the cotton crop in the southern soil. Against the twentieth-century version of this feudal system, the eternal victims, those, for whom cotton was yesterday, and remains today, the rationale for educational deprivation, inhuman living conditions, and outright acts of violence, are allied.

Yet permanence is not all pervasive. There is change, though not in institutions nor in the seekers after power, nor even in the great mass of black people whose fate is controlled by Northerner and Southerner alike. The change has been wrought in the young—in such as Zora Cresswell and Bles Alwyn. Picture Zora, child of the swamp, who had once been seduced by a son of Cresswell. She is a mystic, a dreamer of fairylands and castles. Initially, she harbors an intense dislike of education; however, after traveling north under the wardship of white philanthropists, she begins to educate herself. Change is manifested through a growing awareness of the plight of her people. The sermon of a black minister, which inspires her to devote her life and energy to aiding them, precipitates her return to the South: "Forget yourselves and your petty wants, and behold your starving people. The wail of black millions sweeps the air—east and west the cry, Help! . . . Give up your pleasures; give up your wants; give up all to the weak and wretched of our people. Go down to Pharaoh and smite him in God's name. Go down to the South where we writhe. Strike—work—build—hew—lead—inspire. . . . The Harvest is waiting. Who will cry: 'Here am I; send me!'"[7]

Change is manifested also in young Alwyn. Unlike Zora, he early displays a thirst for knowledge; on his own initiative, he enrolls in a school for black children. His pattern of maturation differs also from that of Zora's. To transcend his former condition, he must travel a lonely, solitary path to manhood, and each episode of his life is but a preparation. The path is paved with disillusionment, trial and error, and constant reverses. One such example occurs in a particular incident concerning his relationship with Zora. When Bles discovers that Zora, beautiful Zora, was deflowered by the son of her former master, he severs the relationship and takes the first step toward manhood: "These days were days of alternate hope and doubt with Bles Alwyn. Strength and ambition and inarticulate love were fighting within him. He felt, in the dark thousands of his kind about him, a mighty calling to deeds. He was becoming conscious of the narrowness and straightness of his black world, and red anger flashed in him ever and again as he felt his bonds."[8]

Education, so important a symbol in this novel, means also to come to grips with the inevitability of interracial strife. Alwyn, residing in the North, becomes a major force in the Republican party. When he is considered for a job as treasurer, the highest appointed position for a black man, he is undone through collusion between jealous Blacks and southern whites. But education entails, too, an awareness of the ways of black folk: "When he looked about him for fellowship he found himself in a strange dilemma: those black folk, in whom he recognized the old sweet-tempered Negro traits, had also looser, uglier manners than he was accustomed to, from which he shrank. The upper classes of Negroes . . . were strangers . . . because of a curious coldness and aloofness that made them cease to seem like his own kind; they seemed almost at times like black white people—strangers in way and thought."[9]

The success of Alwyn's education, the maturation of the boy to manhood, and the central conflict of his life evolve around the mulatto Miss Wynn, who, along with others in her set, were said to prefer "the lighter shades of colored folk." When Alwyn threatens to attack the Republican party for reneging on a campaign promise to support an educational bill, he is offered bribery in the form of Miss Wynn and an appointment to the position of treasurer. Thus the conflict: To violate his principles is to gain Miss Wynn and to achieve success. To abide by them is to lose both. After soul-searching deliberation, the answer is clear: ". . . to be a man! To say calmly, 'No!' To stand in that great audience and say 'my people first and last.'" Bles passes the test, achieves manhood, is now ready to return south to rejoin Zora and their war against the owners of the silver fleece.

They enlist the help of poor black serfs in this endeavor, imploring them to help themselves, by striking a blow for freedom against the power men. At first their appeals are rebuffed because of fear, ignorance, and the divisive efforts of a black minister controlled by whites. Soon, however, the idea of using the swamp to plant their own cotton, of establishing co-operative farming in the black belt is accepted, and the people rise to heroic heights: ". . . Before sunrise, tools were in the swamp, axes and saws and tugging of mules was heard. The forest trembled as by some mighty magic, swaying and falling with crash on crash. Huge bonfires blazed and crackled, until at last a wide black scar appeared in the thick south side of the swamp, which widened and widened to full twenty acres."

The heroism of the black people in the novel, the turn of Zora and Bles from individual pursuits to those involving unity of race, is symbolic of the change taking place among black people between 1853 and 1911 in general and the black writer in particular. The most effective of the black writers were not inclined to accept definitions of the race created by outsiders. Dunbar, of course, was an exception: Personal problems forced him out of step with his race and time. Chesnutt, though all too infrequently, not only challenged the negative images existing in the literature of his time but, in addition, offered more positive ones. Griggs and Du Bois continually challenged the imagists, and though their characters remain wedded to American values and ideals, they are images of thinking black men in an era when such provoked ribald laughter.

Both men mirrored the events of their time. Though but a few years from slavery (thirty-five at the time of publication of Du Bois' novel), black people had begun to create an intelligentsia. The "enlightened men of the race" forced to choose between the program of Washington and that of Du Bois were more likely now to accept the latter, which urged movement outside of the narrow concerns of the black world and into those of the wider world, in order to understand it and to deal with it. Aided in the coming years by *The Crisis, Opportunity, The Negro World, The Messenger,* and other lesser known black magazines, African-Americans began more and more to question the definitions which circumscribed them. This is not to suggest that a millennium had been reached. The twentieth century would have its blacks in black face—black-faced minstrels who painted their faces blacker still, men who acted out the roles of comic buffoon, docile ward, feeble-minded child, and to one another, brute Negro. Yet these were no longer images regarded as symbolic of a race, surely not by Blacks, who had become secure enough and confident enough in themselves to think of each other in broader more human terms. Blacks might go to the theater to see *The Green Pastures,* might laugh at the antics of "de Lawd," but they knew that he and his train were little more than an exercise of the fantasy of white folks, that no such characters existed in the black community, and that even those who pranced and clowned upon the stage were practicing deception upon whites who insisted that they "knew their Negroes."

In varying ways, each of the novelists of the late nineteenth-early twentieth centuries contributed to the growth of this attitude, formed, in part, by increasing cynicism about America and white Americans. Behind such cynicism was a weakening of belief and faith in a country, believed by a majority of whites, in the words of Edward Everett, to be ". . . in its theory perfect, and in its operation it is perfect also. Thus we have solved the great problem in human affairs."[10]

For the overwhelming majority of black people and, in particular, the writers, such a summation of American progress at the beginning of the twentieth century was fallacious, and through protest organizations, papers, magazines, poems, and books, they contributed testimony which proved otherwise. Such efforts were dismissed by ignoring the protesters and their protests. For example, Van Wyck Brooks, in 1921, not long after the demise of the Garvey movement, states, without irony, that unlike such critics as John Ruskin of England and Friedrich Nietzsche of Germany, American social critics had more often tended to praise their country than to criticize it: "There is nothing else in all modern history like the unanimity of praise and confidence with which . . . the American ship of state was launched and manned. In all our long nineteenth-century past, there was scarcely a breath of dissent, doubt, or censure. . . ."[11]

If the criticism mounted by Blacks against the country's values and morals received such sundry disdain, the question arose as to whether or not such criticism was not only futile, but incapable of fulfilling stated objectives. And further, if the voices of concern go unheeded, does this not mandate a re-examination of that society which offers as one of its democratic principles that fair and just grievances are to be heard and adjudicated? If such is not the case, then what is the function of the literary vehicle, once believed by each writer, from Brown to Du Bois, to be to inform the American public of the just grievances of Blacks? Such questions heightened the prevailing cynicism of the times. Many writers, whether stated or unstated, began to entertain the idea that the attempt to gain entry into the American mainstream by Blacks was destined to fail. Thus began slow, but sure, development of a literature which, decade after decade, moved away from its previous objective—to bring about changes in America's evaluation and treatment of Blacks—to a new and veritable radical position—to bring about changes in the minds of Blacks concerning their own status as a people and their survival as a race within the United States.

IV

THE WHITE
MAN'S BURDEN

The Marrow of Tradition, Imperium in Imperio, and *The Quest of the Silver Fleece* were not the agents of change. They were simply records evidencing the fact that change was taking place, theoretical disquisitions in fiction that sought to create images of a "New Negro" for those for whom the old had become a necessary symbol and, through example, to underline the function of the novel as conceived by their predecessors. They were, however, the works of innovators, in a sense that those of their predecessors were not, for education and a wider appreciation of the the problems of the times made the authors more aware of the possibilities as well as the dangers of the world in which they lived. Unlike the earlier writers, they had ideas upon which to feed, contradictory theories concerning methods and ways of engaging in the battle to liberate men's intellects as well as their bodies. The characters they created would linger on in the literature of the twentieth century; but already, in 1916, five years after publication of *The Silver Fleece,* the New Negro whom they symbolized was challenged by a newer image, as the old images of the Plantation school of literature were routed, banished almost completely, from serious consideration by Blacks and whites alike.

The new image was not offered by the writers of the Harlem Renaissance, that period of output and innovation in black literature, but, instead by the efforts of a Jamaican Black, with only a cursory interest in literature. Whether Marcus Garvey read novels or not is open to conjecture; yet no single individual before Richard Wright and Imamu Baraka so affected the literature of his time, caused black writers to shift their emphasis from the middle-class characters, who people the novels of each black writer from Brown to Du Bois, and concentrate upon the wider areas of black life where different characters were in abundance. With the exception of Malcolm X, no individual before or after Garvey did as much to destroy the images of old, to render obsolete and unintelligible the offerings of the imagists. When Alain Locke, philosopher of the Renaissance movement, writes in *The New Negro,* in 1925, that "The day of 'aunties,' 'uncles,' and 'mammies' is . . . gone, Uncle Tom and Sambo have passed on, and even the Colonel and 'George' play barnstorm roles from which they escape with relief when the public spotlight is off,"[1] he is paying an unacknowledged tribute to the success of the Garvey movement.

That this squat, rounded Jamaican with unmistakable black features would become the metaphor of struggle and endurance in the twentieth century for millions throughout the world, the symbol of hope and aspirations for thousands of young black men, and the image upon which future men of literature would draw for portraits of courage and determination is nothing short of phenomenal. Born in Jamaica, West Indies, son of West Indian peasants, and despite his claim of having attended two colleges, poorly educated, he lacked the character, education, and status of such of his eventual adversaries as Du Bois, Walter White, A. Philip Randolph, and Chandler Harris. In addition, none of his previous occupations—printer, editor of magazines—equipped him for the role he would later undertake. What preparation he had, he acquired during a stay in London from 1912 to 1913, when be became fascinated with African culture and history and enamored of the writings of Booker T. Washington.

Before the events which took place in 1917, Garvey himself had no inclination of vying for leadership of American Blacks. His natural constituency, he believed, was in Jamaica, and it was there that he established the first branch of the Universal Negro Improvement Association in 1914. This first venture was not overly ambitious. The major program of the UNIA consisted of plans to construct a chain of industrial educational institutions modeled upon the programs enunciated in the writings of his idol, Washington. Needing funds, and having corresponded with Washington and been granted an audience— Garvey believed the Tuskegean would help him to secure money— he made plans to travel to the United States in 1916. Though the death of Washington occurred earlier in the year, Garvey stuck to his plan, arriving in America on March 23, 1916. Thirteen months later, after making a tour of the United States, he made his first formal appearance before a gathering of African-Americans at the Bethel Methodist Episcopal Church in New York City. This engagement marked the beginning of what Alain Locke has called the "spectacular phenomenon" of the Garvey movement.

The success of the movement, however, is not to be attributed to the charismatic personality of the man alone. As in the cases of Douglass, Garnet, Washington, and Du Bois, events were of equal importance—events destined to bring man and moment together simultaneously and to project the man as more the result than the maker of events. Those that produced the Garvey movement had their beginnings outside Jamaica, deep in the historical experiences of Blacks in America. To understand those factors which produced the "spectacular phenomenon" is to conceive of past and present as replicas one of the other, to confront recurring obstacles in the path of black aspiration, to realize that, in part, the success of Marcus Garvey was due to continuing violence against Blacks in American life, the great migration as a result of this violence, and the growing anger and bitterness of poor Blacks, those whose plight was yet to be taken seriously by either black leaders or black writers.

Blacks were no strangers to the violence which erupted in twenty-six race riots in 1919, the year Garvey first proposed his idea of the Black Star [Ship] Line. Charles Chesnutt investigated the Wilmington, North Carolina, race riot, which took place in 1898 and discovered in the ruin and loss of life by Blacks the germinal idea for his novel, *The Marrow of Tradition*. Enraged by the brutality and merciless killing of Blacks in the Atlanta, Georgia, riot of 1906, Du Bois composed the angry poem, *Litany at Atlanta*. During the same year, black soldiers were attacked in a riot at Fort Brown, in Brownsville, Texas. These were a few of the outbreaks that occurred in the South, yet similar incidents took place in the North, particularly during the year 1919. Put down this year for the riot in Washington, D.C., precipitated by false reports of black attacks upon white women; for the Chicago riot, which topped all others in length of duration, eleven days, complicity of a number of city officials, and total number of casualties, twenty-two blacks and sixteen whites killed and over five hundred of both races wounded. Alongside the massacre in Chicago, outbreaks in Tennessee, Arkansas, and Nebraska appeared as mini affairs.

The reason for most of the riots was that there was no reason, nor was one needed. For public comsumption and sometimes for self-rationalization, reasons were given—black infringement upon white rights, black attacks upon white women, or, as in the Chicago riot, the refusal of Blacks to obey segregation codes. The rationale known to every Black, however, that which needed no explication, was that riots were the repressive acts of white militants who, in regard to Blacks, knew and recognized no distinctions. Middle-class Blacks, mulattoes, poor Blacks, black sharecroppers, and black doctors, all were targets of racial chauvinists. This insight into the white nationalist psyche, coupled with recognition of an inability to engage in all-out warfare, propelled into motion an immigration of a people unparalleled in American history.

From the dust-caked roads and city streets of the South, by boat, train, and bus, and when these avenues of escape were closed, on foot, Blacks made their way to the North, in pursuit of the dream deferred. They were encouraged by such editorials as those of the Chicago *Defender:* "[Leave the region] . . . where your mother, sister, and daughter are raped and burned at the stake; where your father, brother, and sons are treated with contempt and hung to a pole, riddled with bullets at the least mention that he does not like the way he is treated. . . ."[2]

For the most part, those migrating from south to north were poor, more black than mulatto, and their increasing anger and resentment, their growing cynicism about the country, unlike that of the black middle class, found no outlet or recognition in the established civil rights organizations. Hampered by internecine warfare, dedicated to pursuits more favorable to the middle class than to poor Blacks, and saddled with a board of white advisers, the NAACP was regarded by many poor Blacks as The National Association for the Advancement of *Some* Negroes. The Urban League was little more than a service organization, preoccupied with finding jobs for Blacks in the domestic service. At a time, therefore, when resentment among the poor was at its zenith, spirited leadership was forthcoming in large measure only from a Black of Jamaican descent.

The Garvey movement grew as a result of the ineffectiveness of other organizations. By the time of the first convention of The Universal Negro Improvement Association in 1920, and only four years after the arrival of its founder in the United States, the organization numbered over a quarter million active members in the country and appealed to millions more at home and abroad. Aided by its propaganda organ, *The Negro World,* it became the fulcrum point for the discontent of the black poor. Saunders Redding writes: "The Garvey movement cannot be dismissed merely as the aberration of an organized pressure group. The least that can be said of it is that it was an authentic folk movement. Its spirit of race chauvinism had the sympathy of the overwhelming majority of the Negro people, including those who opposed its objectives."[3]

It was an authentic folk movement to be sure, and its hero was "folk" in the way that missed the attention of most black writers. Neither urbane nor overly sophisticated, Garvey, like a country preacher, was a man whose charisma lay in his ability to use the spoken word, to fire emotions, to appeal to man's intuitive, instead of rational, sense. Let the Negro leaders debate fine points of the law, make appeals to Congress, the President, and the Supreme Court, issue indictums from distant offices; from the street-corner podiums and makeshift stands, Garvey brought home the reality of oppression and denial of liberty in clear, concise language, met the people on the street corners and in the meeting halls, away from the stultifying presence of either whites or the black middle class. Identification with this short, squat black man was not difficult for those long ostracized for possessing features they were led to believe unattractive, and Garvey became not only an inspiration but a symbol.

Here upon the stage of the early twentieth century, in the halls and parades of the UNIA, were the New Negroes, as colorful and as inspiring as a well-wrought poem. There were pomp and circumstance in their proceedings to be sure; there were the regality and splendor of the Black Star nurses, the spectacle of the Red, Black, and Green hoisted aloft by thousands of unsmiling, serious black men and women, outcasts from the American mainstream, who chanted the new music, pledged fidelity to Africa—opening their minds and hearts to black men everywhere, enunciating the cry destined to ring with solemn dignity down through the ages, "Up You Mighty Race." The images were alive and moving, and men and women felt their stirring. Black people christened their man-child, Marcus Aurelious; the Red, Black, and Green became the metaphor of man's concern for his fellow man, for humanity and justice. Belief in the beauty of things black replaced shame and embarrassment; hope in life replaced despair and desperation. The old God, who promised much and delivered nothing, was dethroned and replaced by the god of man, the black god, ushered into birth by the cries of black liberation.

To assess the accomplishments of Marcus Garvey, it is not necessary to speak of him as either the "New Moses" or the "Black Messiah." Such terms do little to reveal the true importance of the man. He was not redeemer, but symbol, not savior, but image. In the long march toward freedom and liberation, he personified the hope of millions for whom Canaan had not yet arrived. And he personified their hopes and aspirations even in his failures—when his Black Star Line met disaster through sabotage and a lack of business acumen on the part of himself and his advisers. When the government of Liberia—induced no doubt by the French, British, and Americans—reneged on its promise to allow his members to establish a colony upon its shores, here, still, he symbolized the aspirations of countless Blacks for whom such dreams, let alone successes, were non-existent. And the symbol, withstanding the calumny of enemies and the test of time alike, remained dear to the heart of black men even after, to quote Claude McKay, a ". . . powerful combination of the Negro intelligentsia, aided by wealthy white supporters . . . finally brought about [his] downfall."[4]

However, how does one destroy symbols so meaningful and necessary? To harass the man, indict him, and imprison him, and finally exile him could not destroy what he meant to Blacks, nor halt the forces he had set in motion. Roi Ottley, an observer of the Garvey movement, summed up the example of his life, three years after Garvey's death in London: "Concretely the movement set in motion what was to become the most compelling force in Negro life—race and color consciousness, which is today that ephemeral thing that inspires 'race loyalty'; the banner to which Negroes rally; the chains that bind them together. It has propelled many a political and social movement and stimulated racial internationalism. It is indeed a philosophy, an ethical standard by which most things are measured and interpreted."

Garvey's address made shortly before entering a Georgia prison is more representative, certainly more prophetic: "If I die in Atlanta my work shall then only begin, but I shall live, in the physical or spiritual, to see the day of Africa's glory. When I am dead, wrap the mantle of the Red, Black, and Green around me, for in the new life I shall arise . . . to lead the millions up the heights of triumphs with colors that you well know. Look for me in the whirlwind or the storm. . . ."[5]

The influence of the Jamaican ranged far and wide, touched almost all elements within the black community. Nowhere is this more true than in the case of black writers. Some, like Eric Walrond, were influenced directly, through personal association with the UNIA or contact with the man; others, like Claude McKay, were influenced indirectly. This West Indian poet, credited with having begun the New Negro movement with the publication of the book *Harlem Shadows,* in 1922, has summed up Garvey's influence upon the literary personalities of his day: "If Marcus Garvey did not originate the phrase, New Negro, he at least made it popular. First novels by Harlem writers were published in that period: Jessie Fauset's *There Is Confusion,* Walter White's *The Fire in the Flint,* Nella Larsen's *Quicksand,* Rudolph Fisher's *The Walls of Jericho,* and Wallace Thurmond's *The Blacker the Berry. . . .*"[6] The astute, conservative Benjamin Brawley, a critic usually ahead of his time, was convinced of Garvey's importance as black image to layman and writer alike: ". . . as no other man of the era, he had given to the Negro a new sense of freedom. His influence on the literature . . . was beyond all estimate."[7]

On that fateful day at Atlanta, in the shadow of the jailhouse, Garvey admonished his followers to "look for me in the whirlwind or the storm." Yet it was in the literature of the Renaissance era that his spirit was reincarnated, in the red clay of Georgia, birthplace of the fruit-plum black men and women of Toomer's *Cane,* in the African quest of Cullen and Du Bois, in the racy fiction of Rudolph Fisher and Langston Hughes, in the questioning of McKay's vagabonds and intellectuals, and, in a different way, in the artificial black people who populate the novels of Jessie Fauset and Nella Larsen. Due to the influence of Garvey upon the Renaissance writers, the image of the black artist as a man torn between fidelity to art and fidelity to his race, the wanderer between two worlds, is one already besotted by the age. The image of the black man in these early years of the Renaissance, artist and layman alike, was that of a serious, determined individual, cynical and demanding, wary of white condescension and more assured of his own strength and resources.

Here was the white man's dilemma as well as his burden. Black men, such as those depicted in the Garvey organization, parades, countless newspaper photos, and in some of the literature of the day, constituted a greater threat to different groups of white people than had the Du Bois-Washington debate earlier. Proud, assertive, educated, determined black men, complete contradictions of the stereotypes of old, posed problems for almost every category of whites in the country. Such men were anathema to white intellectuals and white businessmen, lower- and middle-class whites, as well as the professional "friends of the Negro" who had made reputations and fortunes as a result of his condition.

Because of the revelations brought about by the Garvey movement concerning lynchings, the intellectual of Van Wyck Brooks' imagination was called upon either to undergo a moral crisis or shy away from questioning the basic premises upon which the American republic stood. Few chose to undergo such a moral crisis. The emigrés from America in the nineteen twenties, of whom Ernest Hemingway was perhaps the best-known, based dissatisfaction with America not upon

oppression against Blacks, but upon less morally explosive issues such
as corruption in politics and crass materialism. H. L. Mencken, more
pragmatic than most, summed up, by implication, the liberal's dilemma
and rationale for inaction: ". . . Negroes when writing about their
own race made a mistake when they indulged in pleas for justice and
mercy . . . when they based their unjust treatment on the Christian
or moral ethical code. . . ."[8]

Except for areas in which Garvey's association with Africa and his
call for liberation of the continent raised concern about protecting
foreign investments, magnates like Carnegie, Rockefeller, and Gould
were little affected by the movement. To the small businessman, however, now gaining a foothold in the black community, Garvey's insistence that Blacks patronize and service each other constituted a
direct threat. In addition, through civil rights agencies and through
membership in unions, Blacks demanded jobs commensurate with their
educational attainments and skills, thus providing competition for
newly arrived immigrants. Both of these ventures, the buy-black campaign that would affect whites' limited capital and the push for better
jobs, hastened the day when middle-class whites might recognize their
true condition vis-à-vis the magnates and think in terms of protest, if
not rebellion.

To lower- and middle-class whites, the most insecure of Americans,
Blacks presented a mental threat to their well-being and peace of
mind. They lived in a country in which they were as much the victims
of imagists as were Blacks. They were, said every institution of the
country, by virtue of being white, important, knowledgeable, and
powerful. They were the chosen who might become Presidents, business tycoons, or beauty queens. What wrenching of soul must occur,
however, when realization sat in, when they came to understand that
for the most of them, such images were forever beyond their attainments? Few would ever know wealth or power; fewer, still, leave
their mark upon the world; as master races went, most were unable to
approach the image. Given their failures as whites, based upon definitions forwarded in their literature, black men, independent, strong,
and aggressive, caused them not only to question the images which
circumscribe them but also their worth as men.

The newer images of Blacks made visible by the Garvey movement,
however, affected no group in America more than the professed
friends of the African-American. Most were among the groups that
attacked the Garvey movement: members of the Communist and Socialist parties, Jewish intellectuals, and Anglo-Saxon representatives of
civil rights organizations. It was not only their roles as middlemen

between Blacks and the larger society—roles which cast them as peacemakers—that were endangered; but more important, their control of the lucrative market for exploitation of black history and culture energized by the Renaissance movement was opposed by Blacks who argued that those who studied the race and wrote about it should be members of the race. For the Communist and Socialist parties, thinking black men threatened a political turn toward Black Nationalism that would preclude an integrated, white-led revolution.

Each of these groups desired images less threatening than those presented by Garvey; they wanted definitions of Blacks to reverse the trend toward self-esteem and racial awareness. A return to the old images, the aunties, uncles, and mammies, feeble-minded children, darky entertainers, and brute Negroes, was impossible. Not only did the changing times mitigate against such a return, but collusion by Blacks on the prominence of such images was almost impossible to come by in this period of the race's history: the stereotypes of old caused embarrassment and shame to a middle class now preoccupied with race pride. Still, images were needed that would work as effectively as past ones; stereotypes needed to mentally enslave a people anew. Once again, the usually perceptive Benjamin Brawley drives to the heart of the problem: ". . . but while Uncle Tom and Uncle Remus were outmoded, there was now a fondness for the vagabond or roustabout, so that one might ask if after all the new types were an improvement on the old."[9]

Vagabond or roustabout—these offered only a partial solution. The much more effective creation was the primitive, atavistic black savage, still, despite the distance in years from *The Tempest* and *Robinson Crusoe,* a man, not of thought but of emotion, not of hostility but of joy, having no concern for race, but only a total disregard for all save sensuous living, exotic thrills, and sensational experiences: "Wild crap shooters with a whoop and a call/Danced the juba in their gambling hall/And laughed fit to kill, and shook the town/And guyed the policeman and laughed them down/With a boomlay, boomlay, boomlay, Boom."[10] Thus Vachel Lindsay, with a "boomlay, Boom," set the stage for the appearance of the New Negro as defined by white men.

He was, however, not altogether new. The primitive savage, unclothed child of nature, champion of sensuous and sensational living, had made his appearance in the literature and minds of whites long before Robinson Crusoe discovered him on a distant island. Look to Ben Johnson's *The Masque of Blackness,* John Webster's *The White Devils,* and Shakespeare's *Othello* and *The Tempest* for early outlines. Defoe, however, unlike his American counterparts, suggested in the denouement of his novel that Friday (the savage) with Crusoe's help be transformed into an Englishman—an act of assimilationism that Americans would have frowned upon. They were more intent than the Europeans in maintaining the image in perpetuity, not in obliterating it. Therefore, they regarded such character traits as happiness in misery, obsessive sensuality, promiscuity, and complete disregard for the realities of life, when displayed by Blacks, as virtues. For an early validation of this assertion, look into Gertrude Stein's, *Three Lives* (1909).

This book, of which a complete page is reprinted in *Nigger Heaven,* serves as a precursor of "the vogue of primitivism" which reaches its zenith with the award of the Pulitzer Prize to Julia Peterkin for her novel, *Scarlet Sister Mary* (1928). Both books deal with black women in particular and the black community incidentally. In *Three Lives,* half-white Melanctha Herbert, daughter of a black Britisher and a "white lady of some distinction," has come into a schizophrenic inheritance; from her mother, she inherited the civilized virtues, correct standards of living, proper manners, and ladylike qualities; from her savage black father, she inherited nuances and rhythms of her jungle past. Like Scarlet Sister Mary, she is incapable of leading an existence in conformity with the life-style of her mother; instead she must become sexually free, the inhabiter of a world in which joy, ecstacy, and surrendering to human emotions constituted the *sine qua non* of the happy life.

Neither of these books enjoyed a wide audience, either among Blacks or whites. For one thing, the authors were white women and not expected to know the "seamier" more "erotic" side of black life; for another, and more important, neither had reputations for expertise gained from personal association with Blacks; this lack of integration with the subjects of their works mandated questioning of the sincerity of their presentations. This was not the case with Carl Van Vechten (1880–1964), who had impeccable credentials in both the white and the black world. Novelist, critic of music, art, and drama, Van Vechten was a respected, if not highly esteemed, American writer. After publication of the novel *Peter Whiffle* (1922), notes Nathan Huggins, Van Vechten became violently interested in Negroes and began the association with Harlemites which was to endure until his death. His interest in Blacks took the form of philanthropy—aid to black writers —among those who benefited from his friendship were James Weldon Johnson, Nella Larsen, Rudolph Fisher, and Chester Himes. In an unfavorable critique of *Nigger Heaven* (1926), Du Bois acknowledged the author's long-time associations with leading members of Harlem's literary, social, and intellectual set: "The author counts among his friends numbers of Negroes of all classes."

Contrary to Du Bois' assertion that representatives of the black middle class are not depicted in the novel, *Nigger Heaven* includes among its character sketches members of each strata of the black society as the author saw them; Mrs. Albright, possessor of a country home, member of the black upper class; Mary Love, the heroine decidedly middle class—a designation which leads to her dilemma and tragedy. The object of study in Book I of the novel, because of her status she considers herself "a prig" and believes that her class designation makes her "thoroughly out of harmony with her present environment." She is contrasted with Anatole Longfellow, alias the Scarlet Creeper, who occupies the major role in the prologue of the book. Dapperly attired at all times, knowledgeable in the ways of Harlem life, sweet man, pimp, and gambler, the Creeper, as his name implies, is free, easygoing, and colorful. His journey through Harlem on a balmy June day ends where the novel begins (and ends), in a cabaret, and both the man and the cabaret combine to become metaphors of atavistic Harlem: ". . . Expanding his chest, Anatole gazed down the length of the hall. Couples were dancing in such close proximity that their bodies melted together as they swayed and rocked to the tormented howling of the brass, the barbaric beating of the drum. Across each woman's back, clasped tight against her shoulder blades, the black hands of her partner were flattened. Blues, smokes, dinges, charcoals, chocolates, browns, shines, and jigs."[11]

Unlike Mary, the Creeper is not out of step with his environment: He and the environment complement one another. For Van Vechten, each black man has his Creeper running around in his skull; for each, this image of man—egotistical, half-man half-savage, existing in a world of sensuous pleasure, where self-gratification supersedes responsibility to race—is representative. Multiply him two hundred thousand times and you have the race to be born anew after the Garvey movement, the images to appease whites of all persuasion. The Creeper is pleasure principle and phallic symbol rolled into one, a man who has not only found *his* identity but is the measuring rod by which other black characters must evaluate their own. To reach Nirvana each man must feel with the Creeper, share in his lust and pleasure, look at Harlem through primitivist eyes: "Dis place, where ah met you—Harlem," the Creeper informs a woman companion, "Ah calls et, 'specherly tonight, ah calls et Nigger Heaven! I jes nacherly think dis heah is Nigger Heaven!"[12]

The Creeper and Mary are entities to be compared and contrasted. On the side of the Creeper are the Bolita king, Rudolph Pettijohn, and the sex-starved, perverse, black Diana, Lasca Sartoris; midway between these symbols of joy and atavism, stand Mary herself and Byron Kasson—would-be writer and suitor of Mary. On the far side of respectability are Mrs. Albright, well-to-do widow, Olive Hamilton, Mary's roommate, and her lawyer-fiancé, Howard Allison. Outside all groupings and beyond the color line is Dick Sill, a mulatto, soon to pass over into the white race. Despite such an array of characters, the plot of the novel, nevertheless, is simple in execution.

Boy, Byron Kasson, meets girl, Mary Love, and a whirlwind romance is destroyed due to intercession by the other woman, Lasca Sartoris. The major theme, however, is not unrequited love; the central conflicts are inner ones engendered by schizophrenia which forces a choice between a life-style dictated by every man's Creeper within, or one dictated by such mundanities as status and respectability. At stake is a definition of blackness. Both Mary and Byron are opposed to passing, to deserting one's race; and neither wishes to succumb to respectability, to regard himself as completely civilized: "The Negro blood was there, warm and passionately earnest; all her preferences and prejudices were on the side of the race into which she had been born."

Mary's middle-class background and quiet-mannered demeanor contribute to her dilemma. Cherishing an "almost fanatical faith" in black people, she wanted to be like them, to be one of them. So many of their characteristics eluded her, however, made her an outsider, one who wanted desperately to return to the primeval state, to be one with "Savages! Savages at Heart! And she had lost or forfeited this primitive birthright which was so valuable and important an asset, a birthright that all the civilized races were struggling to get back to. She, too, felt this African beat—it completely aroused her emotionally—but she was conscious of feeling it. This love of drums, of exciting rhythms, this naive delight in glowing colour, this warm, sexual emotion, all these were hers only through a mental understanding."[13] Questioning, ambivalent—even self-hating—Mary is incapable of competing with Lasca Sartoris, cannot help Byron solve his problem of schizophrenic dualism, cannot deliver him from respectability to savagery, cannot help him cross the line of his psyche beyond which lay the image of the Creeper. This task, uninhibited, Lasca, possessor of the jungle instincts, she of the hot blood, the passionate, sexual cravings, the sadistic leanings, can perform with the grace and forms of a jungle cat: "I'd like to be cruel to you!"

She engages Byron in lovemaking, ". . . I'd like to cut your heart out. . . . I'd like to bruise you. . . . I'd like to gash you with a knife. . . . Beat you with a whip! . . . She drew her pointed nails across the back of his hand. The flesh came off in ribbons. My baby! My baby! she sobbed, binding his bleeding hand with her handkerchief, kissing his lips."[14]

The symbolic castration of Byron is not lost on the audience. The black intellectual is rendered so effectively impotent by the dominant, savage Sartoris that at the end of the novel, Lasca, having deserted him, Byron resembles a mere shell of a man. Even his attempt to murder his rival for Lasca's affection—the Bolita king—is an act of impotence: Byron fires into the dead body of Pettijohn, who had been expertly murdered by the Creeper. Thus the two characters who survive the end of the novel, are the twin symbols of atavism—Lasca and the Creeper. Not only are they true children of the jungle, but they are metaphors for a people whose one virtue is that they possess no restraining cultural or historical attributes, are acclimatized to a heaven in which: "The music shivered and broke, cracked and smashed. Jungle land. Hottentots and Bantus swaying under the amber moon. Love, sex, passion, hate. . . . Black, green, blue, purple, brown, tan, yellow, white: coloured people."[15]

Impotence and sexuality are the twin themes of *Nigger Heaven*. After the strong, determined black men of the Garvey period, black manhood, for this white writer, is seen as swinging between these two poles, one that of impotence, represented by Byron, the other that of sensuality and sexuality represented by the Creeper. To be Byron is to smell "too much of civilization," to be restrained and restricted. To be the Creeper is to be virile, masculine, uncivilized. To be Byron is to be an intellectual; to be the Creeper is to be a man of instinct and emotion. Move to the new image of black women: to be Mary is to be refined and chaste; to be Lasca is to be daring, promiscuous, and perverse. Given such portraits, is it any wonder that a sex-starved, sensation-starved white America adopted the Creeper and Lasca Sartoris with willing arms, consigning the aunts, uncles, and mammies, the stereotypes of old, completely to the dustbin of American history?

The new images were more than adequate. Creatures of appetite, they were concerned only with their own needs. Such people do not join Black Nationalist movements, dream of returning to Africa, of forging a bond of unity between black men everywhere. They pose no threat to whites, for they have no concept of the deadly warfare continuing daily between black and white America. "Negroes," argues Sartoris, "aren't any worse off than anybody else. They're better off if anything. They have the same privileges that white women had before the bloody fools got the ballot. They're considered irresponsible like children and treated with a special fondness." Like the Creeper, Lasca has "never bothered much about the fact that I'm coloured. It doesn't make any difference to me. . . ."

To all but the most dedicated to racial unity, the symbols of the Creeper and Sartoris, the promiscuous, happy, black man and the sexually perverse, domineering black woman replace the images of black men brought to life by the movement of Marcus Garvey. In but a short time, even large segments of black America, would be more enamored of those who fulfilled the roles depicted in the fiction of Van Vechten, than those personified in the figure and philosophy of the Jamaican. Thus, Du Bois might rail against *Nigger Heaven*—but the railing would be in vain. Black people had come too close to winning a major battle in the war for the control of images, had come too close, with Garvey, of laying the foundation from which true manhood and real revolution might spring. With Garvey gone, the Negro intellectuals rendered impotent, Negro leadership divided, and the Negro middle class confused, the African-American could only look toward the black artist to bring back the stirring images, symbols, and metaphors of the past years, when the Red, Black, and Green symbolized, among other things, black unity, strength, and determination.

The failure of the artist in general in this regard represents the failure of the movement known as the Harlem Renaissance, and in calculating that failure, a large share of responsibility rests with the black novelists. Though influenced by the Garvey movement, the novelists were divided into two groups, the conservatives and the radicals: The conservatives, spokesmen for the black middle class, attempted to draw a thin line between themselves and the "lower classes" of whom the Creeper is representative; the radicals, claiming to speak for the lower classes, viewed Blacks in too many instances through lenses fashioned in the furnace of *Nigger Heaven*. More important, too many of the leading novelists were in hock to Van Vechten, depended upon him for assistance in their publishing ventures. Thus all moved, some with more determination than others, to help resolve the white man's dilemma and to lighten his burden.

The above censure is applicable to James Weldon Johnson (1871–1938). This poet, anthologist, diplomat, and secretary of the NAACP, epitomizes conservative black thought in the period and symbolizes the old virtues based upon status and prestige. Look into his autobiography, *Along This Way* (1933), and the picture that emerges is that of Renaissance man in the classical sense, one imbued with notions of class and privilege, dedicated to the proposition that inevitably reason must triumph over emotion. His one and only novel, *The Autobiography of an Ex-Coloured Man,* was first published anonymously in 1912. Reissued in 1927, two years after the demise of the Garvey movement and one year after *Nigger Heaven,* Johnson had little cause to maintain anonymity. To gain its symbolic worth, *The Autobiography,* with a preface by Van Vechten, must be recognized as the production of a black man, one who knew the race inside out and who was capable of walking the middle ground between the Garveyites and the Van Vechtenites, capable, that is, of representing the black middle class, now on the defensive.

The Autobiography of an Ex-Coloured Man is a Bildungsroman: The reader is invited to trace the life of the protagonist from infancy to adulthood, in the words and thoughts of the protagonist. When he does this with Johnson's unnamed hero, he discovers that the hero was born of mixed parentage—an illegitimate affair between a black woman and a wealthy white man; that he was educated in an integrated school, and that after the death of his mother, he set out to attend college. Along the way, however, money saved for his education is stolen, and he is forced to earn his way by hard work. He becomes a cigar maker, a gambler, and finally, utilizing his skill at the piano, becomes protégé to a wealthy white eccentric. Association with the white patron enables Johnson to move his hero abroad, to Paris, London, and Germany, and to comment upon the diversity among the Europeans. When he decides upon the direction of his future life's work, he leaves his patron and returns to America, determined to go "back into the very heart of the South, to live among the people, and drink in my inspiration first hand. . . ."[16]

The return to his roots, however, is not permanent. Upon witnessing a lynching, the protagonist is filled with a sense of shame and contempt for a people so powerless as to be unable to prevent such acts against them. Due largely to such powerlessness, he decides to move outside of the race into ". . . a larger field of action and opportunity. . . ." With this objective in mind, he returns north, succeeds as a businessman, pays court to a white woman of substance, and after divulging the secret of his racial heritage—a secret accepted by his lover—he marries, has two children, and settles down to life as a white man: "My love for my children makes me glad that I am what I am and keeps me from desiring to be otherwise; and yet, when I sometimes open a little box in which I still keep my fast-yellowing manuscripts, the only tangible remnants of a vanished dream, a dead ambition, a sacrificed talent, I cannot repress the thought that, after all, I have chosen the lesser part, that I have sold my birthright for a mess of pottage."[17]

The Autobiography is a conservative document, leaning heavily toward the ideology of the black middle class. Yet Johnson is a racial conservative who wishes to lend credence to characters drawn in the fiction of Griggs and Du Bois—characters who, though different from the black poor, are proud of their racial heritage. Unlike Fauset, he does not frown upon the desire of the mulatto class for assimilation; like her, however, he argues that those with attributes similar to those of whites comprise among themselves a unique, specific group, and it is here, not in the white world, that such people belong. Nor was he more willing than other conservative Blacks to contest Van Vechten's images. For these, his rationale was simply put: They existed but did not represent the "respectable element" of the race. The importance of *The Autobiography,* therefore, lay in Johnson's attempt to synthesize the thought of the previous period on such topics as the plight of the mulatto, representation of the black middle class, and, for the first time in black fiction, the function of the black artist in the American society.

Johnson developed an attractive portrait of the mulatto, and thus moved beyond Brown, Griggs, and Chesnutt, whose mulatto characters, if not tragic, are the objects of contempt from other Blacks. Their men and women are trapped by historical circumstances, forced, against their will, to choose one world or another. Sometimes they choose the white world, sometimes, the black; yet for each, and Molly Walden is a good example, choice is dictated by assimilationist ideals. The choice of Johnson's protagonist, however, is based upon grounds of expediency. Coercion does not enter into the decision. Though inferior in status to whites, the mulatto is superior in status to Blacks, and thus has the option of becoming a distinct entity altogether. Johnson's mulattoes are not so much concerned with joining the white race, as they are with constituting a new class within the race. For this reason, Johnson has no quarrel with the "peculiar inconsistency of the color question" in which black men and women marry those lighter than themselves. This is "a natural tendency"—the desire of individuals not only to create the distinct race, but to secure "every advantage which complexion of the skin carries. . . ."[18] Thus the tragic mulatto, in the fiction of Johnson, is an image of the past. The mulattoes of the twentieth century have advantages unknown to those of the nineteenth. No longer are they a people straddling two worlds; now, they are exemplars of a new social class. And though Chesnutt foresaw this development, unlike Johnson, he was unable to provide an acceptable formula—one that made mulattoes both a part of, and distinct from, the entire race.

The ability to distinguish oneself from the black poor, however, is a prerogative of the middle class in general—a class which comprises a great many mulattoes. The black middle class had undergone marked changes since the days of Frank Webb. Though achieving and maintaining status was uppermost in their thoughts and actions, they retained more than a superficial interest in race pride and loyalty. With increasing regularity, many realized that the problems confronting Blacks moved beyond class and caste lines. For Johnson, however, a too-close identification with the black poor must be avoided; the middle class must insist on those attainments—education, material acquisition, cultural curiosity—that distinguish them from the poor and move them closer to Anglo-Saxon acceptability: "We are the race," remarks a middle-class doctor, "and the race ought to be judged by us, not by them [the poor]. Every race and every nation should be judged by the best it has been able to produce, not by the worse."[19]

In this disquisition on class, which takes up too much of the novel, Johnson distinguishes three: lower, lower middle, and middle. The lower class, the poor, constitute "what might be called the separate class. . . ." They work in low-grade occupations, "lumber and turpentine camps," and number among their group "ex-convicts and bar-room loafers." This class is more prone than the others to harbor "a sullen hatred for all white men . . ." and "represent the black people of the South far below their normal physical and moral condition." The "second class," the lower middle class, is comprised of servants, washerwomen, waiters, cooks, and coachmen, and are characterized as being "simple, kind-hearted, and faithful." Unlike the poor, they possess a strong fidelity to white people and through them ". . . the whites know the rest of their coloured neighbors. . . ."

The third class, upper middle to upper, is represented by independent workmen, tradesmen, the well-to-do, and the educated. These live in a world apart from other Blacks and, regrettable for Johnson, whites as well. Nothing is more disheartening ". . . than the isolated position into which are forced the very coloured people who most need and who could best appreciate sympathetic cooperation" from whites. These Negroes who refuse to be coupled "with the Negroes of the first class . . . are well disposed towards the whites, and always willing to meet them more than half-way."[20]

It is in Johnson's conception of the function of the black artist that he has left a controversial legacy. No character in fiction, no artist throughout history, has been so willing to surrender the richness of his racial culture as Johnson's protagonist. As a concert pianist, the protagonist becomes conscious of African-American culture: ". . . coloured people of this country have done four things which refute the oft advanced theory that they are an absolutely inferior race, which demonstrates that they have originality and artistic conception. . . . the power of creating that which can influence and appeal universally. The first two of these are the Uncle Remus stories . . . and the Jubilee songs. . . . The other two are ragtime and the cake-walk."[21]

If one accepts this questionable list of contributions, what is the protagonist's own conception of them? They are weapons of war to be sure, but waged in the interests of the black middle class, necessary to counteract the theories that Blacks "are an absolutely inferior race." In other words, black art is a pawn in the larger struggle for recognition from whites and validation of black humanity. To aid in this endeavor the protagonist wishes to surrender his cultural artifacts, to merge the black and white cultural idioms into one, to assimilate the black motif with that of the white. That such is possible, he learns while playing ragtime in Germany. A white pianist, shoves him aside, and taking the theme of ragtime ". . . played it through first in straight chords; then varied and developed it through every known musical form." The protagonist makes his great discovery: "I sat amazed. I had been turning classic music into rag-time, a comparatively easy task; and this man had taken rag-time and made it classic. The thought came across me like a flash—it can be done, why can't I do it?"[22]

The willingness to surrender his cultural artifacts is symbolic, in a larger sense, of the willingness to surrender racial identity—an act he performs at the end of the novel—along with the most important treasure of any people—their cultural and historical artifacts. Thus black art and the black artist alike disappear as distinct entities, as individuals, become American artists, and their productions, American ones. Black artists are the servants of the black middle class, and black art functions as a vehicle to procure them status as Americans: ". . . the future Negro novelist and poet [must] give the country something new and unknown, in depicting the life, the ambitions, the struggles, and the passions of those of their race who are striving to break the narrow limits of traditions."[23]

Therefore, like the protagonist, the black artist and the black middle class are wanderers between two worlds. One, that of the African past, so distant, brought to attention by the efforts of the Garvey movement and Pan-Africanism, and yet, still, symbolically the dark continent, where truer images of those of Van Vechten's novels reside. Closely allied to this world—an essential part of it—is that which denotes slaves and slave ships and melodies wrenched from the tortured throats of a people, and yet which, because of this very history and the manner

of wrenching, remain objects of shame and derision. Garvey might have
sought meaning and beauty in such artifacts as the spirituals, might have
sought to make of black culture the sole possession of black people;
others, however, having approached the Anglo-Saxon norm, wanted
none of the artifacts of the past, those which emerged out of the determination of men, against great odds, to seek release and surcease
for the human soul.

Beyond this world was the other, one of wider opportunity, boasting
of a grandeur which stretched back to the Aegean, which denoted
"the best that had been thought and written," which bequeathed a
legacy of culture and artistic attainment. This world, historically, viewed
the other with amused pity, contempt, or hostility, and erected boundaries which proved almost impervious to assimilationist assault. Yet the
desire to enter, to become a part, to be associated in some form or
manner—even as inferiors—was so intense on the part of some
Blacks that, like Johnson's protagonist, they were willing to barter all
that was essential and necessary to maintain a black identity, outside
that defined by the inhabitants of a world bequeathed Europe and
America by the Greeks and Romans.

This was not true of all black people, nor of all black artists. It was
not true for Martin Delany or Marcus Garvey; for Langston Hughes,
the very idea was unthinkable. Yet the attempt to sacrifice racial
uniqueness and individuality for "American standardization" (read
culture) was embraced by such artists as William Stanley Braithwaite,
Alain Locke, Nella Larsen, and Jessie Fauset. Thus the conflict between the writers of the Renaissance period limited a full-scale assault
upon the new images created to define black people; the writers were
divided into two camps; one, represented by Johnson, Fauset, and
Schuyler, advocated the surrender of black cultural artifacts, in an attempt to become American; the other, represented by Claude McKay
and Langston Hughes, believed that fidelity to the uniqueness of black
cultural experience was necessary, and that the function of the African-
American artist was to serve as caretaker of the cultural heritage.

The problem posed by Johnson's portrait of the artist and the function of black art revolves, in the final analysis, around the question of
definition. Is the black man to be defined in terms of the Euro-American experience or in terms of his own African history, both in America
and abroad? Marcus Garvey had one answer, Carl Van Vechten another, and James Weldon Johnson, yet another. Garvey and Van Vechten are closer to each other than either are in this respect to Johnson:
Both would have advised the black American to seek uniqueness, to cultivate the differences bequeathed him from his African past, though

each would differ radically as to what constituted those differences. For Johnson, however, deviants from the Euro-American norm were non-representative of black people: Anglo-Saxon truth was the truth for all men, and the Anglo-Saxon definition concerning art, values, and morals, having survived the ages, was one which African peoples might well accept even at the expense of losing their own identity.

To the question, What does it mean to be a black man in America? Johnson's answer differed from that of both Garvey and Van Vechten: For Garvey, to be Black meant to be the inheritor of a tradition which reaches beyond the Pharaohs, to cultural artifacts that extol the dignity of the human spirit; for Van Vechten, to be a black man meant to be part of a tradition which reached back to the primeval savagery of the earth's first man, to such distant, exotic places as the Congo, where, in Vachel Lindsay's words, "Tattooed cannibals dance in files. . . ." For Johnson, to be a black man meant to expropriate the cultural artifacts of the West, to become Westernized, to accept a system of values and ethics sanctioned by white men. Between the definitions of Johnson and Garvey lay no middle ground, no room for compromise, and the basic outlines of each produced the division among the Renaissance novelists, which made them unable to prevent the Van Vechten juggernaut, to counter images designed to satisfy the American craving for sensationalism.

V

THE CONFUSION
OF IDENTITY

There were racial paradigms, however, unrecognized by both Johnson and Van Vechten. These lay in the past history of the race, were to be found in the life-style of the poor, and even in the precarious existence maintained by the black middle class, who were forced to walk the tightrope between fidelity to race pride and white acceptance. The past and the paradigms which it offered are seen in the fiction of Johnson and Van Vechten. Both, however, are distortions of the novelists. The Harlem of the one writer differs only slightly from the Harlem of the other, the poor in the writings of one, only in varying degree from those depicted in that of the other. This is in spite of the fact that the poor of Harlem, as Dunbar and Du Bois knew so well, were migrants running not so much away from their past as from the injustices of the past; that they were black people for the most part, wedded to the land—the land of dust and mud-caked soil, of prickly pine trees and wind-singing oaks. Go back to the early history of the race, back before the ordeal of the middle passage, and they are a people at one with the land.

Garvey knew something of this; therefore, he spoke of land, of that which, free and ever free, made man free also, independent and strong. It is this idea that nationalists from that time till this have sought to convey; that to search for the life spirit of black people, to find paradigms of substance and truth, is to think of land and of men once free, now, like the land, free no longer, yet who still retain the vibrancy, majesty, and grandeur of a steady oak planted in rich soil. Jean Toomer (1894–1967) knew this also. This onetime student of mysticism, maternal grandson of a onetime acting southern black governor, who, despite the fact that he never lived up to his promise, was one of the most respected of the Renaissance writers, knew that the life line of his people led to the Nile, back to the land, where ". . . the men, with vestiges of pomp/Race memories of King and caravan/High-priests, an ostrich, and a juju-man/Go singing through the footpaths of the swamp."[1] He knew also that land now was merely a metaphor, an example of what once was, holding still the myths and legends of yesterday; these must be cultivated anew if Blacks are to regain the innocence and freedom which enabled them to survive years of conquest by so many conquerors. This he knew, and in *Cane* (1923), this collage of fiction, songs, and poetry, he sought to tell a people, through myth and legend, symbol and image, of the time that was and the time that existed now; that in the symbol of the sun, in the images evoked by the song, was the connecting link between time present and time past and that this link joined one Black to another—despite national boundaries—making each one with the juju man and the slave, the African princess and the Amazonianlike black women of the South. It is then to the earth that his people must return for paradigms of truer import, the earth to which men must go for rejuvenation, for direction, there where the image and the symbol become flesh: "O land and soil, red soil and sweet-gum tree/So scant of grass so profligate of pines/Now just before an epoch's sun declines/Thy son, in time, I have returned to thee/Thy son, I have in time returned to thee."[2]

Cane is no ordinary book. The very title is symbolic, reminding one of land and greatness; the symbolism of the title is recreated in the structure of the book itself; it is a part of each of the three sections, where are portrayed sketches; vignettes of men and women, some anchored to the land, others, having cast anchor adrift, beset with feelings of wonder, pain, hope, tenderness, and compassion. The journey from the red clay of Georgia in Part One to the stone and pavement of the northern cities in Part Two, and finally back to the sun, dusk, and pine trees of Part Three is the symbolic journey of a race upon whom ". . . the sun is setting on/A song-lit Race of slaves, it has not set/Though late, O soil, it is not too late yet/To catch thy plaintive soul, leaving, soon gone/Leaving, to catch thy plaintive soul soon gone." Here is nothing less than the journey of a people, symbolically away from the earth, and the call to return, once again return.

The first part of *Cane* is devoted to land, to the South, and the major protagonists are earth-women. Look at the sketches of Karintha, Becky, and Carma, Fern, Esther, and Louisa for the joy and hope, terrors and fears associated with the land. For each of Toomer's women in Part One, to live close to the land is to accept the predominance of chance over the absolute, to believe in change and growth, as opposed to stagnation. For those in this section of the novel, therefore, the world is one of pleasure and pain, hope and fear, warmth and hostility: It is a world of limitless possibilities. "When one is on the soil of one's ancestors," writes Toomer, "most anything can come to one."

To understand this idea is to understand not only the first part of *Cane,* but to understand as well the light-years traveled from the perception of black life by Carl Van Vechten and James Weldon Johnson. The life-style of a people derive from their historical and cultural roots; when these are lost, men cease to be men, become artificial and counterfeit. Away from the land, from all that symbolizes possibility, they are mere robots, mechanical men, like those of Part Two, symbolized by the character Rhobert who "wears a house like a monstrous diver's helmet on his head. . . ." For such characters, among whom are Avey, Paul, and Muriel, the funeral dirge has been created: "Let's open our throats, brother, and sing 'Deep River' when he goes down."

Though the seemingly free spirits of Part One are to be contrasted with the mechanical men and women of Part Two, there is a more significant contrast, that between freedom and restraint, between unlimited and limited possibility. The end result of the journey from land, from one's roots, from one's ancestral past means to sever all relationships with the race, to become one with the men and women of the novels of Johnson, Fauset, and Nella Larsen. It means, too, this journey from race, and thus from self, to surrender one's identity, which, once lost, is impossible to regain again. Thus the themes of parts One and Two—people struggling to hold fast to their identity as opposed to those who have surrendered it are combined in Part Three, dramatized in this narrative of man, returning once again to the land, seeking to regain an identity now lost forever.

"Kabnis" is, then, the symbolic link between parts One and Two of *Cane,* serving to complete the movement of the book from south to north, and back to south again. For Kabnis, the prodigal, to return home is difficult. Unlike the man who left, he can no longer hear the whispering of winds ("Night winds in Georgia are vagrant poets") and has forgotten the secret rituals, the promise of life close to earth: ". . . Earth's child. The earth my mother. God is a profligate red-nosed man about town. Bastardy; me. A bastard son has got a right to curse his maker. . . ."

Others, closer to the earth than Kabnis, are, nevertheless, also exiles. Such is Fred Halsey, great grandson of a union between an English gentleman and a black woman. A shopkeeper, born on the land, because of parentage and background, he is not a part of it. There is Professor Layman, teacher and preacher, widely traveled, a silent man, to whom the wonders of the land are also unknown; Hanby, for whom the earth symbolizes what it does for white people—wealth and status: "He is a well-dressed, smooth, rich, black-skinned Negro who thinks there is no one quite so suave and polished as himself. To members of his own race, he affects the manners of a wealthy white planter. . . ." Lewis is an exception! Like Kabnis, an exile returned, he serves as Kabnis' alter ego, is "what a stronger Kabnis might have been. . . ."

The plot of the story concerns the difficulties facing each man as he attempts to come to grips with the artifacts of his past. One, Lewis, capable of hearing the muttering of underground races; the other, Kabnis, unable to embrace even such a symbol of redemption as Lewis, to embrace the land which would resurrect him: "Kabnis, a promise of a soil-soaked beauty, uprooted, thinning out. Suspended a few feet above the soil whose touch would resurrect him. Arm's length removed from him whose will to help . . ."[3] Lewis, however, is attuned to the spirit of the past, can divine in a deaf old man ". . . A mute John the Baptist of a new religion—or tongue-tied shadow of an old"—can reach back into his past, become one with the old man and his people, a "slave boy whom some Christian mistress taught to read the Bible. Black man who saw Jesus in the rice fields, and began preaching to his people. Moses and Christ words used for songs. Deaf blind father of a muted folk who feel their way upward to a life that crushes or absorbs them. . . ."

Lewis emerges as the symbol become substance, the new paradigm, at one with the land and with the history of the race. "Lewis, seated now so that his eyes rest upon the old man, merges with his source and lets the pain and beauty of the South meet him there. White faces, pain-pollen, settle downward through a cane-sweet mist and touch the ovaries of yellow flowers. Cotton-bolls bloom, droop. Black roots twist in a parched red soil beneath a blazing sky. Magnolia, fragrant, a trifle futile, lovely, far off . . ."[4]

Cane provided the model for a literary Renaissance. Though the men and women who people the book are caricatures, they are also paradigms from myth and legend. It is true that Toomer's people are sometimes close to the old stereotypes, true that he argues for them a special kind of primitivism. Yet they are men and women of nobility and grandeur, perhaps oblivious to all but the wonders of the land, or all too ready to surrender their identity. Sketches of life, they represent not life, but the material from which black life has sprung. Images of past and present, they are far removed, in the main, from either those of Johnson or Van Vechten. Only when they assume the guise of robots, while losing their own freedom and spontaneity, only when they seek to become artificial men do they approach the images vouchsafed by James Weldon Johnson. At no point are they likened to the people of *Nigger Heaven,* not even when they are closest to the stereotype; even their sex, their love of jazz and dancing have a wholesome healthy quality, unknown to Van Vechten's characters. Even Toomer's prostitutes are women who feel, who possess a quiet dignity.

Only the Garvey movement serves as an appropriate analogue for the paradigms of black life offered by *Cane.* Both figures, drawing upon the life-styles of the poor, found courage and dignity in their lives. Both found in the land and in those closely tied to it, the spirit of endurance. Despite the fact that Garvey's people walked the streets of the city, they were still only a few steps removed from their roots and, like Lewis, capable still of identifying with the symbols of their past. If the Garvey movement was then the political and social wheel upon which a Renaissance must turn, *Cane* was its literary equivalent; and if the Renaissance was to be such in substance as well as content, then Toomer would have to supersede both Johnson and Van Vechten as literary models for the black writer.

Cane, however, sold "only five hundred copies." Black people, as Hughes noted, did not praise it, and white people refused to buy it. The novel offered aspects of the racial past that both would rather forget. This was true also for black writers. Those who were touched by *Cane*—and some were—felt more akin to those who walked the pavement streets of the city than to those who walked the cane fields of old, and they were incapable of realizing, for the most part, that true images and symbols were possible only if one merged past and present, saw, in the people of today, images of the heroes of yesterday. Add to this the obvious: the specter of *Nigger Heaven* haunted the Renaissance writer as precisely as the specter of Hamlet's uncle haunted him, and the black writer's attempt to break free was as trying as that of the Danish prince.

James Weldon Johnson offered one way; Toomer offered yet another. Johnson's way was that of race division, of separating the "respectable" from the "non-respectable," and of validating, at least in part, the paradigms offered by the Van Vechtenites. Toomer's way was that of the humanist; he was concerned with the race as a unit; he spoke of a communal history and communal roots; he argued that these bound African and African-Americans alike, that in the family of Blacks were colors ranging from plum black to white coconut. That elitism was the choice over democracy had very little to do with the merit of *Cane;* it has more to do with the false optimism engendered, in part, by the new-found black affluence in the period and in the inflated importance of the Renaissance movement.

The disillusionment with America, once reflected by Frederick Douglass, in a conversation with Dunbar, near the end of his life, and that experienced by Gertrude Stein's "lost generation" of white expatriates, affected the black American, only generally, if at all. This peculiar kind of *angst,* the individual stepping outside of the history and culture which nourished him, was not unknown to Claude McKay, and the wanderlust fever early affected Hughes and Toomer. None, however, were willing to foreclose their mortgage upon their American residences. The kind of disillusionment with the country's values and ethics that sent Richard Wright, Chester Himes, William Gardner Smith, and James Baldwin into permanent exile years later was not a part of the sensibility of even the angriest of the Renaissance writers.

The belief not only persisted in Hughes's words that the "race problem had at last been solved through art plus Gladys Bentley . . . [that] . . . the New Negro would lead a new life . . . in green pastures of tolerance created by Countee Cullen, Ethel Waters, Claude McKay, Duke Ellington, Bojangles, and Alain Locke. . . ."[5] But also, that the new century had brought about tangible, though basically, inconsequential gains for Blacks of education and status. Lynching, never to be totally outlawed nor discontinued until the nineteen sixties, came under assault from paid lobbyists of the NAACP who managed at least to secure passage of an anti-lynching bill in the House of Representatives, though the bill met expected death in the Senate. The grandfather clause which limited black voter participation was struck down, and the war, though uprooting millions of Blacks, brought some measure of prosperity to a few.

The black writer could also think in terms of gains. No century had witnessed such strides in the proliferation of material by and about Blacks than the twentieth. Credit for this achievement must go, in part, to the work of Jessie Fauset at *Crisis* magazine and Charles Johnson at *Opportunity*—magazines that not only sponsored the work of new writers but awarded prizes for special accomplishment. Through the influence of white patrons, publishers opened their printing presses to Blacks, as never before. Boni & Liveright, Frederick A. Stokes Co.,

Alfred Knopf, Inc., and Harper & Brothers were among those who published the works of Langston Hughes, James Weldon Johnson, Claude McKay, Countee Cullen, Rudolph Fisher, Jessie Fauset, Nella Larsen, and Zora Neal Hurston. Add to this list, Arna Bontemps, Jean Toomer, George Schuyler, and Wallace Thurman, and the list of published material constitutes a large percentage of the over-all production of black writers in the history of black literature.

These new-won gains for black professional, black middle class, and writer alike affected the views of black people regarding society. Cynicism was still a part of the racial baggage; however, hope, once crushed, sprang anew as a result of the interest in things Black, in what came to be known as the black vogue. Accepting all too readily the promise of a changed society, Blacks, who had previously despaired of ever entering the American mainstream as equals, now thought otherwise—were not James Weldon Johnson and Alain Locke frequent visitors at downtown parties given by white people? Thus separate lodges, schools, institutions, and other black enterprises were regarded as monuments that served to distinguish the middle class from the poor, stood as proof positive of black equality with whites. Many who made the trek from south to north had witnessed whites fleeing Harlem for the Bronx, as they began, like an advancing army, to occupy the once solid white bastion. Yet such people dreamed of the coming years, when their children, if not they themselves, would follow the whites in hot pursuit. More and more the image offered by James Weldon Johnson was seen as the touchstone of the black man's reality.

That such optimism was ephemeral was noted by only a very few. Claude McKay and Langston Hughes questioned the fundamental premise that Negro Heaven, if not *Nigger Heaven,* had been established upon American shores. Changes in the social and political sphere, always for Blacks, tendentious at best, was even more so during the Renaissance. Blacks who attended the parties of whites downtown were few in number, and the whites who came uptown to view Harlem life did so in cabarets from which Blacks were excluded. What seemed to be an economic miracle was destined to last less than fifteen years, and the new-found affluence of the writer proved to be as inflated as the national economy.

Yet the heady atmosphere of progress engendered by the "roaring twenties" prohibited all too many from realizing these salient facts. The most important result was not that the intellectuals and middle class, the writers and Negro leaders, left themselves open for disillusionment in the coming years, but, more important, they attempted to move outside the war for the control of images. Willingness to accept even the implications of *Nigger Heaven*—that Blacks were creatures of emotion and appetite—no matter the amount of qualification—meant to argue that at least *some* of the people were cast in the mold of the Scarlet Creeper and Lasca Sartoris. Though this was not difficult for many to accept, the converse would have to be equally true—that a great many Blacks were symbolized in the philosophy of the Garvey movement and in the poetry and fiction of Jean Toomer. To accept the converse meant, then, to look anew at Blacks left behind in the imagined progress made by the race, to analyze the conditions under which poor Blacks lived. To do so would be to shatter the illusion of a changed and changing America.

The same was true as well in the social and literary sphere. Socially, the war for control of images might be won by accepting the argument that there was no war, that the images of the past, having been dead and buried, had ended the struggle for the right of definition. Distinct images, like distinct races, belonged to the pre-melting pot era of the eighteenth and nineteenth centuries, and the images that bespoke the human condition, that represented man's eternal fight against oppression, were not black, nor white, but American. As a result, the curious notion gained prominence that in a country where race had been, and remained, all important, it was of little consequence except as the background against which one measured forward progress. The writer was free, therefore, to opt for the designation poet, instead of Negro poet, novelist, instead of Negro novelist, suggesting by so doing that one term was of no more importance than the other. In the name of progress, the path pursued by Johnson's protagonist became the accepted one—passing, though not censured, was still considered taboo, however, approaching the white norm by acquiring "Nordic manners, Nordic hair, Nordic art," and an Episcopal heaven not only was not tabooed but encouraged.

George Schuyler (1895–   ) is an apt spokesman for such sentiments. He began his career as a writer for the radical socialist magazine, *The Messenger,* and later wrote for the Pittsburgh *Courier* and the Manchester *Guardian.* He is considered the major satirist of the Renaissance era. His progress, or regression as the case might be, from Socialism to advocate of right-wing causes has drawn rebuke from literary critics and historians alike. A careful reading of his two novels, however, reveals the conservative even as early as the nineteen twenties. *Slaves Today* (1931) is an attack upon the social and political order of the Republic of Liberia. The major theme of the novel is that in the area of cruelty and exploitation, repression and oppression, Blacks are one with whites throughout the world. In that area, therefore, where Blacks claimed moral superiority, Schuyler's findings are that there is little difference between the races. Given this basic premise, it is not surprising that he arrives at the conclusion that the idea of race is historical and artistic "hokum," that black men differed in no fundamental way from whites, and that civil rights programs, riots, and protest marches evidenced disloyalty, subversion, and anti-Americanism. In most of these areas, whether socialist or member of the John Birch Society, he was at one with a great majority of the black middle class.

This belief—that Blacks and whites are similar, but for the exception of a few non-essentials—emerges as the major theme of the novel, *Black No More* (1931). To dramatize this theme, Schuyler satirizes color-phobia among Blacks and whites. "Without a Negro problem," argues Dr. Junius Crookman, "Americans could concentrate their attention on something constructive."

The plot of *Black No More* centers around Dr. Crookman and his remarkable invention which proposes to ". . . Change Black to White in three days." The European-educated physician, a man with status in the black community, is interested in the progress of his race. He subscribes to Negro magazines, is appreciative of African art and artifacts, knowledgeable concerning black history and culture, and proud of the accomplishments of black men from Crispus Attucks to Booker T. Washington. The only flaw in Crookman's character is his marriage, for he is married to an octoroon, almost indistinguishable from white—a notation which calls forth the observation from the author that Crookman was ". . . wedded to everything black except the black woman. . . ." Max Disher, the protagonist, differs from Crookman. He is no race man, is interested in almost nothing black. Analogous to Crookman, he prefers women who are "yella," or, better, white. His preference in terms of women causes him to become involved with the operation, Black No More.

While searching for female companionship of the "yella" or white variety, Max encounters Helen Givens, Georgia beauty, on New Year's Eve, observing the "New Negro" scene in a Harlem cabaret. When he petitions the white woman for a dance, he is rebuffed with the retort, "I never dance with niggers!" Disher, pride wounded, dreams of becoming white in order to pursue Helen. Dream becomes obsession, and Disher seeks out Dr. Crookman and his amazing discovery. The task of making such Blacks as Disher black no more is accomplished by "electrical nutrition and glandular control" and affects all racial features, including the hair. The only flaw in the process, one not yet adjusted, is that the offspring of a married couple will not be affected, may be born Black or white depending upon the color of the male. Disher is successfully transformed into a white man, and remembering that his dream girl is from Georgia, he sets out on his quixotic quest to win her. Along the way he becomes an official in The Knights of Nordica, a white supremacist organization, rapidly gaining in membership and prestige due to the success of the "Black No More" campaign. With his inside dope on "the Negro" question, Max has no difficulty in convincing the Grand Wizard, Rev. Henry Givens, father, incidentally, of Helen, of his expertise on the "Negro menace" in general and Black No More in particular. He is eagerly welcomed into the organization as copartner, and his fortunes soar and decline. He rises to the top echelon in the Knights, marries Helen, makes a fortune, and arranges an alliance between the "Knights" and the Anglo-Saxon Association of America. As a result of the alliance, the two right-wing organizations capture control of the Democratic party, and Disher shrewdly secures the Presidential nomination for his father-in-law, while the nomination for Vice President is awarded the head of the Anglo-Saxon organization, Arthur Snobb-craft. This act precipitates the decline of Disher's fortunes. A discovery, initiated by the Republican party, proves that both Presidential and Vice-Presidential candidates on the Democratic ticket had black antecedents. The discovery, which assures the election of the Republican candidates, also aids Disher. Helen gives birth to a child, showing unmistakable black ancestry. Due to the revelation concerning the elder Givens, however, Disher's duplicity is not discovered, and he forgives his wife for her black heritage. The Knights of Nordica, due to the exposé, cease to be a viable concern, and husband, wife, and father-in-law leave for Mexico with their millions. The President of the equally defunct Anglo-Saxon Association, attempting a similar venture, is captured by a group of rural Southerners, and when revealed as the Snobbcraft of black ancestry, is lynched along with his chief researcher.

Though the operation, Black No More, achieves unprecedented success and prosperity because of the upheavals caused in the social, business, and political areas by the rapid disappearance of Blacks, intense pressure is brought upon the organization to cease its operations. This occurs when Crookman, appointed Surgeon General in the Republican administration, issues a paper proving that those who had undergone the process of Black No More were "two to three shades lighter" than the whites. The irony of the situation is pointed out by Schuyler and the rationale for the demise of Black No More offered as well: "What was the world coming to if the blacks were whiter than the whites?" The roles in the color drama are completely reversed. Dark skin is admirable and desirable; white skin is repulsive and rejected. The whiter-than-white whites are special objects of scorn, and the entire paraphernalia of the society created to deal with the "Negro Problem" reconstructed to deal with the white problem.

The success of *Black No More* is due to the ability of the author to cut through much of the hypocrisy surrounding the color question among Blacks and whites and to move forthrightly to the major problem. If there are fundamental differences between Blacks and whites, in what way are such differences manifested? Each group had, to return to James Weldon Johnson, its cultured and uncultured, its lower, middle, and upper classes. Each its superpatriots, as well as radicals, its conservatives and liberals. Given such similarities, plus a common culture and a common history, the difference then turned upon the ephemeral problem of color. Even here, however, Schuyler argues in *Black No More,* the similarities are more pronounced than the differences; the long line of Blacks willing to avail themselves of Crookman's discovery is proof positive that Blacks agree with whites on the question of the supremacy of Nordic skin.

If then, sane men will admit that color is the desiridatum between people in the American society, and if the majority of both races have assumed the superiority of white skin over that of black, the conclusion is not difficult to arrive at: Blacks must disappear as a racial group and be categorized under the denomination, American. One may, therefore, accept the theory of the superiority of white culture and history. This means to adopt a society constructed along class lines, one in which Blacks of equal education and material attainments join whites of similar achievement against those of the lower classes, black and white. The analogy to the theories of Frank Webb is obvious. Unlike Webb, however, Schuyler is a product of twentieth-not nineteenth-century thought. Webb's Mr. Walters is a man alone, one of such attainments that he stands not only head and shoulders above all Blacks, but above most whites as well. This idea of the titanic hero, the superman, is characteristic of the nineteenth century; the figure of the man alone, high above the herd, appears with regularity in the writings of most early black novelists.

For Schuyler and the twentieth century, however, there were no superrace men, no individuals of towering strength, who had far outstripped others. Such achievement could be accorded, however, to specific groups within races. Thus the philosophy that argued against the individual Black argued in favor of the special group—that the black middle class had far outstripped poor Blacks and moved closer to the image personified by the white middle class. What this meant was that the images of Garvey, Van Vechten, and Toomer could appeal to the need for sensationalism among the black and white middle class, could be accepted as images truly representative of the poor of all classes. Look into American history and literature, in the descriptions of white immigrants, and the assertion is easily verified.

After *Black No More,* the question remains, How does one be both Black and American at the same time? The question is not so simple for Helga Crane, heroine of Nella Larsen's (1893–1963) *Quicksand,* (1928). Larsen, daughter of a mixed parentage, ranked with Jessie Fauset among the most talented of black women writers. Well educated, having studied in America and abroad, she served for many years as a nursing supervisor in New York City. A favorite of Van Vechten, both of her novels evidence his influence, yet, in *Quicksand,* the major conflict which she sets up for Helga, her heroine, is choice between varying classes within the race, each representing positive and negative images.

The plot of *Quicksand* is structured around Helga's quest to discover her true identity, to determine her relationship to whites, the black middle class, and the black poor. The search begins early in her career when, as a teacher in a small college for black women, she hears a white speaker advise students to stay in their places, not to attempt to rise above their station. Infuriated by the audacity with which the speaker attempts to define the black students and, by implication, herself as well, Helga severs her engagement to a colleague and moves to Chicago. She finds employment with a Negro society matron, moves to New York, and establishes friendship with Anne Grey, financially independent and destined to make a promising marriage.

Despite her own background—daughter of a union between a Danish mother and a black father, and her occupation, schoolteacher—identity for Helga cannot be found in the middle-class values of Anne Grey. The argument offered by a onetime suitor, that the black middle class must serve as guides to the new Canaan, leaves her cold: ". . . one of the things that's the matter with us. The race is sterile at the top. Few, very few Negroes of the better class have children, and each generation has to wrestle again with the obstacles of the preceding ones, lack of money, education, and background. We're [the middle class] the ones who must have children if the race is to get anywhere."[6] When Helga receives money from her uncle—brother of her white mother—accompanied by a suggestion that she visit her aunt, Katrina, in Denmark, she leaves America, vowing never to return to the black middle class, to those who wanted to be other than themselves, who wanted to be facsimile imitations of whites: "What they wanted, asked for, begged for, was to be like their white overlords. They were ashamed to be Negroes, but not ashamed to beg to be something else. Something inferior. Not quite genuine. Too bad."

Helga, however, succumbs to the attempt by her aunt and uncle to make her over in their conception of Blacks, to create the living embodiment of the primitive: ". . . She was attractive, unusual, in an exotic, almost savage way. . . ."[7] to fashion her in the jungle image, by bestowing such gifts upon her as a black manilla shawl strewn with great scarlet and lemon flowers, a leopard-skin coat, feathers, furs, and jewelry, exotic perfume, and "shoes with dangerously high heels" in a move to enhance their own social position among the Danish middle class. She balks, however, when the pair attempt to marry her to a Danish artist, who offers the following proposal: ". . . You have the warm impulsive nature of the women of Africa, but . . . the soul of a prostitute. You sell yourself to the highest bidder. I should of course be happy that it is I." Helga's stay in Denmark only makes her less secure about herself as a black woman, less sure to which class of Blacks she really belongs. Attendance at a concert, where she hears black spirituals, interwoven with the classic offerings of Dvořák's New World Symphony, leads her to conclude that she has been too long in Denmark, that she must return to America.

Back home, the countdown to mental catastrophe begins. She resumes her friendship with Anne Grey, now married to Robert Anderson, who attracted Helga's attention when she taught at the girls' college. After impulsively kissing her, Anderson passes up the opportunity to possess her sexually. Helga, as confused now about her identity as a woman as she is about her identity as a Black, distraught and in despair, stumbles into a storefront church. The primitive aspects of the religion of this lower-class institution affects her, carries her aloft on the winds of religious conversion: ". . . A miraculous calm came upon her. Life seemed to expand and to become very easy. Helga Crane felt within her a supreme aspiration toward the regaining of simple happiness, a happiness unburdened by the complexities of the life she had known. . . . Gradually the room grew quiet and almost solemn, and to the kneeling girl time seemed to sink back into the mysterious grandeur and holiness of far-off simpler times."[8]

Helga is seduced by Reverend Green, pastor of the church, who escorts her home after the conversion and whom she later marries and accompanies to a small Alabama town. Here, among the poor Blacks, reality replaces illusion: "For the preacher, her husband, she had a feeling of gratitude amounting almost to sin. . . . What did it matter that he consumed his food, even the softest varieties, audibly? What did it matter that though he did not work with his hands . . . his fingernails were always rimmed with black? What did it matter that he failed to wash his fat body . . . as often as Helga did? There were things that more than outweighed these. In the certainty of his goodness, his righteousness, his holiness, Helga somehow overcame her first disgust at the odor of sweat and stale garments."

By the time the tables are turned, however, by the time the negative values of the marriage and her husband outweigh the positive, she has become too mired in the quicksand of familial life, has been encumbered and trapped by four children. The search for identity ends here, among the poor, and eventual resignation to a life of mental anguish and despair marks the end of her quest. Her ordeal is inconclusive, and the success or failure of her search for identity must be determined by the reader. Helga, dreaming of escape, but unable to execute the plan formulated in her dream, due to the birth of a fifth child, can offer no answers. Not knowing the true nature and experiences of her race, and disdaining both the world of whites and of the black middle class, when confronted with the unromantic side of black life, as Miss Larsen sees it, she is drawn into the mental quicksand of despair and helplessness.

Quicksand is a novel, almost modern in its plot and conflicts. More so than *Black No More,* it seeks to broach the wider question of identity, not the loss of it, but the search for it, and to suggest that this search in a world, race mad, must produce serious psychological problems of the spirit and soul. Helga cannot accept the definition of herself as Black in the terminology of whites or affluent Blacks; therefore, she is forced into a self-destructive encounter with her own fantasies, forced to discover the realities of the world of poverty and desperation. Unlike the black middle class she cannot accept the argument that pigmentation of skin does not indicate a difference in cultural and historical values, cannot believe that the true images of black people do not reside in the "primitive" aspects of lower-class black life.

Thus her romanticism of the "poor suffering Black," in the final analysis, causes her undoing. For her identity cannot be discovered here, any more than it can in the life-style of the middle class or of whites, and the major flaw in the character of Helga is that she knew nothing of her true history and roots. She is incapable, therefore, of maintaining her balance in a world in which conflicting forces demand that she surrender her individuality. Her real conflict is not due to skin color, but to the inability to find self-validation in a world in which all choices are equally reprehensible. That this is the dilemma of Helga Crane does not suggest that it is the dilemma of the author, also.

For though better executed, technically, than *Black No More,* and presenting dimensions of the problem of identity which did not occur to Schuyler, Miss Larsen's novel by implication, at least, suggests, in the fate of the heroine, that the black middle-class values, no matter how imitative, are far superior to those of the white world or to that world of the black poor fantasized in the dreams of Helga Crane. Those who survive the novel, the Anne Greys, the Andersons, and the Vayles, imitative white men and women, though they may be, are conscious of an identity, no matter how flawed, which moves them outside that depicted in the writings of either Van Vechten or Jean Toomer. Theirs is a passive acceptance of the superiority of white images over black, and the ability to accept these minimize psychological difficulties of the kind encountered by Helga Crane.

Thus the middle-class-black reader of the twenties had little difficulty in choosing the fate of Anne Grey, hypocritical and pretentious, over that of Helga Crane, doomed to the quicksand of poverty and want. Anne is, after all, made in the image of James Weldon Johnson's protagonist; she is cognizant of the fine distinctions between the black middle class and the black poor as is George Schuyler; unlike her friend, therefore, she engages upon no quest to establish her identity, stays clear of the life-style so akin to that of those suggested in the fiction of Jean Toomer. The tragedy of Helga Crane and Nella Larsen, as well, however, is that neither knew of the values of courage and endurance depicted in the life-style of Toomer's men and women, and therefore looked upon black life as lived by the poor through the distorted lenses of white sociologists. In their flight from themselves, Blacks have all too often accepted the same images of each other as have whites.

Nella Larsen's second novel, *Passing* (1929), differs fundamentally from the first. In terms of character development, organization, and fidelity to language, the second, divided into three sections—"Encounter," "Re-encounter," and "Finale"—is superior to the first. Though this structure makes for a more well-knit novel, none of her characters possess the stature of a Helga Crane, and Miss Larsen loses both focus and emotional intensity in her attempt to balance Irene Redfield and Clare Kendry against one another. Redfield, representative of the black middle class, fair enough to pass for white, does not do so; Kendry, who passes into the white race, retains her romantic ideas concerning Blacks; like Helga Crane she is attracted by what she considers their primitive characteristics. The experiences of both are juxtaposed in the novel, with the result that Clare's act of passing receives more extensive treatment than Irene's adoption of white-middle-class values.

Though the novel is told from the point of view of Irene Redfield, the basic plot centers around Clare Kendry, daughter of a union between a wastrel black man and a white woman. At the outset of the novel, Clare has become black no more, has married a white man who has contempt for Blacks, hidden her racial background, and given birth to a daughter. Still, she is enamored of all things black: "You don't know," she relates to Irene, "you can't realize how I want to see Negroes, to be with them again, to talk with them, to hear them laugh." The mania for association with black people has caused her to contact Irene, her childhood friend, and to renew the relationship between them. As a result, she is able to associate with Blacks frequently without her husband's knowledge. Irene, however, having marital difficulties of her own, becomes paranoid at the close relationship which develops between her husband, Brian, and the beautiful Clare. The last section of the novel entitled "Finale" is appropriately designated; the events that lead to Clare's death are analogous to the contrived incidents in poorly written morality melodrama.

Unknown to Clare, her husband has been suspicious of her actions ever since she introduced him to her Negro friend, Irene. Clare attends a party at the residence of a Black and, unknowingly, is followed by her husband, who breaks into the party, and confronts his wife: "So you're a nigger, a damned dirty nigger! His voice was a snarl and a moan, an expression of rage and pain." When Clare, self-composed and seemingly deliriously happy as a result of the discovery, makes no attempt to comfort her enraged husband, Irene fantasizes that if Clare is divorced by her husband, Brian may become her target: "She ran across the room, her terror tinged with ferocity, and laid a hand on Clare's bare arm. One thought possessed her. She couldn't have Clare cast aside by Bellow. She couldn't have her free."[9] What happens next is open to conjecture. Clare stands before an open window; pandemonium, chaos, and confusion reign; Irene rushes toward her and "one moment Clare had been there, a vital glowing thing, like a flame of red and gold. The next she was gone." The novel ends on a note of intrigue: Was Clare murdered or did she plummet, accidentally, several stories to her death?

The dramatic intensity of *Passing* is derived from Miss Larsen's contrast between Irene and Clare. Hoyt Fuller, editor of *Black World,* is correct when he argues that to concentrate upon the theme of passing in the novel is to mitigate its worth. Passing, as dramatized through the experiences of Clare, entails secrecy, deception, loss of identity, and eventually tragedy. It means to be separated from a life-style, which, for Clare, as for Helga, offers up romantic images of sensation and atavism, to lose something, in the James Weldon Johnson sense, of one's own soul. Even Clare's act of passing is suspect, based more upon expediency and hope of escaping poverty than upon commitment to a belief in the superiority of Euro-American values: ". . . I wanted things," she explains. "I knew I wasn't bad-looking and that I could pass. You can't know, Irene, how, when I used to go over to the South side, I used almost to hate all of you. You had all the things I wanted and never had had. It made me all the more determined to get them."[10]

Irene's life, by comparison, is superior to that of her friend. Though she has more than a casual interest in "passing," having done so in a small way, in department stores, etc., and, to the reader, seeming at times to resent the color of her husband (tea-colored) and of her son (dark), her interest is merely that of a curious woman, one interested in knowing the ". . . hazardous business of passing, this breaking away from all that was familiar and friendly to take one's chances in another environment. . . ." Possessing the symbolism of the white world, Irene has little reason to completely adopt its images. The wife of a doctor, she has servants, security, and near dictatorial powers over her family. As a black woman, she has more prestige, let alone power, than would be accorded her were she white under similar circumstances. It is this knowledge that induces the paranoia concerning Clare and Brian. For without Brian, the symbols Irene has acquired disappear. Prestige and standing in the black community amount to nothing in the absence of her doctor husband; her plan to send her children to Europe to study, where they will learn nothing of either sex or race, impossible of bearing fruition were Brian to desert her. Her standing in the white community as a representative of "respectable Blacks" and her role as missionary to the black poor must be forfeited with the loss of her husband. In light of her possessions, it takes no great leap of the imagination to believe that Clare Kendry met her death at the hands of Irene Redfield.

Aspects of Miss Larsen's personal life bear heavily upon both of her novels. Like Helga Crane, she was the product of a mixed marriage, and like both Irene Redfield and Clare Kendry, her own marriage was beset by turmoil. Her conflict between possible marriage to a white man and attempting to make a go of her marriage, all combine to present her as one beset by the problem of psychic dualism—the major theme in *Quicksand* and *Passing*—and accounts for her ambivalence concerning the meaning of blackness. Here she is both analogous to, and different from, Schuyler and Johnson. In the final analysis, her characters, Helga, Anne, Irene, and Clare, must either find their identities in the world of the black middle class, or face disaster. Not as partial to this class as either Johnson, Schuyler, or Jessie Fauset, and privy to its hypocrisies and pretensions, nevertheless, she believes that it is far superior to the lower class, and in some instances, for those like Irene Redfield, offers opportunities that the white world does not. Yet, both novels evidence the fact that she was not altogether happy with this special class, that she was capable of understanding, though not forgiving, their shortcomings. They wished, after all, to be both American and Negro, and yet Negro with limitations, defining the term in ways that moved them outside the sphere of less fortunate Blacks.

Like Miss Larsen herself, and Helga Crane, more specifically, theirs is a romanticism based upon repression or ignorance of the true facts concerning the black poor and their life-style. For Helga, nuances of the problem, occasioned by confusion of images, appear; for the black poor are both symbols of atavism and of the Christ figure, the poor suffering wards of American society: "Marriage . . . that means children, to me; and why add more suffering to the world? Why add more unwanted, tortured Negroes to America? Why do Negroes have children? Surely it must be sinful. Think of the awfulness of being responsible for the giving of life to creatures doomed to endure such wounds to the flesh, such wounds to the spirit, as Negroes have to endure."[11]

Read Miss Larsen's novels and discover the disaster which awaits those who search for identity through fantasy—either by passing into the white world or affectuating too close an association with the poor of the black world. In the final analysis it is better to be Irene Redfield than either Helga Crane or Clare Kendry, though happiness is not, and cannot be, the key to the character of either. For the question is not one of happiness for Miss Larsen, but one of survival. Those characters in her novels, beset by problems of identity, are doomed to destruction; only those who accept the fact that identity is a prerogative of a special class of people are capable of surviving. Theirs is not so much the finding of an identity, but the creation of one out of material bequeathed by both the white and the black worlds.

Unlike her colleagues, however, Miss Larsen realizes that there is something unique in the black experience, something which sets Blacks aside from whites: "For the first time Helga Crane felt sympathy rather than contempt and hatred of that father, who so often and so angrily she had blamed for his desertion of her mother. She understood now, his rejection, his repudiation, of the formal claim her mother had represented. She understood his yearning, his intolerable need for the inexhaustible humor and the incessant hope of his own kind, his need for those things, not material, indigenous to all Negro environments."

That Miss Larsen has been characterized by Adelaide Cromwell Hill as one who was ". . . different, even a bit strange, not at all at home with those around her"[12] explains, in part, her ambivalence toward the members of her own class, her romanticism with the black poor, and why the middle class has not readily accepted her as one of its major spokesmen. In pointing out the differences between whites and Blacks, she wavered between suggesting universal similarities between Blacks of all classes, suggesting, on the other hand, that there were lines of demarcation between poor and affluent Blacks that made one a superior group of people, the other an inferior. This was a psychic dilemma which the black bourgeoisie now, at this part of the twentieth century, wished to avoid; and though Miss Larsen was of them, she was not completely with them, did not always sing their praises, seemed not too enamored of the images they had adopted. Thus she was less their spokesman than Jessie Fauset, less the oracle bespeaking their real promise and achievement; and though they did not neglect her altogether, they nevertheless suggested that those, who would know them, look for their true portraits in the works of Jessie Fauset. Miss Fauset, influential editor of *Crisis* magazine, was one of the most respected of the Renaissance novelists, lauded even by Claude McKay, despite her bourgeois Philadelphia background.

As William Stanley Braithwaite observed, she took a "special class within the race" and gave it status and distinction. Two of her four novels, *There Is Confusion* (1924) and *Plum Bun* (1929), suggest the truth of this observation. Miss Fauset, however, had additional objectives. To point out the fallacy of the act of "passing" and to satirize, even more mercilessly than did Miss Larsen, those who chose to become black no more. For her, moreover, Blacks were special people, able to adopt white images while maintaining distinctions between the races. She holds no romantic vision of the black poor, as does Miss Larsen, but believes in the unique ability of affluent Blacks to serve as mentors to whites and missionaries to Blacks. In the foreword to her novel, *The Chinaberry Tree* (1931), differences between the races are played down and the similarities between the white and black middle class extolled. For the problem, simply put, is that white Americans, oblivious to the life-style of this class, are unaware that there are times when Blacks work, love, and attend to the demands of living, without thinking of "the [race] problem." What these people are like in those times, whites do not know; it is the job of the novelist to inform them. For this special class of Blacks are descendants of the early settlers, who played a great part in the building of the republic, men and women, who, though boasting of "no association" like that of members of the Sons and Daughters of the American Revolution, still date their ancestry as far back as other Americans. Naturally, therefore, like their white counterparts, they boast of their old Boston families, old Philadelphians, old Charlestonians. . . . "They are dark Americans who wear their joy and rue very much as does the white American. [They] may wear it with some difference, but it is the same joy and rue."

There Is Confusion, her first novel, which precedes *Quicksand* by some four years and Toomer's *Cane* by one, illustrates her intention to argue in fiction such sentiments as the above. The story centers around two "old Philadelphia families." One is descended from the *nouveau riche,* has gained entry into the "wider world," read white, by hard work and perseverance. The other offers a background marred by the specter of miscegenation, family feuds, and arrogance. Joanna Marshall is a product of the first family; Peter Bye, a product of the other. Joanna, like her father, is ambitious and aspiring; Peter, like his ancestors, at least one of them, is a wastrel, unaspiring and unambitious. The salvation of Peter Bye, through altercation with the spirit of work and progress as exemplified in Miss Marshall and her family, forms the plot structure of the novel.

First, the genealogy: Joel Marshall, father of Joanna, is a man cast in the Booker T. Washington tradition. Son of ignorant, unlettered slaves, he is a second-generation black man, early thrown upon his own by an uncaring society. He begins, however, despite the obstacles, from the ground up. A job as a laborer enables him to save enough money to open a small restaurant. Continued hard work and frugality enable him to move onward, to become a caterer. Having dutifully supported his mother, after her death, now a man of means, he travels to New York and marries a pretty, but not overly ambitious, woman. In addition to being a hard worker and a frugal man, Joel maintains a reverence for the black historical past, never allows his family to forget the contributions of such as Frederick Douglass to the building of the nation. His character is summed up in his own advice to his children: "Nothing in reason is impossible." And one does not think "anything about being colored. . . ."; such an accident of birth no more prohibits success "than being poor, or having some slight deformity . . . having some natural drawback often pushes you forward, that is if you've got anything in you to start with."

Of the four Marshall children—Joanna, Alexander, Philip, and Sylvia—Joanna is closer in ambition and temperament to her father. Those qualities, which pushed the older Marshall to success, push Joanna to want to become the best singer in the world and to take an abiding interest in people "who . . . had a purpose in life." Her character is flawed, however, by snobbery and obsession with success: "With Joanna, success and distinction were an obsession." Snobbery and obsession differentiate her from her father and draw rebuke from Miss Fauset. The middle-class female must be tolerant toward others and willing to forego her own ambitions in deference to her husband-to-be. Before Joanna can become the perfect middle-class model, therefore, she must undergo a baptism, must be cleansed of the evils of snobbery and obsession.

Unlike Joanna, Peter is the legatee of a mixed heritage. His great grandfather, Joshua Bye, was hinted to be the offspring of his white master, Aaron Bye. Without stating the case, Miss Fauset has more than a passing interest in the theme that the result of the admixture of white and black blood produces a mutant upon the family tree. Isaiah, son of Joshua, presents a positive example. He is the embodiment of the spirit of independence of struggle against tremendous odds. Openly rebellious against the tradition that suggests that his race must be hewers of wood and drawers of water, he prospers and becomes the founder of a school for black youth. With his son, Meriwether, however, the negative characteristics of mixed marriage come to the fore. Meriwether, father of Peter, is a bitter man, unambitious, dedicated to the belief that the world "owes me a living." Like his namesake, white Meriwether Bye, he too desires, early in life, to become a surgeon. Yet he soon runs through his inheritance, tires of the hard work and demands of study, and succeeds in ". . . wiping away all that edifice of respectability and good citizenship which Joshua Bye had so carefully built up."

Peter is haunted by ghosts of yesteryear past. The blood of old Isaiah encourages him to dream of becoming a surgeon; that of his father, Meriwether, causes him to seek, instead, a quick, easy path to manhood and success. The closeness of the younger Bye to the attitudes of his father are dramatized by his use of the race question as rationale for his setbacks. Miss Fauset, therefore, underlines the task awaiting

Joanna: Through care and persuasion she must point Peter in the direction of Joshua, away from that established by Meriwether: ". . . this new Peter—this old Peter . . . with the early shiftlessness, the irresolutions of his father, Meriwether Bye, the ancient grudge of his grandfather, Isaiah Bye, rearing up, bearing full and perfect fruit in his heart."[13]

There is little doubt in the mind of the reader, from the moment that Peter and Joanna meet in the novel, that the two are to be saviors of each other, that through Peter, Joanna will be cured of defects in her own character, and through Joanna, Peter will gain his manhood and his rightful identity. This conflict reduces the novel to the level of a nineteenth-century melodrama of love and romance, distinguished, in the main, only by the color of the characters. The resolution of the conflict bears out this assertion. Joanna receives a rebuff and a dressing down from her family, when she is discovered to have brought about the separation between a poor laundress' daughter and Philip. As a result, she surrenders her obsession with ambition and settles for the role of housewife, instead of a career as the ". . . one colored person who sings best in these days. . . ."

For Peter, absolution is more difficult to come by. He must be purged of both unambition and bitterness concerning the racial problem if he is to survive as a successful husband in a black-middle-class union, or become a facsimile of Joel Marshall: "The man I marry," avows Joanna, "must be a man worthwhile, like my father or Philip. I couldn't stand the thought of spending my life with someone ordinary." Before Peter can fulfill his destiny, therefore, he must travel overseas to the war front, confront the white Meriwether Bye, be informed of the importance of his ancestors from the white oracle: "[without them] Aaron Bye would never have got on his feet." This summary of the heroics of his ancestors helps Peter accept his role as a man, without bitterness against his past or uncertainty concerning his future. At the end of the novel, ready to return from the war back to his Joanna, he has grown in "the spirit of racial tolerance and the spirit of racial responsibility. . . . He wanted to live in America; he wanted to get along with his fellow man, but he no longer proposed to let circumstances shape his career. . . . He meant to be a successful surgeon, a responsible husband and father, a self-reliant man."[15]

The technical defect of *There Is Confusion* has detracted from its importance as a major work in the history of black literature. More so than the novels of any of her predecessors, however, that of Miss Fauset sums up the dreams, aspirations, and desires of the black middle class of her time and beyond. She was more in tune with their aspirations than Johnson, Schuyler, or Larsen, knew the images they desired, the portraits of themselves they wanted offered in evidence to the white world of their superior attainments and qualities. Joel Marshall, having risen to prominence through diligence and hard work, is representative of their number. Yet, the progress of the race cannot stop with the likes of Marshall; he is a suitable, but not exceptional, image. The standard bearer of the racial image must be a professional—a doctor, preferably—one possessing the following characteristics: willingness to work hard, to be a loving father, and to refuse to trade upon race bitterness.

Indeed, the salient quality of Miss Fauset's work is the appeal to tolerance on the part of her major characters. Those who are bitter about past treatment of the race must be made to forgive, to realize that oppression against Blacks is specific, not universal. This ability to forgive past transgressions means that her characters are morally superior to whites, are those who believe in and uphold the truisms of the American creed. Far less snobbish than the characters of Johnson or Miss Larsen, those of Miss Fauset are interested in elevating the race. To do this, they offer themselves as examples, suggesting in so doing that they are intellectually and economically superior to other Blacks. Undoubtedly, Miss Fauset is not cognizant of the image she advances! It was one all too real, delineating life as lived in a way that fiction should not. The paradigms she brought to life in *There Is Confusion* were but fictional representations of a class, lacking in too many of the virtues which Miss Fauset held sacrosanct.

There is little doubt, however, that Miss Fauset, more so than her contemporaries, spoke for the black bourgeoisie, past and present. The dream of Frank Webb, of a class midway between whites and poor Blacks, is now realized; the middle class has grown to maturity and received validation in the work of a talented writer. Let others consider the race to be homogeneous; here, in the novels of Jessie Fauset, is proof positive that a special class, differing little from its white counterpart, has finally arrived upon the American scene. This class was no longer beset by problems of psychic dualism like that which affected Johnson's protagonist, no longer sought status and culture by "passing" over into the white race. Images of cultured and respected people can be found now in the likes of Joel Marshall, Joanna and Peter Bye. Angela Murray, heroine of *Plum Bun,* therefore, was far from the mark when she asserted that all the important things in life "were wrapped up with white people . . . because for the present they had power and the badge of that power was whiteness."[16] With the publication of *There Is Confusion,* the remark no longer had validity and the Angela Murrays must come to realize that the symbol of power is no longer whiteness but class, and one is more capable of exercising power in the race into which he is born than in the other, where entry can be gained only through "passing."

This is the lesson Miss Fauset imparts to her middle-class audience in her second novel *Plum Bun*. Angela Murray, third-generation octoroon, has fared better than her sister, Virginia; she has inherited Caucasian features. Unlike Virginia, she has not acquired the black tint of her father's skin, nor his Negro hair, but instead, "her mother's creamy complexion and her soft, cloudy, chestnut hair. . . ." Her endowments from her father are not to be scorned completely, however; he has bequeathed his daughter Angela his "aquiline nose, the gift of some remote Indian ancestors which gave to his face and his eldest daughter's that touch of chiseled immobility." From her mulatto mother, Angela has learned of the joy and freedom inherent in possessing a white skin. Like Irene Redfield, Mrs. Murray delights in playing the game of passing. On one such occasion, while in the company of whites, she is forced to snub her own daughter Virginia. The incident, meant as a forewarning to Angela—one of the consequences of passing is neglect of one's own flesh and blood—nevertheless, does not temper her belief that being Black is ". . . nothing short of a curse." After a conflict between herself and a suitor, Matthew Henson, due in part to the fact that Matthew does not measure up to the white image, has, indeed, inherited his father's "thick, tight, bad hair," Angela, as obsessed with the idea of success as was Joanna Marshall, decides that happiness and success lay across the color line: "I'm going to leave Philadelphia, give up schoolteaching, break away from our loving friends and acquaintances and bust up the whole shooting match."[17]

She travels to New York, changes her name, and becomes involved with two men: Anthony Cross, secretly passing, has chosen a career as an artist, and Roger Fielding, white, wealthy, and opposed to Blacks: "I'd send 'em all back to Africa if I could." The choice for Angela, therefore, is between sensitive Anthony and selfish, egotistical, racist Roger. Initially, she desires Roger and the affluence and power he symbolizes. As for Anthony, she wanted none of his "poverty and perspiration and secret vows. . . ." Roger, however, is dominated by a father who insists that he not marry outside of his class, let alone his race, and Angela's calculated campaign to seduce the young man into marriage causes him to propose something altogether different: "I'm asking you to live in my house, to live for me; to be my girl; to keep a love-nest where I and only I may come."[18] Though Angela spurns the offer, she allows herself to be seduced by Roger, and in hopes of eventually persuading him to accept matrimony, in spite of his father's preferences, she neglects her sister, Virginia, now arrived in New York.

The incident is analogous to that which had occurred earlier between Virginia and her mother. Having promised to meet her sister at the train station, Angela is surprised when Roger appears at the same moment as Virginia. To acknowledge her sister means to reveal her racial background and lose Roger; therefore, she denies her sister. At this point in the novel, the dramatic conflict becomes evident. The reader is asked to view the lives of two sisters, one who deserted her race and her family, the other who maintained loyalty to both. Despite the affront by her sister, Virginia settles in New York, makes her way into association with the class of "the best colored people," and finds as much pleasure in her own race as Angela once believed she might find in the other. Thus the accolades are due Virginia; Angela must come back from the market place of dreams and illusions, must be made to realize that the plum bun resides in the world she has left.

A forgiving Virginia comes to her aid. Through visits to her sister, now residing in Harlem, Angela learns of the "fulness, richness, even thickness of [black] life" in Harlem. Discovery of the "best class of colored people" helps her to understand the importance of the black middle class. This importance is articulated during a lecture by a distinguished black sociologist: "Those of us with money and rank cannot yet go our separate ways—must still help our less fortunate, weaker brethren—[cannot] go our separate ways apart from the unwashed, untutored herd." And in words designed for the eyes of the reader and for the ears of Angela, he argues not for love of race, but pride of race, which enables Blacks to find their own race "beautiful and praiseworthy," to advocate a chauvinism "content with its own type, that finds completeness within its own group."

Shortly after the lecture, Angela refuses Roger, who finally consents to marriage, moves to Harlem, surrenders her identity as a white woman, and makes further discoveries concerning her class and its obligations: "Harlem intrigued her; it was a wonderful city; it represented, she felt, the last work in racial pride, integrity and even self-sacrifice. Here were people of a very high intellectual type, exponents of the realest and most essential refinement, living cheek by jowl with coarse or ill-bred or even criminal, certainly indifferent, members of their race. Of course some of this propinquity was due to outer pressure, but there was present, too, a hidden consciousness of race duty, a something which if translated said: Perhaps you do pull me down a little from the height to which I have climbed. But on the other hand, perhaps, I'm helping you to rise!"[19]

Market is finally done, when Anthony and Virginia discover that they do not love each other. Anthony loves Angela, still, and Matthew and Virginia have come to love each other. Lost on Miss Fauset, but obvious to the reader, is the fact that the mulattoes, Anthony and Angela, and the Blacks, Virginia and Matthew, enter into union with each other and not with their differently complexioned partners of either sex. Nevertheless, the cycle for Angela Murray, from home and back again, is completed, and four lovers, each cognizant of their responsibilities as important members of the race, return to a life, though within the color line, more richly endowed than that beyond it.

Despite tedious prose, overwriting, improbable situations, and contrived incidents, *Plum Bun* ranks with its predecessor, *There Is Confusion,* as one of the more important novels of the period. Without hesitation, Miss Fauset delineates the life-style of that class which she represented, describing in graphic terms the major concerns of their lives. Marriage, security, family, and respectability lead the list, with race pride and interest necessary elements. The successful marriage, of course, leads to the stable family, security, and respectability, none of which is possible without strict adherence to the Protestant ethic. Had the class for which she spoke divined in her philosophy dedication to work and progress as a suitable norm by which one validated his worth, their position might not have been so contemptible. However, they settled instead for an ethic based upon appearance, upon status attained by skin color and one's distance in things material from the poor. Few middle-class-black families would not understand Miss Fauset's intentions, subconsciously or otherwise, in uniting Anthony with Angela and Virginia with Matthew. Pride in race does not mean that one surrender the white aesthetic, that he opt for the formula that Black is beautiful. The successful marriage from which all else might spring demands a union between like peoples, mulattoes with mulattoes, Blacks with Blacks.

In *Nigger Heaven,* Van Vechten describes the black and white world in terms of a theater. Blacks sit above "in our places in the gallery . . . and watch the white world sitting down below in the good seats of the orchestra." The implication that all black people are the same, occupy the same seat in the gallery, was one that spokesmen for the bourgeoisie were determined to counteract. They insisted upon the recognition of class distinction and believed, falsely, that such was important in the over-all evaluation of Blacks by whites. If this were not so, ponder the consequences: one Black differed not one iota from another, and recognition plus better treatment and a chance to live as free citizens were no more available to the middle class than to the poor.

This meant a careful evaluation, once again, of the images, symbols, and definitions accepted as a result of the flight from those displayed in the works of Van Vechten, a questioning of the very idea of the concept of "better black people." In actuality, to be Joel Marshall or Matthew Henson did not obviate maltreatment, nor gain special distinction in the eyes of whites. The image of black men in white masks was scorned and derided by whites who, given a choice between Joel Marshall and the Scarlet Creeper, due to their own psychological needs, opted for the image suggested by the Creeper. Those who flocked to Harlem during the "Van Vechten vogue" did not go to see Joel, for they questioned his authenticity, though he presented no such threat as that offered by the Garvey men, no real contradiction to the black image they had been taught to believe in.

That Blacks should attempt to "become like them" was understandable; that they could never fulfill this ambition—well, the whites knew this even if the Blacks did not. And though some members of the middle class, like the people of Miss Fauset's novels, entertained doubts about the validity of a "special class" founded on caste and class distinctions, the black poor came to believe with most of them that the possession of Nordic skin, Nordic manners, and Nordic culture defined one as human beings. The men and women of *There Is Confusion* and *Plum Bun* became the new models, the new images, for members of the lower class, the Anthonys and Angelas were the paradigms against which they measured their worth. They were well aware of the fact that the Angela Murrays were not images but symbols. Yet even the symbols seemed more acceptable to their mentors, the black bourgeoisie, than the images presented by Toomer and Garvey. Thus, spurred on by the attitudes of the times, created, in part, by the literature of Johnson, Schuyler, Larsen, and Fauset, they joined in chasing the white phantom, with all too often, disastrous results.

No novel illustrates this pursuit of folly better than Wallace Thurman's (1902–34) *The Blacker the Berry* (1929). Thurman, onetime reader at Macaulay's and Hollywood script writer, was considered as one of the genuine intellectuals of the Renaissance era. His novel received little praise upon publication. *Black No More* was more highly praised, though Thurman's novel, also satire, is the better novel, both in terms of technical construction and relevance of content. Moreover, the novel questions the sanctity of the new models presented in the fiction of middle-class writers and assesses the importance and value of such models to Blacks as a whole. In observing the black middle class, the black poor saw a group of people rushing to become like whites, while arguing fidelity to race. What is to be made of Negro leaders who in most cases, as Schuyler observed, were married to everything black except the black woman? In an age in which stage shows and cabarets, frequented by middle-class Blacks and whites, featured entertainment in which black skin, kinky hair, and thick lips were objects of humor for comedian and spectator alike, what were the possessors of such features to think of their own images? Having been led to believe that it was of incalculable advantage, if not to be white, then at least to possess white characteristics, it is not surprising that the poor sought to emulate their tutors.

Such is the case with Emma Lou, black heroine of Thurman's *The Blacker the Berry*. Her grandmother, founder and acknowledged leader of the blue-vein set of Boise, Idaho, believes that those of lighter complexion are a "superior class," who should be rewarded with more "respect, opportunity and social acceptance than the more pure blooded Negroes. . . ." Her motto, and that of her group, is the motto of old: "Whiter and whiter every generation until the grandchildren of the blue veins could easily go over into the white race and become assimilated so that problems of race would plague them no more."[20] For Emma Lou, whose mother mistakenly married a dark man, the wishes of the elders are impossible of fulfillment. Because of her black skin, she is an outcast, hounded on three sides: by a grandmother who holds her in contempt; a mother who blames her for her own unhappy situation; and a stepfather, son of an illicit union between an Irishman and a black washerwoman, who deserts her mother, in protest against Emma Lou.

The psychological results are disastrous for the young girl. Feeling guilt about, and contempt for, her black skin, she attempts to lighten it. She tries bleaching creams, powders, scouring with brushes and soap—all to no avail. Her failure to lighten her skin, coupled with daily rebuffs from mother and grandmother alike, forces her to leave Boise, intent upon finding a mate cast in the image she herself cannot approach. Her first stop is the University of California, as a student. Her rejection here, however, by the university's own blue-vein society, is as severe as was that in Boise, Idaho. Finding neither acceptance nor recognition here, among the lighter members of the race, she moves on to New York, the celebrated home of the "New Negro."

She finds, however, that the New Negro of New York differs little from the "old" Negro of Idaho and California. Indeed, the preference of Harlem men for "high yaller" women is part of a curious triangle peculiar to the New Negro era: the white people come to Harlem to view the new curiosities; the mulattoes try to impress the whites by imitating their choice in everything from drinks to women; and the darker Blacks follow suit in regard to the mulattoes. The example of the supreme irony of this situation is evidenced by the situation of a white actress with whom Emma Lou finds employment ". . . who was playing for the moment the part of a mulatto Carmen in an alleged melodrama of Negro life. . . ."

The actress' example, in addition, points out the ironic intent of the novel. She assumes the guise of a black woman for the short term of her performance, yet she never confuses her real identity, the one she adopts on stage. The Blacks, on the other hand, not only expropriate the roles of others, but act as if they and the identities they assume are one and the same. This leads to a confusion of identity, fraught with dangers for mulattoes and Blacks alike. For not only do the mulattoes have contempt for Blacks of darker skin color; so, also, do the Blacks themselves. Emma Lou is an appropriate example. She is a beautiful woman, black skin and all. Yet, her contempt for her color is shown in the hostility she feels toward those whose color is as dark as her own. She becomes easy prey then for mulatto men like Jaspar Carne, with "teak wood tan skin" and "curly hair," who seduces her, borrows money from her, and leaves; and Alva, with whom she engages in a sadomasochistic relationship until forced to the painful realization that she had been used, had been nothing more to the mulatto than a source of money and sex, that to both him and his friends, she was ". . . a typical black mammy." As a result, having come upon self-awareness, she leaves Alva's household and begins the pursuit of a mate, black like herself.

The problem of the confusion of identity, produced in part by the aspirations of the black middle class, was one of the major preoccupations of Thurman's short life. One of the true Renaissance intellectuals, this preoccupation, along with doubts concerning his own potential and accomplishments, led, one supposes, to alcoholism and death from tuberculosis. Almost alone among his colleagues, he exhibited concern for honesty and distaste for hypocrisy and pretension, realizing that honesty and truth were necessary for a realistic appraisal of the major dilemma facing the race as a whole. There is little doubt that the character Truman, who outlines the dilemma, is the pseudonym for the author: "In an environment where there are so many color-prejudiced whites, there are bound to be a number of color-prejudiced Blacks. . . . For, as you know, prejudices are always caused by differences, and the majority group sets the standards."[21] Earlier, Thurman avowed that one cannot blame Blacks for being prejudiced against each other so long as one believes that white is not only "the symbol of everything pure and good" but the foundation of black religious values as well ". . . the God . . . most Negroes worship is a patriarchal white man, seated on a white throne, in a spotless white heaven, radiant with white streets and white-apparelled angels eating white honey and drinking white milk."[22]

The rationale is not a justification, but an explanation, and this is true also of the novel. Thurman, however, was capable of condemning as well, as his second novel, *Infants of the Spring* (1930), demonstrates. His condemnation here is not of the middle class or the poor, but of his fellow artists. The problem of the confusion of identity is not to be solved by the Alvas or the Emma Lous, the Irene Redfields or the Angela Murrays, but by the artist honest enough and talented enough to engage in the war for the control of images, and thus make unnecessary the kind of confusion which characterizes the lives and thinking of the middle class and their spokesman. The road to truer images lay not in adopting Nordic ones in protest against those offered by Van Vechten, nor in creating a special group within the race, to serve as the reservoir for a new set of images. Instead, a search for paradigms must begin anew, must begin where Toomer and Garvey left off among the black poor, who, despite their own confusions of images, can never approach the Anglo-Saxon norm. Thurman's defense of the magazine *Fire,* which he and others founded, evidences his thought in this direction: *"Fire,* like Mr. Hughes' poetry, was experimental. *It was not interested in sociological problems or propaganda. It was purely artistic in intent and conception. Its contributors went to the proletariat rather than to the bourgeoisie for characters and material. They were interested in people who still retained some individual race qualities and who were not totally white American in every respect save color of skin."

The solution to the problem posed by a confusion of images must be found by the artist. What is needed, therefore, is a baptism, a cleansing of the soul and spirit, one that will remove a predilection for images of things white. Thurman, Hughes, McKay, and Rudolph Fisher, among others, believed in such a baptism, believed in the possibility of resurrecting such as Alva and Emma Lou; they were less sanguine about salvation for such as Irene Redfield and Angela Murray. These contrasting opinions, concerning the black poor and the black middle class, account for much of the conflict between the radicals and conservatives of the period. The younger, radical writers refused to become the spokesmen of the bourgeoisie, championed images found in the life-style of the poor. Like Helga Crane, however, in too many instances, they were romanticists concerning the poor, some too close in descriptions of black life to Van Vechten and as obstinate as the spokesmen for the middle class in touting their new-found images. They failed to recognize the contribution, dubious to be sure, made by the conservatives, and thus foreclosed the possibility of compromise, of a united struggle against the major antagonist.

For the conservative writers, who depicted black men as white men, with few distinctions, made necessary the attempt by the radicals to search for newer images, without following this almost inevitable route, due to the necessity of Blacks of all classes to move outside the definitions forwarded by Van Vechten. Whatever one might think of the images promulgated in the works of Johnson, Fauset, and Larsen, they were as necessary as their opposites in the works of Toomer and the movement of Marcus Garvey. Once these images were scrutinized and questioned, the attempt to create newer, more representative ones might begin. It is not surprising that after such satiric attacks as that of *The Blacker the Berry,* novels concerning "passing" are scarcely ever written by Blacks in the latter part of the century, that the class for which Miss Fauset is spokeswoman disappears from black literature, returning only, in most cases, as objects of derision.

For younger black Americans, those who would appear during the Richard Wright era, novelists who championed Euro-American values, by adhering to the concept of a special class within the race, only magnified the differences between this class and whites and the similarities between it and other Blacks. In postulating men and women outside the color line, they proved how close these were to those within it; in constructing a world based upon hypocrisy and pretension, they were forced, after the depression, to comprehend the hoax they had perpetrated upon themselves. The solution to their problem was simplistic. Their true identity could be found only within their own race, their humanity measured in terms only of that of the most maligned African-American.

No adoption of Nordic manners or expropriation of Nordic culture could change the way whites perceived them, nor rescue them from the oppression directed against Blacks as a whole. To become Angela Murray did not obviate the problems of racism nor bring about equality with whites. Blacks in white masks remained Blacks still, inheritors of a common culture and a common fate. Though these ideas are not clearly stated in the works of the Renaissance writers, radical or conservative, both helped to place them into proper perspective. The question posed, satirically, by Wallace Thurman remained to be answered: Is there truth in the old folk saying that the blacker the berry, the sweeter the juice? The answer was not forthcoming from the Renaissance writers, nor from writers for many years to come; but in their own way, novelists Claude McKay, Rudolph Fisher, and Zora Neal Hurston answered as best they could, due to time and circumstances, in the affirmative. Thus they managed to shift the novel from a preoccupation with the black middle class to a preoccupation with the black proletariat. The answer then to Van Vechten was to meet the white minister of propaganda head on, to retreat not one step from the proposition that the blacker berry did, indeed, produce the more succulent juice.

VI

THE OUTSIDER

If the images and symbols of the Van Vechtenites were the underlying catalysts for movement toward those of Euro-Americans, the obverse was the effect upon the radical writers. They moved in to harvest the crop that Van Vechten had sown, denying always that they were doing so. Yet despite the fact that sensationalism and atavism are characteristics in their works, they were able in most instances to view the black proletariat realistically, in a sense that Van Vechten never could, that Toomer might only approximate. Few of their characters, with the exception of the women of Zora Neal Hurston and Bita Plant of McKay's *Banana Bottom,* ever reach the grandeur or status of the Garveyites. Nevertheless, for the most part, the writers were intent upon portraying the black man as a human being with universal faults, aspirations, and appetites, instead of as a mere shadow image of white Americans. In doing this they borrowed shamelessly from the new socialism, from the naturalism of Émile Zola, Frank Norris, Stendahl, and Dostoevsky, from the perceptions of Toomer and Garvey, and from the history and culture of the race itself

They were creators of a new tradition in black literature—one which centered for the first time exclusively upon those who neither materially nor physically could approach the American norm. This sense of distance between their people and the society depicted the men and women of their novels as rebels if only in the sense that they were antithetical, by nature of their existence, to American standardization and sameness. These were outsiders, though nowhere approaching such stature as those offered in the works of Delany and Wright. Their creators, despite all, were men deeply impressed with the American Experience who believed still in America and its value system. Even those like Hughes and McKay, most impressed by the social miracle wrought by Communist Russia, were Americans still, in their insistence that Blacks loved the country of their birth, despite oppression.

Yet, they were outsiders and despite their refusal to acknowledge this fact, their works depict men and women who, by virtue of their lifestyles, are separated from most of their countrymen, white and Black, and are more likely to search for their identity in the black community, rather than in Main Street, U.S.A., to seek images and symbols once held dear by those who had undertaken the great migration. Look back upon the vagabonds and intellectuals of McKay, the charlatans of Countee Cullen, the troubadours of Langston Hughes, and in a later time, the robust men and women of Zora Neal Hurston, and the age of Richard Wright is almost upon us. The younger writers of the Renaissance period were the bridge linking the new man with the old.

The works of Claude McKay (1889–1948) are seminal in this respect. For most of his life he is an outsider, a cosmopolitan owing fidelity to no God save his own. He is one of the genuine intellectuals of the "New Negro" vogue—a world traveler and a poet, whose book, *Harlem Shadows* (1922), is credited with beginning the Renaissance period—and the key to his works and character alike centers upon cultural dualism—an attraction and repulsion for the artifacts of the Western world. Something of this is apparent in his first novel, *Home to Harlem* (1928). The question he poses in the novel is analogous to that posed in Johnson's novel: Can the black man find his identity in the cultural artifacts of the Western world? For McKay, the answer is difficult to come by. The years since the end of slavery have produced gains only in material and political areas. For those deeper qualities of the human spirit, the new science and technology have brought human ruin and standardization: ". . . Keep your fine feelings," he has one of his intellectual men remark, ". . . but don't try to make a virtue of them. You'll lose them then. They'll become all hollow inside, false and dry as civilization itself. And civilization is rotten. We are all rotten who are touched by it."[1]

Plot is of minor importance in *Home to Harlem;* the action of the novel centers upon the exploits of its two major characters, Jake and Ray. What thematic structure there is centers upon Jake's search for "a little brown girl," Felice, whom he meets upon his return to the United States from a stint in the army and is later separated from.

Discovering the girl in a cabaret on his first night back in Harlem, he spends the night with her, paying fifty dollars for his pleasure. Felice however, unknown to Jake, returns the money to his pockets, where he discovers it after leaving the hotel. His inclination is to go back and strike up a more meaningful relationship. Male chauvinism, however, intervenes and postpones another meeting until the end of the novel: ". . . Guess I won't go back right now. Never let a woman think you're too crazy about her. But she's a particular piece a business. . . . Me and her again tonight. . . . Handful o' luck shot straight outa heaven. . . ." In failing to "go back right now," Jake loses touch with Felice and embarks upon a search for her which takes him through various adventures as sweet man, strike breaker, vagabond of all trades, and railroad porter.

Jake's *carpe diem* approach to life brings him close, never too close, however, to the stereotypes of Van Vechten. Yet, in only the barest of essentials is there any similarity between Jake and the Scarlet Creeper. The Creeper is the pleasure principle personified; Jake, however, is a man of dreams ". . . Ef I was edjucated," he confesses to Ray, "I could understand things better and be proper speaking like you is. . . . And I mighta helped mah lil sister to get edjucated too. . . ." Moreover, confronted by a world ruled by whites and "dictie Negroes," relegated to an environment where violence, decay, and despair constitute the norm, Jake is able to maintain his sanity, to envision paradise in hell itself, to find surcease from a day on the white man's waterfront, or on the white man's steam engines, in nights of gin, women, and song. He is, therefore, as McKay decribes him, one who ". . . stood forth as one of those unique types of humanity who lived alone and were never lonely. . . . He, in his frame and atmosphere, was the Alpha and Omega himself."[2]

The description might have better suited Ray. Like his female counterpart in *Banana Bottom,* McKay's third novel, Ray has been educated in the West and is unable to throw off its influence, to return to his roots, to return to his Haiti. His is the first presence in black literature of the brooding intellectual, who, like Caliban, having been taught the manners, culture, and language of his captors, comes to realize the great gulf created between himself and his own people. Thus, unlike the characters of the novels of Johnson, Larsen, and Fauset, possessing the paraphernalia of the Euro-American world, forces the question which haunts him throughout the novel: To what culture do I belong?

He emerges as a man without a cultural home, existing within a cultural void, retaining not the artifacts but only the memories of a culture far different from that which claims him: "Immediately he was back home again. His father's house was a vast forest full of blooming hibiscus and mimosas and giant evergreen trees. . . . He was a young shining chief in a marble palace . . . and life was all blue happiness. Taboos and terrors and penalties were transformed into new pagan delights, orgies of Orient-blue carnival, of rare flowers and red fruits, cherubs and seraphs and fetishes and phalli and all the most-high gods."[3] What has changed the dream into nightmare? The United States Army, carrier of Euro-American culture, has conquered the island, rendered impotent the sons and daughters of Toussaint L'Ouverture and Dessalines, made servants and coolies of a once proud people, and, spreading culture by means of the bayonet, has destroyed the idyllic dream, made impossible the return home again. Thus unable to discover an appropriate life-style in what appears as the escapist philosophy of Jake, Ray is destined to search always for what once was, to dream of the Haiti before the conquerors arrived.

Both men, therefore, are outsiders in a world ruled by Anglo-Saxons, both have sniffed the narcotic of Western civilization, Jake, less so than Ray, and both, in flight from the rules and restraints of Western culture, flee from the same enemy. The marines and the slaveowners, after all, had this in common: Each prescribed a cultural life-style different from that of the people they conquered. Thus the central point made in *Home to Harlem* is not that one must search for an identity, but an acknowledgment that identity, stolen, lost, or destroyed, is difficult to retrieve. Unlike the actors in the picture show—one of the most revealing scenes in the novel—neither Jake nor Ray will settle for the decorations, the form, the pretensions of those ". . . all dressed up in expensive evening clothes with automobiles and menials to imitate white society people. . . ."

Neither, that is, is willing to accept himself as an image made in the mold of a white man. Listen to Jake's rationale for leaving Harlem, after a brutal fight with a friend, observe the images of white men conjured up in his dialogue, and we are far from the novels of Johnson or Miss Fauset: "Oh, he was infinitely disgusted with himself to think that he had just been moved by the same savage emotions as those vile, vicious, villainous white men, who, like hyenas and rattlers, had fought, murdered, and clawed the entrails out of black men. . . ."[4]

The desire to be one's self is strong in these proletarian characters of Claude McKay, and his people, on the whole, are different from those of Wallace Thurman. Yet, *Home to Harlem* and *The Blacker the Berry* are parts of the same truth; each, like its predecessors, concerned with the loss of black identity. For McKay, however, and this marks the distinction between *Home to Harlem* and other novels, identity for

Blacks can be found only outside of the Western orbit, only when men can return to the gods of their fathers. Interjecting a note of modernity into the novel, men must search for their identity outside of a technological, mechanical-oriented world even as they search for it outside one marred by racism. In *Banjo* (1929), in which Ray appears again as a roving vagabond, McKay has reached some sort of conclusion to the question concerning identity: "Only when he got down among the black and brown working boys and girls of the country did he find something of that raw unconscious and the devil with them pride in being Negro that was his own natural birthright."[5]

The answer, however, was not to be found in *Banjo,* nor in *Home to Harlem.* Neither of these novels takes the reader to the end of the odyssey, neither offers a resolution to the conflict facing the outsider. This was the task of *Banana Bottom* (1933), McKay's third and best novel.

Bita Plant, despite being educated in the Western world, has not forsaken her roots and culture, has maintained fidelity to the past and belief in the cultural viability of her people. That the way home would be found by this young sensitive woman, instead of by one of McKay's intellectual vagabonds, or that the problem of black identity cannot be found in America, but outside, is symbolic of McKay's growing confusion concerning identity himself—a confusion to be obviated in but a few years, when he will find his identity in the Catholic Church, will surrender the god, Obeah, for the most demanding of the Christian Gods.

Banana Bottom might better have been entitled the education of Bita Plant. Raped at an early age by a demented playmate, she is taken into the household of white missionaries, reverends Malcolm and Priscilla Craig. Their rescue of the young girl from her environment is done as a favor to the father, Jordan Plant, an old friend, and from a desire to make the child over in their Anglo-Saxon image: "Priscilla Craig had conceived the idea of redeeming her [Bita] from her past by a long period of education without any contact with Banana Bottom and at the finish she would be English trained and appearing in everything but the color of her skin."[6] Though both husband and wife hold contempt for the culture of the people of Banana Bottom, Priscilla's is more universal, taking in black people everywhere.

The plot of the novel, therefore, evolves around Bita Plant's ability to resist the attempt to rob her of her own cultural roots and substitute those of an alien culture. The choices are difficult ones: On one side, represented by the Craigs, lay the paraphernalia of the Western world —wealth, power, security. In addition, the color problem, so important among Blacks in America, looms even larger here, and Bita is cognizant of the fact that she is black, not mulatto, and that in Jamaica that made a great difference in terms of jobs, security, and status. On the other side, represented by the people of Banana Bottom, lay a culture and history, one more appreciated by the white Squire Genser, than by either the mulattoes or the missionaries. Genser, an outsider, attuned in thought, if not completely in spirit, to the culture of the area, is Bita's confidant and teacher: "Obeah is a part of your folklore, like your Anancy tales and your digging Jammas. And your folklore is the spiritual link between you and your ancestral origin. My mind is richer because I know your folklore."[7]

Due to the influence and counseling of the squire, frequent trips to Banana Bottom, and rebellion against her benefactors by openly flirting with the town rake, Bita severs her life with the missionaries and their culture, resolves the conflict in a release of pent-up hostility over the attempt of the Craigs to transform her into an Anglo-Saxon: "She became contemptuous of everything—the plan of her education and the way of existence at the mission, and her eye wandering to the photograph of her English college over her bed, she suddenly ripped it from its frame, tore the thing up and trampled the pieces under her feet. . . ."[8] Her eventual return to Banana Bottom, after refusing the offerings of the white world, her reunion with her own people and culture, and her marriage to Jubban, worker on her father's farm, are paralleled by the eventual acceptance of the people of the region of their own gods over those of the missionaries. Two years away from his own conversion to Catholicism, McKay can see Bita's conflict and that of the people as well, involving, in more than an abstract sense, the choice of one god over another.

Bita's return to the cultural artifacts of her ancestors is symbolic, on a larger scale, of the attempt by the radical writers to return, if not to their cultural roots, at least to a re-examination of the cultural past, in the limited manner of Toomer and Garvey. They wanted to create images of black men and women outside the concepts offered by the conservatives, and though in too many cases their images bore striking resemblance to those of the primitivists, for the most part, they retain those characteristics peculiar to the black proletariat. Moreover, the cultural odysseys of Ray and Jake, Banjo and Bita, evidence, on the part of the writer, an intention to move toward a realistic appraisal of black life in all its existential trials and tribulations. This meant an acceptance of the idea of the African-American as rebel and outsider.

The chief characteristic of the men and women in the novels of the radicals is not, therefore, their "primitivism" but the desire to regain their cultural paradise, lost to the conquerors. In this, too, they differed from the conservatives. Johnson and Fauset, for example, believed in the sanctity of the white image, accepted the thesis of cultural hegemony as espoused by the Euro-Americans. They were capable, as a result of casting aspersion upon their own past, of believing that other black people, at home and abroad, were less culturally endowed than the middle class whom they represented. The younger writers were more cosmopolitan, more attuned to the currents of the time now moving men and nations alike from preoccupation with Victorian notions of propriety, cultural conformity, and superiority. Like Ray and Bita, they questioned, almost to the man, the assertion that human worth might be defined in terms of skin color or material acquisition. In identifying with the proletariat, they became, also, like the people in their novels, outsiders, and as they moved farther and farther beyond American definitions of Blacks, they became more universal.

Their outsiders were men and women, intellectual enough to seek a return to some metaphysical past, to recognize that something beyond the color of one's skin made him different from the Americans. Not surprisingly, therefore, McKay, the compulsive wanderer, can return with Bita, in spirit, if not in actuality, to the culture of his Jamaican ancestors. His contemporary, Rudolph Fisher, author of *The Walls of Jericho* and *The Conjure-Man Dies,* though unable to accept the philosophy of the Garvey movement, through his characters, Jinx and Bubber, must search for a meaning in the ghetto life, constructed long after the arrival of the first slave ship. Such characters and their creator, knowing not the gods of their ancestors, and yet, not accepting completely the gods of the West, searched for paradise in those areas defined as outside Western acceptance or recognition.

They were simple people, living lives of desperation, yet bearing those lives with the fortitude of their ancestors of old. Not the archetypes of modern black man, they were the forerunners and, in this, constituted the brick and mortar of a new literary tradition.

Of such magnitude are the men and women who people the novels of Rudolph Fisher (1897–1934), this all too often ignored physician turned explorer of the ways of Harlem black folk. The author of two novels and a number of short stories, he contributed the first detective novel to African-American literature—*The Conjure-Man Dies.* To those of a younger generation, the characters he created and the novels he authored are almost unknown, and yet, of the Renaissance writers, more so than Hughes, he is the comic novelist, a forerunner of Ralph Ellison and Ishmael Reed. He created his characters from the material of the Harlem streets, and if not capable of imbuing them with the silent grandeur and dignity with which Hughes often imbues his people, nevertheless, he spreads over them a veneer of humanity, sufficient to differentiate them from those of either Van Vechten or Jessie Fauset. Outsiders to those beyond the Harlem environment, they are images and symbols, which, though distorted, are truer representations than those prescribed heretofore, of men and women far distant from the African gods.

The major plot structure of Fisher's first novel, *The Walls of Jericho* (1928), evolves around one such character. Joshua "Shine" Jones, piano mover, a man of considerable strength and pride, is a man consumed by his own ego. A mock battle ensues between himself and the objects he transports, so much so that he pits his manhood against the piano, "his particular prey, his almost living archenemies." Shine has been successful, in each battle, despite the superstition that "sooner or later the piano took its terrible toll in this dangerous warfare with man. . . ." Success, therefore, inflates his ego to the point where excessive *hubris* becomes the dominant feature of his personality. The stage is set then for the classic confrontation between the man of pride and his nemesis; for Shine, the nemesis is neither white people, whom he hates, nor the "dicties," whom he holds in contempt, but beautiful, statuesque Linda Young. His reputation as a piano mover and a ladies' man make no impression upon Linda; the romance that ensues therefore presents Shine with an unenviable conflict; he must divest himself of hubris or lose Linda. When the "hard man" admits at the end of the novel that "the guy that's really hard is the guy that's hard enough to be soft . . ." the walls of Jericho have tumbled down, deflation of the ego of a proud man has taken place. With the help of Linda, Shine has returned to equal fellowship with others in the Harlem community.

Running parallel with the plot involving Joshua Shine Jones is that involving the transition of the Harlem community. The black population at the turn of the century, as James Weldon Johnson notes in *Black Manhattan* (1930), was situated in lower Manhattan, near the "Tenderloin district." The eventual migration of Blacks uptown, and the resistance offered by whites before they moved farther into the Bronx, is treated with comic seriousness by Fisher. "We won—we won territory," boasts one character. "All the fays had to get out, make way, make room for us. What did they do? Resist of course—why the devil shouldn't they? Clung to their district, tried to recover. And we broke their heads with chimney bricks and bathed their bodies in hot lye."[9]

Fred Merrit, "bushy-headed" mulatto, is the latest of the black invaders. The block to which he sets siege is presided over by a dowager spinster, wealthy champion of all causes. Miss Agatha Cramp, liberal expender of money to foreign liberation movements and humanitarian of the highest order, is, nevertheless, disturbed that her new neighbor is a black man. Merrit, successful attorney, ashamed of his miscegenetic background, has no affection for this white woman or her fellows, in fact, holds the entire race culpable for his condition ". . . I hate fays. Always have. Always will. Chief joy in life is making them uncomfortable. . . ." His purchase of a house in an all-white neighborhood enables Fisher to merge the two plots of the story. The men hired to move Merrit into the house consist of a team, Joshua Shine Jones, Bubber Brown, and Jinx Jenkins. Linda is Miss Cramp's maid. Jealousy, induced by Merrit's association with Linda, cures Shine of hubris, and a fire at the Merrit house, set not by an agent of Mrs. Cramp's, but by someone with a grudge against the attorney, only spurs Merrit to greater determination to integrate the neighborhood. This determination hastens the departure of Miss Cramp and, symbolically, of whites in general.

The seriousness of the two plots is underlined by the jokes, high jinks, antics, and ribald actions of Jinx and Bubber. Knowledgeable in the ways of Harlemites, the two serve as commentators upon the Harlem scene, as well as guides in the mores and folkways of "Jigs, high yallers, and dicties." Devoid of the seriousness which characterizes Jake of *Home to Harlem* and given stature and importance lacking in caricatures of Blacks from Friday to Nigger Jim, they emerge as characters for whom Harlem is filled with innocent fascination. Yet, beneath the comic masks lay the seriousness so much a part even of black humor: "Beneath the jests, the avowed fear, the merriment, was a characteristic irony, a typical disavowal of fact and repudiation of reality, a markedly racial tendency to make light of what actually was grave. . . ."[10]

Though *The Walls of Jericho* is a different kind of novel from *Cane, Home to Harlem,* or *Banana Bottom,* its author has gone to the same source for material as his contemporaries. He, too, has discovered the wealth of artistic potential in the black outsiders, those who lived among others, much like invisible men, separate within the race of which they were a part, adhering to their own mores and folkways. As the radicals were beginning to understand, such characters were symbolic of those for whom life was seldom abstraction, who were forced by years of custom and patterns initiated long ago to live life on a high plane of comedy, seriousness, and chance. They were the realists, despite their Emma Lous and Alvas, and when Fisher added his roustabouts to McKay's brooding intellectuals, this sense of realism descended upon the black novel in a way, heretofore, equaled only in Dunbar's *The Sport of the Gods*.

Here history and prophecy are revealed as the bridesmaids of fiction. Joshua Jones and Fred Merrit, men separated by color, education, and status, are sharers of the same culture, both outsiders in the American society, forged into unity as a result of historical patterns. Merrit, successful attorney, is no more acceptable to Miss Cramp than Shine Jones, piano mover, and despite his status, his life is as restricted and determined as that of his lower-class counterpart.

In the lexicon of the new imagists, of whom Van Vechten is the most important example, there are no terms to define either of them, and those invented by the bourgeoisie are distortions, nowhere bordering upon actuality. Fisher knew this, and thus he included in his colony of outsiders all varieties of black people, each engaged in his own private battle, attempting always to assault the almost seemingly impregnable walls of Jericho.

What was needed from the black novelist—a synthesis of the thought of the conservative writers and that of the radicals—is partly achieved in the works of this comic novelist, where the question of race, ever important, remains understated. In *The Walls of Jericho* and in *The Conjure-Man Dies* (1932), Jessie Fauset joins hands with Claude McKay, James Weldon Johnson with Langston Hughes, dictie with roustabout, one black man with another, each fighting his own Jericho and each engaged with the more tyrannical Jerichos from without. When Fred Merrit, who is fair enough to pass for white, joins hands with Shine at the end of the novel, diversity remains still; it is, however, diversity with uniformity which enables the group, outsiders all, to unite in the pursuit of self-definition.

Fisher's novels are footnotes to the spirit if not the thesis of the Garvey movement. Here also is the realization that black people, despite an accident of history and the passage of time, had roots to which they might return. Such an idea ran counter to the "melting pot" thesis gaining in importance in a decade when European immigrants brought their culture, history, and life-style to America, and in many cases, deposited them in the American vault of sameness and standardization. Rightly so, the radical novelists therefore believed that the major battle of the twentieth century would center around the black man's campaign to maintain a sense of his historical and cultural peculiarity against those forces, past and present, that combined to either assimilate him on American terms or contruct definitions to limit his human potential.

To successfully engage in this campaign meant to turn away from the images, symbols, and metaphors, the myths and legends enunciated for him by a people whose culture and history differed from his own and who could never understand nor sanction the sense of unity which bound one black man to another, even though a sense of diversity and individualism remained ever present. Moreover, to engage in this campaign to the fullest mandated that the black writer recognize the necessity for the creation not only of a new man, but of a new system of values, morals, and ethics, and to do so meant to return to the past to go back to and beyond the holocaust.

For it was here that the quest would have to begin: back with Toomer into time, to the Africa of Garvey's dreams, to the southland of Wylie Henderson and Zora Neal Hurston, to the city streets of Langston Hughes, Claude McKay, and Rudolph Fisher; here must begin the search for the new land, leading to the creation of new values and a more accurate definition of the human condition. Fisher believed that the search might commence in the Harlem of his comic characters; McKay, in the wanderings of his intellectual rebels; Hurston, in the struggles and failings of the men and women of a new South. Each believed, however, that the new world a-coming could be brought into being only by a community of outsiders, those who knew of life and existence, of the travails of man, in a way that those who knew not the god of the African bush people never could. In this connection, the works of Fisher offer their greatest contribution: portrait of Blacks as rebels outside American definitions and terminology. It is a contribution to be fully appreciated in the coming Black Power era of the nineteen sixties.

By the time Zora Neal Hurston (1903–60) published *Jonah's Gourd Vine* (1934), her first novel, Wallace Thurman and Rudolph Fisher were dead, and the forces they had helped to set in motion during the Renaissance were already being undermined by the efforts of the Communist party. The influence of the party on black writers could be seen in the short stories of Richard Wright, some of the poetry of Hughes and McKay. The battle against these new imagists, the successors to the Van Vechtenites, however, lay still some years in the future. In neither of her three novels did Miss Hurston react to the growing attempt by the party to influence the direction of black literature. Like Jessie Fauset, she was well liked by her contemporaries, and her reputation as a folklorist equaled her reputation as a novelist. Of her three novels, *Jonah's Gourd Vine* and *Their Eyes Were Watching God* (1937) are more closely allied to the spirit of the Renaissance than to that of the writers of the coming period.

Deserting the urban setting, already overworked by Hughes, McKay,

Cullen, Thurman, and Fisher among others, Miss Hurston chose in her novels to return to the southland—a region far different from that of Toomer's *Cane* in 1923. Remnants of the old feudal order remain— cotton farming, tenantry, and sharecropping. The modern world, however, intrudes through trains, automobiles, and new ideas concerning the race question. Reading her novel is to be aware of the distance of her people from those of Fisher or his environment. Still, *Jonah's Gourd Vine* is a novel of change.

The hero, John Pearson, is a realist living in an environment haunted still by the ghosts of Harris, Dixon, and Page. It is one in which the images created long ago are still adhered to by Blacks and whites alike and the dramatic tension of the novel is created by the attempt of the major characters to break completely with the definitions of the past. Pearson, itinerant laborer become preacher, son of a white man and a black woman, is incapable of doing so. His wife, Lucy, however, succeeds in breaking free of the images which circumscribe her as a Black and a woman and, in so doing, presents a positive image of black women seen, heretofore, only in such novels as *The Quest of the Silver Fleece* and *Banana Bottom*.

Shortly after publication of *Jonah's Gourd Vine*, Miss Hurston, in a letter to James Weldon Johnson, talked about her major character, John Pearson. She had, she told her colleague, tried to present a different kind of preacher from those depicted in legend and myth, one who was neither comical nor an imitation of white ministers, who was "the common run of us who love magnificence, beauty, poetry, and color so much that there can never be too much of it." She added that the preacher was, outside of his pulpit, a man like other men, and thus "should be free to follow his bent as other men." There can be no quarrel with Larry Neal's observation that in this statement "a definite, culturally determined value system is at work." Yet the question for the reader is whose value system has determined the actions of John Pearson? The implications of Miss Hurston's statement and the actions that unfold in the novel contradict each other; for to suggest that the preacher, outside the pulpit, should be free "to follow his bent as other men" means to condone the actions which lead Pearson along the road to his tragic end—a tragedy manifested by his inability to move beyond the terms which circumscribe him.

Like the tragic mulatto of old, Pearson is marked for tragedy. His stepfather, Ned, utters this fatalistic appraisal: ". . . Dese white folks orta know and dey say dese half-white niggers got de worst part uf bofe de white and de black folks." It is not, however, mixed blood that leads to the tragedy of John Pearson, and here Miss Hurston offers a definition of tragedy peculiar to her black characters alone. Such a concept had never seriously been applied, in its highest meaning, to Blacks. Never seen as men of distinction and nobility—those worthy of a tragic occurrence and having, according to American definition, no place lower than his actual state to fall—few writers thought of the life of an individual Black as bordering upon the tragic. Looking into black history and folklore, however, Miss Hurston is capable of divining a difference between tragedy as defined by the Euro-Americans and tragedy as it occurs in the lives of Blacks. Not being born to power, black men, unlike the Hamlets or King Lears, must travel long, separate roads to status and distinction before pride and ego combine to produce the hubristic act, leading to downfall and destruction.

John begins life as the adopted stepson of Ned Crittendon, whose wife brings the mulatto child into the marital union. The distinguishing marks of his early life are poverty and hard work, coupled with animosity between himself and his stepfather, an ex-slave, who takes out the resentment of forty years upon the mulatto . . .[11] "John is de house-nigger. Ole Marsa always kep de yaller niggers in de house and give 'em uh job totin' silver dishes and goblets. . . . Us black niggers is . . . s'posed tuh ketch de wind and de weather."[12] The hostility between the two causes the stepfather to "bind" John over to a onetime overseer to work his land. Amy, the mother, knowing the overseer's reputation for cruelty, shepherds her son to the plantation from which she had come, to Massa Alf Pearson (presumably John's father) in Notasulga, a nearby town: "Tell im whose boy you is and maybe he mought put yuh tuh work." In addition to putting John to work, the former slaveowner allows him to attend school. In the environment of Notasulga, the future John Pearson is born. He develops a new sense of pride and accomplishment, through learning, and an ability to perform the most difficult and hardest tasks. He meets his future wife, Lucy Potts, and, after a brief sojourn from the plantation, returns to marry her against the wishes of her parents. Yet, the character flaw, so necessary to John's tragic denouement, appears. What elements of the tragic personality might a black man in the southland of the nineteen thirties possess? Pride, arrogance, or excessive jealousy leading to self-destruction were not possible for most Blacks. And though excessive pride, coupled with indecision, had served Miss Larsen well in *Quicksand,* for her male character, Miss Hurston had something else in mind. To find a clue to her thinking is to return to the letter to James Weldon Johnson, to the passage: "I see a preacher as a man outside of his pulpit and so far as I am concerned he should be free to follow his bent as other men." Take into account the sexual promiscuity of Pearson, and the conclusion seems to be that the "bent of other men" concerns sex. Whether intended or not, it is this flaw in Pearson's character that eventually brings about his downfall.

Due to his sexual promiscuity—postmarital affairs with women on the plantation—John is forced to leave. He travels to Florida, where he begins life anew. For a while, the John of old returns, sober, and hard working, apparently cured of the disease of sexual promiscuity. He sends for his wife and children and, due to Lucy's strength and loyalty, moves from town carpenter to minister of the town church and on into the church hierarchy, becoming pastor of an even larger church, to town mayor, and moderator of the State Association of Ministers. The key to his meteoric rise is Lucy, whose contribution is noticed in the words of Pearson's opponent: ". . . If me and him wuz tuh swap wives Ah'd go past im so fast you'd think it de A.C.L. passing uh go'her." Yet the flaw in John's character again asserts itself. Lucy senses the return of John to the ways of old ". . . a little cold feeling impinged upon her antennae. There was another woman."

Lucy, because of her loyalty, courage, and perseverance, stands out as the dominant character in the novel. Not as artificially conceived as the women of the novels of Nella Larsen and Jessie Fauset, nor the frivolous caricatures of the novels of Chesnutt, Griggs, and Dunbar, Lucy is the black woman come to maturity in a new South and a new age. Fidelity and courage are her chief characteristics, her willingness to suffer for her man and her children, an important element in her makeup as a black woman. Viewing her during these troubling times, the reader is made aware that only some supernatural force, something which defies Lucy's ability to combat it, can make complete the tragic ending of John Pearson, can enable him to bring about his own destruction. Here the old South exists even amid evidence of change. At the point where Lucy has brought the sinner to the altar of redemption, when he has broken his ties with "the other woman," Hattie Johnson, Hattie turns to the remedies of old, engages the assistance of the conjure woman, An' Dangie, in the battle for John Pearson's affections. "Stan over de gate whar he sleeps and eat dese beans and drop de hulls 'round yo' feet. Ah'll do de rest."[13]

Lucy, woman of the future, unable to wage successful warfare against the forces of the past and incapable of redirecting the energy of her husband, after a long illness, goes to her grave. Following immediately upon her death, the countdown begins for John Pearson. He marries Hattie Johnson. The once neat home of Lucy and the well-cared-for children fall into disarray. Through innuendo and character assassination, his enemies dispossess him of his positions: moderator of "The Association" and pastor of the church. He turns to carpentry, his old profession, and discovers that the townspeople will not allow him to work. Hattie, like Lucy, a victim of his sexual license, yet lacking the latter's loyalty and patience, deserts him. Finally, he is forced to leave the town of his rise and fall.

The novel might have ended here. Miss Hurston is intent, however, upon making even more pronounced the mortal flaw in Pearson's character. The former minister leaves the town and the past behind him and settles in another, not far distant from the former. Here he meets Sister Lovelace, an older version of Lucy, and begins his rise once again. Yet success in a new town and recognition as a businessman and devoted husband are all jeopardized by the former minister's obsession with sex. Having journeyed to the former town once again and betrayed Sister Lovelace, his new wife, it seems only natural that his final end, his tragic denouement involve the old and new South: "The ground-mist lifted on a Florida sunrise as John fled homeward. The car droned ho-o-ome and tortured the man. False pretender: Outside show to the world. Soon he would be in the shelter of Sally's presence. Faith and no questions asked. He had prayed for Lucy's return and God had answered with Sally. He drove on but half-seeing the railroad from looking inward . . . the engine struck the car squarely and hurled it about like a toy."[14]

Despite structural and formal defects, *Jonah's Gourd Vine* is most important for its depiction of the character of the black woman. Lucy is far from being completely developed as a character. She does, however, contain elements seldom seen in fiction by men which feature black women. Moreover, Miss Hurston, in her portrayal of Lucy, has begun early to deal with the conflict between black men and women, which receives fuller explication in Chester Himes's *Lonely Crusade* and John Williams' *Sissie* later in the century. The conflict centers around two victims of the same oppressive society. Take John and Lucy as metaphors of black men and women. John, unlike his stepfather, the former slave, is set free in a world which denies him the normal route for the pursuit of manhood. According to Miss Hurston, therefore, he must prove his manhood by having sexual relationships with women other than his wife. He has discovered, in other words, that the black man's route to manhood lay in the exploitation of black women. For no other men in the Euro-American society is this true.

It is not too far wrong to suggest that despite Miss Hurston's fondness for John, in him she has substantiated the theses concerning the black man's overt sexuality; if not more sexually potent than other men, he is assuredly more promiscuous. Thus, John, the metaphor of black men, remains, for Miss Hurston, essentially a creature of appetite, insatiable even though offered such a delectable morsel as Lucy Pearson. Her loyalty, perseverance, and love border upon the messianic. What her husband lacks in courage, strength, and initiative, she more than compensates for. The conflicts, therefore, given such personalities can be resolved only when black men correct the defects in character. That this was the author's implicit commentary upon black men might be attributable to her distorted conception of them. The chances are, however, that she was less interested in John Pearson than in Lucy, less interested in the men of her novels than in the women, who receive more multidimensional treatment.

In *Jonah's Gourd Vine* and *Their Eyes Were Watching God,* she views them as modern women, patterned upon paradigms of the past, those of the courage and strength of Harriet Tubman and Sojourner Truth. Far from being the images of old, the willing copartners of white men in the castration of black men, her women are, instead, the foundations of a new order, the leavening rods of change, from whose loins will eventually come the new man. Past stereotypes aside, therefore, her women need only search for greater liberation, move even beyond the stoiclike devotion of a Lucy Pearson, move toward greater independence and freedom. Put another way, black liberation meant burying the old images and symbols that had circumscribed black women along with black men. What is needed, McKay had argued in *Banjo,* "Women that can understand us as human beings and not as wild over-sexed savages." In the context of *Jonah's Gourd Vine* and *Their Eyes Were Watching God,* this meant that both sexes must move collectively outside of American history and definitions. The race, Miss Hurston might have amended Du Bois' statement, will be saved by its liberated black women.

Much of her second novel, *Their Eyes Were Watching God* (1937), centers around the theme of the liberated black woman. In *Jonah's Gourd Vine,* Lucy Pearson, though an improvement over women in previous black novels, is, nevertheless, still the picture of loyalty and devotion. She is a woman hovering always near rebellion and assertion of individuality, yet she lacks the determination or, perhaps, desire to break completely with past mores and folkways. Janie Starks, the central character of Miss Hurston's second novel, has no such problem. She is a more completely developed character, and like her male counterparts in the fiction of McKay and Fisher, capable of moving outside the definitions of both black and white imagists. The problem confronting Janie is presented by her grandmother, aged relic of the past: ". . . de white man is de ruler of everything as fur as ah been able tuh find out. Maybe its some place way off in de ocean where de black man is in power, but we dont know nothin but what we see. So de white man throw down de load and tell de nigger man tuh pick it up. He pick it up because he have to, but don't tote it. He hand it to his womenfolks. De nigger women is de mule uh de world. . . ."[15] The tension set up between adhering to this designation and rebelling against it constitutes the major conflict of the novel.

In rebelling against the definition of black women and moving to assert her own individuality, Janie must travel the route of tradition. The ending of *Their Eyes Were Watching God,* therefore, is in the beginning, and the novel, which gains its immediacy through first-person narration, merges past and present through use of flashbacks. In the opening pages of the novel, Janie, the outsider, returns to tell her own story. She left the town of Eatonville with Teacake, happy-go-lucky gambler and part-time worker who, said the townspeople, was "too young for her." For them, such an act constituted rebellion against old and accepted standards of conduct. For Janie, however, rebellion has brought about a dignity and stature unknown before, has transformed her from a dreamer to an activist, has enabled her to participate in experiences unusual for women of her time.

Consider her background before Teacake. A beautiful octoroon, who, aided by her grandmother and constant association with white children, is made early to believe that she differs from other Blacks, that the image to which she must aspire is one of ". . . sittin on porches lak de white madam. Dats what she wanted for me—don't keer whut it cost. . . ." Thus to become like "de white madam," Janie married men, modeled in the image of the master of the big house. First there was Logan Killocks, who, master of over sixty acres of land, offers security, status, and protection, but not love. After her grandmother passes away, Janie evidences the first sign of rebellion: "The familiar people and things had failed her. . . . She knew now that marriage did not make love. Janie's first dream was dead, so she became a woman.

Killocks, however, is only the first stop along the path to complete rebellion. The next, the most important, is Joe Starks. Egotistical, avaricious, and ambitious, he is a wealthy businessman, mayor of the small town of Eatonville, and a man who is close to the image of the master in the big house: "Take for instance that new house of his. It had two stories with porches, with bannisters and such things. The rest of the town looked like servants quarters surrounding the 'big house.' . . . It made the village feel funny talking to him—just like he was somebody else." Years with Joe Starks, however, convince the octoroon that the image depicted in the philosophy of her "Nanny" was one of stagnation and circumscription, one which denied freedom. This realization, long before Starks's death, had caused "her image" of him to come tumbling down, to shatter. And yet ". . . looking at it she saw that it never was the flesh and blood of her dreams." Joe Starks's death does not fill her with remorse but, on the contrary, brings a feeling of relief. It is not, she related, that I worry over "Joe's death, I just loves this freedom."

Freedom is a man named Teacake. Like Janie, he is an outsider and in the eyes of the townspeople a ne'er-do-well, who has no business becoming familiar with "somebody lak Janie Starks." Janie, however, is somebody like Teacake. His search for a life-style outside that prescribed by tradition is as determined as hers. His commitment to a life of chance, to living by the roll of the dice, to moving outside of conventional values, stirs the rebellious spirit in Janie, enables her to move completely outside the prescriptions of past mores: "So us is goin off somewhere and start all over in Teacake's way. Dis ain't no business proposition, and no race after property and titles. Dis is uh love game. Ah done lived Granma's way, now ah means tuh live mine." For Janie, this means to live a life-style which runs the gamut from gambling dives to bean picking, traveling from one end of Florida to the other. The rewards are that she is able, finally, to obey the inner voice, to experience things she "wanted to see and know." Teacake is cast in the mold of such vagabonds as Ray and Banjo and, thus, is not only capable of accepting Janie's new-found freedom as a woman, but of encouraging it. Adventures with Teacake complete the liberation of Janie Starks. At this point, she is ready to return to Eatonville, to tell her tale, to become a symbol of rebellion for others. Thus, the separation of Janie and Teacake is required.

The two are separated when Teacake meets death at the hands of Janie. During a hurricane and a flight down river in a "two hundred miles an hour wind" when "the sea was walking the earth with a heavy heel," Teacake is attacked and bitten by a wild dog. A few weeks after the hurricane, evidences of rabies appear. In an accompanying maddened seizure he attacks Janie, who reluctantly shoots him. Freed by a judge and jury who label the shooting incident as self-defense, she returns home. The little girl who played with white children so often that she became confused about her identity, who accepted, in part, a definition of herself, handed down from tradition via her grandmother and reinforced by the actions of the two husbands she outlasted, finally broke free of the images offered by both whites and Blacks, moved to validate her own womanhood in new terms. Neither sexual object, nor shallow imitation woman of the big house, she emerged from the novel as modern black woman, as strange and alien to American thought as the new men of the literature of McKay and Fisher.

Their Eyes Were Watching God, a novel of intense power, evidences the strength and promise of African-American culture. Miss Hurston, like Fisher, Toomer, Hughes, and McKay, went to the proletariat to seek values, to create and recreate images and symbols that had been partially obliterated or distorted through years of white nationalist propaganda. Her characters were outsiders in America because they were the inheritors of a culture different from that of others. It is true that, unlike Bita Plant, they have no Banana Bottom to which to return, are incapable at this point of time in recognizing the existence of the god, Obeah. They remain, however, oblivious as well to the gods of the Euro-Americans and are thus nomads in a world where identity for black people is founded upon the theology of such modern-day saints as Vachel Lindsay and Carl Van Vechten.

Yet the novel functions as an antithesis to *Nigger Heaven.* For Miss Hurston's characters, sex, atavism, joy, and pleasure do not constitute the essence of a people who must continually wage warfare for their very existence. The Lasca Sartorises and the Scarlet Creepers are revealed not only as vicious stereotypes when measured against Teacake and Janie but as cruel figments of the white imagination, created in order to enslave men anew. In addition, the novel also repudiates the values and images bequeathed black literature in the works of Johnson and Fauset. Fidelity to Euro-American values, to prosperity and status, are equally as enslaving and debilitating: Irene Redfield, a symbol of the new slavery in much the same way that Lasca Sartoris is. Both sanction an identity based upon stereotypes of the past; neither, like Janie Starks, is capable of "hearing the murmur of underground voices." For Miss Hurston, therefore, the path to liberation is not to be found in either the surrealistic hell of *Nigger Heaven,* or in the sterile imitative heaven of *There Is Confusion.*

Janie Starks, however, is not the completion of the new paradigm, but only evidence of an important beginning. After returning to the town from which her search for freedom began, she remains an outsider and yet is not able to continue her rebellion beyond the immediate present. Like Teacake, she, too, is dead to the realities of the world in which she lives. For though the white world remains more symbol than actuality for her, it is in actuality that it is oppressive. Thus the questioning, restless spirit which led to rebellion against the tradition that circumscribes her, due to race and sex, must lead her to challenge the equally restrictive patterns that deny physical freedom. This was the task of writers more talented and more angry than Miss Hurston, and that Janie Starks does not measure up in this respect, detracts neither from her importance as a character nor from the importance of *Their Eyes Were Watching God*.

The novel, over-all, is a fitting document with which to begin a final discussion of the Harlem Renaissance. Coming six years before *Native Son*, it marks the end of a period in African-American literature, in which the black writer engages once again in the task of freeing the minds of men from the stultifying images created in the works of the descendants of Page, Harris, and Dixon. It suggests that before men can move outside of the traditions and mores which seek to enslave them anew, they must become outsiders in the true sense of the term. Salvation for black people can come, therefore, only when they have taken the existential plunge outside cannons which affront man's sense of decency and justice: To be an outsider is to be removed from the paradigms of the past and to be one with men, from ancient times to the present day, whose history and culture have been distinguished by a hatred of injustice and oppression and who have fought, long and hard, against man's tyranny, physically or mentally, against man.

Thus the critical reporters who place the death of the Harlem Renaissance movement in 1929—the date of the stock market crash—were no more accurate than those who argue that it continues to the present day. More accurately, not only did Fisher, McKay, and Hurston carry on the spirit of the movement well into the thirties but of all the blows dealt against it none were powerful enough to inflict a death blow until the publication of *Native Son* in 1940. This is not to minimize the effects of the forces that sought to topple the movement, forces which ranged from the lack of clearly defined ideological perspectives, on the part of the writers themselves, to the stock market crash which brought on the depression. There was no single ideological premise adhered to explicitly by one writer or another, and the internecine warfare that ranged between proponents of varying literary ideas have been recorded in such works as "The Negro Artist and the Racial Mountain," *A Long Way from Home,* and *Infants of the Spring.*

This lack of ideological agreement was coupled with the dependence of most of the writers upon white sponsorship, and though this support was not as widespread as often believed, it was important enough to preclude ideological unanimity. Along with dependence upon white sponsorship were too many interracial parties at which literary discussion of the kind designed to foster independent black creativity was hardly forthcoming. The stock market crash which heralded the collapse of the American economy, therefore, only pointed up the major weaknesses of the movement, the inability of the people involved for instance to establish publishing institutions of their own. Because they were in hock to white publishers, once the depression was under way and the vogue in things "Negro" had ended, contracts for new books by black authors were few. All of these were contributing factors to the demise of the movement; none, however, in and of itself was sufficient. For the final deathblow, one must turn to Richard Wright and *Native Son,* while proper credit must be given the Renaissance writers for helping to pave the way for the efforts of Wright and his followers.

Their interests in black culture, their attacks upon the imagists, though tacit and not co-ordinated or sustained from one work to another, and their insistence upon new directions for black writers created the atmosphere for *Uncle Tom's Children* and *Native Son* and made acceptable the existence of the outsider. The works of Wright and his followers are indebted to the cultural foundation established by these writers—one that sought a value system from within the black community. At the apex of this system is a fidelity to a black life-style as lived by the urban black poor, one that demanded literature capable of exploiting the problems and concerns of that vast majority of Blacks unable to approximate the Euro-American norm. Out of this life-style had come courage, endurance, and rebellion against things as they were, and it is these which become the salient characteristics of black characters in the fiction of 1940 and beyond. Moreover, the assault upon the new images created by the early twentieth-century propagandists had been launched, though not often so vigorous or calculated as one might have wished. Still, the characters of Hughes, McKay, Fisher, and Hurston, despite their limitations, were antithetical to those in the works of their white contemporaries.

In refusing to sanction negative images which depicted black folks, the Renaissance writers continued the efforts begun by such novelists as Sutton Griggs and, in so doing, added to the importance and stature of the movement. Even the conservatives—Johnson, Fauset, Braithwaite, and Brawley—refused to accept in total, either socially or literarily, the images of black people offered up by Van Vechten. As ridiculous to the modern sensibility as many of the characters in the novels of Johnson and Fauset may be, they are attempts by the authors to unveil new images before the American public. Thus, *The Autobiography, There Is Confusion,* and *Passing,* despite the intentions of their authors, only served to reinforce the argument that the search for black identity must begin with those characterized by Langston Hughes as the black poor, who care not "if they are like white people or any one else."

Here, among the poor, was the stuff of real tragedy; here the everyday themes which lead to a realistic art; here, still operative, though in muted form, the old cultural value systems that sustained a people for centuries. In the everyday world of the black proletariat was tragedy, hope, and faith, the ingredients of life which had helped to create the great art of the spirituals. Hughes, undoubtedly went too far in romanticizing them, for here, too, as first Miss Larsen and then Thurman demonstrated, are universal characteristics of avarice, enmity, and greed. Yet, the essence of the black man's major conflict against America—man torn between hope and despair in a world which held out promise, while every one of its institutions shouted the obverse—was enunciated more clearly here than anywhere else. In the streets of Harlem and in the cane fields of Georgia, the American dream lay prostrated; yet those who walked the streets and toiled in the fields clung to life and hope, refused to believe that man was less than what their biblical prophets had told them he was, continued to believe that at some time the veil would be rendered and the victims go free.

The return to the concerns of the black proletariat, initiated by Marcus Garvey, meant the departure by the novelist from the characters and themes of old. Gone were the aristocratic men and women of the novels of Frank Webb, Charles Chesnutt, and Sutton Griggs, and though the half-white imitations of the conservatives are still to be found in the latter part of the period, they are overshadowed by the representations of the black poor. All of this demanded a new sensibility and it is this, though not fully developed, that was most operative among the radicals. For however romantic and fanciful, Garvey's insistence upon a return to the glory of Ghana, Songhay, and Ethiopia, and Toomer and Hurston's championing of those who lived in the first home away from home was to return to an existence buried now in the recesses of memory. It was to return to a state of supposed racial innocence which meant to return to the cultural artifacts of long ago. For there was, as Imamu Baraka, among others, was to point out in the later years, a culture that had sustained Blacks long before and after the holocaust, and it is this culture which the best of the Renaissance writers sought to explore. In so doing, they were successful in moving the novel away from the path of assimilationism, to prevent once again the ascendancy of literature designed to make the black man a white everyman.

This is not to say that the new-found sensibility was not limited in scope. There is much truth in Sterling Brown's accusation that the real life-and-death struggle of the black poor was glossed over, that the bitterness and resentment of men and women, not cognizant of the literary movement in their midst, was not explored, that the frustrations and hostilities, soon to come to fruition in the Harlem riots of the thirties, were not analyzed. Furthermore, with the exception of Bita Plant and Janie Starks, none of the characters are entirely free from the stultifying attraction of the commercial and material forces of the society; none, in other words, are outsiders as a result of choice. Thus the heightened sensibility stopped short of exploring the full range of possibilities in the African-American experience and depicted the outsider, all too often, as a man cast adrift by the society, rather than one who, out of a sense of concern for humanity, sought consciously to desert the Sodom and Gomorrah of the Euro-Americans.

Yet, the novelists of the period were vanguard men and women, and in this role they performed well. They attempted to clear the forest of old dying trees, to plant new seeds, though they were unaware of what kind of plant these seeds would give birth to. Few were aware that only a few years distant and the Jakes, Bubbers, Rays, and Banjoes, the Bita Plants and Janie Starks would appear in the roles of Bigger Thomas and Lutie Johnson. Their men and women were way stations along the route which led to new creations, and this in essence was what the movement was all about. The new image, fully developed, however, does not appear in their works, though they, like their counterparts of the nineteenth century, predicted his coming. Theirs was the questionings and the doubts, the first full-scale exploration of what it meant for Blacks to live in an alien and hostile culture, given the unwillingness to accept definitions forwarded by that culture as the price for its recognition. They were not conscious rebels, but questioning ones, and in this respect they left a legacy for future writers. Their men and women, for example, were not completely Clotels or Mr. Walterses, not all Henry Blakes or Josh Greenes. They were characters somewhere between, rebels within limits, maintaining faith and belief in the past. Read their novels, and the portraits of Vachel Lindsay, E. F. Stribling, Gertrude Stein, and Van Vechten appear as grotesque distortions in comparison, nowhere approaching the paradigms of old, those offered in the true-life experiences of Frederick Douglass, Harriet Tubman, Nat Turner, or Marcus Garvey.

For the Scarlet Creeper and Lasca Sartoris were little more than the alter egos of their creators, more white than Black, and from such images sane black men have always fled. The black writer of the Renaissance, in the main, fled from them and, though to a limited extent, into a greater awareness of his own heritage. In so doing, he pointed the way toward a tradition in literature based upon cultural diversity instead of cultural sameness. Janie Starks's repudiation of the role of mistress of the big house is the most telling symbol of the determination of black Americans to turn from facile imitation of white cultures; Bita Plant's surrender of Western values and religious tenets, to return to those in the religion of the god, Obeah, suggests the culmination of two centuries of attempts to move beyond the American image makers to return to a past of greatness and promise, to create out of the material of a great history, a timeless and enduring literature. Whatever the faults of the Renaissance writers—and they were many—their novels were footnotes to those of the coming years.

VII

CHRIST IN BLACK FACE

When Richard Wright published "Blueprint for Negro Writing" in *New Challenge Magazine,* in 1932, the task of undoing the work of the Renaissance writers had begun. His statement, like much of the criticism of the writers of the period—that his predecessors were little more than "prim and decorous ambassadors" humbly begging whites to recognize black humanity—was not altogether true. This description applied to many, and James Weldon Johnson, Nella Larsen, and Jessie Fauset come quickly to mind. The best of the radical contingent, however, in Langston Hughes's words, attempted, to the best of their ability, to describe black life unashamedly without overt consideration for the opinions of white people.

 Long before Richard Wright, therefore, black writers had accepted "the nationalistic implications" of their own lives and of those about them. They did not believe, however, that nationalism should be either dependent upon, or infused with, Marxism. They realized, and Toomer, Hughes, and McKay are good examples, that the road to nationalism led over alien images to the adoption of more positive ones. Wright realized this himself, noting that nationalism was rife among the black middle class and black people in general, though unstated and undefined. However, he argued, in addition, that ". . . a simple literary realism which seeks to depict the lives of these people devoid of wider social connotations, devoid of the revolutionary significance of these nationalist tendencies must of necessity do a rank injustice to the Negro people and alienate their possible allies in the struggle for freedom."[1]

Nationalism, in other words, must not be an end in itself, but merely the instrument by which one entered the larger society.

Wright's article supplied a partial rationale for the about-face of the American Communist party on "the Negro question," which occurred at the Sixth World Congress in 1928. During the Garvey years, the Communist image makers depicted Blacks as simply Americans, non-homogeneous as a race, beset by twin evils—capitalist exploitation and economic imperialism. They attempted to negate the nationalistic implications of black life by arguing that because race prejudice was the result of capitalist exploitation and imperialism, the solution to the black problem led not through nationalism but through the integration of black and white workers in the United States, who embraced the struggle against "capital."

By 1928, the successes of the Garvey movement had forced the party to look more closely at Black Nationalism and to evaluate the danger it proposed to the theory of integrated revolution. In that year the Communist International averred that Garveyism, like Ghandism, was inimical to the revolutionization of the Negro masses, primarily because the movement was a form of Zionism, advancing the slogan "Back to Africa" instead of advocating struggle against American imperialism. Such a dangerous ideology, which proposed a separate black nation, was to be strongly resisted. The shift, in 1928, from all-out opposition to tacit acceptance was not a shift to black Garveyism, but an attempt to limit nationalism, to fit it into the framework of integrated revolution. The party adopted as a working proposition the thesis that Blacks in the southern part of the country constituted a separate nation and were, therefore, subject to development in the fashion of minority groups in the Soviet Union. It argued that there were legitimate forces that might serve as the foundation for developing "a Negro nation." This limited acquiescence to Black Nationalist ideology, however, was granted always in the belief that Nationalist aspirations were to be controlled and directed by the party, which is to say, by white Americans: "The Communist party . . . must consider itself not only the party of the working class generally, but also the champion of the Negro as an oppressed race, and especially the organizer of the Negro working-class movement."

When the party moved outside of economic and social considerations to take cognizance of black culture and black writers, it sought to utilize both in an attempt to achieve integrationist objectives. If nationalists of the Garvey persuasion saw in the cultural artifacts of black people paradigms of heroism and grandeur, for the party theoreticians the nationalistic culture of African-Americans was based upon suffering and abnegation, manifested in physical characteristics, language patterns, and thought, which, before 1863, had so stunted "these people" culturally, as to force them "into the category of an incipient nation. Differences in physical characteristics were less sharply apparent; a common tongue (English) had been developed; they all lived compactly together under the evolving aegis of slavery. Here lay a condition fallow for the birth of a national psychology."[2]

The black writer, to return to Wright, could help implement the Communist program by creating "the myths and symbols that inspire a faith in life." To do this, however, meant not to attack the imagists nor those who historically and, at present, sought to define black humanity, but instead black writers of the past: "There is little in recent Negro poetry that would lead one to believe that the poets are conscious of the Negro masses," writes a party functionary. "They do not echo the lamentations of the downtrodden masses. Millions of blacks are suffering from poverty and cruelty, and black poets shut their eyes! There is not a race more desperate in this country than the black race, and Negro poets play with pale emotions."[3]

The party leveled its attack, therefore, not upon the successors to Van Vechten—among whom the party itself was one of the most important—but against those black writers who attempted to develop images and symbols based upon the positive, not the negative, aspects of black culture. Such literature, in most instances, did not depict the race as downtrodden, nor black people as suffering debilitations of the spirit or loss of humane characteristics as a result of oppression and exploitation. More likely it remembered the heroism engendered in the fight against oppression by those who ran away, fomented rebellion, and even committed suicide than those who were maimed and twisted by the experience. The Renaissance writers wrote of a resilience in black life and refused to accept the argument that the major feature of black culture in America was suffering and degradation. Historical novelists like Du Bois and Bontemps refuted this argument consciously, others, perhaps, unconsciously; all refused, however, to accept the image of the dehumanized Black, crippled as a human being by the economic and imperialistic forces of "world-wide capitalism."

"How many John Henrys," asked Wright parroting the party line, "have lived and died on the lips of black people? How many mythical heroes in embryo have been allowed to perish for lack of husbanding by alert intelligence?"[4]

The answer, to a great many, does not lead to Wright's conclusion that the reason lay in the writer's cowardice or in his distorted perceptions. It suggests, only, that before the recreation of such images was possible, the successes and the excesses of the Renaissance years had to be undergone, that Mr. Walters had to be demolished as an acceptable image, and that the protagonists of such novels as *The Autobiography* be revealed as white, not black, caricatures. The sensibility able to create the modern John Henry could arise only after that which created Jake and Ray, Bita and Janie had done its work. The legacy left their successors by the Renaissance writers was to move forward in creating images and symbols erected upon the principles of nationalism. Such a legacy dictated literature which spoke of black people, as a whole, as a separate nation, yet, one that allowed for no Messiahs, individual or collective. Society as a naturalistic construct was more germane to white writers during the period preceding World War Two than to black writers.

To "create the values by which black people were to live and die" meant, as Wright was later to discover, that the naturalistic theory of literature, as forwarded in the writings of Zola and Dreiser, and adopted Jake and Ray, Bita and Janie, had done its work. The legacy left their *Friends, The Sport of the Gods,* and *Blood on the Forge,* had to be modified and eventually discarded altogether. The argument for a deterministic universe for black people meant only to supplant one religion with another. Where Christianity held out vague promises of a heaven beyond death, the determinist program of the naturalists relegated Blacks to a life absent of meaning or purpose. It repudiated the examples of Douglass, Brown, and Garnet, not to mention scores of others whose lives argued that man, not society, was the final determiner of his destiny. From the naturalistic theory, first expounded upon by a black writer in the works of Paul Laurence Dunbar, comes the image of the black man as eternal victim, a plaything of Americans, relegated to a life of suffering and tribulation. The white liberals and the Communists added an addendum: Salvation in a naturalistic universe —a contradiction in terms—was possible through the arrival of a white deus ex machina. The new image of Blacks, conjured up in the minds of the successors to Van Vechten, therefore, was as the bearers of eternal angst, the Christ figure in black face, the metaphor for suffering humanity, in short, as Richard Wright described him, America's metaphor.

Given the racist nature of the society, facts to substantiate almost any hypothesis based upon the oppression of Blacks are not difficult to come by. The Communists found such an arsenal of facts ready at hand after the stock market crash of 1928. The depression was a great catharsis! The black middle class, which had grown to prosperity during and preceding the first war, found its newly arrived at status in jeopardy. Neither previous conditions of importance nor skin pigmentation prevented integration among Blacks on the bread lines or on the relief roles; here black doctor rubbed elbows with black stevedores, society matrons, with maids and kitchen girls. Whatever privileges were to be awarded went to whites not Blacks, as America looked out for its own. Statistics on employment among Blacks and whites during the depression years reveal that "unemployment among Negro workers in the cities was in some instances twice as high as among white workers."[5] In some cities, Houston and Detroit are examples, black unemployment doubled that of white, and in the South, where the unemployment picture was more positive due to the prevalence of Blacks in agricultural work, in terms of job security, African-Americans lagged far behind whites. In 1937, at the height of the New Deal experiment, unemployment among Blacks trailed unemployment among whites in the ratio of almost two to one. As a result, at a time when white Americans were destroying milk and oranges and slaughtering livestock, Blacks already close to the subsistence level, were pushed even closer.

The result of the economic holocaust for Blacks meant a lessening of the emphasis upon class distinctions that had occurred during previous years. The portrait of rural and urban dwellers painted by Wright in the documentary, *12 Million Black Voices* (1941), had relevance for Blacks of all classes. The breakdown of class distinctions did not mean, however, a turn toward conscious nationalism. Bread took preference over ideology, and black middle class and black poor alike, privy to the same statistics and facts available to the sociologists and the Marxist theoreticians, began to view their problem in terms formulated by these white groups: "By placing progressively greater emphasis on such problems as relief, unemployment, welfare and housing—matters of growing importance for Negroes because the economic debacle bore most heavily upon them as a group—the Party made some rather impressive gains among the race. . . ."[6]

If the black problem could be viewed in terms of economic exploitation, white liberals and the party could view Blacks as the vanguard of a proletarian revolution, designed to usher in the classless society, due to the fact that they were the most brutalized, dehumanized, and exploited element within the country. The revelation that 52.2 per cent of all black families were on relief during the second term of the Roosevelt administration, and the continual lynching and mutilation of Blacks, north and south, lent credence to the party's argument, suggested, indeed, that at the basis of the black problem in America was a ruthless, inhuman capitalist society.

It is not surprising, therefore, that black and white co-operation occurred in many industrial areas of America, that Blacks joined whites on picket lines, took part in integrated strikes. Nor is it surprising that the proletarian literature of the period, represented by Scott Nearing's novel, *Free-Born,* portrays a black hero whose parents have been lynched and whose sweetheart has been ravished and killed and who joins the proletariat in the crusade for "a free world under working class control."[7] Such novels suggested that the Communists had taken the naturalistic theory of literature and embellished it with a Marxist denouement—substituting the socialist heaven for damnation and perdition. Black literature that did not follow this line, that did not depict the African-American united with his white working-class colleagues, that did not point out the depressing conditions faced by Blacks as a result of the economic disaster, that did not present the image of the prostrated Black, doomed without the aid of white allies, that did not offer examples of the black worker in conflict with an oppressive America, was either irrelevant, or written by bourgeois reactionaries.

Wright's assertion in *12 Million Black Voices* complements the forces and ideas combining in the thirties to create symbols, images, definitions, and proscriptions of Blacks as enslaving as those offered by the propagandists of old. If, he writes, Blacks had "been allowed" to participate in the growth of America, presumably on integrationist terms, the texture of black life, let alone the patterns of the country's traditions, the status of art, and the sanctity of laws, might have been vastly different.[8] The key words in the statement are "allowed to participate," for here, the society is both savior and destroyer. For the Communists, it was the latter; it had the potential to make men into effective participants in the social order as presently constructed; however, it made them objects of oppression. Nevertheless, it was the final arbitrator of man's destiny, the final determiner of his worth. Blacks, on the other hand, all too often, regarded society in terms of salvation, the doler of meager pittance from the relief role. Like the Communists, they too believed that their fate rested in the hands of the Americans. At a time when the black masses succumbed to the chicanery of Father Divine and Bishop Grace, the belief in a Messiah far more capable of philanthropic undertakings was not surprising. The times called for art, therefore, which argued that the American society would be operative for Blacks when the new revolution was completed, images that depicted the black poor as vanguardsman of this revolution. Such images were possible, however, only after Blacks discovered that their interests were the same as those of "oppressed people the world over" and integrated under the leadership of whites in order to erect the new society. The fact that Blacks—given the success of a proletarian revolution—would have to demand of the Socialists and Communists rights as black men, and enter as such into the mainstream of the new society, seemed lost upon white people, who ignored the question from non-ideologues in the black community as to whether or not the Communists and the Socialists, like the capitalists and the oppressors, were not white also.

Even Wright acknowledged this concern. Some Blacks, he reported in *12 Million Black Voices,* found it not only impossible to work with white people but believed that it was futile to think of salvation in terms of American mores and folkways. The distrust of Americans is so great, he added, that Blacks form "intensely racial and nationalistic organizations and advocate the establishment of a separate state . . . in which we black folk would live. . . ."9 And the best of the black writers, despite the insistence upon a naturalistic literature, infused with a Marxist denouement, found it difficult to adhere to literary rules based upon superficial realities, which said little about the reality of black life in America. Move outside of William Attaway—the most important of the novelists to view the black problem in Marxist terminology—and the major writers, Wright, Himes, Petry, and Smith, are ambivalent Marxists at best, strongly anti-Marxists at worst. Unable to accept the image of the black man as Christ figure or eternal victim, they improved upon the images left by their predecessors. They added conscious motivation to the characters of their outsiders and, in so doing, created images which angered and shocked their liberal and Communist critics and advisers.

More important, they remained independent men and women, less influenced by whites than were the writers of the Renaissance; though, for the most part, they were integrationists and avowedly antinationalist, their works propounded the most healthy of nationalist doctrines: that man's fate is not predetermined—that Blacks will not be saved by societal architects whether white Communists or white advocates of the New Deal. That instead Blacks must save themselves, must view themselves as modern men, adrift in a hostile universe, having no allies outside the race, forced to imprint their own sense of humanity and decency upon the chaos and tumult of the times. The ideas are not new, nor the images they call forth. Both are products of black life lived, always, on the high plane of alienation and rebellion. In the main, William Attaway (1912–   ) was untouched by such ideas. This one-time vagabond and hobo turned novelist was influenced by a variety of factors, few of them specifically related to Black Nationalism. His first novel, *Let Me Breathe Thunder* (1939), was influenced as much by his own personal experiences as by John Steinbeck's *Of Mice and Men*. His second novel, *Blood on the Forge* (1941), bears the imprint of the Marxist propaganda of the thirties, though in many cases his people are based upon realistic paradigms of black life. Both novels differ from those of the past, the first in its choice of characters, predominantly white, the second in depicting the dislocation of black men during the great depression and their subsequent fate couched in naturalistic theory.

Attaway's first novel was reportage, the product of a man setting down his experience in fictional form. The second demonstrates maturity of form; here the author has a firmer grip upon his material, has concretized his ideas and learned more about the function between structure and content. The first novel was written from the point of view of the first person, enabling the author to achieve immediacy by focusing attention to the action of the novel through the narrator's eyes. This form, however, negated meaningful attempts to delineate character, made almost impossible vast rhetorical or descriptive sweeps. Written in five parts, the movement of the second novel is from south to north and back to south again, the major characters following the route of the great migration, as Attaway dramatizes the experiences of black men who trekked north to the steel industry in the middle of the twentieth century.

The plot of the novel centers around the Moss brothers, Big Mat, Chinatown, and Melody, hard-up farm hands caught up in the economic misery brought on by crop failure and the depression. The initial story begins in Vagamond County, a part of the southland which differs from that in the fiction of Jean Toomer and Zora Hurston. Vagamond County is the South of brutal white riding bosses and cynical white plantation owners, like Mr. Johnson, who adheres to the old notions concerning Blacks. There are three reasons, he relates, why only "niggers work my land . . . they ain't bothered with the itch; they know how to make it the best way they kin and they don't kick none."[10] Times, however, have changed and, unknowing to Johnson, men have changed with them. Up north are steel mills, and down south are agents of the men who own the mills, imploring such men as Big Mat and his brothers to desert the land. When Big Mat, after a violent altercation with the riding boss, has visions of the white man awakening "to lead the lynch mob against him," he and his brothers accept the offer of the mill agent, desert the farm for the steel mill.

The motivations which drove the Moss brothers from the South are analogous to those which had precipitated the black migration. For such men, the South of their birth had offered little nourishment, had helped them to erect no defenses useful against a hostile alien environment. Confronted from birth with oppression by southern landowners and brutality, as a result of rigid segregation, each black man was born into the universe as an outsider, and the marrow of rebellion was soaked into his bones like milk from a mother's breast; the defenses erected, as a result, form the patterns of their adult lives. The Moss brothers will transfer such patterns from south to north only to meet disaster.

Take Big Mat, darkest of the brothers, a brooder, powerful and strong, who long ago had visions of preaching the word. The South gave him an infertile wife, a hatred of whites, and a disbelief in everything except his own brute strength. When such attributes as hatred and brute power are transferred from south to north, they become the agents of his downfall. His brothers, on the other hand, are even less equipped to deal with life in a different environment. Chinatown was "a man who lived by outward symbols." Long ago he accepted the stereotypes applied to him, believed that the images constructed by southern propagandists were accurate, never constructed a mirror within which he might validate his humanity. He is forced, therefore, to seek some semblance of his worth in outward things in order to stave off complete dehumanization: "When I jest little Chinatown, I seen the way things is an I know I got to have somethin to make me feel like I somebody. So all the time I dream about a gold tooth, shinin and makin everybody look when Chinatown smile."

For a picture of Melody, one must look to the prototypes offered by Banjo of the novel by that name and Jimboy of *Not Without Laughter*. Each is a man who, deeply wounded by life's experiences, seeks to escape by choosing the life-style of the atavist. Song, laughter, and dreams are the major artifacts of life; they are defenses erected by powerless, defenseless men in order to protect themselves. Melody, for example, never had problems which could not be resolved either by strumming away on his guitar or of dreaming of the new world to come: ". . . the hills ain't red no more. There ain't no crab-apple trees squat in the hills, no more land to hoe in the red-hot sun—white the same as black."

In one family, Attaway has presented the most important stereotypes of black men handed down through literature and history. Melody and Chinatown are images of the past. They represent men forced, by the exigencies of living, to compromise with injustice and to stem their inner rage and tumult by grasping symbols of support, either outer or inner. In this sense, both are creative, forced to construct necessary props in order to maintain sanity in an insane world. Though in the course of the novel, Chinatown loses his eyesight and Melody, his gift for songs and dreams, neither, like Big Mat, loses his sanity, comes to view white society as possessing no codes, legal or moral, that they are bound to accept.

How indebted Attaway is to Richard Wright for the portrait of Big Mat is not known. *Blood on the Forge* appears one year after *Native Son;* Big Mat is born after Bigger Thomas has reached maturity. Both characters, however, present paradigms of black men who move outside the old prescribed roles. For both there are archetypes in history—Nat Turner and Denmark Vesey, for example—but with the rare exception of Josh Green, few such in black literature. What was necessary to bring the image of the new man into existence was the revelation that the old lines of defense erected by Blacks could not survive in the modern world, that the resources of dreamers and songsters were useless in a world where power was man's ultimate defense against oppression and exploitation. For such men as Big Mat, none of the old values offer hope for survival, nothing that he has experienced in the South, nor will experience in the North, can erase the years of anger and rage. In a world where man has been cursed by God—Mat believes that the inability of his wife to bear children is such a curse—there are no values to which one must ascribe. Anarchy and chaos, therefore, are loosed upon the world, and man, free of the restrictions imposed in a God-ruled universe, must create artifacts anew to assure his survival.

Following in the footsteps of those who undertook the migration, the Moss brothers travel, allegorically, from the old to the new world. The new world is one of iron and steel, of black men and white men pitting their brains and strength against unnatural forces; it is a world of whiskey and women, of hostility and anger, one where men engage their physical resources against the alien forces represented by the machines, where strikes and strikebreakers abound, and where madmen are almost indistinguishable from the sane. In this new world, the defenses of each of the brothers break down. After lonely, isolated days in the mill, Melody is incapable of finding salvation in song; no longer able to play the music of his heritage. Chinatown, the man who had hoped to validate his humanity by displaying the wealth in his mouth, falls victim to the machine, loses his eyesight, and is plunged into eternal darkness.

One by one the brothers are symbolically castrated, rendered impotent. Only Big Mat moves outside this analysis. Though he too is destroyed, the forces which render him impotent are as much his creation as that of the machine. Unlike his more passive brothers, he is driven by a compulsive anger and rage: anger and rage occasioned by the involuntary rupture from the land, and anger and rage too at the riding bosses and landowners who drove him away, at the dry, dust-caked soil that would not allow him to feed his family, at the God who cursed him by making his wife fallow. Mat, therefore, like the machines he services, becomes a force unto himself, relying upon brute strength to replace the values handed down from his cultural past. "For a long time Big Mat had been empty, like a torn paper sack inside. But all of that was over. He had begun to heal his ruptured ego with a new medicine. That medicine was a sense of brutal power. A few careless words from a police deputy had started that strange healing. This Monday would complete the cure. That the cure might be deadly was too deep a thought for him. The only thing he felt was a sense of becoming whole again. . . . Today he would be the law—the boss. . . ."[11]

The old defenses work no better, however, for Mat than they do for his brothers. Obsessed with the past of riding bosses and lynching mobs, Mat joins the men who own the machines when a strike ensues, becoming deputy sheriff—the riding boss created anew in black face—dedicating himself to violence and vengeance. Such a dedication, however, cannot save Big Mat, in the way it saves Bigger Thomas and Bob Cross. Attaway does not have enough faith in his character to accept him as the black outsider become rebel. He is still naturalist enough to posit a universe void of hope, where no defenses allow man to cope with his isolation, still liberal enough to believe in the integrated revolution. The words put into the mouth of a white sheriff after Mat's death are as much Attaway's as the sheriff's: "Sure is a shame that big nigger had to go and git himself killed. But I don't reckon we kin pin it on nobody. . . . He was game, all right, but crazier'n hell. That's the thing 'bout nigger deputies—they're fightin the race war 'stead of a labor strike."[12]

The difference between Big Mat and his brothers is that, for him, the race war *was* the major battle. Somehow, one senses that Attaway wishes this were not so. Rereading the novel, one comes away with the idea, missed at first, that Attaway would have preferred a different Mat, one able to move beyond the violence which formed him, to create new and different modes of living. In this role, he might have become like the character Smothers, a warrior against the machine which destroys every one but Mat. Smothers, its major antagonist, is sucked up in the hot lava of the erupting machine, soaked up with the fire and fumes, his bones used as watch fobs to be distributed to the surviving workers as everlasting reminders of the superiority of the machine to man. The machine crushes Chinatown and Melody alike, white and black workers, old and young. Big Mat in contrast, however, meets death because he has no defenses that will prevent his inner obsessions from destroying him. At the moment he assumes the guise of the riding boss of old, at that point, his author has turned away from the conflict he thrust upon him—black man at odds with a white world—and sought to render him impotent because of his unwillingness to unite with his fellow man in a futile war against the machine.

In reality, however, only two options are open for a black man like Mat—death with glory or eternal rebellion; and Attaway's inability to accept either option, to see the black man after the great migration as having no recourse but to create new modes of living, to carve new values and ethics out of the marrow of violence itself—it is this which ruins an otherwise brilliant novel and prevents any salvation for black men outside that envisioned in the Marxist formula. All that remains, therefore, after the death of Big Mat is doom and despair climaxed by the last scene in the novel: Returning home to Vagamond County, Melody and Chinatown meet a black soldier, blinded like Chinatown, not from the steel mill directly, but instead, from the steel of war.

Blood on the Forge is a well-written novel. It deserved the plaudits of critics past and present. It is a structurally sounder novel than *Native Son,* and the inner mechanics—symbols and images of life, death, and destruction—work as effectively for Attaway as they do for Wright. Yet, Attaway, unlike Wright, has accepted the argument that themes of universal import take preference over those of more parochial import; that is, the conflict between man and the machine is more universal than that between black man and a racist society. Under the influence of this argument, despite the coming years of the Hitler madness, the continuing brutalization of Blacks by whites, the incarceration of Japanese citizens by Americans, and the struggle of the darker peoples of the world against white colonialism, Attaway wants to deny universality to the most universal phenomenon in world history. Moreover, he wants to make Big Mat, Chinatown, and Melody into more fully developed images of the vagabonds, Step and Ed, men in conflict with a hostile environment forced to find new modes of living, yet unable to do so.

This despite the fact that Attaway lives in a universe marred by turmoil and dissension. The depression, as he knows so well, has brought men to the brink of revolution, the migration made it impossible for people to survive by the patterns of old. In such a new world, Melody and Chinatown, of course, are doomed; hedonism and paganism, twin evils for black men, are useless in a world in which the race war is an eternal given. This is not so for Big Mat; in a world of violence and turmoil, violence is the norm, and the man who tempers it with the proper humanism has come close to constructing a new ethic. Attaway could not accept this idea. There is too much of the naturalist in him, too much of the sociologist; he adheres to a code that preaches universal brotherhood, yet one that refuses to acknowledge the historical fact that such has been achieved only when one man possessed guns as powerful as the other. When Big Mat exchanges the Bible for the sheriff's cudgel, he has leaped across centuries of black history into the modern world. Attaway, however, cannot accept him, recoils in horror from his own creation, attempts to convince the reader that excessive rage and compulsive anger have driven Mat to become more insane than other men, that violence represents not redemption for him, but vengeance, and that the race war, unlike other wars, must be fought out on the high plane of moral niceties and meaningless epithets. "At the moment," noted Wright, "when a people begin to realize a meaning in their suffering, the civilization that engenders that suffering is doomed." Realization may lead in one of two directions. The first is that of the Communists, white liberals, and "Negro leaders." Oppression engenders a sense of nobility and heroism in those who undergo it, transforms them from mortal to martyr, makes man one with his Christ. The other direction is that pointed up in the philosophy of the revolutionary; oppression leads to violence, through which man attempts to transcend his personal anguish to become a metaphor for oppressed men everywhere and, by resorting to violence, attempts to outlaw both violence and oppression. The difference is between men who are willing to die in the cause of liberation and men who are willing to be killed in the same cause.

Big Mat fails on both counts. Oppression against him, north and south, has been all too pervasive for Attaway to depict him as a Christ figure, yet, paradoxically, not so severe as to fit him for the role of revolutionary. Big Mat remains, therefore, in literary purgatory, suspended somewhere between the Christian heaven and the revolutionary hell, an incomplete man, unable to face the new world a-coming. His death is as meaningless as his life, and though this may well be the key point of this naturalistic novel, it does not come to grips with the realities of black life.

The responsibility, in this instance, is that of the author. The road had been cleared for him and his followers. The men of the Renaissance were circumscribed by limited knowledge of craft, dependence upon white publishers and readers and a small black reading public. Attaway, on the other hand, faces a situation in which a growing black reading public is coming into being, dependence upon white publishers lessened, the mastery of craft been achieved, and the new imagists nowhere as powerful or influential as the old. What distinquishes this period from the preceding one is the independence of the black writer from the new imagists, an independence which leaves the writer free to honestly record the black experience. *Blood on the Forge* fails to adhere to this new spirit. Attaway backs away from Armageddon at sight of the flames. What might have become a novel representing man's courage and strength, becomes one instead which consigns him to doom and damnation. Given the author's ability to focus on dramatic events, to effectively interweave symbolism and imagery into his narration, to construct logical and orderly plot sequences, one might have expected a novel equal to that of *Native Son*. Expectations, however, are unfulfilled and one turns with eager heart and little remorse from the literature of blind men and Christ figures, leaves the black martyr nailed upon the cross of irrelevance, consigns his corpse to the Communists and liberals, and turns to the rebels of Richard Wright, Chester Himes, Ann Petry, and William Gardner Smith.

VIII

THE BLACK REBEL

By the time Richard Wright (1909–60) was fifteen years old he had been an alcoholic, lived in three different home environments, been a spectator to southern violence (an uncle was lynched when he was ten years old), and had seen and remembered more acts of man's violence against man than most men could even imagine. When he left the South at an early age, he was intent upon discovering whether or not he, a part of the South, could be transplanted to an alien environment and there grow differently, become healthy, "perhaps to bloom." He did not know that the roots of oppression had sunk too deeply, that the effects of what he had known and seen had left indelible marks upon him, that because of his experiences in the southland, he would never know peace, never be free from a very real paranoia.

This is so, even though he leaves America in 1946, journeys to a new land, attempting to leave racism behind, to find a humanism different from that found in the land in which he was born, or the Communist part in which much of his thinking had been forged. His exodus from regions and nations, from ideologies and philosophies, makes him the first of the conscious black rebels. He realizes that peace between black men and white men is an impossibility, that in a world where heaven is defined in the terminology of either Christ or Marx, the salvation of Blacks entails a loss of innocence, acceptance of the frightening reality that life must always be lived on a fever pitch of desperation.

He had been robbed of his own innocence at an early age, had lost the romantic wistfulness with which he gazed upon a strange and incomprehensible world. For these reasons he was able to move beyond the pessimism, lack of faith and commitment to the human spirit, evidenced in the works of Attaway, to avow that black men, in order to deal with a hostile environment, must become articulate enough to analyze it and to form judgment about it. Salvation, he believed, if possible, would come only when one understood the nature of the forces arrayed against him: "Themes for Negro writers will emerge when they have begun to feel the meaning of the history of their race as though they in one lifetime had lived it themselves throughout all the long centuries." This is the message of *The Outsider, Uncle Tom's Children, Lawd Today,* and *Eight Men;* it is the lesson also of the prose works, *Black Power, Pagan Spain,* and *White Man, Listen.* More specifically, however, it is the message of two novels written eighteen years apart from one another, yet remaining the same, despite different casts of characters and changes in locale; *Native Son* (1940) and *The Long Dream* (1958) are garments woven from the same cloth.

Native Son begins with a shrill, penetrating noise—the harsh sound of an alarm clock. Like the herald in an Elizabethan drama, the clock calls the audience to rapt attention, forcing it to focus on the novel's major protagonists, the Thomas family, consisting of four members—two sons, one daughter, and a mother. It is a rodent, however, not the alarm clock that rouses the Thomas family, galvanizes it into action. Women scream, chairs topple, and the oldest of the boys, Bigger, prepares to wage a mock epic battle with the rat. The battle between Bigger and the rat symbolizes the coming battle between the young man and a hostile environment. Consider: the rat leaves the safety of his hole and is immediately confronted with danger. He has moved beyond the boundaries established by the family, and his presence has disrupted the tranquillity of the universe. He is hunted down and destroyed. Bigger, in the course of the novel, undergoes a parallel experience. When he leaves Chicago's South Side, when he moves into an alien environment, he too disrupts the tranquillity of the universe and as a result must be destroyed.

The analogy, however, cannot be pushed as far as Dorothy Canfield Fisher, in her introduction to the novel, wishes to push it. Bigger Thomas is not a rodent, but a man who feels deeply and who is intuitively aware of the differences between his life-style and those of others. He cannot accept the hole to which he has been consigned; when threatened, he cannot even retreat there for security, for the power that controls him exercises that control nowhere more effectively than there. He is a black man trapped as much by his own acute sensitivity as he is by the "white mountain" which symbolizes his condition. His acute sensitivity is the key to his character. He is incapable of comprehending the world as a rational construct. A sensitive young man who feels more often than he thinks, he is forced to deal with an irrational world, through intuition.

To understand *Native Son* and Bigger Thomas, the reader must deal with them on an intuitional, emotional level. For to accept the world as a rational construct means that one will never understand Bigger or the environment in which he lives, never comprehend the true meaning of the murders he commits nor the sensation bordering upon elation which accompanies his accepting responsibility for them. To accept the murder of Mary Dalton, for example, means that the reader must willingly suspend rational belief and accept the idea of a universe in which all values have been turned upside down, in which murder is not a mark of man's inhumanity, but of his humanity, not an act denoting the degenerate, but the hero, not an effort at self-destruction, but an attempt to validate manhood. In short, one must understand, that the murderer of Mary Dalton is a young man of great sensibility.

The murder of Mary Dalton is the high-water point of the novel, the catalyst that propels Bigger upon the search for manhood. Everything before is prelude: the altercations between Bigger and his family; plotting robbery with neighborhood friends; the job as chauffeur to the Dalton family, where he is subjected to the obsequious behavior of Mary and her friend Jan. After the murder, the plot of the novel takes a clearly defined form; the three books are united into one complete whole. It is this act that moves Bigger from a state of innocence to one of maturity, that unleashes the man within the boy. The frightened boy of Book 1, who cannot muster enough courage to rob a white man's store, after the murder, becomes, in Book 2, a man of strength; he not only commits murder, he also attempts extortion, holds his own against the Chicago Police Department, attempts to pin the crime on Jan, the Communist, and murders his girlfriend, Bessie Mears, an accomplice in the extortion plot.

After Book 2, having revealed Bigger as a character of substance, having brought him through the grueling experience of self-awareness, the final book of the novel, and the actions it includes, seems anticlimactic: Bigger, captured by the police, the subsequent trial in which he is defended by the party lawyer, Max, his sentence to die in the electric chair are all preordained from the actions in books 1 and 2. Not even his final declaration of manhood, the proclamation hurled to his lawyer and to an uncaring universe alike, "What I killed for, I am," is surprising to anyone but the lawyer. For Bigger Thomas had murdered Mary Dalton, white and rich, and had thrown the universe into chaos and confusion.

The murder of Mary, alone, however, does not accomplish this feat. Mary Dalton is merely the symbol of oppression, the "white mountain" personalized in one naive, simplistic human being. Around her the American race mythology has been constructed and, because of this, no crime that a black man could commit would strike a more telling blow at the society than her murder. Further, no crime could bring about such a cartharsis as that which enables Bigger to move so far outside American mores and values and to create a new ethic for living.

Think of the murders Bigger might have committed, rank them on the scale of importance. The murder of a black man or woman—Bessie, for example—would cause no disruption of the universe; the murder of a white man has caused ripples, brought about retaliation. The murder of a white woman, on the other hand, brings all forces of the society against the black murderer immediately, makes him an international outlaw, bestows the kind of infamy upon him reserved for the depraved and the mad.

The question of the authenticity of the murder—murder or accident—has provoked endless controversy. Wright, by accident or design, supplied the motive for the controversy by attempting to make the crime appear both spontaneous and determined, forcing the reader to characterize it as either a grotesque mistake or a gratuitous murder. To understand the world in which Bigger lives, however, is to believe, with Max, that his every waking moment was a preparation for murder, to recall afterward that he accepts responsibility for it as such, refuses, himself, to regard it as an accident and, as a result, leaves the reader no other choice than to accept the act for what it is. For all else considered, even as murderer, Bigger is more humane and compassionate than the society which hunts and inevitably punishes him: He has accepted the responsibility for his crime; others remain blind harbingers of death, unwilling to accept responsibility for their many crimes against humanity.

This is the comparison—between Bigger and the society in which he lives—that Wright wishes the reader to make. Had he not imposed the murder of Bessie Mears upon the structure of the novel, the comparison would have held without serious contention. Bessie's murder receives little consideration by critics, black or white; she is said to be merely a red herring, a device used by the author to point out the hypocrisy of the society: The state, unable to discover the corpus delicti in the case of Mary, whose body has been burned to dust, wheels the dead Bessie into the crowded courtroom, allowing the black woman to substitute for the white even though Bessie's death is unimportant in determining his fate; it is for the murder of Mary Dalton that Bigger must die.

But this is the most disconcerting act of the novel, serving primarily to substantiate the integrationist rhetoric of Communists and liberals. A poor black boy commits two murders. One victim, white, is the daughter of a wealthy capitalist; the other, black, is uneducated and oppressed. In Marxist-liberal theology the moral is simple: Because the victims are both black and white, the argument that Bigger's was a blow against racial oppression cannot hold. What is closer to the point is that to live in a world of violence mandates that one lose all perception of race and color; for to accept violence as the ultimate solution to the American racial nightmare is to produce the psychotic, for whom no color or racial demarcation line separates one victim from another.

The rationale against black vengeance and retribution does not hold, however, because the murder of Bessie Mears is the weakest incident in the novel. To murder this woman, of his color and race, means that Bigger severs all ties with the universe, becomes a man completely alone. Further, for a Black to murder another is to commit the most heinous of crimes, to substantiate the argument made by Attaway, in *Blood on the Forge,* that the black man who engages in violence becomes so obsessed with hatred and rage that he is incapable of distinguishing between friend and foe, not able to separate the oppressor from the victim. On this level Bigger fails as both rebel and revolutionary.

The reader, therefore, is confronted with the choice of two Biggers: one before the murder of Bessie Mears, the other, after. The Bigger Thomas prior to Bessie's murder is, to paraphrase Cleaver, a man who is in violent rebellion against the white world; he is a man so hurt and enraged by the psychological damage of white racism that he rebels against the entire white society. The Bigger after the murder of Bessie, on the other hand, is as much the brainchild of Communists and liberals as he is of Richard Wright; he is the man who gives credence, through his act, to the argument that warfare against society boomerangs into warfare against oppressed and oppressor alike, that the murder of a white woman leads inexorably to the murder of a black one, that the black rebel who moves outside of American ethics and values becomes alienated from his own race, that the murder of a black woman leads equally to the conclusion, "What I killed for, I am."

It is this Bigger, however, that the modern black sensibility will not accept. The Bigger who remains as paradigm, as positive symbol, is the Bigger who cannot dream of America as other than a "white mountain" of oppression, who, to find order in the universe, must impose it himself, who cries out in rage, anguish, and pain: "Half the time, I feel like I'm on the outside of the world peeping in through a knot-hole in the fence." The Bigger acceptable to black readers is he who knows, intuitively, that "outside of the world" is the proper place for a sensitive black man to be. To accept this Bigger is to repudiate the Marxist-liberals who demand that the symbol of black man in the latter half of the twentieth century be that of the Christ figure, the martyr for whom violence enacted against, not reciprocated against, is a mark of distinction. However, if black men know any God, today, it is not He of charity and forgiveness but the God of Douglass and Nat Turner, He of fire, thunder, and retribution. But more: Each black man knows that the universe in which he lives has been a violent one since birth, has made of his life and the lives of those around him a daily game of Russian roulette, and that such a universe can be confronted only when black men move collectively to accept violence as a new ethic, as a force for change, as the only instrument capable of bringing about the just society.

To accept this Bigger finally is to accept the reality of the world of the twentieth century. Two years after publication of *Native Son,* Europe's war became world-wide and validated the practicality of the ethic of violence as ten thousand *Native Sons* could not do. The orgy of violence culminated in one frenzied night of American derangement when the atomic bomb blasted millions of yellow men into senseless oblivion. With the advent of this catastrophe, to paraphrase Karl Jaspers, man found himself alone in the universe sans God, living in a world of chance, aware that the morning might bring unexpected disaster. The stable, ordered universe was now beyond comprehension, and man's survival was dependent upon his intuitions, his insight; the world created by the rational intellect bordered upon the brink of ruin. Thus World War Two and its aftermath sanctioned murder and violence as a new ethic, one which enabled men to survive in a psychotic world. In this respect, that which had served Bigger well in the Chicago slums enabled nations to survive the holocaust. In this war all values were reversed: Right became wrong, good became evil, and murder and violence the key to salvation and redemption.

The ethic the world came to accept, however, was that acknowledged by Bigger throughout his life. For him and those like him,

World War Two was merely the eternal war raised to the height of universality. Hitler's racism was only another form of the American variety, the dangerous expeditions undertaken by Blacks into Asian and European theaters of war similar, in a personal sense, to past expeditions into Mississippi or New York City. Wherever the theater of war, the black man was always in mortal danger: The black man in America, noted Wright, "lives always in expectation of an attack, and he is seldom disappointed."

Wright understood and accepted the ramifications of this war, and the images he projects of men moving inexorably toward Armageddon, therefore, invoke sympathy and pride. Sympathy because his hero has not truly discovered a means of dealing effectively with a hostile society, has become rebel, though not revolutionary; pride because his heroes differed so fundamentally from those of either the old imagists or the new, differed, that is, from the Scarlet Creeper and Lasca Sartoris, and the Joe Christmases and Dilseys as well. In the aftermath of World War Two, when Blacks throughout the world move for freedom and liberation, to read *Native Son* is to realize that one is in the presence of new and powerful images; that Bigger Thomas will be surpassed. It is to know, and to realize also, that without *Native Son* this point of maturation might not have been reached, that black men might have continued to receive from their writers only vague glimpses of the reality hidden behind the illusion, that only by accepting violence as an ethic might black men chart the path to salvation. *Native Son* is the model for the novelist of the nineteen seventies. This is true, in another way, of *The Long Dream,* published during the author's self-imposed exile in Europe. The novel resembled *Native Son* in enough essentials to draw the rebuke from one critic that "Wright exaggerated the position of the Negro in the United States; conditions had changed drastically and for the better; he had lost touch with reality because he lived in France."[1] The truth of this charge can be determined, however, if one makes an analogy between the novel and the autobiography, *Black Boy* (1945). Both are Little Richard's Almanacks, maps, and guidebooks on the way Blacks must order their lives in the twentieth century. In each section of *The Long Dream,* Wright intimates that he does not believe that the lessons have been learned. The life and experiences of Fishbelly substantiate this belief. He is born into a world in which survival necessitates that he remold the weapons of the past into instruments capable of dealing with the future. He differs from the fatherless Bigger in that he has a father, one capable of passing such weapons down to his son. The role of Tyree, the father, and his attempt to educate his son in the ways of the white world make the novel more than Wright's critics have averred—a poor echo of *Native Son* and *Uncle Tom's Children.*

Whatever Wright's intentions, characterwise, Tyree Tucker is the major protagonist of the novel. Fishbelly, it is true, carries the rhetorical load, is pinpointed at the scene of each episode; from his viewpoint the novel unfolds. Yet it is the intensity, strength, and weakness of Tyree, the changes he undergoes almost before the readers very eyes, that provide the dramatic import of the novel. He draws attention, initially, because of his seeming obsequiousness, the rigid control exercised over his feelings and emotions while dealing with whites. For three quarters of the novel, the reader will be fascinated by him, angered by him, forced to think longingly of the days of Bigger Thomas. In the nineteen sixties, during the embryonic black revolt, it is difficult to comprehend the tremendous fear that seemingly dictates his every action, understand that he truly believes that he is haunted by ghosts of old, that the major conflict between the races centers around the white woman, that, for this reason, laws are made against Blacks and sheriff's posses ride.

Nor can a case be made for him as a positive image. This is not because of his promiscuity, that he seems cut too much from the cloth of John Pearson, that he seems to believe that sexual prowess is one barometer of black manhood. Yet, he rings all too true as a symbol black men have spent centuries attempting to run away from. More so than any other black character in the literature of his day, he is close to Mr. Walters, believes that Armageddon might be staved off by he who possesses property and wealth: "I'm a man! I got a business, a home, property, money in the bank . . . is my life bad?"[2] Tyree Tucker has done well indeed! Ambitious, though uneducated, he learned well the patterns of southern life. In each city, there are two towns, black town and white town. Both are ruled by whites. Black town, however, is parceled out as fiefdoms to those Blacks skillful enough and loyal enough to whites to assure prosperity for both.

Clintonville is one such town. Tyree, funeral-parlor owner, is the surrogate ruler, having achieved this position by exploiting black people for whites, chief among whom is the corrupt police chief, Cantley. In addition to his funeral-parlor business, and in alliance with a colleague, Doctor Bruce, and Cantley, Tyree owns the Grove House of prostitution. The image Wright wants to invoke of Tyree is crystal clear; he is a scavenger, a pimp, profiting from the living and the dead as well. Yet, for Tyree, there are obligations and responsibilities. His position demands the loss of human dignity and freedom. The

esire to care for his family and to give his son the education he
never received means that he surrenders his manhood. This is drama-
ized each time he whines, cavorts, and Toms in front of Cantley.

Yet, Wright would have the reader sympathize with him. He sees
Tyree as an artist, one who has perfected the art of survival, who has
discovered the key to dealing with white folks: "Obey em! . . . Don't
dispute em! Don't talk back to em. Don't give em no excuse for
nothing. . . . Say 'yessir' and 'nawsir' to em. And when they talking,
keep your mouth shut." In this universe, life depends upon man's
talent at mimicry, his ability to perform roles perfectly, to be continuously creative, to lie to white people who want and expect the
lie; survival means that one must act in such a manner that one's
performance becomes flawless, while being able at all times to distinguish between the role and one's own identity.

Tyree is the master mimic, and the talents he exercises so well, he
wishes to pass down to his son, in much the same way that one leaves
a rich inheritance. He knows that money and power are not enough to
save any black man in Clintonville, that along with these one must
develop specific ways of hearing and seeing, a sixth sense, functioning
like an antennae, to ward off danger. One must so condition his
emotions and responses that he can respond, mechanically, to the
lightest whim of his adversary. Such are the strengths of Tyree's
makeup; they are the weapons with which he has learned to fight
and survive. These, in modified form, therefore, he desires to pass on
to his son, who had no tradition, mores, and past guidelines to sustain
him. Those possessed by Tyree must be learned anew by each generation, are codified in no tabernacles; they are based more upon
instinct than rational comprehension. And though they are part of a
tradition of creativity and survival, Fishbelly initially holds them and
his father in contempt. Having undergone a brutalizing experience at
the hands of whites and witnessing his father dissimulate before his
tormentors, he concludes that ". . . no white man would ever need to
threaten Tyree with castration," for he "was already castrated."[3] Fishbelly is forced, therefore, to search for his own means of survival, to
create modes of living which enable him to combat his own fear and
terror.

Fishbelly's evaluation of his father, however, in light of his own experiences need re-evaluation. Like the reader, he has never seen a
threatened Tyree, never known Tyree when his ethic did not work,
when the old value system between white and Black did not hold,
when mimicry would not suffice to stave off danger. When the Grove
House of prostitution catches fire and over forty people are killed, an

investigation is launched. Fearing implication, the police chief demands the canceled checks, proof of his complicity in maintaining the house of prostitution. The checks are Tyree's weapons. One batch he turns over to the police chief. The other he passes to a liberal reformer. Unknown to either the reader or his son, he secretes another batch with his mistress. Under attack, the old Tyree has disappeared and a new one has emerged: "You see me crying and begging," he tells his son, "well that's a way of fighting. And when that way don't get me nothing I have to do something else." After Tyree is gunned down by the police, the question for the reader is whether Fishbelly has learned the painful lesson his father sought to impart, is capable, in Tyree's words of going "it alone."

The long years of education Fishbelly has received from Tyree have been directed to such a moment as this. The time would come, as Tyree knew so well, when he would be forced to transgress the code between whites and Blacks and be punished by death. The result was that his son would be forced back upon his own resources. As a dissimulator, Fishbelly is a dismal failure. It is not that he still harbors contempt for his father's way of fighting, nor that he has not perfected the art of dissimulation. For Cantley, he is an unknown quality, "one of those new niggers," not easily understandable. Try as he may to imitate the style of his father, Fishbelly cannot. He runs the funeral parlor, wants to continue operating houses of prostitution, to do business with Cantley. On the other hand, he wants to keep a trump card, much as his father had done; he wants to hold out some of the canceled checks Tyree's mistress had secreted before leaving Clintonville, to blackmail the chief; yet he cannot.

The reason is not that Fishbelly has not learned his lessons well, but that he is, as Cantley pointed out, a "New Negro." The unwritten covenant between Tyree and Cantley was based on mutual trust. The white man sanctioned those wishes of the Black, which had nothing to do with social equality, after the black man had prostrated himself. The rules of this ritual—prostration, self-castration—mandated that the black man never question the fairness of the ritual, never debate the wrongness or rightness of his surrender of manhood. Yet Fishbelly has early looked upon the face of death and, since doing so, come to question the rituals by which black people live, wants to know why some people live in security and peace, while others live in dread and terror, why the demarcation line between white town and black is manhood. Tyree was willing to barter manhood away for momentary rewards; Fishbelly wishes to hold on to his even while performing the act of dissimulation. It is this difference between father and son that provokes fear among those who trusted the father: ". . . the white folks," an employee of the funeral parlor informs Fishbelly, "think you're after them and they're scared . . . you're not like Tyree. You say the right words, but they don't believe you."

As a result of the inability of the police chief to believe Fishbelly, because he refuses to admit possession of the remaining checks, a white woman is sent to his apartment; he is charged with rape and jailed for two years. In jail he sums up the effects of his education, realizes, finally, that his father had not failed him, nor had he been an errant pupil; instead, something in him was missing, "some quality of character that the conditions under which he had lived had failed to give him. Just beyond the tip of his grasp was the realization that he had somehow collaborated with those who had brought this disaster upon him."[4] This realization, evidencing, perhaps, that the lessons of the father had been well learned, forces Fisbelly, once out of jail, after surrendering the checks to a reform movement, to leave America, to become an alien, exchanging one strange and incomprehensible land for another.

The education of Fishbelly Tucker is now complete. The long trek from adolescence to manhood is over. Without familial support or security, he is now a man alone, forced to apply his education in a new and different environment. The success of Tyree's efforts toward the education of his son can be properly evaluated only in the distant future, wherein Fishbelly must attempt to deal, creatively, with new problems arising as a result of his exile. In one aspect, however, the teachings of the father can be called imminently successful. Fishbelly survived the South, learned much from the examples set before, and escaped the region with his life and his sanity intact. This was the objective of his education, toward these ends Tyree was the stern taskmaster, with this goal each element of the black community was in accord: Americans educate their children to become professionals; Blacks educate their children to survive the Americans.

Far then from being an anachronism, as some critics have charged, or outdated according to subject matter, *The Long Dream* speaks to Blacks with a relevance that complements *Native Son*. It too is a novel, which, however incompletely, demonstrates the precarious peace between Blacks and whites in America and argues anew the proposition that the evils which confronted the father have not diminished, continue to plague the son also. It suggests that survival for the black man depends still upon a sixth sense—an awareness that, overnight, moves him from the ranks of the innocent to the ranks of the mature. It validates the world of chance, the world in which African-Americans have always lived, and repeats the lesson learned, from Douglass through Garvey, that for Blacks the American society has never been a stable, ordered construct, that whatever order was possible would have to be imposed by the people themselves. Look deeply into the pages of *The Long Dream,* and what emerges is a black fable, now, in this period of the twentieth century, more fact than fable. The black man awakes in the morning to find an assassin sitting in the doorway of his home, rifle cocked, aimed at his heart. Each day the assassin sits, the black man approaches the door and hesitates. Finally, one morning he opens the door, accepting the fact that the assassin will always be there, knowing that whether the rifle fires or not is dependent upon the whims of the assassin.

The education of the black child, therefore, must proceed always with cognizance of the eternal assassin. This is the theme dramatized in *The Long Dream.* Tyree has learned to live with him, to accept the threat of life or death which the assassin holds over him. He has come to grips with an absurd world in which man proves his manhood through violence and terror. It is exactly this situation, however, that Fishbelly cannot endure. The perpetual state of terror, the daily confrontation with the assassin, causes him to question the nature of the universe, God, and the society that spawned him. It is this questioning which leads him along the road to rebellion; his education, unlike that of Tyree's, will cause him not to tolerate the assassin, but to try at least to escape him, at best to kill him.

Among Wright's five novels, *The Long Dream* ranks second to *Native Son.* In neither novel has he provided totally new images, given complete pictures of modern-day black man. For more important than his character descriptions is his analysis of society, his willingness to speak of the terrors of black life inflicted by the proponents of white nationalism, his refusal to seek rapprochement with a nation that continues the holocaust against Blacks begun by their ancestors. Outside of Bigger Thomas and Tyree, his characters are far less important than the society they daily confront. Thus the significance of the novels taken together is that they complement each other: *Native Son* demonstrates how black men must live and die in urban America; *The Long Dream,* how Blacks have lived and died in a South far different from that shown in the fiction of Jean Toomer or Zora Hurston. Together they reiterate the theme that terror, intimidation, dread, and oppression constitute part of black truth in America.

This is a lesson that neither Blacks nor whites wanted to learn. Americans, Wright related, have never been able to accept my truth, and the reason is, one supposes, that to do so is to accept the fact that America has not changed, that the nationalist sensibilities that led to the first holocaust exist still, that no black man can know with certainty that in the next hour he will not be assigned to the wall, forced to face the firing squad of anonymous assassins. This does not mean, as Baldwin and Ellison would have us believe, that because the lives of Blacks are circumscribed by terror and fear, the eventual result is inaction. Far from it; none of Wright's characters are inactive; each refuses to accept the designation as non-human beings. Most are rebels, are sensitive men, who will make no peace with a world ruled by terrorists, who will never acquiesce to the reign of injustice in the universe, who will demand at all times from the God of man, a just accounting.

The final judgment upon Wright's importance in the area of black literature rests upon *Native Son*. Bigger Thomas is the compilation of a number of images, awaiting only the temperament and insight of Wright to bring him to life. Strip the nihilism and self-hate from his personality makeup and he is part Douglass and Brown, part Du Bois and Garvey; in our own day, he is part Malcolm and Stokely, part Rap Brown and Martin Luther King, Jr. A legend in black history and folklore, he remains something inside of ourselves which must be exorcised; he is the race demon who must be confronted, contended with, before black writers are free to create newer and more powerful images. The creation of Bigger Thomas made impossible further portraits of images culled from the white imagination. Neither the Marxists nor liberals were happy with him; both wanted more Big Mats, clamored for more images of the Christ figure, wanted martyrs and saviors; the black man as rebel was outside of their comprehension.

Dorothy Canfield Fisher's introduction to the novel affords an example. Unable to accept Bigger as a rebel, conscious or otherwise, she sees him as a madman, one to be lobotomized with the scalpel of the naturalists. He has been turned into a schizophrenic, incapable of distinguishing between right and wrong, by a society which holds out promises of achievement while at the same time assuring black failure. The madness of Bigger, unlike that of Joe Christmas, is occasioned by the Pavlovian universe in which he lives. Conditioning has been so effective that when he rebels, it is not so much against man, but against situations and conditions. Push this thesis far enough and the major antagonist of *Native Son* is not man, but some ephemeral entity called society, environment, etc., and Bigger's hatred against whites is the result of his own paranoia. True to the Marxist-liberal doctrine, this assessment removes responsibility from where it belongs, places it upon inanimate things, and suggests that the animosity of black men against whites is based upon nothing so much as sheer fantasy.

Yet, the antagonists for Bigger, despite Wright's condescension to

Communist rhetoric at the end of the novel, are always seen in terms of "them," for it is not society, but "they who never gave me a chance." The America he sees is the real America, comprised of real, live enemies from all stations in life, of all persuasions. Each, the white Communist liberal and segregationist alike, dons the assassin's role, sits outside the doorway of the Bigger Thomases of America, and it's the collective actions of whites, tacit or otherwise, that has made necessary the dream of a new universe. Here, all values and definitions are obsolete; the demarcation line between right and wrong is obscured, the man who steps outside the old ethical system of the West, who adopts the proposition that in a world ruled by white men violence is given, becomes not madman, but rebel. In a universe where violence is the norm, the madman is the sanest man of all.

Yet Bigger Thomas remains an image to be surpassed, and *Native Son* a novel in need of future emendation. Incapable of introspection and thought, Bigger Thomas too often resembles a mechanical puppet guided through myriad experiences by an expert puppeteer. He remains too much a man of emotion and intuition to deal adequately with a world in which technology has become man's new instrument for brutality against other men, and his lack of knowledge concerning the world in which he lives, and the forces he must daily confront, cannot be compensated for by reliance upon feeling and intuition. Neither should *Native Son* be considered the model for future black writers; it is merely the starting point along the way to novels of more complexity, those which analyze in greater detail the problems confronting black men in a technological age. The world of the nineteen seventies differs markedly from that of the forties—Blacks throughout the world have made this so—and the prescriptions for living, enunciated in *Native Son,* no longer suffice.

For when all is said and done, Wright remained a moralist and *Native Son,* an optimistic novel. Bigger's rebellion is not against American morality but, instead, against laws and rules that forbid him entrance into the mainstream of American life. At this point, he is a rebel who seeks not to destroy evil so much as to make an accommodation with it, and though his motivations are realistic for his time, in this they are absurd. Absolution for Blacks can come only when they have stepped outside the house that Caesar built and rendered unto Caesar that which is his. To do so requires guidelines different from those enunciated in *Native Son,* and a rebel more articulate and knowledgeable than Bigger Thomas.

Criticism of *Native Son* by Blacks, however, are seldom based upon Bigger's viability as a realistic image, or *Native Son*'s fidelity to truth concerning the black condition. Their critiques usually center around the argument that Wright neglected the "other world" of Blacks, did not pay proper respect to the black middle class. Blyden Jackson, a critic in the tradition of William Stanley Braithwaite, some years after *Native Son,* issues the classic rebuke, without mentioning the novel by name: "Negroes are more literate now than they ever were. They earn more money. They are better housed. They dress better. They certainly look better. And none of these changes came overnight. Yet, during all the long years while a race was acquiring strength and consolidating hard-won gains, Negro literature has been perpetuating a literary fallacy. The prototypic Negro hero has been not only bitter, but broken."[5]

The kind of novel and the kind of hero that Jackson and other black critics of his persuasion demand have usually been the rule, not the exception, in black literature; here was the material of the novels of the conservatives, here were depicted the images of respectability and progress, so appealing to whites and the black middle class. The attack upon Wright and the novelists of his bent, therefore, is that such characters as Bigger Thomas, being one-dimensional, must be denied altogether; they are more representative of aberrations among Blacks than realistic images, more parochial than universal to the race as a whole. James Baldwin, capable during times of greatest ambiguity of echoing the conservative critics, argues, somewhat contradictorily, that no such character ever existed.

Charges that Bigger was non-representative of black men, that *Native Son* was a novel of only parochial import and interest, might be leveled against Wright, with some degree of justification, depending upon the conservative attitude of the critic. Bigger, after all, was poor, uneducated, hostile, and a bitter contradiction to the one-dimensional characters portrayed in the fiction of Jessie Fauset and James Weldon Johnson. Yet to make this charge against Chester Himes's (1909–) character, Bob Jones, and the novel, *If He Hollers Let Him Go* (1946), is more difficult. Himes knows the black middle class, in a way that Wright did not. Before embarking upon a long and productive career, which resulted in over ten books, half of which are detective fiction, he was a member of that class in actuality, if not in temperament. He presents, therefore, as the hero of his novel, a Black of middle-class stature, with education, good employment, good marriageable prospects, who yet, all too often, sounds like Bigger Thomas: ". . . with the white folks sitting on my brain, controlling my every thought, action, and emotion, making life one crisis after another, day and night, asleep and awake, conscious and unconscious, I couldn't make it. I knew that unless I found my niche and crawled into it, unless I stopped hating white folks and learned to take them as they came, I couldn't live in America, much less expect to accomplish anything in it."⁶

Bob Jones is the central character in *If He Hollers,* a novel concerned with the powerlessness of the black-middle-class intellectual. The dramatic structure, centered upon powerlessness, determines the tone, the hard-boiled style, and the first-person narrative that allows the reader direct access to the thoughts of the protagonist. Though, all too often, it is clear that Himes, like Wright, is pulling the strings for his character, forcing him to think and act as the author wishes him to, for the most part Bob Jones speaks through his own emotions and communicates something of his hostility, anguish, and dread.

Jones is the product of the black migration that occurred during wartime when jobs in defense plants were available on the West Coast. He leaves Ohio for California, secures a job in the Atlas shipyard, and, against the wishes of his immediate supervisor, is elevated to leaderman—a job of token reponsibility—as a result of a presidential order forbidding discrimination in federal employment. He is better educated than the white men who serve over him—he is the product of two years of college education; nevertheless, his job is symbolic; he has been promoted, according to the supervisor, to minimize trouble between black and white workers. The role of racial adjudicator, however, is one that Jones does not want. He wants, instead, to be able to perform his job, supervise men, give orders, and contribute to the war effort. Anything less, he surmises, would be an acknowledgment of his own powerlessness.

His predicament is crystallized in the person of Madge Perkins, white "peroxide blonde" from the South, who comes to symbolize Jones's powerlessness as both man and leaderman. Though Jones has a supervisory position, when he needs help on jobs that cannot be performed by his own crew, he must appeal to whites. Invariably, the whites refuse to work under a black man. Such a request and refusal brings about the initial altercation between Jones and Madge. Madge not only refuses to work with the black leaderman, she calls him a nigger—an act which leads Jones to retaliate in kind. Further evidence of powerlessness is demonstrated when he is demoted from leaderman to mechanic as a result. Added to these are a series of other incidents —all registering negatively upon Jones's self-esteem.

In despair over having lost his position, Jones joins a crap game between Blacks and whites. His luck is unbelievably good—so good that one white player, Johnny Stoddard, who loses most heavily, during an argument, attacks him from behind, knocking him unconscious. The second incident involves his fiancée, Alice Harrison, mulatto, daughter of a prominent black Californian. Jones escorts her to an all-white restaurant. The two are served reluctantly and seated near the door of the pantry. After dinner they are told by the manager not to patronize the restaurant again. En route to visit Alice's girlfriend, the two are stopped by highway policemen. Insults and sarcastic remarks are aimed at Jones and his fiancée, and his inability to protect her is dramatized in the taunting behavior of the policemen and the passive acceptance of Jones.

Quips by Alice, contrasting his color with her own, and her acceptance of a date with a white male coworker enrage Jones, cause him to search for objects to vent his hostility upon. He thinks of Madge Perkins and Johnny Stoddard. Stoddard, he singles out for murder; Madge, he decides to make love to. After obtaining the white woman's address from a coworker, he locates her, living alone, in a white neighborhood. She allows him into the apartment after feigned resistance, teases him with her white body—first offering, then withholding it! At the point of submission, however, she utters the words that send Jones into immediate panic: "Rape—just the sound of the word scared me, took everything out of me, my desire, my determination, my whole buildup. I was taut, poised, ready to light out and run a crooked mile. The only thing she had to do to make me stop was just say the word."[7]

Consequent humiliation at the hands of Madge, his inability to avenge himself upon Stoddard, plus the fact that his job is taken over by a white man, whose education and experience are inferior to his, drive home the fact of his powerlessness, force him to acknowledge his impotence: "I could see the whole thing standing there, like a great conglomeration of all the peckerwoods in the world, taunting me 'Nigger you haven't got a chance.'" Jones accepts this evaluation of things, proceeds to make up with his girlfriend, and to accept his inferior status in the shipyard. However, the figure of Madge intrudes once again. When he stumbles upon her asleep on a ship, in one of the cabins, she prevents him from leaving. He refuses the offer of her body and in retaliation, Madge sounds the alarm: "Help! Help! My God, help me. Some white man, help me! I'm being raped." After a brief escape, Jones is caught, beaten senseless, brought before a judge, and after the president of the shipyard deters Madge from pressing charges—charges that would have proven embarrassing to the shipyard—Jones is allowed to enlist in the United States Army.

Despite overt similarities, *If He Hollers Let Him Go* is far distant from *Native Son* in terms of theme and character development. By 1940, the war against Fascism in Europe had revealed the Fascism in America itself. Citizens of Japanese descent were herded into concentration camps; Blacks were still lynched on the average of one a month. The integration experiment in industry, promulgated by A. Phillip Randolph's threatened march on Washington, failed, due to the reluctance of those in authority to upgrade black workers in defense plants. The united front campaign of the Communist party resulted in the bartering away of black interests, and many black Americans, like Bob Jones, were convinced that Americans would rather lose the war than to treat black men with dignity.

Concomitantly, however, the war produced an upsurge in economic gains for African-Americans. Those on the home front benefited from work in factories, defense plants, and in, heretofore, closed government bureaucracies. Black men comprised part of Roosevelt's "kitchen cabinet," and a few held other prestigious posts in the Administration. Many Blacks engaged in a new migration, one which led north and west, and as prosperity came to them in increasing numbers, the old middle class, based upon caste and position, was replaced by a new breed, those who, like Jones, had managed to claw their way to respectability and were determined to settle for nothing short of true manhood rights. The differences between the old and the new black middle class are explored by Himes. The old are represented by the Harrisons: smug, obsequious, wealthy, fair-complexioned, and professional. Their credo remains unchanged. "White people are trying so hard to help us; we've got to earn our equality. We've got to show them that we're good enough; we've got to prove it to them. Southern Negroes are coming in here and making it hard for us. . . . We can't get everything we want overnight and we can't expect the white people to give us what we don't deserve. We must be patient; we must make progress."[8]

Such a credo belongs to a dying world, one which only such critics as Blyden Jackson would care to resurrect; further, it serves to pinpoint the vast gulf separating the new middle class from the old. Despite the fact that Blacks dress better, eat better, are better educated, and better paid, these changes have not brought about similar changes in treatment accorded them. The new society desired by the Harrisons, based upon the Booker Washington formula, has not come about. The country, which fights Fascism abroad, openly practices Fascism at home, and the changes in economic and material areas—whatever changes there were—have not ended oppression, let alone discrimination, though Blacks die on foreign battlefields. American tryanny and oppression have been directed not only at Blacks of little education or financial standing, not only at the Bigger Thomases, but at the Bob Joneses as well. It is this lesson that the black middle class and their spokesmen, novelists, and critics have been unwilling to learn.

Despite structural flaws and inept characterization, *If He Hollers Let Him Go* succeeds as a novel and serves to complement *Native Son.* The rage and anger of Bigger Thomas is universalized in the person of Bob Jones, black everyman, demonstrating that the line between the intellectual and the uneducated Black, in terms of opportunity and treatment, is thin indeed. Himes might have made the point more forcefully, had Jones not accepted the right of the society to castrate him, had he not adhered to superficial values, as readily, though not as completely, as the Harrisons.

Psychological analysis of character is Himes's major forte, and the source of much of the power and strength of the novel, as well as a primary cause of its weakness. Jones is such a central character that not only are all impressions filtered through his mind, but, because of this, other characters receive faulty analysis. In addition, his problems are so important that relationship with others, on a human level, are seldom explored by the author. The break up of the affair between Alice and Bob is well presented, yet the dynamics of the relationship itself remained unexplored. Jones's difficulties and disagreements with the Communist party are stated but not examined, and Madge is so obviously a symbol of a degenerate, though alluring, America (the siren song) that what might have been a realistic examination of relationships between black men and white women never takes place. Loose threads dangle about in the novel, waiting to be meshed together, to be woven into a more substantial garment.

Lonely Crusade (1947), Himes's second novel, is the more substantial garment. The areas, left unexplored in *If He Hollers,* receive fuller exploration here. Moreover, in this second novel, Himes is as interested in relationships between individuals as he is in the individuals themselves. This interest takes him into areas previously ignored by other black writers—the conflict between Blacks and Jews, personified in debates between Abe Rosenberg, party member, and the novel's protagonist, Lee Gordon, the sadomasochistic relationship between black men and their wives, and the conflict between the black intellectual and the Communist party. The labor scene remains Himes's special milieu, and the plight of the middle-class-black intellectual, his primary concern. These interests lead him, once again, into creating a novel in which plot is incidental.

The time period represented in the novel is 1943. Lee Gordon, college graduate, after numerous attempts, secures the most important job in his life—organizer in the Comstock War Plant during wartime. His task is to organize black workers in favor of the union and against management, in a forthcoming election to determine worker representation. He is encouraged in his job by Joe Ptak, his boss, yet he fears entering into competition with whites: "The elation at having secured this job was now replaced by the frightening realization that he, a Negro, was holding it—that he had once again crossed into the competitive white world where he would be subjected to every abuse concocted in the minds of white people to harass and intimidate Negroes."[9]

Gordon's fear of whites is manifested in the inferior position he holds in regard to his wife. Though he is the college graduate, Ruth is able to obtain employment more quickly and of a more prestigious nature. Not only this, but marriage to this capable black woman has produced a sadomasochistic union. Gordon feels incapable of protecting his wife, so much so, that he often looks into "strange restaurants," to discover the presence of other Negroes before entering with her, in order to avoid embarrassment by whites. The result of such paranoia is that the relationship between them degenerates and Gordon seeks companionship with Jackie Forks, a white woman.

His relationship with Jackie symbolizes the predatory relationships existing between himself and other characters in the novel—Foster, owner of the Comstock plant, Luther, a Communist organizer, and Lester, an embittered ex-schoolteacher. Each wants to use Gordon for his own purposes. Foster, for example, a man who "considered being an American the greatest thing of all," has no fear of the coming election, does not believe that the union can be successful in his plant. His overtures to Gordon, his offer of money and position, designed to separate Gordon from the union, are based solely upon his desire to take from the union . . . "their favorite colored boy."

Unlike Lee, Luther accepts Foster's offer, works for both, the party and the management. A pragmatic, unscrupulous man, he has total disdain for moral or ethical standards. He uses his white mistress, Mollie, as a meal ticket and punching bag. He regards the Communist party as a white man's organization to which he owes no allegiance. His contempt for Foster and the Comstock organization is revealed through his act of dissimulation before whites, the fawning and condescension with which he dealt with them. For Luther, his mistress, Foster, and the party were necessary to satiate his greed for money. His example forces Gordon to re-examine his own moral ethic, to arrive, tenuously, at the position that ". . . the one rigid rule in human behavior was to be for yourself and to hell with everyone else . . . ," for Blacks could never attain honor, and integrity was for fools only. Better, then, that he believed "in the almighty dollar, the cowardice of Negroes, and the hypocrisy of whites, and he would never go wrong."[10]

Yet Gordon is incapable of adopting the amoral position of Luther McGregor, for to do so is to sanction murder. Here, Gordon retreats from his newly adopted position. When an agent of Foster taunts Luther and Gordon with large sums of money, in an attempt to impress upon Gordon the importance of being a member of the Comstock organization, he is shocked into immobility as Luther, on sight of the money, ". . . rose like a great black monster," killed the agent, and began calmly to search for a means of disposing of the body. The incident brings home to Gordon the stark reality of the world in which Luther lives: "Unemotional and undisturbed as a man without a soul, without sense, without a nervous system, moving through a world where there was no retribution, no right, no wrong, no God, he looked about for a mop, and finding none, went through the doorway into the next room."

Like Luther, Jackie's interests in Gordon are dictated by selfish concerns. Wanting greater recognition and security from the party, she agrees to snare Gordon into the Communist organization, using her body as bait.

Gordon, however, believes that her interest in him goes beyond party duty and obligation. When a traitor is discovered within the party ranks and Gordon brings charges against Luther, the party, unwilling to accept Luther as the traitor, settles upon Jackie instead, expels her. Gordon moves to defend her, offers his protection. He deserts his wife, only to discover the true nature of Jackie Forks. For not only was her relationship with him founded solely upon party duty and obligation, but the white woman, even in the most intimate moments between them, had always erected the barrier of color: "I'm white, Lee—white! Can't you understand that?"[11]

The flaw in Gordon's character is that he does not understand. Like Bob Jones, he cannot comprehend fully the world in which he lives. His lonely crusade is a search for meaning and understanding. Despite the fact that he too is Black, Luther and Lester remain outside his range of understanding. So too does race tradition which engenders natural suspicion of all things white. Lacking this, Gordon never fully understands Jackie, professes love for her even after she has denigrated him. He forces himself into her apartment, after Luther's murder of the Comstock agent, and reveals the details of the incident. Her betrayal, informing the police, brings no hatred or hostility, but pity, does not sour him upon either the woman or the world, does not convince him that human brotherhood is impossible. On the day of the election, therefore, Luther having been killed by the police, Gordon hides near a sound truck, watching the men being refused entrance to the polling booths. Ptak, the union leader, is felled by one of the guards barring the workers, and Gordon leaves his hiding place, picks up the fallen banner, and marches at the head of an integrated union. This symbolic example of white men and black men united at the end of the novel does not offer, as Himes wished, a picture of optimistic race relations; instead, the incident serves to underline the inability of the protagonist to comprehend the world in which he is fated to live.

Despite an implausible ending, *Lonely Crusade* is a more fully developed novel than *If He Hollers Let Him Go*. What the book lacks in style and organization is more than compensated for by variety of themes and conflicts between characters—some, almost novel with Chester Himes. One such example, that between Blacks and Jews, is posited by Himes in almost contemporary terminology. In a debate with Gordon, Abe Rosenberg represents the Jewish attitude concerning Blacks, while Gordon represents the obverse. Central to the debate is Rosenberg's insistence upon nationalism, one that fails to gain approval from the integrationist aspirant Black: "Isn't it the best society," asks Rosenberg, "that provides cultural autonomy for all the racial and religious groups?"

The conflict between Blacks and the Communist party receives paramount attention. The party affects Blacks in different ways. For Bart, who has risen high in the structure, Communism has not destroyed his sense of racial identity: "Though Bart was a good Marxist, at times, he was more Negro than Communist." For Luther, the party offers status he could receive nowhere else and enables him to profit materially. For Gordon, having undergone negative experiences at the hands of the party, it represents the epitome of treachery, hypocrisy, and deceit. The most telling criticism against the party is offered by Ruth, Gordon's wife: "What they apparently can't see is that I like being a Negro regardless of what color I am; that I like being an American even more so and that I wouldn't exchange this democracy I live in for all the utopias they can possibly picture. . . ."[12]

Ruth's attitude toward the party reveals her attitude as well toward the American society, pointing up the difference between herself and her husband and leading to the central conflict of the novel—that between the black man and the black woman. Black women might well entertain love and respect for America; black men, the primary object of its scorn and hatred, cannot possibly do so. The conflict between the two, therefore, is based upon their variant perceptions of the society. For Lee, America is chaotic and disordered, a place where he is unable to protect his wife, to fight its attempt to use her to invalidate his manhood. Ruth receives largesses, in terms of jobs and status, unattainable by Gordon. She is awarded the roles of provider, protector, and sometimes authority figure. Not surprisingly, Gordon is forced first into panic, then into bitterness, and finally into committing acts of brutality.

Rage against the white world becomes rage against its surrogate, who, unwillingly, becomes the tool of the forces arrayed against him. Not able to understand her own part in the castration of her husband, Ruth cannot divorce Gordon the brute from Gordon the victim; the lines between black husband and black wife, therefore, are irreparably dissevered. Because he cannot find a sense of his manhood in his wife, Gordon is forced to search for a way of salvaging his sense of self. That he sees salvation in the union between himself and Jackie Forks is ironic and points up the extent of his desperation. Jackie pinpoints Gordon's dilemma, drives to the heart of the black man-white woman association at its most primary level: "I wonder," Gordon asks her, "why white women are so much more affectionate to Negro men than our own women are?" Jackie's reply is instant and to the point: "It's only in your mind. . . . In your mind we are the ultimate."[13]

Gordon's desperation has led him to accept the stereotypes of black women and white women, to accept the American mythology without questioning, and, severely wounded in the war against the society in which he lives, out of fear and an instinct for survival, he seeks to become American by adopting the symbol of American attainment: "She was," he thinks of Jackie, "the kind of American whom even Hitler would have welcomed—fair, Aryan, and a pure-blooded gentile. . . ." The possession of Jackie, therefore, equals possession of the American dream, and Gordon, torn between love and hate for his country, can only find salvation in this woman created in the image of the dream. Yet, Himes knows, though Gordon may not, that Jackie is more reality than dream. Hers is a pathological hatred of Blacks, which has made her ". . . so much ripe flesh . . . good only in America for getting some Negro lynched."

The major conflict of the novel, however, is that involving Lee Gordon and himself. Intellectually better endowed than Bigger Thomas, psychologically more capable of repressing his emotions than Bob Jones, his inability to understand the nuances of his own position in America and to understand the strength of his racial traditions lead him to seek salvation in the symbols and images of the white world.

The search for understanding and meaning that propel him through the novel is partially fulfilled at the end, when he realizes that the problems he encounters, the conflicts which rend him apart are not peculiar to him alone: that the world in which he lived had foisted upon him false definitions concerning himself and his race: ". . . he, Lee Gordon, a Negro, was either normal or subnormal. And if he was normal, he would have to rise above the connotation America has given to his race. He would have to stand or fall as one other human being in the world."[14]

Despite this realization, Gordon remains, basically, a man alone, and this feature of his character is representative of that of the men and women who people Himes's novels in general. Bob Jones, Lester, Luther, and Lee Gordon are alienated from Blacks and whites. Unlike Jake and Bita Plant, they have not chosen alienation, desire nothing so much as to be accepted on American terms, the tension of their lives formed by a forced separation from the culture they desire to be apart of. They do not even possess—with Johnson's protagonist—the status of wanderers between two worlds; for though they possess the necessary qualification for entrance into the societal mainstream, they are rejected and forced back upon themselves. Yet they differ from their predecessors and contemporaries in that they are intellectuals more capable of reflection than of action. They are alienated, in part, because of their superior intellects and sensibilities, because they can give form and substance to the range of their rage and hostility in a way that men of intuition and feeling cannot. They are incapable, however, of understanding their position in the world. Educated though they may be, they remain oblivious of their own culture and history. Thus naïveté abounds; the belief in an integrated society, in a universal brotherhood predicated upon equal respect for men of all races and cultures, and the assumption that the war against Fascism abroad will spell disaster for that against Fascism at home. Such beliefs Bigger Thomas would never entertain. To maintain them in light of the contrary examples afforded by American history means that at some point—in a confrontation between reality and illusion—the characters must gain greater insight into the black situation.

The inability of Himes's protagonists to do this makes them psychologically disturbed men, often consumed by self-hatred and self-abnegation. They are, however, more accurate portraits of black intellectuals and the black middle class than supposed in the theology of Blyden Jackson, for they are torn between the human desire to be accepted by the society which bred them and an equal repulsion for the practices of that society. Beneath their obsession with the American dream lay a reservoir of hatred and contempt for America, which must inevitably lead in coming years to an intense questioning of the basic premise upon which the dream has always rested. In presenting such portraits, Himes has secured his place in black literary history. Finally, he has added new dimensions to the character of Bigger Thomas—intellect and reason—and succeeded in showing us the necessity of the catharsis yet to come, the revelation which still awaits us: that in this society, there are no demarcation lines separating one black man from another. The recognition of this fact is a prelude to the fiction of the sixties and seventies, and it is as much to Chester Himes as to Richard Wright that the young black writers of the present are indebted. After *If He Hollers* and *Lonely Crusade,* ideas of superior Blacks and inferior Blacks are to be found only in the imagination of such black men as Blyden Jackson.

If the novels of Richard Wright served as a model for his contemporaries in terms of form and content, the characters of Chester Himes, with slight variations, serve as models for black writers yet to come. Few would disavow Wright's analysis of society, would deny that the result of living as a black man in America meant that one existed in a world where all values had been introverted; neither would many dispute Himes's assumption that rage and hostility, enmity and fear were universal within the black psyche, elements in the makeup of poor and middle-class Blacks alike. Thus to call Himes a follower of Wright is true only to the degree that Himes shared Wright's belief in the stunting, limiting capabilities of environment. In the area of character delineation, however, Himes, himself, is an innovator, and his contemporaries may be deemed his followers as well as followers of Wright.

Two black writers might have been influenced by each. Ann Petry (1911–) and William Gardner Smith (1942–) are one with Wright in their concept of America; yet both are close to Himes in terms of character development, have moved beyond Bigger Thomas, to deal with characters of some status and education. They are of differing temperaments and talents. Miss Petry is the more accomplished craftsman. She is a master of the metaphor and the image, proficient in the creation of suggestive art. Her style varies, ranging from the sharp, crisp idiom of the black community in her first novel, *The Street,* to the stilted language of the English romantics, as exemplified in *The Narrows*. Smith is more expert at understatement, better able to dramatize action than to describe it. Though not as successful as Miss Petry in delineating character, the movement of his narrative is more fluid, and his ability to focus on important details and explicate them in simplistic language is one of his stronger points. Both are distinguished for two works dealing with the plight of Blacks after the war years, *The Street* (1946) and *The Stone Face* (1963).

The Street has been compared to *Native Son*. Given a change of characters, some critics have argued, and the work is little more than a carbon copy of its predecessor. There are similarities to be sure. Both Wright and Miss Petry wrote in the naturalistic idiom, both were interested in the effects of environment upon the psychological makeup of characters; both were aware of the images handed down from the past, knew firsthand the damage incurred when men accepted definitions of themselves not of their own making. In terms of style, both are descriptive and analytical, more proficient in describing action than dramatizing it; neither is adept at handling dialogue. Here, the similarities end. Miss Petry, a Northerner, was born of bourgeois stock, college educated, and less prolific than her contemporary. Her major output consisted of two fine novels, *The Narrows* (1953) and *The Street*. In its own right *The Street* is a powerful and provocative work, exploring areas that Wright, taking his reader for granted, did not venture to explore. Most important, Miss Petry is more interested in the effects of the environment upon her characters than she is in the characters themselves.

The characters are products of the street; their lives are dominated by forces beyond their control. Take Lutie Johnson, the protagonist, for example. Her difficulties commence long before she moves to the street, 116th, situated in Harlem, New York. Marital problems brought on because she is able to find work, while her husband is not, lead her to the street. Overly ambitious, she refuses to heed the advice of a former employer, "It's best that the man do the work when the babies are young," and accepts a sleep-in job in the home of the Chandlers, a wealthy white family. Here in this non-black world, she finds affluence and plenty; she also finds degeneracy, suspicion, and hostility. The husband is an incurable alcoholic, and the wife, a promiscuous woman. Nevertheless, Lutie is more attracted by the Chandlers' middle-class status and affluence than repulsed by their failures as human beings. After listening to lectures on the Protestant ethic from Mrs. Chandler, she arrives at the conclusion that any one who worked hard enough could be rich and prosperous: ". . . these people had wanted only one thing—money and more money—and so they got it." She imparts this philosophy, through letters, to her husband.

However, Jim Johnson, the husband, is a proud man, and his inability to rise to middle-class status is not due to his lack of initiative but to his racial background. His attempts to provide for his family are thwarted by a society which treats the Chandlers one way and the Johnsons another. The former may live in the world of rising stock prices, accumulated dividends, and swollen bank accounts; for the latter, however, the choice was between work with dignity or no work at all, and work, with or without dignity, was difficult to come by. Unable to support his wife and child, forced to live off the earnings of his wife, whom he sees only occasionally—in order to save money Lutie limited her visits home to weekends—Jim takes up with another woman. When Lutie, summoned home by her father to take stock of the situation, discovers her husband and his lover together, she terminates the relationship, and moves into the home of her widowed father. Due to his licentious behavior, she is forced to search for a different environment in which to raise her son. She moves to 116th Street! Lucy must share equal billing in the novel with the street. With metaphorical clarity, Miss Petry paints a frightening portrait of this antagonist in the opening pages of the book: "There was a cold November wind blowing through 116th Street . . . it did everything it could to discourage the people walking along the street. It found all the dirt and dust and grime on the sidewalk and lifted it up so that . . . the dust got into their eyes and blinded them; and the grit stung their skins. It wrapped newspaper around their feet, entangling them until the people cursed deep in their throats, stamped their feet, kicked at the paper. The wind blew it back again and again until they were forced to stoop and dislodge the paper with their hands, and then the wind grabbed their hats, pried their scarves from around their necks, stuck its fingers inside their coat collars, blew their coats away from their bodies."

In light of the awesome natural forces arrayed against the protagonist, *The Street* takes on the dimensions of a mock-heroic epic. Lutie must wage warfare against an impregnable foe that has rendered all before her either passive or helpless, that has, somehow, achieved a life of its own, become sovereign in its own right, complete arbitrator over the destinies of people. In quixoticlike fashion, she is determined to wage warfare against it, despite her knowledge that for others the battle has long since been over, that those, like Mrs. Hedges and Boots Smith, have their made peace with it, while others, like the super and Min, continue to suffer anxiety and frustration, are completely at its mercy.

Once a vagrant, scouring garbage cans for food, Mrs. Hedges, aided by Mr. Junto, a Jew, has come to terms with the street. Junto is the most powerful man in the area; his power derives from the houses of prostitution established and run for him by Mrs. Hedges. Knowing the street as Junto never could, Mrs. Hedges knew that it would provide many customers from among men who, in hating whites and being unable to relieve their frustrations, sought escape and were willing to pay for it. A female pimp, who desires to please Junto at all costs, when the Jew becomes interested in Lutie, Mrs. Hedges seeks to procure her for him. The case of Boots Smith is analogous to that of Mrs. Hedges. With the aid of Junto, the musician has also made terms with the street. No longer an inhabitant—he maintains an apartment on Sugar Hill—he makes his living as a bandleader, entertaining the street's inhabitants who flock to Junto's cabaret for surcease from the white world. Like black men from Josh Green to Bob Jones, Smith harbors a hatred so intense for white people that he . . . "wouldn't lift a finger to help em stop Germans or nobody else."

Mrs. Hedges and Smith are privileged persons on the street. They are not untouched by its filth, crime, and poverty, but aid the street in its vendetta against others, are leeches forced to play such roles by a hostile society. Given a different environment, each might have succeeded on his own merits. Yet, Boots's talent will avail him little in a profession where black musicians suffer from want, while less talented white ones move toward fame and riches. Given Mrs. Hedges' entrepreneurial skills, energy, ability, and a white skin, she might have created a capitalistic enterprise, might have become, like the Chandlers, a purveyor of stock market receipts and dividends. Only when measured alongside such inhabitants of the street as Jones, the super, and Min, his common-law wife, do the two appear to occupy exalted position.

Jones, a middle-aged, lonely man, who has worked in apartment houses for so long that he has come to represent the underground forces symbolized by the street itself, survives mainly on fantasies. The long years have taken their toll of his self-esteem, and the quest to regain a sense of his manhood takes the route of sexual fantasy: ". . . he had developed the habit of spending his spare time outside the buildings in which he worked; looking at the women who went past, estimating them, wanting them."[15] Min, more representative of a type than of an actual character, is legend in black life, if not in black fiction. A lonely woman, unable to secure a mate, she is the ghetto's eternal victim, preyed upon by men and merchants, charlatans and jackleg ministers alike. The long years of working for white people have given her little except sore feet, an old clothes chest, a belief in the inevitability of things, and a quiet, passive acceptance of her own condition. She desires little from the street, wants only to hold on to what little she has.

Understanding the awesome power of the street, knowing what it has done to its other inhabitants, despite the odds, Lutie engages in rebellion against it. She is confident that she can protect her young son, Bub, and herself from its power, believes that she can thwart the forces, both human and inhuman, waged against her. When Jones, obsessed with the desire to sleep with her, attempts rape, she is rescued by Mrs. Hedges. Enraged, the super seeks revenge. He coaxes Bub into rifling the mailboxes of occupants on the street. Lutie, unaware of the super's actions, continues to flatter Smith, who has taken an interest in her, and whom she believes represents passage from the street.

Unknown to either Smith or herself, however, she has been chosen by Junto. The bandleader is informed that he is to stay away from her at the risk of losing his job in the cabaret. He weighs the options in this fashion: "Balance Lutie Johnson. Weigh Lutie Johnson. Long legs and warm mouth. Soft skin and pointed breasts. Straight slim black and small waist . . . not enough. She didn't weigh enough when she was balanced against a life of saying 'yes sir' to every white bastard who had the price of a Pullman ticket . . . one hundred Lutie Johnson didn't weigh enough."[16] Thus Smith joins Mrs. Hedges as Junto's procurer. Taking advantage of Lutie's need for money, when Bub is arrested for breaking into mailboxes, Smith sets up a rendezvous between Junto and Lutie at his Sugar Hill apartment. Lutie is unaware that she is supposed to sell her body to the Jew for money. When the discovery is made, she becomes enraged, sees Junto as the metaphor of all her ills, wants to commit murder.

It is Smith, however, upon whom she eventually unleashes her rage. After being repulsed, Junto leaves the apartment! Smith attempts to force Lutie into sexual activity. The rage, previously directed against the white man, emerges again, moving beyond Smith to encompass the street and the white world at large. Out of this sense of rage, she surrenders finally to the street, leveling a quickly grasped candlestick in futility, not against Smith, upon whom she rains blow after blow, but upon ". . . the dirty crowded street . . . the rows of dilapidated old houses, the little lost girls in Mrs. Hedges' apartment; the smashed homes where the women did drudgery because their men deserted them . . . she was striking at the white world which thrust black people into a walled enclosure from which there was no escape. . . ."[17] Defeat is registered! Lutie steals money from the fallen Smith and, forsaking her son, leaves for Chicago.

Like *Native Son,* the value of *The Street* lay in its realistic analysis and appraisal of the American society. Racism is the major problem between Blacks and whites, the final determiner of the actions of Johnson, Jones, Min, and Boots Smith. Every societal institution, from the educational to the armed forces, operates upon racist codes and duplicates the pressure exercised upon the people by the street. The cyclical phenomenon dramatized at the end of the novel offers only one example. His mother gone, Bub is remanded to reformatory school to learn other ways of dealing with the street, to become a facsimile of Smith or his father. That few other options are open constitutes a tacit agreement with the liberals and Communists and accounts for the major flaw of the novel.

For *The Street* backs away from a denouement. Having painted the portrait, Miss Petry does not revarnish her work, does not add color to her painting. She moves beyond the social Darwinists, insisting upon salvation of her people along classical lines: Change the society and there will be no Juntos, Boots Smiths, Mins, or Joneses. Yet, given the hopelessness of the world she depicts, given racism as a fact of life, given the fact that those who might change society are unwilling to do so, the solution is apparent: The Lutie Johnsons can be saved only by the Lutie Johnsons! Only through collective action can the street be cleared of the Juntos and Hedgeses and made viable for human life; only when Blacks move to establish power and control over the institutions that govern their lives will this street and the society at large cease to be agents of oppression.

This analysis speaks of a different kind of novel than that written by Miss Petry, and the reasons may be due to her own ambivalence. She will not retreat from the premise advanced by Douglass that racism in America is not an eternal given, that conscientious men and women cannot eradicate it from the social structure. Yet, to examine Junto and the Chandlers is to arrive at the conclusion that she had little faith that such people would move to bring about freedom of opportunity for all. In fact, she suggests that to entrust the salvation of Blacks to the hands of such characters means to opt for the status quo. Not surprisingly, therefore, Lutie Johnson is a rebel in her own right, refusing to accept the argument of her own impotence, refusing to allow herself to march calmly and passively to certain destruction. Lacking power to substantially alter the course of her life, nevertheless, she denounces injustice and oppression, moves, ineffectually to be sure, to improve her condition. Through Lutie's example, Miss Petry suggests, despite her ambivalence, that to accept the premise of *The Street*—that America is an oppressive place for black people—is to begin the exploration for realistic ways of combating the deterministic universe.

In so doing she has paved the way for future black writers, by pointing out the closed nature of the society, and freed even the protest novelist to move to other dimensions, to examine the relationship between black man and black man, instead of those that primarily concern man and society. The novelists who move toward exploration of this new conflict—James Baldwin, Ralph Ellison, John Williams, and John Killens—have been freed by their predecessors, among whom, Miss Petry ranks very high indeed. For, despite its intentions, *The Street* has made unnecessary literature based upon the naturalist or determinist philosophy, has mandated, instead, literature that assigns the responsibility for man's fate, not to institutions or environment, but to man himself.

In this respect, William Gardner Smith's novel, *The Stone Face,* is a transitional novel. Though he draws upon material already covered by his predecessors, and though his rebels are cast in the mold of those of Wright and Himes, he appears more attuned to the modern sensibility than his predecessors. His rebels are more advanced men, come close to approaching the revolutionaries found in the novels of Delany, Sam Greenlee, and John Williams. His milieu is international, his setting American and Europe, and his primary concern, the search for a black identity. An author at the age of twenty, Smith has not lived up to his promise, though *Last of the Conquerors,* his first novel, and *The Stone Face* represent superior efforts. Like Wright, he too found permanent exile in France.

The structure of *The Stone Face* contributes to any explication of the novel. The book is divided into three parts, "The Fugitive," "The White Man," and "The Brother"; each is a necessary step forward in understanding the character of the hero, Simeon Brown. Part One deals with Simeon Brown's past. The Philadelphia-born expatriate lost an eye in the early years of his life due to a brutal, unwarranted assault by Chris, a white youth. The incident left Brown bitter and resentful, and the image of Chris's face, imprinted upon his psyche, serves as his metaphor for American racism. Chris and America are one in having no compassion, generosity, or love, of hating and denying everything conducive to life; "This was the terrible face of antiman, of discord, of disharmony with the universe."[18] The recurring image of the "stone face," in the form of racist acts by white men, pushes Brown close to murder and, finally, to exile. In one such incident he is worked over by Mike, a white policeman, who tells him that "this is a white man's country"; in another, he is accosted by a white sailor while walking a coworker home. These incidents, and his inability to shake the image of the first stone face, propel him to Paris; here he hopes to put the stone faces and the violence accompanying them behind him. From this point the story begins.

In Paris, Brown joins the African-American expatriate colony, and falls in love with Maria, Polish, who suffers from fear of blindness. In many instances, her life in Poland, where she watched her family being led to the concentration camps and to execution, has been similar to Brown's. Her ambition is to become an actress, visit Hollywood, and make a lot of money, "and have a car." Along with others of the expatriate colony, Benson, novelist, Babe, bookstore owner, Harold, composer, and Doug, who works for the American Embassy, Brown and Maria are outcasts enjoying respite from the brutality of their native environments. Of the expatriates, only Benson remains bitter, has not made his peace with French society. Harold is the only one of the group who seeks to return to America. His interest is in art, not race, and his ideas of the function of the artist resemble those later advanced in the writings of Baldwin and Ellison: "Temporary causes and problems are the death of art": those bound to causes should "go get a gun and fight and leave art alone." Babe finds a measure of peace in Paris, unknown before. A onetime member of the NAACP, he soon realizes that the goal of integration is fruitless, that the objective of too many Blacks is assimilation into American society, and that few would agree with him that "they [white people] was my enemies, there was a fight on, a long war been going on since they took the first slave there, but what kinda war was that when your aim was to be *integrated* into the enemy!"

Despite past maltreatment, only Brown, among the expatriates, is aware of the war being waged on Parisian soil. The treatment of Algerians in France parallels the treatment of Blacks in America, and though France maintains a policy of racial acceptance toward Blacks, the policy is inoperative in the case of Algerians. Thus one of the functions of Part One of the novel is to depict the ordeal undergone by the Algerian people in France and draw a parallel not only between the treatment accorded them and Blacks, but also the commitment of the Algerians to liberation and the non-commitment of the Blacks. More sensitive than his fellow expatriates, living consciously with the memory of so many stone-faced men, Brown comes to feel a kinship with the oppressed Algerians.

His first encounter with them, however, is not positive. He defends a prostitute, who unknown to him had stolen money from an Arab; the man is arrested. In subsequent meetings with the Algerians, in particular with Ahmed, a student, and Hossein, member of the FLN, Brown is first taunted because of the difference in treatment accorded him and that accorded the Arabs, called contemptuously a "white man" and subsequently informed of the ordeal daily undergone by Arabs at the hands of the French. The plight of the Algerians is further explored in Part Two; here also is dramatized a growing awareness, on Brown's part, of the nature of oppression and its universality. In the relationship that develops between Brown and Ahmed, the former, not only learns more about the suffering of the Algerian people, but gains a heightened awareness of himself as an African-American. Oppression is the common bond between them, and Brown discovers this fact when he escorts two of them to a French restaurant. The Arabs are unwelcomed and insulted, and Brown, who stands up for them, is asked not to visit the restaurant again. Such incidents, his friendship with the Arabs, and his frustration concerning the relationship between Maria and himself lead him to examine his role as an expatriate.

Maria, though in love with Brown, is more enamored of her career. Under the tutelage of a director who has amorous designs upon her, her career begins to expand. Her main concern is about a forthcoming operation she fears will leave her blind. Yet when Brown proposes marriage, neither marriage nor fear of blindness account for her ambivalence. Having survived the ordeal of the Nazis, Maria seeks a life of escapism, where one is "Cut off from the troubles of the world." Her desire for peace and stability coupled with Brown's growing awareness of the universality of oppression present him with a dilemma. He had come to Paris to escape violence; yet, he found violence everywhere dogging his path. News of the incidents taking place in Little Rock, Arkansas, the faces of the men, who stand guard against the entrance of black children into the school, bring to his mind the faces of Chris, Mike, and the sailor. News of the Congo rebellion in which black men war against black men and his growing appreciation of the Algerian condition have made no longer possible any hope of escape like that envisioned by Maria. His reply to her is strained: "That kind of life might not be possible for a Negro if he thinks and feels."[19] He had arrived at the conclusion that the only difference between the French, Germans, and Americans was the accident of nationality, that wherever they were, there too were the stone faces. Further evidence to support this view is not difficult to come by. When he learns through Ahmed, that Hossein has been arrested by the police, and that he, Ahmed, is returning to Algeria to aid in the struggle there, the import of Ahmed's subsequent remarks makes impossible Brown's continual existence as an expatriate: "I can't sit by, comfortable, while the others take the hard blows."

Parts One and Two delineate the central conflict of the novel—that involving the protagonist and his own conscience. Presented with an environment in which he might live free from racial restrictions, and carrying memories of one that was racially restrictive and oppressive, where does choice lie for the sensitive black intellectual? Smith has loaded the argument against his protagonist. For once, having been subjected to violence and oppression, the thinking individual cannot help, theoretically, but to arrive at the conclusion that racial freedom for the individual is impossible without freedom for all men. The environment, which offers such to Brown, denies it to others, if not because of color, then for some other equally ridiculous reason. For Brown to be truly opposed to oppression, therefore, means to champion freedom everywhere, to regard victims the world over as brothers one of another.

Aptly entitled, "The Brother," Part Three examines the conclusions reached tentatively in parts One and Two. The series of events, leading to the final denouement, form one connecting link in the final determination of Simeon Brown to rejoin the ranks of the oppressed and underprivileged. Maria and Brown drift farther apart after her successful operation, and her career moves from bit parts to roles of more consequence. In a letter, severing the relationship, Brown points out the indecision concerning his own life: ". . . I love you but you have a career and your own life to lead; I feel I have another kind of life before me, though I'm not sure what it will be yet." The death of Ahmed, who returns to Paris to engage in a protest march against a curfew restricting Algerians to their apartments after daylight, hastens Brown's final decision concerning the direction of his life.

The French police react to the non-violent demonstration by the Arabs by clubbing and beating men, women, and children. Numbers of people are maimed; some, including Ahmed, are killed. Brown, witnessing the clubbing of a woman with a baby in her arms, is transported back to Philadelphia, back to the stone-faced men from whom he had run away: "He saw it as clearly as though it were only inches from him—that face he knew so well, the face in America he had tried to escape—it was Chris, Mike, their face." He rushes to the aid of the woman, is arrested and thrown into prison with the Algerians. This and similar experiences during the night bring about the final realization and determination. The faces of the French policemen, of Mike, Chris, the Nazi torturers at Buchenwald, of the men who formed the mobs in the South, of Afrikaner and Portuguese were the same faces; so long as such men existed, peace was an impossibility, for "Wherever this face was found, it was his enemy; and whoever feared or suffered from or fought against this face was his brother."[20] The end of the novel finds Brown deserting the expatriate colony and preparing to return to America.

The Stone Face is a novel of prophetic import, forecasting the changes in black perception during the years of the sixties. The period after the Supreme Court decision in Brown *versus* Board of Education, the Emmet Till slaying, the ordeals of black youngsters, undergone in such places as Little Rock, and the emergence of Malcolm X and Martin Luther King upon the political landscape have helped to produce the kind of conscious wrestling and introspection leading to an awareness of the condition of the African-American. Such awareness is possible only after the theory of society, or environment, as man's major antagonist has been transcended. The major conflict in Brown's life is not between him and the environment, but between himself and his own conscience. Moved away from the limiting effects of American racism, placed into an environment of relative peace and security, he must still come to terms with the reality of the universal threat to liberty and freedom, must grow to recognize his unity with all mankind. The lessons learned through experience transform him from a fugitive to a revolutionary. Thus Smith's formula for the making of a black revolutionary: from hatred to awareness to rebellion to revolution.

Awareness, a key word, is the one dimension missing from the personality makeup of Brown's fictional ancestors, Bigger Thomas, Lee Gordon, and Bob Jones. Each is limited by parochialism, hampered by an inability to perceive of themselves in a positive sense and to relate their condition to that of the race as a collective whole. They were existentialists, individual men, prototypes of the ego men of the European novels, fighting solitary battles against societal restrictions, hoping to secure salvation, not for all men, but for themselves. Thus, they were less well-developed characters than Simeon Brown, though improvements over those offered in previous periods of black literature. Brown surpasses them, as images for the modern black mind, at that point where he reaches out to embrace the Algerian experience, to make himself one with the oppressed people of the world, to subscribe to the philosophy of such prophets as Frantz Fanon that those who comprise the wretched of the earth constitute a collective brotherhood against tyranny and oppression.

Smith's movement away from much of the deterministic thought of his predecessors marks another forward advance for the black novelist. Brown's conflict, though psychological in nature, points to a lessening of the tendency to think of society as the objective corelative for the actions of black people. In this case, society as major antagonist, as architect of men's actions, is less important in determining man's fate than reason and conscience. Thus the major war is not that of man to free himself from an imagined naturalist environment, but to free his mind from the limiting effects of old myths and legends, distorted symbols and images. To do so means not only to arrive at an awareness of one's own strength and potential but also to join as one with the oppressed of the world, seeing them not in the image of the downtrodden of old, but as the vanguardsmen of the better world to come. For black people this means to identify with a majority of the earth's people, with those who confront identical problems of exploitation and oppression. When the black novelist seizes upon such images to people his works, the black novel moves into the universal arena, and the black character becomes the representative of struggling humanity everywhere. Smith was not the first to conceive of such dimensions, and his critical articles evidence the fact that he was oblivious to many of the ramifications of his own work. Yet, he had the vision and foresight to realize that the novel, having come so far since Brown and Webb, despite more emendation, must return, inevitably, to the novel as conceived by Martin Delany. *The Stone Face* is a more modern, updated version of its nineteenth-century predecessor.

IX

OF RACE AND
RAGE

William Gardner Smith and Richard Wright were anathema to the
new imagists—the academic "scholars" and critics who demanded of
the black writer that he wrap the "race problem up in symbol, images,
plain niceties, and downright lies." These new imagists differed from
the old, from the liberals and Communists. They held no fondness for
Christ figures and black martyrs, desired no images of pitiable, mas-
ochistic Blacks. What they demanded of the black novelist was the
creation of images that were "universal . . . more than Negro . . .
human beings." As for the novel itself, the classic statement regarding
its composition and function has been forwarded by Herbert Hill in
an introduction to William Demby's *Beetlecreek: "Beetlecreek* is a
highly imaginative work, rich with symbolic meaning and suggestion
and concerned with questions of good and evil that go beyond race."[1]
   Because every good novel—and some not so good—is concerned
with the question of good and evil, one is not too far wrong to suggest
that the critic's true affection for Demby's novel is his belief that it
"goes beyond race." Though such phraseology is part of the terminology
of the academic scholars and critics, none are quite sure what it means.
For many, it means novels different from those of Wright and Smith,
novels that do not focus upon the black problem in America; for others,
it means that the novelist must consider the black character as an in-

dividual preoccupied with individual problems instead of those of the group. For others, it means that the novelist must forego concern with racism and its effects upon his characters—a concern that limits the work to "narrow parochialism." For others, to advocate the egalitarian principle is to argue the cause for integration on the artistic level, if not on the social and political. Admittedly, social integration is an impossibility, yet experiences and life-styles might be integrated through the medium of art. The objective of such suggestions is to move the black novel from its status as a weapon in the interests of black people to an instrument for the propagation of lies and half-truths, in order to stifle the rising awareness of Blacks in the intellectual and social areas of the black communities, to prevent the emergence of such sophisticated, determined Blacks as depicted in the novels of Delany and Smith. Two recent novels lend themselves to this kind of evaluation. *Invisible Man* (1952), by Ralph Ellison (1914–) and *Another Country* (1962), by James Baldwin (1924–). Ellison, whose first and only novel won him the National Book Award in 1952, is an astute jazz critic, and—as his collection of essays, *Shadow and Act* (1964), demonstrates—a competent literary critic as well. These attributes have been overshadowed, however, by the success of his novel. In each case, the white critics and academicians, like Herbert Hill, have read their own meaning into the novel and stopped far short of a realistic explication.

After acknowledging the fact that Ellison displays remarkable creativity in the area of suggestive language—of metaphors, imagery, and surrealism—the most descriptive comment about *Invisible Man* is that the novel has—and this is the only word for it—soul. The idiom is that of African-Americans evidenced in the rhetorical excesses of the black preacher and the racy idiom of the ghetto street. Characters, excellent facsimiles of black people who have survived a precarious American existence, move in and out of its pages. Go into the streets of *Invisible Man,* into the homes of the black people portrayed therein, and the rich sounds are those of the community itself. Pathos, anger, joy, hope, resentment—Ellison has managed to capture it all. *Invisible Man,* therefore, is as much a novel about its people, their mores and folkways, as it is about the nameless protagonist who occupies the reader's center of attention.

In fact, the task of the protagonist is to introduce the reader to the immense color and pageantry in black life; to narrate the movement of black people from slavery to the modern era; to make of time a collage in which one might glimpse the fluidity and variety of the black experience. Having completed such tasks, having taken the reader, via his own imagination, through the labyrinthine corridors of the black experience, though not achieving visibility, the quest undertaken at the beginning of the novel, the protagonist undergoes a catharsis, discovers the richness and fullness of his black heritage. This picturesque novel, therefore, depicts, through allegory, the history of the black man's trials and errors in America; dramatizes his running the gauntlet of American pretensions, suffering from the attempt by white Americans to define him, to construct roles for him, and to create images and symbols to which he must adhere. The modern-day Cain, thus, is a black man, rushing not so much from his sins as from those who offer him eternal facelessness and invisibility. To discover that the world for black men is one of immense possibilities, despite the power of the imagists, constitutes an awareness that moves allegory close to actuality.

A search for the dominant theme of the novel leads not to the sources sighted by Ellison—Dostoevsky, Melville, or T. S. Elliot—but to a passage from Du Bois' *The Souls of Black Folks:* "After the Egyptian and Indian, the Greek and Roman, the Teuton and Mongolian, the Negro is a sort of seventh son, born with a veil and gifted with second sight in this American world—a world which yields him no true self-consciousness, but only lets him see himself through the revelation of the other world. It is a peculiar sensation, this double consciousness, this sense of always looking at one's self through the eyes of others, of measuring one's soul by the tape of a world that looks on in amused contempt and pity. One ever feels his twoness—an American, a Negro; two souls, two thoughts, two unreconciled strivings: two warring ideals in one dark body, whose dogged strength alone keeps it from being torn asunder. The history of the American Negro is the history of this strife—this longing to attain self-conscious manhood to merge his double self into a better and truer self. . . ."[2]

The concept of the mirror image is central to the theory of psychic dualism—the phrase applied to Du Bois' analysis of the black dilemma. Children live in a universe where sensory impressions are daily imprinted upon the psyche; their growth may be influenced by any number of such impressions, which often take the form of things seen and heard. Images of himself form the essence of the child's being in the younger years, that period of time when he is most susceptible to influences from those who represent power, either in the immediate family or from outside. Images, both positive and negative, sift through his mind; some are retained, make lasting impressions; others are discarded. In either case, for an evaluation of himself, for evidence that he is like other people, the child peers into mirrors constructed by those who symbolize power and influence.

The black child, however, knows that he is different from white people in terms of color and history, yet he is confused as to the quality of that difference because he has been told that such differences are negative, and that to validate his humanity, he must accept the roles and images prescribed for him by those in power and authority. The history of the black American, therefore, has been one of ambivalence concerning the value of the images projected in the American mirror and doubts about the authenticity of those existing somewhere in the collective conscious, awaiting recreation by the novelist or the historian. The protagonist of *Invisible Man,* therefore, is both novelist and historian, recreator of images and destroyer of myths. His narrative is the sociological thesis of Du Bois given lyrical and allegorical form.

In addition to a "prologue and epilogue," the novel is divided into four parts. The situation in which we encounter the protagonist in the prologue is analogous to that in which we encounter him in the epilogue. He lives a symbolical underground existence, situated on the border line between Harlem and the white areas of Manhattan, in the basement of an apartment house, rented exclusively by white people. With mechanical ingenuity, he has managed to light his apartment by hooking into the main electric feeder line of the Monopolated Light and Power Company. The narrative of how he arrived at this position awaits the telling, and like the old ex-slave, freed after the Civil War, the protagonist aches "with a compassion to tell his story, one that will merge past and present, end and beginning." Central to both is an ambivalence concerning the images and symbols of Black as opposed to American life.

This theme, ambivalence, assumes shape and form in the first segment of the novel, which might be termed "down South." In this first home away from home for the African-American, the pattern of life, defined by the outsider as rigid, is instead quite fluid. The roles one is called upon to play by white Southerners vary from black man to black man, and this assortment of roles is passed from father to son. The oral history, on the other hand, often presents roles that clash with those provided by the Americans, presents images of positive import. The result is confusion concerning the roles one is to play in relationship to white people who represent authority. In the first segment of the novel, the protagonist is offered his choice of four roles, each validated by white Americans. The first, suggested in the dying words of his grandfather, is that of the wily slave, expert at displaying obsequiousness in dealing with white folks: ". . . overcome 'em with yeses, undermine 'em with grins, agree 'em to death and destruction. . . ."[3] The second and third roles, those of darky entertainer and Christ figure, come directly from whites. The final role, engaged in by the protagonist up North—ward of the American society—is one bestowed, not by southern racists, but by northern liberals.

Before the protagonist can achieve visibility—an identity, uniquely his own—each of the roles must be rejected, the images, personified by men up North and down South, who legitimatize such roles, rejected as well. To reject the role of the Christ figure or savior of Western civilization means to reject Mr. Norton, the white trustee of the college which he attends. Norton holds a twentieth century—Marxist—view of the protagonist, believes him to be his savior and foreteller of his fate. Like white philanthropists since the end of the Civil War, he has contributed to such black institutions as that attended by the protagonist —those which teach out individuality and teach in conformity. Some, like Norton, have become altruistic out of feelings of guilt and personal sickness—Norton has an Oedipal fixation upon his daughter— and thus perceives Blacks as bearers of the guilt and shame they are unable to bear alone. This explains, in part, Norton's fascination for the black Trueblood, a man who has committed incest with his own daughter and become expectant father to both his pregnant wife and child.

The protagonist, however, has little understanding of the Nortons of this world, though he is willing to reject the role Norton has prescribed for him and to accept that personified in the figure of Dr. Bledsoe, the crafty old president of the State college, who is a living exemplar of the image of the wily slave, a dissimulator par excellence, "a spy in the enemy's camp." He has learned to yes 'em to death and to overcome 'em with lies. To the whites he is a mere tool; a meek, mildmannered, subservient darky. To Blacks he is the fictional Uncle Tom made flesh. Throughout the protagonist's encounter with Bledsoe, the racial craftiness of the educator is contrasted with the ignorance and naïveté of the protagonist. When the protagonist offers an excuse for allowing the white philanthropist to visit the quarters of Trueblood, —he had been ordered—Bledsoe's reply is crisp and tort. "Ordered you? . . . He ordered you? Dammit, white folks are always giving orders, it's a habit with them. Why didn't you make an excuse. . . . My God, boy! You're black and living in the South—did you forget how to lie?"[4]

The central flaw in the protagonist's character is that he has never known how to lie, has never been able to understand the nature of black survival in America, nor the roles Blacks were forced to play. When he is expelled from the college by Bledsoe and supplied with bogus letters of introduction to northern white industrialists, his punishment is due primarily to ignorance in regard to the social mechanics of the South. He had been offered choices of a number of roles. Each, though limiting his individuality, is necessary for survival. Yet he cannot understand the examples offered in the warning of his grandfather nor in the person of Bledsoe, cannot understand, that is, that he must ". . . learn to look beneath the surface. . . . Play the game but don't believe in it. . . . Play the game, but play it your own way. . . . Learn how it operates; learn how you operate."[5] Having failed in the attempt to live as a black man in the South, the protagonist travels north.

His initial experiences up North precipitate the eventual movement from naïveté to awareness and bring him into confrontation with Ras the Exhorter and Brother Jack, two symbols of roles as limiting and restrictive as those encountered down South. During his first days in the North, he is made cognizant of the true nature of Bledsoe, made to realize by the son of an industrialist that the letters the former president had given him as recommendations for employment were designed in effect, to "keep this nigger boy running." In addition, finally securing a job in a paint factory, he is involved in an accident which lands him in the company hospital.

The doctors, armed with modern machines, capable of producing frontal lobotomies without operation, want to transform him into a robot, make him live only as he has to in complete integrity, experience "no major conflict of motives and what is even better, society will suffer no traumata on his account."[6] The machine, in other words, will succeed where the teachings of his grandfather, Norton, and Bledsoe have failed, make him live only as he has to in complete integrity, experience "no major conflict of motives and what is even better, society will suffer no traumata on his account."[7] The roles and images they prescribed, or sanctioned, meant that the protagonist accept only one facet of the racial reality—impotence and helplessness. The objective of the doctors, however, is to see that he functions without emotion or past memory, surrendering his true identity for one of nebulous distinction; that he see himself always through the eyes of others; that he surrender the double consciousness so important a part of the racial memory. The attempt at mental castration fails. Besieged by questions from the doctors after his operation, though confusion of identity persists, aspects of the racial memory remain. Though unable to remember either his own name or that of his mother, he is capable of recalling images of Buckeye the rabbit and Brer Rabbit, remnants of his cultural history. Thus the machine men fail to rob him of his identity—he had never had one to begin with—

but help to bring him nearer maturity; he is not rendered impotent, but mentally stronger: "I was no longer afraid. Not of important men, not of trustees and such; for knowing now that there was nothing which I could expect from them, there was no reason to be afraid. . . ."[8] The operation has prepared him for his experiences in black Harlem.

He is prepared also to accept the life-style of black people in a way that he had not been before. In Harlem, he meets Mary Rambo, a part of the southern soil transported north, a link between the old world and the new, not merely a person but a force, "like something out of my past," which prevents him from "whirling off into some unknown." In the rich underground world of Harlem, Mary Rambo symbolizes the environment of "hot, baked Car'lina yams," so syrupy and bubbly that they melted on the way to your mouth; of chitterlings and fried peas, mustard greens and black-eyed peas, pig ears and ham hocks, of down-to-earth black men and women, of tenderness and tragedy, of sadness and joy. The acceptance of this underground world, of this different culture, induces greater awareness: "To hell with being ashamed of what you liked. No more of that for me. I am what I am. I wolfed down the yam and ran back to the old man and handed him twenty-five cents. 'Give me two more . . .'"

Tragedy, an important element in the life of Harlemites, brings the hero into contact with the brotherhood and into conflict with Ras the Exhorter. The eviction of an aged couple from their apartment is the catalyst. The eviction of the couple, and the placing of their meager belongings upon the sidewalk by city officials, spurs the protagonist to make an eloquent speech defending the two and moves the gathering mob to rout the dispossess servers. The speech brings him to the attention of the brotherhood, who succeed, finally, in convincing him to become district spokesman for the Harlem area. Reluctantly, he moves from the home of Mary Rambo, takes a downtown apartment and, with the aid of young Tod Clifton, assumes his duties. Due primarily to the work of Clifton, idealistic leader of the youth group of the brotherhood, the protagonist increases the organizations' standing and prestige in the black community. Success in this area precipitates the first serious conflict between the forces of the brotherhood and those of Ras the Exhorter. The encounter is psychologically disturbing. Ras and his followers break up a meeting held by the brotherhood and violence ensues. The Exhorter, in a position to kill Clifton, lectures the youth leader instead; the lecture affects both Clifton and the protagonist. Expressing brotherhood based upon race and skin color, Ras exhorts the two to join him in an attempt to make Harlem a better place for black people, offering in addition, the prophecy, that when the white people have finished using black people "they turn against you."

Though the prophecy of Ras rings true—the protagonist is demoted, due to trumped up charges—the protagonist was attracted to the brotherhood, not only because of its program concerning Blacks, but more specifically because of its imposed sense of discipline, its fidelity to pattern: "Life was all pattern and discipline and the beauty of discipline is when it works. . . ." Pattern, however, is another, more sophisticated euphemism for role, and that which the brotherhood assigned to enforce obedience was far more encompassing than those previously encountered down south. The rational restructuring of society —the aims of the brotherhood—meant also the rational structuring of individual conscience, the permanent loss of freedom, identity, and racial bonds; the assignment to a lifetime of invisibility. For Blacks, it meant, the acceptance of the will of other men, complete abandonment for all times of individuality and responsibility, the personification of the image of the docile, helpless ward.

Tod Clifton somehow recognizes this fact, deserts the organization, and steps outside of history. In a liberating gesture, in an act of repentance for having accepted the brotherhood's theology, he sells sambo dolls on a street corner—parodies of his own self-hated image. Having been torn between the ideology of the brotherhood and that of Ras, between actuality and illusion, he accepted illusion; thus his penance is the selling of dancing dolls, which cavort and grin at the pleasure of the string puller and, finally, death at the hands of the police. The protagonist reaches Clifton's point of awareness much later, through events both symbolic and actual. He discovers that the chairman of the brotherhood, Brother Jack, the apostle of scientific determinism, of discipline and rationality, has a glass eye, symbolizing not only the blindness of the brotherhood, but the hollowness of such concepts as well. Actual awareness comes about, when, in an attempt to escape the followers of Ras, he assumes the guise of Rhinehart, numbers runner, pimp, jackleg minister, and briber—a man capable of being all things to all men. In this experience, where he is mistaken for Rinehart by a number of people, he becomes cognizant for the first time of the fluidity of the black world, realizes, too, the absurdity of the theology of scientific determinism in human affairs: Life was fluid and real and for black people, more so than for any others, one of unlimited possibilities.

Rank *Invisible Man* among the twenty best novels published in the last thirty years. It is rich in imagery, myth, and legend, adorned with suggestive, figurative language, and infused with the wealthy language and life-style of a people. Like Baldwin's *Go Tell It on the Mountain* and John Killen's *Youngblood,* the novel is primarily concerned with the education of its protagonist whose growth from innocence to maturity involves a journey through American stereotypes and images. As such, the novel looks ahead to the seventies, to writers equally intent upon recreating the legends, myths, and folklore of a people.

Though the strength, vitality, and beauty of the novel derives from its subject matter, race, critics, white and Black, with verbal assists from Ellison, argue that the novel is "one which moves beyond race" to deal with a common culture and to postulate the possibilities inherent in American society for all men, irrespective of race, religion, or color. The novel, in this analysis, manifests the frontier spirit as defined in the writings of Mark Twain, the theory of self-reliance as learned from Emerson, and the existentialism of Dostoevsky and Camus—all pointing toward man, not as a member of a specific racial or religious group, but as an individual. Thus Ras, in this view, is symbolic of an alien ideology, much like that represented by the Ku Klux Klan, offering values that black men, if they are to join the American mainstream, must denounce. This is a veiled argument for assimulationism— one which leaves out of consideration a great portion of the novel.

For to accept this view—and Ellison has done nothing to counteract it—is to suggest that the protagonist's journey through history has been in vain, his descent underground, futile. The values he seeks are not to be found in his own cultural history and heritage, but in that of a nation which purports to be one, indivisible, sans specific races or cultures. To accept this thesis is to accept a narrow view of art. For art is as much a celebration of the racial heritage as it is of life, and black life, even within the limitations of oppression, is rich in heritage and culture. *Invisible Man* sanctions this argument by contrasting the values of oppressed and oppressor. Thus two value systems are operative: one, the possession of those who have moved out or been forced to move outside American history; the other, the possession of those trapped within it. The values of tenderness, humaneness, hope, and promise, those which concern man as a human entity, are possessed only by certain black characters in the novel. To them is awarded courage and dignity under fire, the existential attempt to carve meaning out of absurdity. Look again at the portrait of the slave who finds love and hate in a world where hatred is the norm; at the insane who discover joy in a joyless society; at the Bledsoes, even, the self-centered men, struggling to retain power within a closed society; at the idealism of a Tod Clifton; at the concern of a Mary Rambo for the human condition, and here, the moral ethic is personified; the black men and women of *Invisible*

Man are universal symbols of man's desire to retain his humanity even under the most severe oppression.

No such argument can be made for the white characters. Look at the men who fill the hall where the smoker takes place; look at Norton, young Emerson, Brother Jack, the white women who offer their bodies to the protagonist—no redeeming human quality is to be found. Each character is obsessed with his own ego; each suffers from personal sickness; each is a victim of fantasy and illusion. Norton has an Oedipal attachment to his daughter; young Emerson hates and fears his father. The women are depicted as sex starved and frustrated, and Brother Jack evidences the worst characteristics of rational man: cold, pragmatic, concerned not with human improvement, but with power. Each is, therefore, a victim of his own history and culture. None are free to experience the immense possibilities of life, to step outside the confines of their own history, to view the world as a new frontier, or life itself, as cause for celebration. Their history is the record of man's transformation from humanist to machine man; their legends are used up, their myths destroyed, their creativity stifled. Placed alongside those to whom the Christian God never came, they resemble nothing so much as pagans, knowing neither their god nor his offspring. Their history and culture have left them in a world bounded by walls of narrow parochialism.

Given this analysis of *Invisible Man,* the central flaw in the character of the protagonist, that which mars an otherwise superb novel, is to be attributable more to Ellison's political beliefs than to artistic deficiency. For given the contrast between the two worlds, that of whites and that of Blacks, the protagonist is unable to discover his identity in the world of promise and hope, is content to hang, symbolically, midway between paradise and hell, when he might leave his underground sanctuary and emerge as a black man. Like the hero of *The Autobiography of An Ex-Coloured Man,* Ellison's protagonist chooses death over life, opts for non-creativity in favor of creativity, chooses the path of individualism instead of racial unity.

It is this choice, individualism as opposed to racial unity, that forms the connecting link between Ellison and the European existentialists and makes him one with James Baldwin. He has bought the propaganda of the academic critics, accepted the image of the faceless, universal man, trapped in the narrow world of his own ego. He has accepted, as well, the modern idea of a raceless world, despite the fact that those who have proposed such an existential solution to the problems of human kind have never stepped outside of their own race, religion, or nationality. Faulkner remained a champion of white supremacy until his death; Camus and Malraux fervent advocates of French hegemony. Neither attempted to move beyond race or nationality, neither thought of himself as an individual—as opposed to the collective entity. Whenever the interests of the race or nation were threatened, each opted for the race or nation, not for the individual, and refused to move beyond "the narrow parochialism" of nation or race.

Ellison's tendency to act the role of Rhinehart to his white critics and supporters, however, cannot be made to obscure the importance of *Invisible Man*. For despite its assimilationist denouement—Ellison's social and political credo—the novel remains a remarkable one and anticipates much of the creative direction of the coming years. The heroism and courage of the racial past, the pomp and pageantry to be found in racial customs, the richness of varying life-styles, and the struggle of men and women to escape the limiting definitions of outsiders—this is the fruit of *Invisible Man*.

If the "real" Ralph Ellison is to be found in the pages of *Invisible Man,* and not in the rhetoric of his public and critical documents, the obverse is true for his contemporary, James Baldwin (1924–   ). Baldwin is as much a product of the civil rights movement of the fifties and sixties as he is of the voluminous collection of works that have helped to establish his literary reputation. Long before much of America read *Notes of a Native Son,* the sensitive, pained face of Baldwin graced the TV networks, and in eloquent, concise diction, he presented the black man's indictment against America. Such public exposure clouded critical perspectives in relationship to Baldwin's works; the one-to-one correlation between the rhetorician and writer was made, the words and phrases uttered in debates and news conferences obscuring, all too often, careful attention to the words and phraseology in the writing itself. As a result, the real James Baldwin has remained buried in ambiguity for over ten years.

The history of black literary criticism holds few ironies equal to this: Ralph Ellison, whose works are counteropposed to the theories of the modern-day imagists, has come under fire from Black Aestheticians, mainly because of his rhetoric, while James Baldwin, whose works support much of the propaganda of white image makers, past and present, has been praised, primarily because of his rhetorical statements. Eldridge Cleaver, whose essay, "Notes on a Native Son," contains a great deal of nonsensical bombast, was among the first to recognize an important aspect of Baldwin's works. Observed Cleaver: Baldwin is guilty of a profound hatred of Blacks and a "shameful, fanatical, fawning sycophantic love of the whites." It is possible now, after the tumult of the sixties, to examine more closely Baldwin's celebrated rage and to conclude that it was always a personal rage, one more concerned with the individual "I" than the collective "we," a rage born at times out of a subconscious desire to be, if not white, then, certainly, less black. ". . . the most crucial time in my own development," he writes, "came when I was forced to recognize that I was a kind of bastard of the West; when I followed the lines of my past I did not find myself in Europe but in Africa."[9]

Here begins the narrative of cultural ambiguity leading to the conclusion that the artifacts of Western culture ". . . were not really my creations; they did not contain my history; I might search in vain forever for any reflection of myself. I was an interloper; this was not my heritage. At the same time I had no other heritage which I could possibly hope to use—I had certainly been unfitted for the jungle or the tribe. I would have to appropriate these white centuries. I would have to make them mine." What this meant was that eventually the cultural interloper would arrive at the conclusion that a hatred of black people was based, perhaps, upon the fact that they had not created the cultural artifacts of the West "because they failed to produce Rembrandt."[10] The ignorance of black history and culture, the condescending, negative criticism of the ancestral home, the contempt for Blacks based upon the same criteria as that used by whites, the obsession with expropriating the artifacts of another culture, and the oneness of thought with those from Thomas Jefferson to Daniel Moynihan who regard Blacks as bastards of the West—illegitimate people at best, interlopers at worst—these are the themes that pervade the essays and novels of James Baldwin.

Undoubtedly, his own life experiences have contributed greatly to his observations and beliefs, and these experiences are honestly depicted in three volumes of essays and an autobiographical novel. Here is depicted also the terrible tension in Baldwin's life and work: the refusal to accept his status as a black man equal to Euro-American man and an obsession to claim European history and culture as his own. The tension has led him to view Blacks in the images prescribed by whites; at one time they are seen as victims of the American social system; at another, as saviors of Western civilization. This tension is nowhere evidenced more so than in *Another Country* (1962), where Baldwin surrenders to the American image makers and joins in sanctioning images and symbols, now created anew, by white nationalists of the modern era.

Another Country marks a detour from the path charted in varying degrees by Wright and Ellison. The novel evidences a tendency on the part of the author to return to themes of yesteryear. Wright offered an image of Blacks as embittered and rebellious; Ellison added other dimensions: intellect and creativity. In both cases the image that predominates is one of man outside the hypocrisy and pretensions of a corrupt society. With Baldwin, however, the black novel travels back to the worst of the assimilationists, moves, in creation of images, to the primitivism of Carl Van Vechten, and compliments the literary propaganda of white liberals and the Communist party. His idea of the black world as atavistic and sensational owes much to the rhetoric of Van Vechten and his modern-day sympathizers, and the image of the black man as the Christ figure is a product of the Communist and liberal rhetoric of the thirties and forties.

Another Country, essentially the story of jazz musician, Rufus Scott, supports each of these assertions. Scott is led to take his own life as a result of the degradation imposed by his black skin, the inability of his white friends to understand and to love him, and as a result of his own self-shame and hatred. He is incapable of existing in a world alone, of carrying the heavy burden of blackness, and thus, without love and support, has become one of the fallen, one of the crushed. ". . . Entirely alone, and dying of it, he was part of an unprecedented multitude."[11] The Rufus Scott confronted in the beginning of the novel has traveled the gamut from happiness to despair, been brought low, and stands badly in need of human companionship. When he plunges off of the George Washington Bridge, what appears to be suicide is actually murder; Rufus has been murdered by an uncaring, unfeeling white society. For such unconcern—defined by Baldwin alternately as innocence and human ignorance—the society, or its representatives, must pay. *Another Country* thus becomes a novel of vengeance and redemption.

Book One of this three-part novel establishes the outlines of the plot, introduces the reader to victim and victimizer, hints at vengeance and redemption to come. The trip to suicide/murder begins for Rufus when he meets Leona, white Southerner, who deserts her husband and comes north. The relationship that rapidly develops into sadomasochism reveals Rufus's lack of self-confidence and hints at the paranoia engendered by his black skin. Real or imagined altercations with neighbors, landlords, and visitors to Greenwich Village, where the couple lives, force Rufus to a recognition of his own impotence: Unlike his friend Vivaldo, he is unable to protect his white girlfriend. "The lowest whore in Manhattan would be protected as long as she had Vivaldo on her arm. This was because Vivaldo was white."

Rufus, however, is not white and animosity and hostility are directed toward him because of his relationship with Leona. The white woman becomes, therefore, an object of the rage and fury he is unable to unleash upon the white world. But she is merely the object; at the core of the musician's rage is an inability to accept the fact that he is equal to white men, to arrive at a definition of himself outside that vouchsafed by the white world. This inability on his part has led to fear, bitterness, and hatred, and pushes him toward physical brutality against this symbol of his oppression, brings him low, and makes it impossible for others to understand him. He is the mystical problem child, the worst personification of the images produced in the fiction of white writers, lacking even the nobility that rage produces in Joe Christmas, to be compared to William Styron's Nat Turner—a man embittered not because of racial oppression against his people, but against that fate which made him Black and, consequently, one of the fallen multitude.

The love-hate relationship between the two results in a nervous breakdown for the girl. She is remanded to her family, forced to make the trek back to the South, and disappears from the pages of *Another Country,* assigned the fate of staring "at the walls of a narrow room; she would remain there forever." Leona gone, Rufus begins the final descent into despair and degeneracy. He disappears from the village, lives on scraps and handouts, prostitutes himself in homosexual relationships, and acknowledges his hatred of whites: "How I hate them— all those white sons of bitches out there. They're trying to kill me— they got the world on a string . . . and they tying that string around my neck, they killing me."[12] The string is tightened even more severely on the night of his return from the underground existence, and he plunges, headfirst, off the George Washington Bridge. His is a death that need not have been. Suicide is the term used; given the fact, however, that his death might have been prevented, that it was, at least, gratuitous, suicide might be defined as murder resulting from the inability of one man, white, to love another, Black. On that fateful night, two people, both white, might have prevented Rufus's death. Yet, neither Vivaldo Moore nor Cass Silenski were capable of understanding the depth of his despair, could make the transcendental leap across the prism of their own egos to offer the proper comfort and understanding.

Vivaldo Moore, a writer, whose inability to perceive Rufus's discomfort is highlighted by his failure to understand the characters in his novel, is the jazz musician's closest friend. The two shared board, bed, and girls together, and developed a relationship that "transcends" race. On the night Rufus returns from isolation, his thoughts are directed toward Vivaldo, "the only friend he had left in the city, or maybe in the world. . . ." Though not as close a friend as Vivaldo, Cass has managed to gain the affection of Rufus through acts of kindness and friend-ship. Middle class, married to a writer, Richard who has prostituted his art by publishing pulp material instead of a serious novel, she too is so preoccupied with her own concerns that she is unable to divine the needs of Rufus. On the fateful night of his death, therefore, his white friends desert him: Vivaldo, to shack up with his girlfriend, Jean; Cass, after giving Rufus money, accompanies her husband home. Much later, in hindsight, Cass sounds the cryptic note of the novel: "I wonder if there was anything—we—any—one—could have done."[13]

This note is echoed later in the comments of Vivaldo and Eric Jones, the absent protagonist, who shares top billing along with Rufus in the novel. Subconsciously each of his friends acknowledges guilt for his death—guilt occasioned by unknowing, which, for Baldwin, might be defined as innocence. Such innocence, historically, has led the Rufus Scotts of the world to an unnecessary doom, and for this, as it is in the Old Testament, the sinner must pay. The structure of the novel be-comes apparent. Rufus, dead, remains the center of consciousness for each of the characters, exerting a power over their lives he had not exerted before his death. For the remainder of the novel, he will haunt the memories and actions of all those who had known and failed him, of Cass and Vivaldo, of Eric and, to an extent, of Richard.

The influence from beyond the grave, however, takes on corpo-real form in the person of the musician's sister. Ida Scott is the instru-ment of vengeance and redemption. Embittered by the death of her brother, she establishes a relationship with Vivaldo, whom she meets at Rufus's funeral. The relationship, consummated in Book One by sexual intercourse, results in a common-law-marriage situation. Beau-tiful and wise beyond her years, talented as a singer, she becomes the black in-residence for the white people in the novel. She reminds them of their sins against Blacks, is the conscience of those who have little conscience, the eyes for those who cannot see. She blames the death of her brother upon Cass and Vivaldo, and her motivation for seeking revenge is summed up near the end of the narrative: "I felt that I'd been robbed. And I *had* been robbed—of the only hope I had. By a group of people too cowardly even to know what they had done."[14]

The means of exacting revenge—having an affair with a TV pro-ducer, intended to infuriate Vivaldo, and lectures on the plight of Blacks designed to shame Cass—throw the novel into utter confusion. The whites must not only be punished, but robbed of their innocence as well, made to acknowledge the instability of the world in which they live. Sin must be avenged, but the sinner must be redeemed, the fallen resurrected; reality must replace illusion, and for Baldwin there are two poles of reality in the Western world—one occupied by Blacks, the other by homosexuals. Both are Darwinian mutants, the new people whose modes of living and capacity for understanding make them the logical antithesis to a nation of people grown comfortable and uncaring as a result of materialism and technology.

Dunbar's *Sport of the Gods* and Van Vechten's *Nigger Heaven* are literary antecedents of *Another Country*. Both depicted the "underground existence" of Blacks and suggested the two-tier structure of the American society: Blacks constituted one layer! Because of their underground status, they were centers of knowledge and awareness; they knew the fundamental art of survival, were capable of living a life of sensationalism and atavism, despite the terrible American ordeal. The other layer is comprised of whites, those above ground, who have lost the natural lust for things of pleasure—for jazz and sex, and for laughter through pain. In modern terms, they are the squares who having strayed from their primitive state are unconsciously striving to return to it. The images derived from those who comprise this societal structure—Lasca Sartoris and the Scarlet Creeper—with few exceptions, disappeared from the fiction of black writers until James Baldwin who, at the height of the civil rights movement, updated them in ways that would have astonished even Van Vechten. He added dimensions derived from the existential jargon of the American and European writers and, in so doing, prophesied the hippie generation, some few years in the future. Blacks, the centers of knowing, therefore, are differentiated from, and awarded greater status than, whites, the innocents, who desire to do something "dirty and they knew that you knew how. All black people knew that." Yet contradictorily, there arises in the novel, the note of black salvation, the idea that perhaps whites might rescue Blacks from the dirt and degradation of life: "I've often wished," Ida tells Vivaldo, "you'd left me where I was. . . . Down there in the jungle, black and funky—and myself."[15]

The comparison between blackness and the darker side of Homo sapiens is not new: Examples can be found in Greek and Roman philosophy, in biblical canon, in the works of thinkers from Count Gobineau to Bertrand Russell. In this association, which borders everywhere on Freudian psychology, the desire for sexual freedom is universal. Blacks—and Mailer's image in "The White Negro" is a good example—are walking phallic symbols, denizens of the regions of sex and lewdness, where "dirty things" are not only practiced but accorded the status of respectability. They are distinguished from whites, therefore, by a greater degree of freedom, a greater knowledge of jazz, drugs, and sex. The things that Rufus Scott knows—the dark mysteries of such jungles as Harlem—Ida, a black woman, victim of black and white males, knows even better.

More so than any of his contemporaries, Baldwin has accepted the prevailing negative stereotypes of Blacks—the debasing, inhumane images—and attempted to tar them with the brush of grandeur. Their atavistic characteristics, on the other hand, are directly related to their treatment as Blacks in America: "They keep you here," Ida explains Harlem to Cass, "because you're Black. . . ." To be born Black is, at one and the same time, damnation and salvation, and the white world, if it is to confront its own atavistic yearnings, must acknowledge this creation of its darker personality. Only those, therefore, who are willing to make such a confrontation, of delving into the world of sex and atavism, of knowing the terrible penalties—and rewards—occasioned by being Black, are capable of resurrection.

Despite the assertions of white critics, *Another Country* is not an avowal of Baldwin's hostility and rage against whites; rage and hostility there is, but it is due to the fact that he is not accepted by whites, even though he has accepted *their* definitions and stereotypes of other Blacks. He is steeped in the literature of Henry James, Dostoevsky, Camus, and Hemingway; yet, neither in the novels nor the essays does he evidence knowledge of the history and culture of black people. Of black history, he is totally ignorant, and of black writers before Richard Wright, oblivious. It is ignorance that has led Baldwin to argue the theory of societal determinism in a way that those black writers who ascribed, in part, to the naturalist position did not. Rufus and Ida, computerized artifacts, owe their being to the American society, have no identity so long as it withholds acceptance. Yet to be accepted by such as Cass is to be accepted by squares, by the damned, by those who are punished for not knowing: "How," asks Cass, "can you blame us if we don't know?" The confusion is germane to Cass and reader alike. Whites are unable to regard Blacks as human beings because they can never know what it means to be Black; yet, for not knowing the unknowable, they are censured anyway. What is evident, therefore, is need on the part of the author for recognition and acceptance by whites. This need makes *Another Country* a very personal and a very private novel; it is Baldwin's most articulate plea for love and understanding from his fellow white Americans.

Whatever promise Baldwin might have evidenced after *Go Tell It on the Mountain* (1953) is questionable after *Another Country*. In the latter he has recreated the black protest novel, sought to make black once again a vehicle for raising the awareness of white people. For, more so than *The Fire Next Time* (1963), *Another Country* is an epistle addressed to whites, warning them that their cathedrals, time honored by history, face ruination at the hands of savages, that salvation for the society at large is possible only after the savages are redeemed, scrubbed clean of blackness, and allowed to integrate into the modern world. Like the old evangelical preacher, Baldwin seduces and threatens his flock; he admonishes them to join the church of the Christ militant, to move among the sinners and proselytize in order to bring others to the tabernacle of the Lord. There is too the dire prediction of things to come: If men forego the opportunity to erect the new Canaan, they face the coming day of vengeance and recrimination of death, doom, and destruction. Thus strip away the more sensational features of *Another Country,* and the integrationist ethic is revealed; to be elevated to human kind, Blacks must be made one with the society, must desert the legacy of the cultural past.

The contemporary black writer, however, was likely to bury his *Another Country,* to ridicule its example, both in terms of its integrationist denouement and its distortion of images and symbols. He was more likely to adopt the position that literature and politics were antipodal arms one of the other and that the function of the black novelist was not to educate white people but to liberate Blacks. In so doing he moved toward a literary creed based upon the tenets of Black Nationalism and the works of a group of young critics, called, in some quarters, Black Aestheticians, offered assurance that the move would continue. The critical writings of Askia Muhammed Toure, Imamu Baraka, Maylama Karenga, George Kent, Stephen Henderson, and Hoyt Fuller, to name but a few, evidence the change in literary perception since *Another Country.* In varying ways, each of these critics conceives of a literature whose major preoccupation is to make black people in America aware of the fact that Blacks, wherever they are, are an African people.

X

WHITE NATIONALISM

The anthology *Black Fire* (1968), by Imamu Baraka (Leroi Jones) and Larry Neal, was one of the more important publications in the new era of black literature. Like its predecessors, *The New Negro* (1925) and *The Book of American Negro Poetry* (1922), it was a guideline for the new literature which broke with many of the treasured standards of the past. Included among such standards was that which restricted the dimension of a work of art by defining the term. The critic Robert Bone writes: "Art is not life; it is not a branch of politics; it is not to be used as a front for any cause however just. Art is a different kind of human activity from politics—more or less valuable, depending on one's point of view—but in any case different." The critic moves from this premise to lecture the black writer: "To respect this distinction is the beginning of wisdom for the Negro novelist. The color line exists not between the covers of a book but outside, in the real world. . . . Let the Negro novelist as citizen, as political man, vent his fury and indignation through the appropriate protest organizations, but as novelist, as artist, let him pursue his vision, his power of seeing and revealing, which is mankind's rarest gift."[1]

Black Fire was the black writers' answer to the arrogant assumption of white critics that they might continue to define the terms by which others came to grips with the world they lived in. Fundamentally, the book was a coming to age of a literary movement, which owed much to the novels of John Killens, William Melvin Kelley, and Richard Wright, to the poetry of Askia Muhummed Toure, Don L. Lee, Sonia Sanchez, and Ishmael Reed, to the publishing ventures of such magazines as *Liberator, Umbra, Journal of Negro Poetry,* and *Negro Digest* (now *Black World*), and to the establishment of Imamu Baraka's Black Arts Repertory Theater in Harlem in 1954.

The Black Arts Theater project was short-lived; yet, like the magazines, it provided an invaluable training ground for new black writers, many of whose works were represented in *Black Fire*. Situated in Harlem, the theater brought the artist into direct contact with black people, thus erasing the usual line existing between artist and public. This proximity of the artist to his people made for perceptions impossible to achieve from an isolated position in a studio apartment downtown or in a suburban home. The experience of knowing empirically the subjects of his work forced the black writer to the conclusion that a unity existed between himself and black people, unparalleled by that between any other groups in the American society; he discovered, if he did not already know, that their pain and laughter were his and that their courage and strength under siege were the most universal traits of man. In all of this, he gained a most valuable insight into White Nationalism.

These were sophisticated men and women of great talent; many had been lauded by the black press. All were familiar with more overt forms of White Nationalism—that displayed in the propaganda of such as Harris, Page, the Communist party, and white liberals, which sought to control and define Blacks by manipulating the images, symbols, and metaphors of their experiences. Yet many had assumed that such activity was a relic of the past, that whites had begun to look at Blacks through different, less tinted glasses. What many began to realize in 1964, and what all acknowledged by 1968, was that white nationalists had only shifted their propagandistic emphasis, not discontinued previous practices, and moved now with more zeal than before to destroy the new black consciousness coming to growth in the nineteen fifties and sixties.

Definitions are in order. White Nationalism is a subtle or overtly held belief in the superiority and dominance of the cultural artifacts of men of white ancestry over those of peoples of different skin color. Colonialism and racism are synonyms. Their guiding ethos is the belief that white people are "God's chosen people." It is supported by militancy which takes the form of oppression, condescension, and pretension. Its major text of reference is the Bible, its major medium of propagation, Western culture; its adherents are united in their universal contempt for people with different color and culture, and it operates on what might be called the identification theory of history. The premise is here advanced that the great achievements of man, in the arts, sciences, literature, medicine, etc., were made by whites. Thus even the most ignorant, non-productive, non-creative white claim a kinship with those who achieved in the different areas, might be said to identify, on the basis of skin color, with artists and statesmen. Not only whites, but some Blacks, have accepted the superiority-by-identification theory. Writes Baldwin: "These people [white villagers] have made the modern world, in effect, even if they do not know it. The most illiterate among them is related, in a way that I am not, to Dante, Shakespeare, Michelangelo, Aeschylus, Da Vinci, Rembrandt, and Racine. . . ."[2]

Believing in such a theory, men like Ronald Berman are able to speak of Blacks in America as residents of ". . . a community of the lost"; to assert that the black condition is adequately depicted in such texts as *Manchild in the Promised Land* and *Another Country,* and to argue that Blacks are more morally corrupt than whites; intellectually, more backward, much more insensitive to others; and much more brutal. This community of the lost, therefore, is "an irremedial community" inhabited by a form of life that "is, finally, separate and invincible to *our* [italics mine] pieties."[3]

The virus of White Nationalism is spread through such instruments as guns, tanks, images, and symbols. It was advanced by colonial powers—English, French, German, and Belgium—during the eighteenth and nineteenth centuries, first by forces of arms, and then by the Bible, which pointed up the difference between the images of the oppressed and those of the oppressor. Total victory was not complete, however, until the colonialists had established educational institutions which mandated that the subject people replace their own cultural artifacts—religion, history, literature—with those of the nationalists. Blacks who adopted the symbols of nationalism—dress, manner, speech, disdain for their fellows—were made partners, of sorts, in white nationalist ventures and often became the most ardent defenders and rabid propagators of the faith.

The colonialist experience was refined by the American nationalists. After slavery, the method of subjugation was almost totally one of propaganda. Guns and tanks were always available, mobs ready and at hand. To continue the subjugation of black people, however, white nationalists in America relied heavily upon manipulation of images, defining definitions, and committing acts of historical distortion. The black man's inhumanity was not only the central argument of the men of old, the southern defenders of slavery, but even more so, it is of primary importance to the nationalists of the contemporary era, of such as Berman, Norman Mailer, Irving Howe, Robert Bone, and William Styron, men whose writings have raised anew the banner of white supremacy and black inferiority. Descendants of the Harrises, Dixons, Pages, Lindsays, and Van Vechtens, their task, in the America of the latter part of the twentieth century, was no less important than that of their historical counterparts—to propagandize the virtues of White Nationalism by any means necessary. For these modern-day propagators of the faith, literature was, also, their medium.

The reaction by Blacks, however, as evidenced by *Black Fire* and the Black Repertory Theater in the cultural and political arena, was more pronounced than in days of the past. The artistic movement of the sixties, the cultural arm of the Black Power revolution, began the most determined assault upon White Nationalism in American history. Believing that one cannot divorce politics from art, the black writer accepted the critical findings of such men as Karenga, Fuller, and Lee, which argued that art must be, not only political, but functional and relevant to a particular people in a particular society. They moved to accommodate and complement the activities of such activists as H. Rap Brown, Malcolm X, and Stokely Carmichael and, as the drama and poetry of the years between 1965 and 1972 illustrate, evidenced in both the cultural and political sphere a profound knowledge of the meanings, operations, and dangers of White Nationalism. From this perspective, Imamu Baraka writes in 1970; "We are not Black Nationalists because of the devil, we would be Nationalists if no devil ever existed."

In the latter part of the twentieth century, therefore, the stage was set for a full-scale war between the proponents of White Nationalism, those who believed in man's dominance by men of white pigmentation, and Black Nationalists, those who believed in the natural right of the freedom of all men. Echoes of the battle still resound, even after the abortive move for civil rights in the last fifteen years. Despite the failures of the civil rights movement, without it, the hope-filled years between 1954 and 1965, the crucial confrontation, might not have come. Those were the years when men sought not to destroy evil, but to reach an accommodation with it, not to demand an end to the excesses of White Nationalism in the interests of humanity, but in the interests of themselves and their progeny. They were, for the most part, young and idealistic, mainly interested in reform, in making technical changes here and there in the existing order. Their great mistake—and that which led to the many failures of the movement—was to underestimate the tenacity of White Nationalism and its appeal to the majority of white Americans.

The civil rights movement of the fifties and sixties may be divided into two phases. The first is characterized by those who believed the impossible dream, who thought that accommodation with White Nationalism was possible. Their beliefs were strengthened by the Supreme Court decision in Brown *versus* Board of Education. This phase came to an abrupt close in 1965 during the Meredith March, when the phrase Black Power was articulated by the young men and women of SNCC and CORE, and is characterized by the knowledge that one cannot make an accommodation with the forces of evil, nor barter manhood rights for intangible gains.

Despite its failure, the first phase was a gallant effort to temper the excesses of White Nationalism. Riding home from a day's work on December 1, 1955, Mrs. Rosa Parks was not interested in forcing a confrontation with White Nationalism. She was intent only on sitting in the one available seat on a segregated bus in Montgomery, Alabama. This simple act of defiance, of heroism, given the place and circumstances, was instrumental in ushering in the age of mass demonstrations and freedom rides, of interjecting, briefly, into American history, a sense of courage and decency. Equally as important, the act of rebellion projected Martin Luther King, Jr., upon the national stage, gave new stature to such organizations as the NAACP, CORE, and the Urban League, and enhanced the prestige of others like SNCC and the Nation of Islam. Indirectly, the act paved the way for the elimination of most legal segregation from the South, the success of the Black Power movement, and the emergence of Malcolm X and the Nation of Islam as forces in African-American life. In addition, the act produced, what Martin Luther King, Jr., called "a new dignity" among black people. After the battles waged throughout the South, after confronting mobs of vigilantes, sheriffs, deputies, and dogs, after the deaths of men, women, and children, a new meaning was added to the term heroism by men and women who became paradigms of determination and hope for black writer and black populace alike.

Their appeals to conscience, however, availed little, and their heroism is marked more by the courage of the fine men and women who participated in the movement than by a few, mostly intangible, gains. William Miller offers these incomplete casualty statistics: "Sylvester Maxwell was castrated, multilated, and lynched in Madison County. . . . SNCC worker James Travis was wounded by gunfire. . . . Dewey Greene's home was fired into by a shotgun. In Clarksdale, a negro drugstore was smashed. . . ."[4] Add to this number the dead and mutilated, Mack

Parker, Jimmy Lee Jackson, James Reeb, Viola Liuzzo, Chaney, Goodman, and Schwerner, four children in Birmingham, Medgar Evers, the unnamed bodies found floating in the Mississippi River, and, finally, the murder of Martin Luther King, Jr., himself, and the balance sheet in terms of progress remains blatantly unequal.

The pragmatic gains of the movement by no stretch of the imagination justify such violence, though black and white historians are all too ready to hail as remarkable the gaining of access to white-owned lunch counters and stores by Blacks and the outlawing of discrimination in transportation and voter registration. Such "achievements" did nothing to change the basic power relationship between Blacks and whites, meant very little for poor Blacks, north or south, in terms of better living conditions, and made no lasting impression upon the disciples of White Nationalism. In a sane universe, the death of four black children is a ridiculous price to pay for the integration of a restaurant! The real gains, as Martin Luther King, Jr., realized, lay elsewhere: "Our real victory is not so much the desegregation of the buses as it is a new sense of dignity and destiny."[5] He explains further: ". . . the resounding shout of the Negroes' protest had shattered the myth of his contentment. The courage with which he confronted enraged mobs dissolved the stereotype of the grinning, submissive Uncle Tom. Indeed, by the end of a turbulent decade there was a new quality to Negro life. The Negro was no longer a subject of change; he was the active organ of change."[6]

The death of the old images and symbols, in the minds of most black people, was not due solely to the activities of the southern legions of Martin King. Equally important were those men and women in the urban areas of America for whom the tangible gains of the Southern Crusade meant very little, the intangible gains a great deal. The men and women who participated in the rebellions of the latter sixties in America's major cities were no less heroic than those who marched from Montgomery to Cicero, and it is due to their heroism that the new phase began. They were spurred by the same sense of dignity and pride, motivated by the same desire for freedom from oppression, as were their southern counterparts, and as instrumental in forging a new sense of pride among African-Americans. In the memories of black people, their battlefields are as famous as those upon which King's legions marched: Harlem, Jersey City, Watts, Detroit, Newark, and Washington, D.C. In the area of violent confrontation—an attempt to limit the oppression of White Nationalism —they differed from the Southerners. The men who followed Martin King were non-violent practitioners; they were dedicated to a philosophy that argued that containment of violence could result from self-sacrifice and, in too many cases, self-prostration. The men and women in the urban areas realized with Frantz Fanon that violence can be ended only by violence and that, in a world ruled by white men, non-violence was a dangerous philosophy, one which did not limit violence but encouraged it.

The movements, north and south, prepared the way for the Black Power revolution, an old philosophy dressed in modern garb. For black people the concept needs no definition or explication. Go back to the Animal Tales, those relics of a far-way African ancestry. The symbolic confrontation between master and slave evolves around black power; in their militant beauty, the spirituals advance no themes so fundamental as black power, and the concept is alive in the oratorical literature of such giants as Garnet, Douglass, and Remond. Even in the poetry and novels of those infiuenced by Western ideology, the concept is a constant theme, ranging with varying emphasis from George Moses Horton to Langston Hughes, from Martin Delany to Richard Wright.

As I have written previously: "Dig deep into the rhetoric of black power, and you will unearth a world in which men of all ethnic, racial, and religious groups live together in a communal society, share communal affluence, and sup from a communal trough. Its adherents prophesy the day of the coming millennium when the existence of the millionaire and the hungry man will have come to an end, when no man will live in a mansion or a rat-infested tenement, when no man will possess more of the earth's bounties than his neighbors." Moral in tone and intent, black power envisions a world far different than that constructed by the Euro-Americans, one which encourages man's faith and belief in man.

Black power, therefore, not only represented a turning point for the civil rights movement in America, but it sounded the gong for the opening round in the battle against White Nationalism and had international as well as national importance. The concept spoke to the needs of the oppressed throughout the world, and its proponents attempted to forge a common bond of unity between themselves and those whom Fanon has called the wretched of the earth. The cardinal tenet of the concept, stated by Carmichael and Hamilton, has been sanctioned by revolutionaries everywhere: ". . . we must first redefine ourselves. Our basic need is to reclaim our history and our identity from what must be called cultural terrorism, from the depredation of self-justifying white guilt. We shall have to struggle for the right to create our own terms through which to define ourselves and our relationship to the society, and to have these terms recognized. This is the first necessity of a free people, and the first right that any oppressor must suspend."[7]

The full dimensions of the war between the proponents of black power and White Nationalism in the cultural areas were not pronounced until after the successes of the new, young writers, whose works were published, mostly in black magazines, until Imamu Baraka deserted the East Village hippie cult for Harlem nor until publication of the book, *Black Fire*. The young writers of the sixties and seventies differed from their politically activist counterparts; they had no such armies as those led by King, possessed no organizational skills such as those possessed by the brilliant followers of Elijah Muhammad. Words were their chief weapons and, they came to realize, were used against them today as they had been used against their ancestors yesterday. Action followed realization!

As intensive, vigorous, and heroic the war being fought on the dust-caked roads of Albany, Georgia, and the asphalt streets of Newark, it was the wrong war, fought not against the major, but the minor, adversary. The Bull Connors and Sheriff Clarks were programmed men, acting more upon impulse than thought; they performed the roles layed out for them, attempted to force recalcitrant Blacks to adhere to the stereotypes of the past. They were unable to fathom these new Blacks, could not understand men and women so far outside the old images. Therefore, they resorted to the weapons which had proven successful in the past, to violence, terror, and murder. Nor were northern whites more prepared to deal with Blacks who projected images different from those fixed in white minds. The urban guerrillas were a more puzzling bunch than even their southern counterparts, willing to risk their lives and to undergo violent confrontation in the quest for liberty and dignity. When these Blacks, north and south, accepted Malcolm X, H. Rap Brown, and Stokely Carmichael as their heroes, opted for the theology of black power, adversaries more sophisticated than the Sheriff Clarks and Bull Connors entered the fray on behalf of White Nationalism. Their weapons, too, were words, and they used them unsparingly as they set about to undo the revolution in conscious awareness, brought about during past decades, in an attempt to bring back the years of the supremacy of the idea of white superiority and black inferiority.

Such men are legion in the minds of black writers and critics. Note among their number, Selden Rodman, Theodore Gross, Herbert Hill, Fred Ehrenfeld, Richard Gilman, Louis Simpson, and Norman Podhoretz. Primarily northern liberals, their books and articles in my opinion, attempted to negate the images of Blacks now being recreated in the streets of America and beamed to the world via television and radio. To the man, they adhered I believe to the definitions of old, were granted the status of prophets, mainly because they were Northerners, not Southerners, critics and professors, not red necks and laborers. What might be called their acts of castration were performed not in the dark of the dusk-clad night, but in the pages of *Commentary, Dissent,* and *The Atlantic Monthly.* Under the guise of artists and critics, they were, I suppose, intent upon the intellectual rape of a race of people, and the success of their efforts would come full blown in the nineteen seventies and the re-election of Richard Nixon. In all fairness, however, such men as the above-named, one might conjecture, were not creators or originators; they were followers, not leaders, men of lesser talent than those who began as early as the fifties to publicly champion the old images of Blacks. Of these latter, three stand out with more prominence than others. They are the logical descendants of the Van Vechtenites, Communists, and social writers, and among their many publications, "The White Negro" (1959), "Black Boys and Native Sons" (1963), and *The Confessions of Nat Turner* (1966) were the three designed to begin a return to the images and symbols of the white imagination.

"The White Negro" ranks among Norman Mailer's most popular essays. Frequently anthologized, published in both magazine and pamphlet format, it has found its way into the homes of students, laymen, professionals, and social planners alike. On the surface, the essay appears to argue for assimilationism, to suggest that an existential leap across the color line by Blacks and whites has occurred, that the age-old tendency of Blacks to conform to white images has been reversed, and that whites, instead, have accepted the images depicted by Blacks. Observations of the hip cult, the beat generation, the people who populate the novels of Jack Kerouac and James Baldwin provide the foundation for reflection upon the new transvestites—whites who wish to exchange their status for that of Blacks. It is the image Mailer draws of Blacks that forms the credo of his nationalist thought.

The brave men and women of King's army notwithstanding, the neat, professional members of the Nation of Islam to the contrary, the image of Blacks presented by Mailer in 1959 is the same as that presented in *Nigger Heaven* in 1926: "It is . . . no accident," he writes, "that psychopathy is most prevalent with the Negro. Hated from outside and therefore hating himself, the Negro was forced into the position of exploring all those moral wildernesses of civilized life which the square automatically condemns as delinquent or evil or immature or moribund or self-destructive or corrupt. . . . But the Negro, not being privileged

to gratify his self-esteem with the heady satisfactions of categorical condemnation, chose to move instead in that other direction where all
situations are equally valid, and in the worst of perversion, promiscuity,
pimpery, drug addiction, rape, razor slash, bottle-break, what-have
you, the Negro discovered and elaborated a morality of the bottom. . . ."[8]

Van Vechten did not go so far, and the reason was due not only to
the difference in genre. The earlier writer was more interested in producing counterimages to those proposed by the Garveyites, while
Mailer, the contemporary white liberal, is intent upon destroying a
movement as well, using art as a political instrument, warning white
Americans that despite the attacks upon American morality by such
as King, despite the paradigms of courage and endurance exhibited by
the freedom riders, sit-inners, and passive protesters, the image of
Blacks is represented best by those who subsist ". . . for their Saturday
night kicks, relinquishing the pleasure of the mind for the more obliga-
tory pleasures of the body. . . ."[9] The model for white Negroes, however, operates on a dual imagistic level. He symbolizes, on the one
hand, the utmost in depravity and perversion—"black as sin, black as
the devil"—while his knowledge of perversion and depravity make him
the twentieth-century Christ figure, capable of leading men not to the
contentment and complacency of heaven—which for Mailer resembles
a white middle-class surburban village—but to the excitement, terror,
and existential undertakings of hell. Through a metaphysical leap
which does credit to sophists of old, Mailer inverts the societal values,
giving to perversion, promiscuity, and degeneracy an *élan vital* of their
own, making of black people the truest metaphors of this substratum
of human existence. Clearly then, the black people who frequent the
imagination of Mailer, are pimps, prostitutes, sexual pariahs, purveyors
of jazz—the new religion—and self-haters, who differ from whites in
being, like Ida Scott, privy to the dark, dreaded desires of each human
heart: the acolytes of the religion of Satan, creating disciples by every
nuance of atavistic life-style from jazz to language: "Add to this the
cunning of their language, the abstract ambiguous alternatives in which
from the danger of their oppression they learned to speak 'Well, now,
man, like I'm looking for a cat to turn me on. . . .' add even more the
profound sensitivity of the Negro jazzman who was the cultural mentor
of a people, and it is not too difficult to believe that the language of Hip,
which evolved, was an artful language, tested and shaped by an intense
experience . . . was able to express the existential states of the enlisted man."[10]

The problem is not Mailer's fanciful (or fitful) imagination. What is plain is that his friendship with Baldwin has taught him little more about black people than friendship with Baldwin taught Styron. Mailer's is the same as that of the racists of old, with the exception, perhaps, that he believes his black charges are destined to undertake the white man's burden. It is equally clear to any black reader of the essay— even Baldwin found it obnoxious—that the author knows as little about the history of jazz as he does about the African-American life-style, that he is incapable of understanding the historical meaning of such black men as Carmichael, Brown, and Malcolm, that he must see them, through the limited prism of his own history, as admitted exceptions in contradistinction to the pimps and hustlers, who constitute the norm. It is not surprising, given this distorted vision of Blacks during the time of chaos and turmoil, that "The White Negro" became must reading in almost every college English course in America. And only those of little imagination could believe that the reason was that white professors were interested in propagating the ideas of black-white miscegenation. The reasons were far more sinister. Many agreed with the underlying theme of the essay, which advanced the argument anew that Blacks were sexual primitives and, given overdeveloped sexual instincts, coupled with limited intellectual capacity, added to a long-established reputation for immorality; therefore the cries of "integration by sixty-four" were not to be taken seriously; integration, after all, is possible only among moral equals.

Mailer took liberty to the point of arrogance with the history and culture of a people about whom he knew little, and this fact was ignored by the academicians. They accepted "The White Negro," for the most part, with the critical acclaim rendered *The Klansman,* despite structural flaws, overwriting, formalistic chaos, and inadequate research in the fields of jazz and history. Fidelity to form and historical accuracy, however, were deemed unimportant in evaluating this nonfictional work. What was more important was that, by recreating the image of old, the essay aided in distorting the images of young black men now being created in the literature and through the ordeal of the street. Given the choice between two images, the black man as moral anarchist, and the black man as moral example, white academicians opted for the former.

With the same lack of critical acumen or inquisitiveness, academicians embraced black images in the works of Irving Howe and William Styron. Unlike Styron and Mailer, Howe is one of the academicians' own stars. Not only does he hold professorial rank in a university, but he is a man of literary attainment, knowledgeable in the area of literary research in a way that Styron and Mailer are not. His friendship with Richard Wright led him to become incensed at the literature of Baldwin and Ellison: Neither, in Howe's opinion, paid proper respect, granted due credit to the example set for them by their onetime confidant. He wrote the essay "Black Boys and Native Sons" as a result— an essay whose ramifications extend beyond the area of literary criticism. Viewed carefully, the essay, which purports to defend Richard Wright, succeeds instead in propounding the worst of the American stereotypes—that of the bad nigger.

The major premise of the essay differs little from that of "The White Negro." White oppression has created a black man with clearly definable psychological traits. Unlike other Americans, he has been relegated to the status of a subhuman, and he exists in an environment where violence is the sine qua non of life: ". . . violence is a central fact in the life of the American Negro, defining and crippling him with a harshness few other Americans need suffer."[11] Grant this premise, and we are far here from the thesis proposed in Fanon's *Wretched of the Earth:* Violence serves as a cathartic, one capable of bringing forth revolutionaries, philosophers, and saints, as well as murderers, degenerates, and criminals. Yet the former roles are impossible for the black man in Howe's theology, for the violent nature of his life makes him one with Bigger Thomas: "Brutal and brutalized, lost forever to his unexpended hatred and his fear of the world, a numbed and illiterate black boy stumbling into a murder. . . ."[12]

Try as one might, it is difficult to correlate Howe's reality with that unfolding in the streets of America. By 1963, the civil rights movement had gathered full steam. Those Blacks attempting to inject a sense of morality and decency into American life were second cousins, if that, to Bigger Thomas as Howe conceived him. Subjected daily to violence on a mass—instead of as previously on an individual scale—theirs was the way not of the murderer but of the martyr. With remarkable creativity, they transformed the violence enacted against them into an instrument of passive resistance and achieved a sense of manhood and dignity, not through stumbling into murder, but by absorbing the worst of violence and terror. As representatives of "bad niggers," the civil rights demonstrators fared very badly. Howe's reality, however, is immune to alteration, even when his knowledge of black life is questioned: "Everybody," Ellison raised his voice in rebuttal to the essay, "wants to tell us what a Negro is, yet few wish, even in a joke, to be one. But if you would tell me who I am, at least take the trouble to discover what I have been."[13]

Ellison, whose rhetoric assumes a strident militancy whenever he is attacked personally, knows what the life of a black man "has been" and the black man who has emerged as a result: a product of diverse experiences, of a cultural tradition that has taught him to retain his sense of decency and humanity even in the face of violence, that has taught him ". . . to deflect racial provocation and to master and contain pain." The paradigm to be drawn from this description is not to be acknowledged by northern liberals, here, at this point of time. What is needed are counterimages, those of brutal and brutalized Blacks, which deny a common humanity and reduce the revolutionary to the status of a criminal. How else does one manage to obscure the past of Douglass and Brown, for example, or negate the present of Malcolm and Carmichael, men who thought of violence not as a brutalizing, but a liberating, norm? How else does one reinforce white egos and champion anew the white man's great burden—managing in the process to define "the nigger" again into his place—without adhering to the stereotype of either the black man as sexual terror or black brute?

Howe is enamored of his own vision, and no number of rebuttals can alter his reality. The Black of his fantasy is one who grew up in oppressive America as a subhuman animal, desperate and hating, part man, part beast who, by being such, evidences the power of white America, to make black men into what it wishes—Christ figures or Bigger Thomases: "What then," asks Howe, "was the experience of a man with a black skin, what could it be in this country?" To suggest that Howe could not possibly know, because he is not Black, would have been considered by the academicians to be the epitome of arrogance. He is a respectable American critic: His credentials have been validated by *The New York Times Review of Books* and *Commentary* magazine. Because he is white, he is able, accordingly, to view the black situation objectively; because he is Jewish, more capable than others of empathizing with the black man's experience. For these reasons, what is contested most often in Howe's essay, by black and white critics alike, is not his image of Bigger Thomas as the black everyman (Ellison's rebuttal, for example, seems designed only to prove that *he* is not like Bigger Thomas) but his arrogant insistence upon literary criteria for black writers.

Thus the irony of "Black Boys and Native Sons" is missed by critics of all persuasions: The Bigger whom Howe depicts is not he of Wright's creative imagination but of Irving Howe's. Brutal and brutalized, Bigger may be, and yet, as James Emanuel has noted, he is a much more sensitive young man than those who oppress him. His capacity to feel deeply redeems him, transforms him from blundering murderer into inept revolutionary. It serves also to contrast his humanity with that of the Daltons whose insensitivity is symbolized by the blindness of Mrs.

Dalton. Thus beyond the anger and hatred, as Emanuel points out, is the sensitivity and feeling, long a part of black history and heritage; a sensitivity, known to Blacks from David Walker to Malcolm X, that precludes acceptance of one's condition as defined by southern bigots or northern liberals: ". . . the most serious problem . . . that faces any Negro," writes Imamu Baraka, "is that for so long now the white man has told him that his, the Negro's version of America and the world, is shameful fantasy."[14]

For too much of America, true reality in regard to black people is that as defined by the Mailers, Howes, and Styrons. Given the necessity to defend White Nationalism, under attack at home and abroad, the situation could not be different. Thus the works of such writers suggest that Martin King and Malcolm X are counterfeit Negroes at best, admitted exceptions at worst. The real images of twenty million or so black people are those personified by the hipster and the brute. What is characteristic of both is that they are moral and intellectual inferiors to whites, that they live by the exigencies of the body, not by those of the mind, that they are so possessed by sexual promiscuity and hatred that they pose little or no serious threat to the continual hegemony of White Nationalism. Such a message was welcomed in the halls of academia and in the councils of mobs as well.

"The White Negro" and "Black Boys and Native Sons" were academic tracts, designed for intellectuals. *The Confessions of Nat Turner*, by William Styron, on the other hand, was designed for the American masses. It was written for white people at large—for klansman and college professor alike and, given the rapid changes taking place in the American social order, it was a novel demanded by the times. From the moment the civil rights movement turned from pursuit of integration to pursuit of Black Power, from the moment aggressive black men, armed not with the King James Bible, but with copies of *The Wretched of the Earth,* appeared, it was necessary that such a book as *The Confessions of Nat Turner* be written and adopted as the definitive commentary on black revolution and revolutionaries.

This book, which has been called, erroneously, a "history," is counter-history. It is the product of a white man lacking the courage to confront history as revealed fact; one who must, instead, deal with it as fable and myth in an attempt to sanction the image of the "good, loyal darky." It is a book that could have been written only by a liberated Southerner, a descendant of the literary and social pretensions of John C. Calhoun and William Faulkner, men who could not bring themselves to believe that the people whom they had attempted to unman had survived the attempt and did not seek their love and affection but, if anything, their lives. Mailer might view Blacks as sexual pariahs; Howe might depict them as aggressive white-haters. Northern liberals, whose daughters and neighborhoods are relatively safe from such creations, are freer to indulge in such fantasies, believing that distance prevents them or theirs from becoming likely victims of their own imagination. For Styron and white Southerners in general, such fantasies are difficult to retain without modification, due to their ofttime close proximity to black people. The black man as sexual pariah, therefore, must be downplayed as an image in order to assure the safety of white womanhood. Thomas Nelson Page, secure in his person, by the presence of the Ku Klux Klan, Knights of the White Camelia, and other vigilante organizations, could afford to fantasize about the "brute Negro." Styron, however, faced with racial confrontation in the present, when black men seem to be demanding an eye for an eye, out of fear as well as guilt, must deny those stereotypes of his forefathers, as well as those of his liberal counterparts, and create one from his own imagination.

Nat Turner is this creation. Part homosexual, part white man, hater of Blacks and admirer of whites, he is a revolutionary without a cause, a slave who has "A kind Master," a man who, though he might have organized a rebellion which took over fifty lives, has no tangible reason for doing so: "For see here, Reverend," Gray, the amenuensis, says in astonishment, "that's another item the people can't understand. If this was out-and-out tyranny, yes, if you was maltreated, beaten, ill-fed ill-clothed, ill-housed—yes. If any of these things prevailed, yes. Even if you existed under the conditions presently extent in the British Isles or Ireland . . . the people could understand. Yes. But this ain't even Mississippi or Arkansas. This is *Virginia* in the year Anno Domino, 1831, and you have labored under civilized and virtuous masters."[15] The revolutionary of Styron's imagination, therefore, rebels not against real, but imagined, injustice, is not sure, despite the times and travails of himself and others, that his rebellion is justified. Like a black Hamlet, he questions not only the mystical revelation handed down from his God, but also fidelity to his own humanity. For what does one make of the slave who ponders the wheres and wherefores of killing his master, who denies the most human longing of men in bondage: "An exquisitely sharpened hatred for the white man is of course an emotion not difficult for Negroes to harbor," Nat admits, and yet, ". . . if truth be known, this hatred does not abound in every Negro's soul. . . ."[16]

Such sentiments need stating anew in this the age of black discontent. The argument that men necessarily hate and despise their oppressors is one that must not be applied to Blacks in America. This appears, in the context of the novel, to be no recently arrived at position: It is historical and evidences the fact that the modern-day black revolutionary has moved no farther in this regard than his ancestors, is still more apt to love and fear white men than to hate them: "Ask the average Negro," Turner lectures, "if he is prepared to kill a white man, and if he says yes, you may be sure that he is indulging in the sheerest brag."[17] Killing white men, of course, is one thing, and to read *The Confessions* accurately is to point out the unlikelihood of this course of action. Yet the desire to sleep with the daughters of white men is another matter. This is, to follow Styron's line of thinking, the objective of every virile black man, a desire held covertly or overtly, most tenaciously by black rebels and revolutionaries. Here is displayed the copulative theory of revolution. Blacks may write of oppression, complain of social injustice, fear the knock on the door in the dark of night, write poems and prose to the God of black power, speak of liberation and freedom. These, however, are simply code words, felicitous arguments which mask the real objectives. Revolution for Blacks is based upon nothing more tangible than a desire to seduce the master's daughter, to be one with the sentiments expressed by their revolutionary paradigm of old: "Take her here on this bank by this quiet brook. Spend upon her all afternoon a backed-up lifetime of passion. Without mercy take your pleasure upon her innocent round young body until she is half mad with fright and pain. Forget your great mission. Abandon all for these hours of terror and bliss. . . ."[18]

"What," asked an exasperated white woman, during a freedom march, "do you people want?" The answer is found in the pages of *The Confessions of Nat Turner* and validated by the success accorded the book by an American public, seldom disposed to read books. The novel became a best seller, won the National Book Award for Fiction, was hailed by critics as far distant in ideology as James Baldwin and the editors of *Time, Newsweek,* and *The New York Review of Books.* The standards of literary excellence demanded by white critics of black novelists—fidelity to language, unity of plot, good character development, objectivity, and commitment to truth instead of propaganda— were waived in the case of *The Confessions,* which, according to these standards, is a second-rate novel. Leave aside the question of genre—a historical novel, which does not even remotely bear upon historical truth—neither the characters of Turner, Hark, nor Margaret Whitehead ring true even as imaginary people of the nineteenth century. In terms of dialogue, the inconsistency is blatant; Nat sometimes sounds like an Old Testament prophet, at other times, like Mailer's black hipster. Stilted writing, tortured metaphors, and forced symbols which could escape only the most literally naive abound: "Why," asks the liberal Miss Whitehead, "do you call yourself a nigger . . . ? I mean it sounds so—well, so sad somehow. I much prefer the word darky."[19]

Yet it is the symbolic import of Margaret Whitehead, which obscures for white critics, all other flaws in the novel. Move from the historical Nat Turner to his counterparts in modern-day America; neither can differentiate between the term darky and nigger; neither can differentiate between freedom and lust, between desiring liberation from oppression or sexual union with the daughters of the oppressor. When one understands that Margaret Whitehead is the most counterrevolutionary weapon of all, that she is the Achilles' heel of each black revolutionary, one need have little concern about the protestations of black militant leaders, nor fear the recent riots and rebellions as little more than the antics of frustrated, neurotic children. One year after the emergence of Black Power, whites needed not art but a soporific; *The Confessions of Nat Turner* supplied this need.

XI

————◆◄◇►◆————

REVOLUTIONARIES, THREE

The success of such tracts as "The White Negro," "Black Boys and Native Sons," and *The Confessions of Nat Turner* is proven in the literary and political arenas. Two of the best-selling novels of the seventies, *Rabbit Redux,* by John Updike, and *The Tenants,* by Bernard Malamud, are attempts to validate the images described by their contemporaries. In *The Tenants,* an embittered black intellectual, incapable of writing fiction, brutalizes his white girlfriend and so enrages his Jewish helpmate that the two engage in a violent death struggle at the end of the novel. The black man as brute, sexual pariah, and copulative agent is more pronounced in Updike's novel. Not only does the character move into the home of the protagonist, but he also intimidates him, hooks his young mistress on drugs, and eventually destroys her. In the area of politics the ugly bellicosity of the southern mobs of the fifties and early sixties has been replaced by the cold pragmatism of the Nixon men. Such men reflect the sentiments of those who man the picket lines in the North to prevent the entrance of black youngsters in schools, who order such mass executions as that at Attica, who sanction the unlawful persecution and imprisonment of members of the Black Panther Party, and who assist Jewish liberals in attacks upon open admissions programs and open-occupancy statutes.

To argue a one-to-one correlation between the "backlash" against black expectations and white writers would be erroneous. Yet, to suggest that by distorting images, by depicting a people as subhuman, and by adding to the storehouse of falsehoods concerning race, the writers helped to produce the atmosphere for white militancy, north and south, is not. The images which have provoked violence by whites from Los Angeles to Forest Hills are those described in the works of their critics and writers. Few of the combatants have misunderstood the underlying message in the works of Styron, Mailer, and Howe—the nigger must be put back into his place and kept there. The militancy as well as such messages presented serious problems for black writers. Though few were apolitical, fewer still viewed politics as an integral, aesthetic component of the literary work of art. Those who admitted a connection all too often viewed the politics of black literature as springing from the same source as that of white literature: Many sanctioned the images, symbols, and metaphors depicted in the works of their white contemporaries. Eldridge Cleaver and Julius Lester championed "The White Negro"; James Baldwin cried exultantly that *The Confessions of Nat Turner* had "begun our common history." *Manchild in the Promised Land, Another Country,* and *Soul on Ice* were black versions of white works, written, one supposes, more to demonstrate the intelligence of the author than to contest the definitions presented by men with no knowledge of black life-style, history, or culture.

What was needed, therefore, was a new political ideology, one that addressed itself to black people throughout the world. And what was needed from the black writer was not only articulation of the new political ideology but a determination to destroy the images and symbols of the past, too many of which were held sacred by Blacks. In short, a commitment to the tenets of Black Nationalism was demanded of the writer, for nothing short of such a commitment could validate his function as a purposeful agent of his people. Like Tod Clifton, militant young revolutionary of Ellison's *Invisible Man,* the black American, having traveled the integrationist path and been rebuffed by bigot and white liberal alike, had no other option than to leap outside the history and culture of the West; the function of the writer was to aid in this endeavor. This thesis, embraced by more black writers than care to admit it publicly, is responsible in part for the about-face of the black novelist from the nihilistic, assimilationist route prescribed by too many of his ancestors and contemporaries. He rejected the image of the black man as white Negro, turned away from themes that depicted the helpless, castrated Black, piteously appealing to white America to alter his condition. Instead, the themes were those that depicted the courage of Blacks under fire, that told of the rich heritage of black culture, that echoed the slogan of Frederick Douglass that those who wish to be free must themselves strike the blow. This change in direction was occasioned in part by the dignity and confidence gained as a result of the civil rights and Black Power struggles; in part as a result of the entrance of the new African nations into independence, and more important, perhaps, by the paradigms offered in the persons of Martin Luther King, Malcolm X, and Imamu Baraka, each a revolutionary, each in his own way, through example, adding impetus to the new politics and the new literature as well.

Martin Luther King was neither an anomaly nor an exception. There was something in him of the stubbornness of Richard Allen, founder of the African Methodist Episcopal Church, creating the instrument, which soon fell into the conservative mold from which King would attempt to rescue it. There was something of the pacifist and moralist William Wells Brown in him also—a commitment to things of the spirit and a belief that in a world ordained by God, right and justice must prevail. Yet, he was closer perhaps to Henry Highland Garnet, whose reputation, secure among the men of his time, has been eclipsed by the formidable reputation of Frederick Douglass. Nevertheless, Garnet remains the most appropriate historical paradigm for the activist black minister and he and King have this in common: Both were respected, feared, and hated by their contemporaries and both were forced to deal with the conservative elements in their ranks. Garnet demanded greater militancy from the conservatives; King, on the other hand, attempted to minimize the militancy of his youthful followers in the civil rights movement, while steering clear of the defeatist, archaic position of the NAACP and the Urban League.

Each man brought to the overwhelming problem of his day—slavery for Garnet, racism for King—a moral integrity, which made for different, yet, in many aspects, similar ideologies. Garnet advocated the liberation of black men by any means necessary—a position which takes him closer to Malcolm X than to King. King, on the other hand, believed that the means should justify the ends, that liberation achieved through violence would mean only that, at some future time, the revolutionary would be forced to remove his rifle from the rack once again. Garnet believed that the new society was possible only when the old had been destroyed; King believed that the new society was possible if men dedicated themselves to make necessary changes in the old. Garnet had too little influence upon the politics of his time for one to gauge the accuracy of his thought. King, however, articulated his position from Montgomery, Alabama, to Cicero, Illinois, in an attempt to influence the events of his time.

The influence has all but waned in the years after the death of this Southerner who as a child had looked at life from the vantage point of a middle-class Black. As such he had known little of the daily acts of trial and tribulation, of the tragedy of the lives of the majority of his people. He had been headed toward a doctorate in theology and a ministerial position in the church of his father. How could he have imagined, in 1955 even, when he accepted leadership of the Montgomery Improvement Association, a middle-class organization led by a middle-class minister, the existential trials to come: years of confrontation with southern police/dogs, wrangles with northern vigilantes, local black leaders and politicians, the Justice Department, and the FBI? Or the periods of achievement, the pilgrimage to India and the shrine of Ghandi, recipient of the Nobel Prize for peace, and, finally, most important, martyrdom in the minds of black men everywhere? Garnet, the more imaginative of the two, might have had some inkling of his destiny; King, almost assuredly, did not.

His lack of imagination, of creativity, accounts, in part, for his failure to understand the nature of the forces arrayed against him and explains his belief in much of his own rhetoric concerning morality and the appeal to conscience. "Beyond the pragmatic invalidity of violence," he wrote, "is its inability to appeal to conscience . . . power and morality must go together, implementing, fulfilling, and ennobling each other. In the quest for power I cannot bypass the concern for morality. . . . Non-violence is power, but it is the right and good use of power. It can save the white man as well as the Negro."[1] Much too often, this Baptist minister spoke of black men undertaking the white man's burden, of saving the advocates of White Nationalism by suffering, which came close to self-prostration. Garnet would have advised black men to save themselves; for King, the salvation of white men was equally important: "Let us be those creative dissenters who will call our beloved nation to a higher destiny, to a new plateau of compassion, to a more noble expression of humanness." He had faith in such sentiments and he held this faith even up until that fateful night in Memphis, Tennessee. It was part of his moral canon; it helped to sustain him during the days in the Birmingham jail, helped him to confront southern rednecks and northern vigilantes, enabled him to forgive the misguided black woman who plunged a letter opener into his chest; it was responsible too, in part, for the many compromises he made with white power brokers. It was this faith, so alien to American thought and history, that spelled his doom and hurried the dark night of retribution and death in Memphis.

White violence and militancy brought him to Memphis the first time, and black resistance brought him back again. The initial journey was made when a strike by black sanitation men drew rebuke from the town mayor. The strikers marched in peaceful protest and were met with white violence. King was called in. Between March 18 and March 31, he made three forays into Memphis. Two were directly related to sentiments such as those articulated by one young marcher, sentiments that presented King with the old dilemma, given added emphasis by the rhetoric of Black Power: "I'm a radical . . . before Henry Loeb [the mayor of Memphis] will listen, the garbage has to be in the street, not in your backyard. . . . Preaching and money raising are fine. Somebody has to do it. But there are some *men* out there. We've got to do some *fighting*. Not marching—*fighting*. And when you talk about fighting a city with as many cops as this city's got, you better have some guns. You're going to need them before it's over."[2]

The dilemma between recognizing the injustices that argued for abandonment of the non-violent philosophy, and the moral stance adopted in support of it, plagued King throughout his career. More than once he was forced to acknowledge the fact that the philosophy was operative only during demonstrations and marches. Yet, he was forced to war with elements even within his own organization which favored the policy of Douglass and John Brown as opposed to that of William Wells Brown and William Lloyd Garrison. Until King journeyed north, into Cicero, Illinois, he managed, due to his prestige, to maintain passive resistance as an acceptable doctrine. The foray into Cicero was his Waterloo. The defeats he and his legions suffered here did much to legitimatize Malcolm X and the advocates of Black Power. The adventure into Cicero, in addition, made King's attempt to buttress the non-violent philosophy at Memphis, anticlimactic. Long before he reached Memphis the appeal of his philosophy had waned among black people, and his book, *Where Do We Go from Here,* is marked by the theme of a leader rushing to catch up with his followers.

The moral edifice upon which King had constructed his passive-resistance campaign—that white Americans could be seduced through appeals to conscience—was destroyed on his first expedition into a major city, north of the Mason-Dixon line. Northerners, who cheered his exploits in the South, who lent him moral and material support, were quickly to desert him in the aftermath of Cicero, ignoring the argument made by social commentators like Gunnar Myrdal and Alex Rose, who agreed in principle with King, that "northern white leadership has relied too much on tokens, substitutes, and Negro patience. The end of this road is clearly in sight. The cohesive, potentially explosive Negro community in the North has a short fuse and a long train of abuses."[3]

The southern movement was a way of placating the North, of keeping sacrosanct and inviolate the real areas of influence and power in America. When King declared a southern victory of sorts, and moved his campaign north, the liberals panicked. They foresaw the specter of the kind of integration they had championed for the South enacted in their own region, and they successfully hurled down the gauntlet of defiance in Cicero, Illinois.

Their success made King's position as a leader, as well as moral philosopher, untenable. Unfortunately—and this was unfair—he was considered by many of the younger, more brighter elements in the black community as little more than a southern version of Roy Wilkins. By 1966, he was more revered as an antiwar leader than a civil rights leader, and the non-violent army he had assembled had splintered into pieces. Even in the South, where non-violence, for practical reasons, had long been part of the black man's struggle, many had followed the example of the Lowndes County Black Panther Party, had adopted the slogan, Black Power, and openly advocated self-defense. In addition, his return to Memphis to lead a non-violent march was in direct response to outbreaks of violence during his earlier presence in the city.

". . . If you want to," he remarked in January, the year that began the drama and suspense, the poetry and death, which culminated in Atlanta, "say that I was a drum major . . . say that I was a drum major for righteousness. . . ."[4] This speech, filled with prophecy and foreboding—"all I can leave behind," he stated, is "a committed life"— would have appealed to the ever-brooding Garnet. His forte, like King's, was oratory, and he too excelled in the sombrous, cadencelike inversions of the Baptist preacher, in the flamboyant gestures and the feltforce tension of words. And Garnet would have appreciated also, the foreboding of the coming months, the hurried pace exhibited by King and his staff, as if there was a great necessity to take care of unfinished business, as if the mark he had left on the psyche of his people was not compensation enough for his short life.

Left his mark he had. His forays against white nationalism from Montgomery to Chicago had punctured the mythology of America as a haven for the poor and destitute, had rendered to shambles the vaunted mythology of the American dream. None of this was lost on the new black writers, many of whose consciousnesses were shaped by his ordeal. He had placed his faith in white America and had been rewarded by the sterile inactions of its intellectuals and critics; moreover, the intransigence of white college professor and white porter alike was convincing evidence that rapprochement between Blacks and whites in America on any level, save that of power, was impossible. Such a truth had never escaped Henry Highland Garnet and one supposes that in the deeper recesses of his memory, had King allowed himself to remonstrate upon the nature of the Euro-American, it might not long have escaped him. Despite his disagreement with the young men who followed Brown, Carmichael, and Malcolm, *Where Do We Go from Here* evidences the fact that he was closer, ideologically speaking, to them than he was to the old men of the civil rights movement. Where many such men had looked to the march on Washington as a culmination of a historic effort, King saw it as significant in charting a more militant direction than that championed by his organization.

He did not know what that direction was; what is essential, however, is that he understood the necessity for change. This attitude was negated by the events in Memphis. "Like anybody," he said on the night before his death, "I would like to live a long life. Longevity has its place. But I'm not concerned about that now. I just want to do God's will. And he's allowed me to go to the mountain. And I've looked over, and I've seen the promised land. I may not get there with you, but I want you to know tonight that we as a people will get to the promised land."[5] The words cannot describe the sudden break from the rostrum, the fall off balance into the arms of a companion, the quick stare of despair and anguish that enveloped the face. That he looked, in that moment, as Henry Highland Garnet must have looked after delivering his admonition to the slaves to arise in rebellion is merely historical conjecture. One thing, however, is true, and it is this which has inspired the new poets and novelists: There was about him, in these final hours, neither the aura of the hippie, brute, or happy darky, but, instead, that poetic aura so often associated with the romantic revolutionary, who contemplates the violent death in order that violence may be ended upon the earth. There was, in short, the aura about him of a black poem.

He was a poem, however, too long shaped and formed in the model of the black middle class, who have consistently tended to pattern their beautiful young poems upon white failures. Only when he stepped outside of such a designation, when he reverted to cadences of the soul-stirring preacher, when he demanded that the signing of the spirituals be a part of the ritual of his organization, on those few times when he donned the clothing of black workers in Birmingham and Selma, and when he sat down to a dish of soul food without shame or consternation, only then did he leap the bridge between the black haves and the black have-nots and become, in a literary sense, the poem of his people.

He differed in this respect from his contemporary Malcolm X. Malcolm was *always* close to the people, always, in a sense, representative of the poetry of their lives. In all the roles he played throughout his lifetime—pimp, convict, minister, and revolutionary—he remained close to the people, whose language he knew and spoke so well and whose symbols, metaphors, images, and tendency to hyperbole, he understood. If the paradigm for King was the militant Garnet, the paradigm for Malcolm can be determined only after he has traveled his ordeal of fire as a young man. The son of a militant father, whose murder helped to bring on the mental breakdown of his mother, he was orphaned at an early age to the state. Surviving this ordeal and finally moving out on his own, the only analogy to be found between him and Douglass before the point of manhood was that both had been enslaved. Douglass by chains and irons, Malcolm by the propaganda of the imagists: "Like hundreds of thousands of country-bred Negroes who had come to the northern black ghetto before me, and have come since, I'd also acquired all the . . . fashionable ghetto adornments—the zuit suits and conk. . . ."[6]

The propaganda had sunk so deeply as to make those days in New York and Boston—the days of Detroit Red—among the most regrettable of his distinguished career. Ironically, Big Red, pimp, numbers runner, gambler, drug dealer, was a less hounded man than the minister of Elijah Muhammad; the man who dealt death and dope to his people, less feared than the man who attempted to save and elevate them. When he is finally sent to prison, it is not because of crimes committed against the black community but because he has had a long affair with a white woman: ". . . It was the same even from our court-appointed lawyers. . . . I said to one lawyer. 'We seem to be getting sentenced because of those girls.' He got red from the neck up. . . . 'You had no business with white girls.' "[7]

In Concord Prison his brother first introduced him to the Nation of Islam; at this point he began to assume characteristics that allow comparison with Douglass. Both men were barely literate at the age of twenty. Both were incensed by injustice and outraged at the unequal status between Blacks and whites. Both were men of action instead of men of reflection; both were controversial men, who broke eventually with the policies of men they had formerly embraced; though Douglass found entree into the highest councils of the Republican party, still, he like Malcolm, was feared and mistrusted by his government. The writings of each—the autobiographies and the collected speeches—demonstrate the remarkable intelligence of self-educated men.

Each man arose to prominence via much the same vehicle: Douglass, the orator, having few peers, presented the case for his people from hostile rostrum to hostile rostrum. Malcolm, after prison, after becoming chief minister of the Harlem Mosque, also took to the stump in defense of his people. Like Douglass, he was gifted in oratory and, with quick wit, steely phrase, and cutting rejoinder, argued the case against racism on three continents. Their experiences are set down in the books dealing with their lives, and no two autobiographies in America offer better evidence against the charges made, historically, by the imagists. The images that emerge are representative of black men throughout history; some like Garnet and King rose to national prominence; most achieved eminence only in the minds of loved ones. Yet both groups of men and women constitute the most appropriate source for the symbols and images of a black literature.

"I don't think anybody," Malcolm wrote, "ever got more out of going to prison than I did." Prison accomplished for Malcolm what slavery did for Douglass, what intuitive insight did for Garnet and Garvey: It afforded him the opportunity to study, brought him into contact with the teachings of Elijah Muhammad, and afforded him an insight into the nature of his antagonist, one that escaped King for most of his life. King's emphasis throughout his career was upon moving forward within the system. In *Where Do We Go from Here,* he argued that the civil rights movement was designed to secure rights, long withheld from black men, who were American citizens. His was the quest for civil rights, a narrow, parochial quest, that virtually ignored the suffering of two thirds of the world's darker people. He was unable to view the black man's struggle in America as merely part of a wider one, to understand that the quest for civil rights in the nineteen seventies must be the quest for human rights, and that to think in such terms meant to conclude that Blacks were among the majority of the people of the world, not the minority. In thought, and sometimes in public utterances, he was capable of formulating a universal theory of oppression; yet he remained, until his death, primarily a local Baptist preacher, unable to understand that the struggle by Blacks in America was the struggle of black men everywhere.

These facts of black life, the prison-educated Malcolm understood. He knew that the power that controlled black people in South Africa, Angola, Mozambique, and even in some of the newly liberated African countries, was the same power that controlled Blacks in America. He knew that the Euro-Americans had extended their power and influence into every area where different people resided, and used that power to keep the indigenous people in ignorance and poverty. He knew that the major conflict, nationally and internationally, was one of race, not class, and that such a conflict was incapable of solution through such methods as marches, name-calling, or futile acts which passed for revolution. "Time and time again," he wrote "the black, the brown, the red, and the yellow races have witnessed and suffered the white man's small ability to understand the simple notes of the spirit. The white man seems tone deaf to the total orchestration of humanity."[8]

At the height of his maturity, such insights make him one with Douglass and, like the earlier abolitionist, he too achieved the eminence of a paradigm, became a model for millions of oppressed and enslaved: "In each place his spirit settled," writes Imamu Baraka, "something was turned on, and over. A beginning, an ending."[9] If the line from Garnet to King ended with the death of King, the line from Douglass to Malcolm continues in those whom he inspired; in the young SNCC people—integrationists turned nationalists—and in the young men and women in the southern and northern communities who continue, even after his death, to revere his name. His insistence upon the separation of those who symbolize moral order and principle from those who symbolize chaos and tyranny, his argument to black men that purification/salvation meant the creation of a new nation ended the fanciful crusade among thinking Blacks for integration even as it renewed the quest for an energetic Black Nationalism.

Once he realized that nationalism under Elijah Muhammad could not grow and flourish outside The Nation of Islam, that it would be bounded by a religious ideology which minimized it as a political force, and that as such it had little appeal to black men throughout the country, he sought to change the direction of "The Nation." Failing in this endeavor, he moved outside, became the leader of his own organization, set out to develop his own kind of nationalism. His was a moral nationalism and its fundamental tenet was that black men were more humane than their white counterparts; that wherever black cruelty, brutality, and hatred toward other Blacks appeared, the West had been there, had left its Bibles and textbooks. His was a nationalism, however, which caused him to extend the hand of brotherhood all too quickly, caused him in that brief visit to Mecca, to attempt to exonerate some men from the crimes of which all were guilty: "Throughout my travels in the Muslim world, I have met, talked to, and even eaten with people who in America would have been considered 'white' but the 'white' attitude was removed from their minds by the religion of Islam. . . ."[10]

In her excellent book, *Garvey, Lumumba, Malcolm: Black Nationalists—Separatists,* Shawna Maglangbayan points out Malcolm's lack of historical perspective: "Unfortunately, as so many of us today, Malcolm X was not informed about the monstrous plight of millions of black men, women, and children subjected to the most degrading forms of oppression in the various Arab-dominated portions of the Middle East and North Africa."[11] Like Douglass, who discovered his own Mecca among the white abolitionists, so did Malcolm discover his among those who momentarily extended the colorless hand of brotherhood. Douglass outgrew his affection for white abolitionists, though, later in his life, he renewed his alliance with white radicals in the Congress of Presidents Grant and Johnson. Malcolm, however, died too soon to repudiate much of what he had accepted on his pilgrimage to Mecca, too soon to realize that ". . . our personal religious convictions (or absence of them) should play no role whatsoever in determining the political orientation of a struggle such as ours, which is purely political, socio-economic and racial."[12]

Yet, despite this, he became the symbol of black manhood for the poor and discontented and for the affluent and satisfied alike, and his example extended from one end of America to the other. Eldridge Cleaver, George Jackson, H. Rap Brown, Stokely Carmichael were influenced by him, and each sought in his own way to fashion his actions and thoughts in accord with Malcolm's, to chip a plank from his cross. Part of their attraction for him was due to his universal outlook, that which included all black men. Like King, he had gone to the mountain and looked beyond; yet, unlike King, what he saw was a new nation coming into being, one created by black men, and this nation, shaping, forming, and molding a newer, more humane universe.

"The Negro leaders whom we accept," a Jewish leader once remarked, "are Bayard Rustin, Roy Wilkins, and Whitney Young." Black people must be ever indebted to the wisdom that caused him not to mention H. Rap Brown, Stokely Carmichael, or Malcolm X. From his statement, however, we learn much about the workings of the white nationalist mind, understand why such men as Mailer, Howe, and Styron must attempt to transform reality. Look again at their images of Blacks and each is imbued with the characteristics of Western man —greed, lust, hatred, immorality, ignorance, and egotism. In the black communities, men with such characteristics are the "admitted exceptions," yet they are elevated to the status of metaphors of a people everywhere, readily accepted by white Americans because they are, in reality, white Americans' own creations. There are truer metaphors of black men—those which have come down through the ages—paradigms of men who exemplify man's love for his fellow man, architects of a system of values and morals which might yet make the earth worth living upon. They are those, unlike the anointed of the Jewish spokesman, who have touched black people deeply, helped them to reshape their lives.

Malcolm was not the greatest of these. He had not the power of Booker Washington, the organizational skill of Garvey; he knew less about history than Stokely Carmichael, was less pragmatic than Sufi Abdul. Still, there is no black man in America, whose courage he did not call into question, whose conscience he did not stir, whose manhood he did not enhance, whose commitment he did not challenge. And there is no black man for whom he is not a symbol of courage and determination, for whom he is not the finest example of black aspirations. That his stature has increased after his death is unimportant. Those, who remember the man in the vibrancy of his youth, know that he lives still, that like Garnet, King, and Douglass, the revolutionary import of his life was that he remains a reminder to Blacks of what was and is, not what white men are willing to accept.

After King and Malcolm, Carmichael and Brown, after the sacrifices of countless numbers of Blacks during the civil rights struggle and the Black Power Revolution, a sensibility was needed to transform their deeds into words. Architects of the mind were necessary, those imbued with the same courage and determination of the above-named. The examples of King and Malcolm must not be allowed to go the way of those of Garnet and Douglass, Delany and Du Bois; no black child should grow up in America unconscious of the life and times of Malcolm X and Martin Luther King, Jr. To prevent this occurrence, what was needed was not so much a new art, as a new artist, one who was willing to take his chances by stepping outside the literary theorems of Henry Fielding, Henry James, T. S. Elliot, James Joyce, Theodore Dreiser, and Jean Paul Sartre. In addition, perceptions were needed, not so much into the nature of art as into the nature of the interrelationship between the people and the artist. Such a perception for the black artist would lead inconclusively to the fact that the artist and the people were one, distinguishable only in terms of life occupation. The inability of the black artist to recognize this fundamental observation accounts for much of the sterile writings prior to the nineteen fifties. The failure was not so much in terms of craftsmanship, of the mastery of form and structure, as it was in perception: "Having read all of whitey's books," admits Imamu Baraka, "I wanted to be an authority on them. Having been taught that art was what white men did, I almost became one to have a go at it."[13]

The Barakas differ from others; they "almost became one," and one supposes that it was due to the examples of men like King and Malcolm that they did not. Others were not so fortunate. They became little more than the black ventriloquist dummies of the Mailers, Howes, and Styrons, many of whom knew of black life and black people only from the books and magazines written by white men. Others, incapable of claiming such ignorance, distorted their perceptions for material gain, pimping off the life and death struggles of a people to the applause and adulation of white publishers, academicians, and critics. There were still others, ever willing to allow the reality of other mortal men to suffice for their own and unwilling to challenge the statements and arguments of those whose only contact with black life was through their maids, students, and servants. In the past, such men were less fortunate than those of the present: They had their Douglasses but could not fathom their greatness; they had their Du Boises but were incapable of understanding them. Having almost become dead men, they were more comfortable with the ideas and examples of dead men, did not recognize the paradigms of their own culture and history. In the northern black communities, in the rural South were, and are, millions of Garnets, Douglasses, Kings, and Malcolms waiting only for the kindling stroke to give them life, only, in most cases, for the artistic sensibility capable of introducing them to a new reality.

Few writers possess greater sensibility in this regard than Imamu Baraka. Despite the uninformed statements of white critics, he is not the first of the black-warrior poets; William Wells Brown retains that honor. He is not the first to realize that literature and politics are merely extensions one of the other; that distinction belongs to Martin Delany; he is not the first to understand that culture is a vehicle for the liberation of a people; Du Bois realized this fact early in his career. He was, however, the first black writer of the modern era to invoke the African Gods of old, the first to be so inspired by the example of Malcolm X that he issued the call for the most noble of all undertakings, the creation of a Black Art:

> Let Black People understand
> that they are lovers and the sons of
> lovers and warriors and sons of
> warriors. Are poems and poets and
> all the loveliness here in the world.
> We want a Black poem. And a Black
> World.
> Let the world be a Black poem. . . .[14]

Baraka is our Du Bois reborn in the nineteen seventies. The distance from Great Barrington, Massachusetts, in 1868, and Newark, New

Jersey, in 1934, calculated in terms of years and miles, may appear long. Black people, however, most often measure distance in terms of accomplishment and compare men and women to one another in terms of their dedication and efforts on behalf of their people. In this respect, similar characteristics appear between the poet of yesterday and the poet of today. Both were activists; neither believed that art was something men practiced behind closed doors, in the sitting room. Both believed in the determination and courage of black people; both were analysts turned moralists, and though Du Bois floundered about for most of his life searching for a value system, one which took him even, unfortunately, into the Communist party, his younger legate discovered one outside Western ideology. It is this that marks the essential difference between them.

The similarities overshadow the differences! Remember Du Bois leaving Fisk for work during school vacation, going into the Tennessee Valley, among the people for the first time, discovering the beauty and pain of their lives. Great Barrington afforded him few such moments. There were few Blacks in the region outside the Du Bois and Burghardt klan; the scholar-poet, therefore, grew up in virtual isolation from Blacks. Only after he had gone to the mountaintop and discovered such people as John and Josie did realization come and was *The Souls of Black Folk* possible. For Baraka, living in Newark, New Jersey, occasions to observe the life-styles of Blacks were many. Yet, Leroi Jones, not yet Imamu, knew of their strength and beauty only intuitively, looked at the people, as black intellectuals sometimes look at them, as helpless wards of a white society.

The vision was not enhanced through association with institutions of higher learning that served only as conduits of white nationalist propaganda. Nor was a new dimension added by the move from Newark to Greenwich Village, from anonymity to respected poet and playwright. The plays, *Dutchman, The Slave,* and *The Toilet,* are powerful dramas, yet they are history examined and retold, not history embellished with an ideology different from that of Western playwrights of the modern era. They were, even more accurately, variations upon themes pronounced in black literature before, themes to be found in the rhetoric of pretender and revolutionary alike. It was necessary then for Jones also to go to the mountaintop, to begin the pilgrimage to his mythical Tennessee, to leave the Great Barrington of the mind. In 1964, thirty-two years after the demise of the Harlem Renaissance, Jones came home to Harlem. With talented colleagues he founded the Black Repertory Theater and, like his older contemporary, set out to learn firsthand about the souls of black people. Listen to his speech in front of the Hotel Theresa, shortly after becoming director of the new theater, and from this moment in time, he has ceased to be Leroi Jones, moved even farther from the West than his literary ancestor, become Imamu Baraka: ". . . black people have, and must realize that we have, our own standards and references for judging the world. And we must begin to make use of them and regard what the white man says as dealing with another reality, because we know, we black people know, what our reality is. Look out your window, or into your heart, you, you know who and where you are. You know what you feel. You know what you have to do: And let no white man or imitation white man tell you differently."[15]

Both Du Bois and Baraka came home, each to his own Harlem; it was Imamu however who perhaps gained greater insight into the nature of the Western world, discovered the Achilles' heel of White Nationalism. He learned that in the West, form must always take precedence over content; the obverse would mean to reveal too much. One must, therefore, accept the mythology surrounding the lives of such men as Washington, Jefferson, and Lincoln, because to analyze the lives they truly lived would destroy them as heroic images. One must accept the moral postulations of such as Edgar Allan Poe, William Faulkner, Norman Mailer, and William Styron, without questioning the moral imperatives by which they live. But, also, one must forget that the culture that produced Tolstoy produced Stalin, that which produced Goethe produced Adolf Hitler, and that which produced Henry David Thoreau produced Richard Nixon. To accept such myths is to choose White Nationalism over Black Nationalism, to opt for death over life.

Imamu opted for life over death and in so doing became the finest example of black artist and human being. Though his contributions in the area of literature are remarkable, his contribution in the area of commitment is even greater. He has stepped outside the embrace of Western culture, dared to embark upon a road different than that of his predecessors and contemporaries, chose the philosophy of Maylana Karenga over that of Immanuel Kant, the example of Du Bois over that of William Faulkner, chose *Black World* magazine over *The New York Times Review of Books,* Southside Newark over Asbury Park, and became spiritual leader of a people instead of prophet of their doom. The choice was made despite the temptations, the bribes offered in the form of wealth and recognition by the white literary establishment. Leroi Jones had accepted their largesse; Imamu Baraka was to have none of it. In scrutinizing the gift offerings of the Americans, he did as Du Bois had done before: granted to Caesar that which was his, turned from downtown to uptown, and provided the black writer with the model of the poet who not only serves as the poet of his people, but whose poetry evidences the best aspirations of a people. The transformation from Leroi Jones to Imamu Baraka meant the rejection of one culture and the acceptance of another.

Nowhere in his works is the transformation more visible than in the two volumes of essays, *Home* (1966) and *Raise Race Raze Rays* (1970). They are compilations of works written over the years; both are insights into the growth of artist and man: "I have been a lot of places," he writes, in the introductory essay to *Home,* "and done a lot of things. And there is a sense of the prodigal about my life that begs to be resolved. But one truth anyone reading these pieces ought to get is the sense of movement—the struggle in myself, to understand where and who I am, and to move with that understanding." *Home* is about movement, about the struggle of a poet—the prodigal son, as McKay once put it—to return and then again return to the roots of his existence. The white novelist had written that one could not go home again; Baraka was determined to come home, knowing as Thomas Wolfe could not have known, that for the black writer all that was required to journey home again was that one burn up a great many dead images, symbols, and metaphors along the way. The book, *Home,* does not completely accomplish this; it is, however, a beginning.

The poet of "Cuba Libre," of the essay-letter to Jules Feiffer, of "Black Is a Country," of "Myth of a Negro Literature" is a poet not of direction, but of analysis. Like his contemporaries—and James Baldwin comes readily to mind—Jones is the emissary from the black world to the white, serving as the pin-prick of its conscience, reminding it of dues yet to be paid: "The lives and destinies of the white American," he writes in "Black Is a Country," "are bound up inextricably with those of the black American, even though the latter has been forced for hundreds of years to inhabit the lonely country of black. It is time we impressed the white man with the nature of his ills as well as the nature of our own. . . ."[16] But, too, he is representative of the individualism so championed by the West, the man outside all racial groupings: "The idea of the all black society within the superstructure of an all white society is useless as well (even if it were possible). We *are* Americans, which is our strength as well as our desperation. The struggle is for *independence* not separation—or assimilation for that matter. . . . I want to be independent of black men just as much as I want independence from the white. . . ."[17]

Here also, however, one senses the prodigal, pictures the poet struggling to gain a sense of direction, encounters a man not altogether comfortable with the niche into which he has settled. The writer who pronounces with utmost certainty, in "Myth of a Negro Literature," that "A Negro literature, to be a legitimate product of the Negro experience in America, must get at that experience in exactly the terms America has proposed for it, in its most ruthless identity" is the same writer who avers in "Black Writing," "Let no one convince any black man that he is an American like anybody else."[18]

Such contradictions comprise the volume, *Home,* and as one follows the prodigal from 1960 to 1965, he witnesses a profound change in human consciousness. The writer is incapable of being grasped, of being pigeonholed, put into one niche or another. At one time he is the angry poet, at another, the poet of reason, at all times, the analyst. Sometimes he is the integrationist; at other times, the nationalist; sometimes the individualist, most times the poet of the people. In these early essays, those before 1964, he resembles a questioning, not yet assured, Du Bois, coming down from Great Barrington, wading into the water with the people and, though not joining in the baptism, knowing that, soon, he must return and then again return. The essays from 1965 onward are those of returning. They point the prodigal back home, return him to the baptism. The movement begun in the essays "Last Days of the American Empire (Including Some Instructions for Black People)" and "The Revolutionary Theatre" reaches fruition in "The Legacy of Malcolm X," and "The Coming Nation." There is at this point the remarkable wedding between poet and revolutionary; here is the sensibility brought to bear upon the black situation. We must, he argues in the essay on Malcolm, understand what culture and cultural attitudes are, and how national consciousness is involved with each, if the example of Malcolm is to be understood, "and why the Black man must now move in that direction since the world will not let him move in any other way." Understand this, and the realization is close at hand that Blacks possess by "the energies of historical necessity" a national black consciousness, a living future, the shouldering to power of "Black Culture," and finally "Black Ideals, A righteous sanctity, out of which words are built."

The journey home is completed, the preacher become the teacher, the poet, the poem, Du Bois reincarnated: "Art, religion, and politics are impressive vectors of a culture." Because culture is described by art, the artist must know the black sensibility as it exists in America, and because religion elevates culture and because God is man in ideal form, "the Black Man must idealize himself as Black. The Black man must seek a Black politics, an ordering of the world that is beneficial to his culture, to his interiorization and judgment of the world. This is strength. And we are hordes."[19]

From the moment the prodigal returned home in 1965, a new chapter in black literature was begun. The years between 1940 and 1952 may well be called the age of Richard Wright, who dominated the literature and gave it direction. The years from 1965 to the present belong to Imamu Baraka. It is the time of the black arts, the time when men seek to return art to the people, when the artist and the people realize at long last that they are one. It is the time of inspiration and hope, of new dedication and new attitudes, a new-found sense of awareness. It is the time of Don L. Lee and Sonia Sanchez, of Askia Muhammed Toure and Mari Evans, of Toni Cade and David Lorens, of Ronald Milner and Ed Bullins, of Ishmael Reed and George Cain. It is the time of nation men engaged in the arduous task of creating a nation, and it bears the indelible stamp of Imamu Baraka.

Change would have come had there been no Baraka. There would have been a rise in black consciousness—a new perception by the African-American writer. Black men would have moved toward construction of a new nation, would have formulated the concept of the Black Aesthetic. The old barriers between art as artifact and art as functional instrument would have been torn down; black writers would have attempted to write a peoples' literature, to construct peoples' institutions. All of this would have occurred had Baraka never existed. Baraka, however—and this is his greatest strength—brought to black art a new sensibility, capable of moving beyond the ideological premise erected by Malcolm and his followers, cementing the bond between art and revolution, and detecting in the life-styles of black people a value system far different from that of Western man. This value system is the connecting link between the essays in *Raise Race,* the unifying concept which draws the book together into a coherent whole and unites the disparate elements. The value system was not created by Imamu; he is merely the artist translating long-held theorems and beliefs of black people. For as it was in *The Souls of Black Folks,* so too it is in this twentieth-century version; the heroes are black people whose trials and tribulations have been heightened and dramatized by the artistic sensibility; it is they who demonstrate the courage and determination which leads, inevitably, from Newark's courthouse in 1966 to Newark's City Hall in 1970.

Home was a search for roots and direction. *Raise Race* is the celebration after the search has been concluded. The prose is that of the assured man, the stance that of teacher and novelist; "The Black poetry in America is the poetry of the changing, evolving peoples. The living beings, the relatives of the most ancient men on earth. Our feeling and understanding began at the beginning of the planet, and we rise understanding this, and our songs, our images, go from there to here. There are no mists over the African Empires. The obscuration of our world has ended. We're here again."[20] Look back at the volumes of essays since *The Souls of Black Folk*. All have been footnotes to Du Bois' monumental work. This is as true of *Notes of a Native Son* and *White Man, Listen* as it is of *The Black Situation* and *Home*. None of these essayists had managed to improve upon Du Bois' vision; each had merely in some way complemented it. The sense of double consciousness, the image of the prodigal at home and not yet at home, of the black intellectual attempting to merge his better self with a truer one, of Blacks attempting to maintain a dual identity in a world which sought to grant them none at all runs throughout each of these books. *Raise Race,* however, moves beyond *The Souls of Black Folk* and, in so doing, becomes its logical successor. Once and for all, the old question of identity and the conflict of the dual psyche is ended. Salvation for Blacks lay outside the Western orbit! Images, symbols, and metaphors of Blacks are not to be found in the mirrors of Western man. "We have our music. We have our art. We have our athletes. We have our religions. We have our black science, older than any on the planet. We have our beautiful people able to do anything and make anything and bring anything into being. . . . We will make cities . . . beautiful thrones of man and testaments to the ecstatic vision of the soulful."[21]

The duality found in the works of Baraka differs from that found in those of Du Bois. Du Bois accepted, all too readily, Western pretensions. He believed that the Shakespeares, Michelangelos, Platos, and Kants were not isolated examples but metaphors of the strength of Western culture. This led him to believe in integration, in the merging of black and white cultures. Only later in his life was he to realize with Baraka that one does not make bargains with the devil, that the devil honors no bargains, will effectuate no meaningful compromise. Thus he remained wedded to Western ideals and pretensions, even though he himself was the best example of the alienated isolated man, outside its history and culture. His inability to realize this made it impossible for him, like Baraka, to envision the new nation: based upon new images, with a spiritual foundation "Without a spiritual underbase, and value system speaking thru and from and out of us, Black sun, the shattering flame of possibility lurks to create itself, blinds already the dumb, halts the lame. . . . A new value system was what the way was prepared for."[22]

The millennium had not been reached. For the first time, however, Blacks had come unbelievably close. The political and literary leaders of the past had left a heritage consisting of a few political pamphlets, records of their life experiences, and made a beginning in the area of codified instruction to black people and black artist alike, in such works as *The Souls of Black Folk, The Condition, Elevation, Emigration, and Destiny of the Colored People of the United States, White Man, Listen,* and *White Man's Burden.* Taken all together, however, they add up to a set of position papers. None articulated singularly the function of the artist; none, likewise, foresaw the coming nation. *Raise Race,* therefore, has the distinction of being the literary Koran, the philosophy of the moral and the just, the Ten Commandments calling a people to sacrifice, struggle, and success. A new world is coming to birth, and a race of people, collectively, have arisen to take control, to return the earth to those who walk with the gods of the people. But there is much more in this collection of important essays. Read such pieces as "Poetry and Karma," "What the Arts Need Now," "Black Art, Nationalism, Organization, Black Institutions," "Meanings of Nationalism," and "Nationalism vs. Pimpart." Here is description, analysis, and direction. Here is challenge, prophecy, and commitment; here is the path which leads back from the long nights of desperation and despair: "We must demand the spiritual by being the spiritual. The Largest Work of Art is the World Itself. The potential is unlimited. The consciousness of men themselves must be raised. The creation of cities. Of Institutions. Governments. Treaties. Ceremonies. Public Rituals of the Actual World. The Nation. These are the only things worthy of the true Black Artist's consciousness. . . . Black Art must be Collective, is the spirit of the whole Nation. It must be Functional, it must have a function in the world to Black people. It must also commit Black people to a struggle for National liberation."[23] From the souls of a great people had come the message of old, shaped and chiseled after the examples of those who had survived numerous holocausts; it was a message embellished with the awe and grandeur of time; it had been sung by black men in the cotton fields of southern plantations, heard by Douglass on the abolitionist's rostrum, noted by Du Bois as he came down from Tennessee to the farmlands, issued anew in the call of Garvey for a new nation, sounded aloud in the old biblical inversions of Martin Luther King, transformed from message to symbol by the courage and commitment of Malcolm X, and structured and codified through the sensibility, commitment, and devotion of Imamu Baraka. In 1970 the message and the people became one: We are an African people and, thus, a loving and just people, committed to the salvation of the human spirit, to the improvement of the human condition; we are practitioners of the Black Arts, advocates of the Black Aesthetic, and builders of the new nation; we are those who walk the way of the new world.

XII

————◀◆▶————

THE WAY OF THE NEW WORLD, PART I

The marriage between the cultural ideology of Imamu Baraka and the social and political ideology of King, Malcolm, and the advocates of Black Power formed the unifying structure of much of the literature of the nineteen sixties and early seventies. This is as true for such genres as drama and poetry—the major concerns of The Black Repertory Theater—as it is for fiction. The writers who contributed to *Black Fire* were intent upon directing black literature away from the academic theorems and formulas of the past. Not only did they engage in the war for control of definitions, they also developed ideas and concepts destined to produce cultural awareness among black people and limit the influence of white art on the black writer. The change in the literature between 1952 and 1972 was all inclusive; it touched each genre and bore most heavily upon the African-American novel. The change in focus and content was given added impetus by the poetry of Gwendolyn Brooks, Langston Hughes, Askia Toure, Larry Neal, Sonia Sanchez, and Johari Amini, to name a few. As a result, the novel became less artifact than vehicle, less the medium for expressing one's personal angst than the medium for expressing the experiences of a race.

The change manifested in the novel was apparent as early as 1954, when John Oliver Killens published the novel, *Youngblood*. This story of drama and tragedy, of hope and commitment was overshadowed by the angst-ridden novels of James Baldwin. Yet, of the novels produced between 1954 and 1970, it is the first to deal with the mythology of race and history, somewhat, outside the American dimension. A novel of power and beauty, it advances images and metaphors of Blacks which will become familiar in future years and is instrumental in bringing about the new Renaissance—one differing from the old in that new writers were no longer willing to substitute black reality for white reality. Men like Ronald Berman might champion images and symbols depicted in such works as *Manchild in the Promised Land* and *Another Country,* might seek to offer these as metaphors of black people. The new generation of writers, who were apt to shun all literary and social offerings by whites, without close, detailed scrutiny, rejected such models as more relevant to white than to black life.

They were, these new Renaissance men, about creating images, symbols, and metaphors strikingly different from those which had been sanctioned heretofore. In their novels, the black man as brute, happy darky, or Christ figure is rarely found. The character, Youngblood, a metaphor for millions of Blacks, north and south, became their model for the black image. A man who inhabited a world far different from that of such literary predecessors as Bigger Thomas, he was more knowledgeable about it and its pretensions. He was determined to carve his own sense of reality out of the American environment, and though he still clings, precariously, to the Western version of the promised land, his commitment to his people is unmatched by any characters in black literature since those of Delany, Griggs, and Du Bois. The renaissance of the nineteen twenties offered no such models. In a sense, it was a movement awaiting a midwife; that, of the present time, is almost full grown, and such characters as Youngblood sustain the argument of Hoyt Fuller, who, more than any other person, has midwifed the new renaissance into birth. . . . They [Black Writers] are fully aware of the dual nature of their heritage, and of the subtleties and complexities; but they are even more aware of the terrible reality of their outsidedness, of their political and economic powerlessness, and of the desperate need for unity. And they have been convinced over and over again, by the irrefutable facts of history and by the cold intransigence of the privileged white majority, that the road to solidarity and strength leads inevitably through reclamation and indoctrination of black arts and culture.[1]

Today's black novelist, for the most part, has accepted Fuller's observations along with those of Karenga, both which point out the manifold objectives of black art. For Karenga, the first objective is that Black Art ". . . must expose the enemy, praise the people and support the revolution." Second, it must be functional—provide new images. "We need new images, and oranges in a bowl or fat white women smiling lewdly cannot be those images. . . . the real function of art is to make revolution, using its own medium." Third, it must be collective: "In a word, it must be from the people and must be returned to the people in a form more beautiful and colorful than it was in real life."[2] Such theorems are more proscriptive than descriptive; they are made after evaluation of the works of numbers of black writers brought to attention and prominence as a result of the revolution of the sixties. These writers constitute an enormous and varied group, and no study can hope to encompass them all in a single section or single volume. They have, each in his own way, contributed to the raising of consciousness by producing new images, to counter those which have circumscribed Blacks since the middle ages.

Their art does expose the enemy, praise the people, and support the revolution; and for images and symbols—and *Black Fire* is a good example—they have gone to the people themselves. Men and women of varying talents, interests, degrees of commitment, and sensibilities, they have moved the black novel into new areas of expression, made race the central characteristic of their work, and derived themes from the mythology and history of the race. They are impossible to categorize. Some were at work during the period eclipsed by Baldwin and Ellison; some are new writers, brought to birth as a result of the political movement in the streets; the works of some are satiric; the works of others border upon realism; still, those of others upon surrealism. Some have written only one novel; others have written as many as six. Some have denounced the new movement; others have vigorously supported it. Though the works of all cannot be evaluated at this point in time, the works of a representative few evidence the changes made in the literature from the past to the present and present a forecast of the literature to come. In the works of John Oliver Killens, John Williams, Ernest Gaines, and William Melvin Kelley, a new tradition is begun, one which depends for its viability upon black perceptions based upon black definitions of reality.

John Oliver Killens (1916–   ) is the spiritual father of the new novelists. It is his direction—more so than that of Ellison—that the young writers have followed. He is the first of the modern period to begin anew, with conscious determination, the quest for new definitions, to attempt to give new meanings to old cultural artifacts. Of his three novels, *Youngblood* is the pioneer in this respect. Yet, equally as important are the two novels, written some ten years apart, *And Then We Heard the Thunder* (1962) and *The Cotillion* (1972). Differences in setting and plot are apparent in the two works; yet, on one level, the novels share similar themes and situations, deal with the same conflict—the attempt at self-education by each of its protagonists. Both Solly Saunders and Yoruba must move from a preoccupation with the self to embrace black people everywhere; from concern with their individual status as victims of the American society to an awareness of their own strengths and egos. Each must begin the study of history, must find there the artifacts which sustained their forefathers, and, having done so, manifest a love toward black people at home and abroad. More so than any novelist in black literary history, Killens is the novelist of love.

The example that would seem less likely to prove this assertion is a novel about war. The genre of the war novel lends itself, most often, to preoccupation with death and pain. Often it is the novel of despair, courage, heroism, and failure—each manifested by hatred and hostility. If love intrudes at all, it is usually either on an individual level or on the level of loyalty to cause and country. This is as true of war novels written by whites—*The Naked and the Dead* and *Catch 22,* for example—as those written by Blacks. Killens had moved outside such parochialism, and through the education of his major protagonist, Solomon Saunders, has written a new kind of war novel. Here, love emanates from the self and becomes all inclusive. In a key statement of the novel, after reading Richard Wright's *12 Million Black Voices,* Saunders avers: ". . . if I'm proud of me, I don't need to hate Mister Charlie's people. I don't want to. I don't need to. If I love me, I can also love the whole damn human race. Black, brown, yellow, white."[3]

And Then We Heard the Thunder is a story, in general, about the men of the 913th Amphibian Platoon during World War Two, and, in particular, about the raising of the conscious awareness of Saunders. The novel, divided into four parts, moves on two levels. The first level is that of protest and depicts the struggle of black Americans to validate their manhood while fighting a war against Fascism at home and in distant lands. The second level is that of black awareness and black assertion. Black men must attain manhood, not only through daily combat with Fascism, but also through experiences which bring about a realization of their oneness with other Blacks. One level, the first, is dramatized through the exploits and adventures of members of the platoon; the other through the experiences of Solomon Saunders. The dual nature of the book is attributable to the fact that Killens speaks to two audiences simultaneously, one, white, the other Black.

The men who comprise the 913th are no ordinary crew. They are Blacks and whites thrown together by the exigencies of war in a way they would not have been during times of peace and tranquillity. For the Blacks of the platoon, among them, Joe Taylor, affectionately nicknamed Bookworm by his friends; Larker (the quiet man); Grant (the Black Nationalist); and Ray (the black opportunist), ambiguity about the nature of the enemy and the war is paramount. Fannie Mae Brandon, sweetheart-to-be of Saunders, early articulates the men's concern: "Where is the enemy? Who is the enemy? Why should we discriminate? A fascist is a fascist and a cracker is a cracker. The war is everywhere we find it."

In Ebbensville, Georgia, where the men are sent for basic training, the war rages unchecked between themselves, mores and folkways of the South, the military police, and their commanding officer. Epithets are frequent: "Get out of here, nigger! Godammit!" Captain Charles J. Rutherford, commanding officer of H. Company of the Fifty-Fifth Quartermaster Regiment, threatens a new recruit: "If I had my forty-five with me this morning, I'd blow your goddamn brains out."[4] Condescension, displayed in the words and actions of Lieutenant Samuels, executive officer of the company, adds a further dimension to the war, "We're in this thing to make a better world for all of us to live in. I'm a Jew. I don't say I know what you folks are up against. I mean I don't know precisely, but . . ." The war rages continuously in the minds of black soldiers: "They put me in this cracker army against my will," avers Pfc. Scott, "and they got the nerve to put me under a peckerwood officer and send me to Georgia. Them Japs and Germans ain't done me nothing. These crackers is my natural enemy."[5] In a letter addressed to newspapers, the President of the United States, and to Negro organizations, Corporal Saunders and Pfc. Taylor enunciate the major elements of the war. The company is composed of black men, yet all of the officers are white, mostly from the South, and bigoted. The company commander deals with his men in a fashion befitting a Nazi general. The soldiers suffer insults and physical abuse by the town and military police. The letter avails little except to result in the transferral of the entire company—including the commander and executive officer—to another front—Monterrey, California, where the war resumes with the old intensity.

The war between Blacks and whites rages most intently, however, on the front line—in the Philippines—during confrontation with the Japanese. Assaults on their manhood are collective and individual.

The black GIs are prevented from attending a Red Cross-sponsored dance and manhandled for attempting to do so. Rumors concerning their sexual bestiality, their inferiority, and their physiological attributes are spread among the Filipino people. The most humiliating act of all is the creation of a course in Information and Education, designed to remind the black soldiers that the war against Japanese militarism and Fascism is as much theirs as it is that of white soldiers. The final war, violent in nature, occurs in Australia. After being wounded in a destructive battle with the Japanese, surviving members of the company are transferred to Australia to recuperate and convalesce from their wounds. The war against the Americans, however, does not change in emphasis or intensity for the black soldiers. The Australians treat the men with kindness and compassion; and such treatment moves the United States Army to action. In order to prevent relationships between black men and white women, the clubs and bars frequented by Blacks are ordered closed. Others are either off limits or segregated. Club-swinging MPs have, seemingly, followed the men from Georgia to Australia, and incidents between them and the military police are frequent and numerous. When Quiet Man Larker is arrested and beaten after the men attempt to reopen a club, ironically named The Southern Cross, the final war occurs.

Killens, the superior craftsman, has carefully led the reader to the final confrontation. There are two wars being fought by Blacks, one a mock war, the other, the real one. Both involve the maiming and killing of men and both are fought against Fascism. Thus the Battle of Bainbridge, deleted from American history books, is as important as the Battle of Iwo Jima or the Battle of North Africa; it is a war not for territory or material gain, not to subject or to oppress a nation or its people; it is a war for manhood. The ferocity of the war, which eventually involves regiments of men on both sides, equipped with tanks and guns, is highlighted by a radio report: "People of Bainbridge were blasted out of their Sunday morning complacency by the war which has finally come to our town. Down in the heart of the commercial district in South Bainbridge, a full-scale battle is raging between the Americans, Blacks and whites. . . ."[6] Bainbridge, thus becomes the symbol of universal holocaust. The surviving members of the company will never forget their ordeal, will remember always the final war. The heroism displayed here will be duplicated once the men return to the war against Fascism at home. The most important result of the Battle of Bainbridge, however, is the unity of the black soldiers, the degree of concern manifested by one black GI for another.

The war against American Fascism leads, inevitably, to black consciousness and awareness.

The import of this assertion is evidenced in the character of Solomon Saunders, Jr. Black everyman, his inner conflict results from ambiguity concerning loyalty to America, individuality, and the fidelity to racial norms. Though he is a victim of Americanism, one who learns, empirically, of oppression, for most of the novel, he remains committed to American ideals, even believes in the war against Fascism abroad. ". . . I believe we have a stake in this war. . . . If Hitler won, the Negro would lose the ground we've already struggled for."[7] He maintains belief as well in the primacy of the individual over the race. College educated, he desires the American dream—home, car, good position—and the Army is viewed as a means toward these achievements. Not surprisingly, therefore, he initially considers his fellow inductees, Taylor, Scotty, and Larker, as inferior to himself, men who are obsessed with the problem of race. Given the novels of the twenties, those of Johnson and Fauset, Saunders would have been an admirable character, one who demonstrated that some Blacks were enterprising, ambitious, and loyal.

Time and circumstances, however, dictate that Saunders confront the realities of black life. He must undergo an education designed to teach him that the American dream can be had only if one is willing to surrender his manhood and forego the necessity of collective responsibility. His education takes place on a personal as well as societal level. When Saunders returns from escorting Fannie Mae Brandon home—with whom he has fallen in love, despite being a married man—he is brutally accosted and beaten by both the Georgia police and the military police. Subsequently, in California, he is jimcrowed along with others from an army canteen, denied admittance to a company dance, though previously invited, when his color becomes known, threatened with demotion by his company commander for protesting racist acts. Despite such incidents, he retains belief in the old faith, reminds the nationalist, Grant, that black men too are Americans. Realization, however, comes through an incident far less personal: one which moves even beyond the context of Black and white. During an air-raid attack by the Japanese, a Filipino woman, whom Saunders has named the Madonna, is killed, along with her young child and dog. Saunders, who had never cried before, who had maintained the archaic theory of the survival of the fittest, who had believed in looking out for "number one," is moved to tears at the sight of the woman's face, the mutilated body of the child, and the mangled form of the dog. Epiphany is reached, here, in this orgy of violence and death; the faces of the woman, child, and dog could be found on those of the world sufferers everywhere.

It is an epiphany which leads the once egotistical Saunders from a concern with individual pursuits to universal ones, and empathy with this image of beauty and suffering lead him along the road to racial awareness. Once he had refused to follow the dictates of his own conscience. Promises of promotion and a chance to attend Officers' Training School forced him to aquiesce to the unrealistic demands of the Army; he had collaborated in teaching the course in Information and Education to his men, despite his knowledge that the course was needed, not by black soldiers, but by white ones. After the epiphany, he gains new strength and determination. The death of his wife and child shake him profoundly but do not destroy him. Given a chance between attending Officers' Candidate School and leaving the Army, he chooses the latter. After reading Wright's *12 Million Black Voices,* the education is completed; Saunders recognizes his affinity with all black men: "This is me," he remonstrates. "Black me . . . Proud black American me, whose ancestors came from great Africa. Not arrogant, but just beginning to be proud of the specialness of black me. No bleaching powder, no hair slick-em up. Just the me I see in the mirror when I shave. . . ."[8]

The final chapter of the education of Solomon Saunders is highlighted by the Battle of Bainbridge. Here is the supreme test; he is forced to choose between individualism and racial unity, between the American dream and black reality. His wife dead, Fannie Mae Brandon has promised to marry him. He might remain in the Army, go to Officers' Training School, or be released from service with no blemish on his record. To join the mutinous black army at Bainbridge would make either alternative impossible. He was not implicated in the initial skirmish, learned of the ensuing war only after the fact. Any decision to enter would be a personal one. He decides to join his comrades, to risk all in the final war against American Fascism abroad, knowing that at last ". . . All his escape hatches from being Negro were more illusion than reality and did not give him dignity. All of his individual solutions and his personal assets, Looks, Personality, Education, Acceptance, Security, the whole damn shooting match was one grand illusion, without dignity." He had arrived at the conclusion that to sign a separate peace treaty with Captain Charlie would not guarantee "safe conduct through the great white civilized jungle. . . ."

Such realization leads to the inescapable conclusion that racial unity is of primary importance. Whatever happened to Saunders happened to him because he was black: position as company clerk, condescending respect from some fellow officers, promotion to sergeant, exclusion from canteens and dance halls, and assaults upon his person by whites. Worse things did not happen to him as they did to others, only because of circumstances. Therefore, the war in which he enlists at the end of the novel, both metaphorically and actually, is not a personal but a collective one, and what is demanded of each warrior is not only valor and courage, but love and respect for one another. These are the qualities demanded by Killens of one black man for another, and the primary characteristic of comrades in arms is love for each other. It is a first principle for the author and constitutes the overriding theme of *And Then We Heard the Thunder*. Men may be designated by race, by the uniforms they wear, by their status in a platoon, company, or battalion. Black men may even be designated by the color of their skin; yet, to be a black man means to evaluate oneself by different criteria: It means to be cognizant of one's past, to opt for the collective "we" over the individual "I" and to love each black man as one loves himself. Only in this way can the long night of oppression and tyranny be ended, can a people move to create the new world.

This thesis has drawn fire from Blacks and whites alike. Killens, asserts Blyden Jackson, has moved from integration to separatism, despite the fact that Killens does not opt for a closed world, does not advocate racial chauvinism. *And Then We Heard the Thunder* is not a novel of racial hostility, not one that attempts to create negative images of another people. The novel simply reiterates the message of thousands of young men and women in the streets of America, who demonstrate against Fascism, that it is more important to be Black than American, that one cannot be the latter until he accepts himself as the former. But more so, the novel opts for a new world and agrees, with Fanon, that only the wretched of the earth, those more capable of love than others, are able to bring it about: "I'm putting my money on that large minority known as colored people," Saunders remarks, "three quarters of the world's population."

Yet, in all of this, Killens creates no images of racial degradation, conjures up no suffering, pitiable black Messiahs. Though his men and women are not unaware of their dual position in society, none is willing to surrender his heritage and culture; his women are neither tyrants, prostitutes, nor frivolous imitations of white Miss Americas. His men are neither Bigger Thomases nor Rufus Scotts. His characters, like his images and symbols, are drawn from a different black reality, one which bespeaks a tradition of sacrifice and courage. These values are symbolized in the persons of Fannie Mae Brandon, Bookworm Taylor, Quiet Man Larker, and, finally, found in the person of Solly Saunders.

Each shares, not only a common history, but common racial experiences which evidence love and commitment, each for the other. It is not accidental that in each of Killens' novels the name of Harriet Tubman is invoked. Not accidental at all, for here is the symbol of courage and sacrifice, the metaphor of racial struggle and commitment; it is in Harriet Tubman that one finds the image of love and hope, of selfless devotion and of dedication to collective, instead of individual, responsibility. And it is this image, reflecting these qualities, that makes *And Then We Heard the Thunder* much more than simply another war novel.

The qualities—courage, sacrifice, love, commitment, and hope—pervade each of Killens' novels. The truth of this statement is evidenced in *The Cotillion.* The two novels between *And Then We Heard the Thunder* and *The Cotillion—Sippi* and *Slaves*—deserve more critical attention than they have received. Both are inferior novels, however, in comparison with the first two; yet, like *The Cotillion,* they are free of overwriting, drawn-out scenes and incidents, and serve as preparation for *The Cotillion.* Both evidence a greater control by the author over his material, the lack of which casts structural blemishes upon *Youngblood* and *Thunder.* These two earlier novels are marred by repetition of incidents and, all too frequently, similarity of action. The tendency toward sentimentality is also strong, and both novels suffer the fate of all big novels from *Clarissa* to *War and Peace:* a lack of focus upon a central plot, and the inability to portray, in multidimension, the numerous characters included in such works. Killens' novels suffer little as a result of these defects; however, having corrected them, *The Cotillion* emerges as his best work.

Killens, it appears, has recognized some of his own shortcomings. In the opening pages of *The Cotillion,* Ben Ali Lumumba informs the audience of his artistic intentions. The novel, designed by whites, which relies heavily upon such essentials as "Angles of narration, points of view, objectivity, universality, composition, author intrusion, sentence structure, syntax," etc., is not capable of portraying the black experience. Therefore, Lumumba, the author's persona, has decided to write his book in "Afro-Americanese . . . Black idiom, Black nuances, Black Style. Black Truth. Black exaggerations."[9] The Western paradigm, in short, cannot contain the nuances of the black experience, has no standards for a life-style which tends toward oral interpretation and which leans heavily in the direction of subjectivity and exaggeration. There is little argument here with form and structure as concepts; what is suggested is that neither can be guided by fast, empirical rules, that both become meaningful and relevant in the eyes of the reader.

Killens suggests, therefore, a one-to-one relationship between reader and writer. Form depends as much upon the perception of the reader as it does upon the technical skill of the writer. What this means is that the novel is viewed as a collective, not an individual creation. The vogue of literature which owes much to Laurence Sterne and James Joyce—one to which too many black writers have been attuned—has long held the audience to be less important than the work of art itself. In arrogant fashion, they have considered the relationship between writer and audience as analogous to that between lord and vassal: "It took me twenty years," Joyce is supposed to have said, "to write *Ulysses;* it should take a reader double that time to read it." In contrast, for Killens, and an increasing number of black novelists, form and structure take shape only under the scrutinizing gaze of the reader. The novel, therefore, cannot be the sole possession of the artist or an intellectual elite. It belongs to the people and becomes universal to the extent that it holds meaning for the people and, as in the case of the black novel, turns inward to the cultural artifacts shared in common by a great number of black people: to such rare artistic elements which comprise the early folklore, jokes, shouts, puns, the dozens—all displayed in such favorites as "Shine" and "the Signifying Monkey"—in addition to an all-encompassing black style, idiom, exaggerations, and truths. Based upon such literary suppositions, *The Cotillion* is a novel written with black people in mind.

The novel has been called "a black comedy." This is true on one level; however, on another, it is too narrow a description. Like black life in general, *The Cotillion* verges upon the tragic and the comic. For even in exaggeration of characters and incidents, there is all too much truth for comfort, in the foibles and human mistakes of the people, too much accuracy and realism. The novel is saved from nihilism by the love of the author for his subject; it is this which enables him to use satire as a means of producing greater unity among black people via the medium of laughter. The central focus of the novel, therefore, is upon the black community, upon the pretensions and illusions of its inhabitants. The plot is a shared one, easily discernible to black professional and black layman alike.

The plot centers around the Lovejoy family and involves the education of the mother, Daphne, and the arrival at the age of blackness of the daughter, Yoruba. Definitions are not difficult to come by in Killens' works. True blackness is, in *The Cotillion,* what it was in *Thunder* and *Youngblood:* Love for race which, beginning there, evolves into love for all humankind. With the exception of Mathew Lovejoy, the father, each of the main characters, Daphne, Yoruba, and Lumumba, suffers from self-doubt and inability to express love for black people, despite class and position. Though the extent of the malady differs for each, it is the same malady, and all are in need of a cotillion—a coming out of one's self into a newer and better self. The malady of self-love and self-doubt is quickly discernible in Daphne Lovejoy. West Indian daughter of a white landowner and his black mistress, she lives in a world of illusion. Aristocratic and stately in appearance, she believes that, with a little luck, she might have been a queen or some other such high personage, and thus she looks with disdain upon the uncouth, unclean folk whom she considers her inferiors. She has borrowed demeanor and comportment from the manual on how white people act, and so has developed contempt for "bad hair," "dark skin," "black colleges," and black people in general. Despite the facts of her own background, she dwells in the make-believe world of pretended ancestral pride and *hauteur* and has distinct ideas about the raising of her daughter, "a beautiful girl, despite the fact that she inherited her father's color and his looks."

Years of self-doubt have led her to prepare her daughter to be white, and her failure in this regard constitutes one of her many crosses. Not only did she prevent Yoruba from drinking coffee, which might make her black skin blacker yet, but she kept her out of the sunlight and away from beaches and attempted to counteract the influence of the father, ". . . who was Black and didn't have any better sense than to be damn proud of his Blackness." Mathew Lovejoy serves as the foil for Daphne and the model for Yoruba. Self-doubt and self-hatred are not part of his makeup, and if Daphne is enamored of all things white, Mathew has reached the pinnacle of black awareness, enamored of those things black, conducive to racial harmony and love. His personality is summed up in Daphne's contemptuous remark that, being Black, Mathew insists upon living "a black life," an objective shared by the daughter, Yoruba. Young, attractive, and sometimes contemptuous of her mother, she is trapped between the illusions of her mother and the reality of her father's vision. Young, vibrant, and becoming increasingly aware of her own beauty and self-worth, she sums up her conflict in her own thoughts: "How do you tell your mother you don't want to be a lady? That you would rather be a good black woman?" Yet, the ambivalence is still there; the choice between pretension and reality, father and mother, meant a choice between ladyship and womanhood.

However, Yoruba, too, is afflicted with the malady of self-doubt and an inability to accept the realities of the black experience. The disdain and contempt she evidences for her mother's point of view shows how far she must travel to realize true blackness. Lumumba, in a key statement of the novel, enunciates the standard, which, not only Yoruba, but Blacks in general should adhere to. The statement is as much that of the author as it is that of the character: "Am I so damn delicate that I'm scared that in rubbing elbows with my Black Bourgeoisie brothers and sisters more of them will rub off on me than of me rub off on them? If I'm that insecure, my Black-Consciousness must be pretty thin and superficial. I mean, they're part of the Black and Beautiful thing as much as anybody else. Every father's child of us has been brainwashed with the whitewash."[10] Yoruba's "coming out," therefore, means an acceptance of her mother, and thereby the acceptance of the oneness of black people, and true blackness means a commitment to educate the Daphnes of the world, to undertake the act of dewhitewashing.

This is the job, too, of the writer, and here, Lumumba's role in the novel takes on added significance. He is the prototype of the new black artist, a man wrestling with his own problems, attempting to come to grips with personal failings and, yet, one who believes in art for peoples' sake, in the oneness of all black people, and who is capable of understanding that the Daphnes and the ladies of the Femmes Fatales —the organization which sponsors the Cotillion—have succumbed to whitewashing more extensively than other Blacks and are in need, therefore, of teachers, not cynical critics. He views his function as an artist as being not only to recreate the uncreated consciousness of the race, but also to serve as teacher, soothsayer, and messenger to the people. Thus, his function is twofold. First, he is the narrator, intruding into the novel at will, commenting upon people and events, and putting each in proper perspective. Second, he is the central character, the hero, not only uniting the varied elements of the novel into a comprehensive whole, but also responsible for transforming "the Cotillion"— the black folks' imitation of a white peoples' ceremony—into a vehicle for black unity. The latter function demands a major upheaval in the thinking and perceptions of the black bourgeoisie.

The old and "honored" families who comprise this group are those who have gained status among Blacks as a result of skin complexion and professional occupation, which includes not only doctors and lawyers, but numbers bankers, postal clerks, gamblers, and hospital attendants. On the whole, the group seems immune to change. The decision by the wives of the "professional men," who comprise the Femmes Fatales, a fancy woman's club in Brooklyn, to open their yearly Cotillion ceremony to Blacks, who measured up to the middle-class norm neither in skin complexion nor professional parentage, evidences not change but missionary fervor. Even upon this point—opening up the Cotillion to outsiders—the group is beset by conflict. Only because of the tenacity of Mrs. Beverly Brap-Brap, wife of a leading undertaker whose funeral home housed some of the best crap games in Brooklyn, and Mrs. Patterson, stately dignified matron with missionary zeal, is the decision made to ". . . go beyond the boundaries of the socially elite of Brooklyn's first families and to choose some of our ladies from the ranks of the culturally deprived of Harlem. . . ." The culturally deprived includes Yoruba. Her entree into the select group results from the acquaintanceship between Daphne and Mrs. Patterson—both members of the prestigious Brooklyn Memorial Episcopal Church.

However, for her, the old conflict, highlighted earlier in the novel, remains. Both Lumumba, her boyfriend and guide, and her father view the Cotillion ceremony as pretentious and imitative. Yoruba shares this view. For Daphne, on the other hand, the Cotillion is viewed as the ultimate activity of those who have gained status and respect in society. Further, the thought that her daughter has a chance to become like "white ladies" fulfills the need of her own status-starved psyche. Though Yoruba wants desperately to sever all relations with the Cotillion, she does not want to offend her mother. She is in need of a deus ex machina, and here, Lumumba fulfills the role. He shaves off his beard, casts aside his dashiki for Ivy League clothes, and ingratiates himself with Daphne. When an occasion arises for the three to be present at a white Cotillion, Lumumba has little difficulty in persuading Daphne to accompany himself and Yoruba—as workers—to see how the white folks live and behave.

Daphne is shocked into partial awareness by the antics of those she had so long admired from afar. In the palatial estate of the white folks on Long Island, at the coming-out party for white debutantes, the scene is reminiscent of a Roman orgy. Buffet-table fights are common; people eat with their hands instead of with eating utensils; drinking, boisterousness, and free sexual play add to the atmosphere. The attempted seduction of her own daughter by a drunken participant, coupled with all that she witnesses, draws, afterward, this admission from the crestfallen Daphne: "I'm so happy we go out to that Long Island fete. It was for true the last illusion. I ain't never really loved white people. I was just too respectful of them, cause they got all the power. But the damn thing out on Long Island was the end of the journey for me."[11]

Yet, the journey to black awareness has only begun. When Daphne argues that the black Cotillion does not have to resemble that of the "sick white people," that it can be performed with dignity and elegance, Lumumba is spurred to action. He enlists the aid of Pam Jefferson, one of the more unpretentious of the young Brooklyn socialites, along with Yoruba, to plan a different kind of Cotillion than the one given previously by the Femmes Fatales. He convinces the two to substitute African dresses for evening gowns, that instead of wigs and straight hair, they should wear naturals, that their mannerisms should approximate those of the African women of old. After demurring, questioning, and reflecting, Yoruba comes to understand how the term cotillion might be redefined, made relevant to black people: "Coming out! Yes! Coming out! I am a debutante coming out of my old self into a new society." And, adds Lumumba/Killens: "She felt cotillionized for real. It was her grand debut into the maturation of her Blackness. The true rites of Cotillion had begun for her. Metamorphosis."

The metamorphosis is not Yoruba's alone. As the girls and their escorts invade the Cotillion in African dress and hairdo, pandemonium breaks loose. A near riot is averted when Lumumba, seizing the microphone, implores the crowd to give up the images of yesterday: "Black brothers and sisters, come out of the cotton patches. . . . all you Toms and Aunt Jemimas. Follow us to liberation! Be done with false illusion. Come with us to the real world!"[12] The effect of the action of Lumumba and his cohorts, however, are not to be measured so much by the shouts of approval which come from many in the audience, nor by the line of people forming behind him and Yoruba, but by Daphne who, forced to make a choice of her own, demonstrates the success of her education. One one side stood Mrs. Patterson, imploring her to leave this madness. On the other, arms outstretched, beckoning her to join the crowd around them, stood Yoruba and Lumumba. "Lady Daphne stood there for an endless moment—torn between the old and new, between illusion and reality. All her life she had lived sincerely in a world of dreams and fancy. Where indeed was the really real world? With Miss Prissy or Lumumba?"[13] When Daphne joins the crowd following Yoruba and Lumumba, her education has been completed and the cotillion has been an unparalleled success.

The success of *The Cotillion* as satire at its best is due to Killens' ability to effectively dramatize the wide desparity between illusion and reality which distinguish his major characters. In so doing, he is never as cutting as Ishmael Reed—perhaps the best black satirist since George Schuyler—nor as sentimental as William Melvin Kelley appears to be in the novel, *Dem*. Killens' wit and humor are directed at conditions, not at people, and this singular element counts toward his success. For the novel that attempts to inform, through the ironic juxtaposition of illusion and reality, demands a sensibility capable of compassion and understanding. Anger is not enough. Condescension must be avoided; chauvinism succeeds only in distorting reality. What is needed is what George Meredith called a love and sober realization of the weakness of one's fellows, which allows the writer to assume a kinship with the human spirit.

But needed in addition is a realization of, and faith in, the strength of one's fellows, a belief in *their* capacity for change. The opposite belief was held by too many black writers in the past who believed that change for black people was impossible, that if change came at all, it would be manifested in the society itself. The fate of Blacks, therefore, did indeed rest upon the good intentions of the American people, and the age of the new man was impossible unless America underwent a major metamorphosis. This meant more than simply allowing the nation to define the individual; it meant, also, to deny the individual a sense of his own strength and a belief in his own possibilities. Blacks appeared, in this evaluation, therefore, not so much as wards of the society but as its products as well. Literature, which accepted this thesis, directed its message toward white Americans, spoke of the conditions under which Blacks were forced to live, and predicated change upon change in the country at large. Having never accepted the basic premise—that black people are incapable of change—Killens has written a different kind of novel and broken completely with previous modes of thought.

He is all too willing to grant to Caesar that which is his, while demanding, conversely, that Caesar do likewise. He is not interested in saving white America, nor in reminding the editors, readers, and contributors to *Commentary* and *Dissent* of their commitment to fair play and equality. White people in the novel are depicted neither as Messiahs nor arch villains. When they are allowed to intrude into the work at all, it is only to point out to black people the fallacy inherent in accepting *them* as models of emulation. Daphne's illusions about white people have helped to bring about self-hatred and self-doubt; in like fashion, this is true on different levels for Yoruba and Lumumba. All have accepted the message from the imagists, old and new, that the surrogates of the Western gods are those of white complexion.

The acceptance of this idea is pervasive, though not exclusively so, among the members of the black bourgeoisie, symbolized by the Femmes Fatales. They have surrendered their birthright, willingly neglected the rich heritage of their African forefathers and black pioneers—all in an attempt to become like a people they know only from a distance. Yet, in the works of Killens they remain "brothers and sisters," who have as great a claim to "blackness" as others and are not, therefore, the only targets of the satirist. Pretentious black revolutionaries; Blacks who harbor contempt for mulattoes; artists, who champion black awareness in order to deceive the people, are equally censured. In the harangue of Billy "Bad Mouth" Williams, pretension of all kinds is excoriated: "Black brothers and sisters, it's time we chased the Bible-toting money changers out of the holy place of worship. We got to get our own houses clean before we can worry about taking care of Whitey's." *The Cotillion* is a satiric novel, calling upon Blacks to replace all the money changers, no matter the designation they answer to, and to join in a mutual housecleaning to purify the air of the black community.

To categorize Killens by labeling him an integrationist or separatist is to understand neither the man nor his work. Go back to *Youngblood,* his first novel, and the major progression is in terms of form and structure. In content, subject matter, and emphasis, Killens has moved only a short distance, if at all, from his first novel. The overriding theme of each of his works is the coming out of his characters into black awareness, the discovery of their black heritage. That he was among the first of the contemporary novelists to write of proud black men and women has not been overlooked by those young writers, who realize that he was among the first to challenge the images and symbols prescribed by the manipulators of the word and the first to break with those championed by members of the Wright school.

More so than the people of Ralph Ellison, his are far removed from past and present stereotypes of Blacks. They are not the middle-class sycophants of old, nor the brainless revolutionaries of the present. They are such men as Bookworm Taylor, Quiet Man Larker, and Mathew Lovejoy, whose characters are delineated by the extent of their love and faith in black people. It is this love and faith the author has shared with his characters from *Youngblood* to *The Cotillion.* The Youngbloods, father and son, the Lovejoys, mother and daughter, Saunders and Lumumba all have this in common; they must be made conscious of their own strength and move to confront a changing world in the manner and style of their creative ancestors. They must move from a preoccupation with self to a preoccupation with the race in general, and they must come to realize that they possess a heritage as enduring and as ancient as the Nile.

Such awareness determines the ascent to manhood and womanhood. None can attain this highest level of human achievement without recognizing his own potential, without finding in the models of black men, past and present, paradigms worthy of emulation. On the bookshelf which lines Lumumba's "pad," historical personages suggest the authenticity of this assertion. There are books by Du Bois, Frazier, Hare, Douglass, Mitchell, Wright, Fanon, Williams, Baraka, and Killens himself. Along with many others—Harriet Tubman and Nat Turner, for example—these are models who have been ignored due to the constant propaganda barrage by those who argue that Blacks have no history and culture. Each of Killens' characters, therefore, has the potential to join such men, and each has the inner strength to confront the American nightmare. None are products of the American society, and each, like Saunders, once cognizant of tradition, can step outside the images, symbols, and definitions which circumscribe him and move to a realization of his own limitless power. At a time when the novel throughout the world celebrates the emergence of the antihero, Killens reasserts the value of the hero, argues, that is, that heroism lay in the attempt to produce a better world for oneself and his people, and that the telling mark of the hero is his love for people.

One may score technical debating points against each of Killens' novels. If the plot sequence seemed too involved in *Youngblood* and *Thunder,* in *The Cotillion,* it seems too slight to support a major satiric venture. Overwriting, a defect in the previous novels, is less in the latter, though some scenes and episodes are stretched out too long and others receive inadequate attention. Sentimentality, though minuscule in *The Cotillion,* mars the earlier novels, and Killens' difficulty with dialogue is corrected only in the later work. To evaluate the novels based upon these defects, however, is to subtract from the richness of the works in terms of language and content, to ignore moving passages of prose in the earlier novels, and to ignore the diversity of black language styles utilized so expertly by the author in *The Cotillion.* The technical faults of Killens are those of exceptional novelists from Fielding to Kafka, and to point them out does not detract from Killens' substantial achievement in the novel form.

Killens' determination to opt for reality over illusion, no matter how devastating that reality may be, marked another area of achievement for the black novelist. For to make such a determination meant to face certain truths about America itself, to believe with Ferdinand Celine, that "the greatest defeat, in anything, is to forget, and above all to forget what it is that has smashed you, to let yourself be smashed without ever realizing how thoroughly devilish men can be. When our time is up, we people mustn't bear malice, but neither must we forget; we must tell the whole thing, without altering one word—everything that we have seen of man's viciousness. . . ."[14] The statement, however, needs emendation. Realization of the evil committed by men and nations alike may help to free the individual from long-held myths concerning the nature of both, and move him closer toward effectuating his own liberation.

The intent of Celine's statement and the emendation lead to the major function of the novels of John A. Williams (1925–   ). Like Killens, a prolific writer, his novels, from *The Angry Ones* (1960) to *Captain Blackman* (1973), evidence a steady progression from protest to assertion, from a feeble optimism to a hard-learned reality. If his first novel, *The Angry Ones,* is mired in the protest tradition, it is because he had not realized in 1960 that his strength lay in the synthesis of fiction and history, rather than in "unrelieved protest." Two of his novels, *The Man Who Cried I Am* (1967) and *Captain Blackman,* synthesize fiction and history and, in so doing, complement Celine; while, at the same time, they validate the three principles of Karenga that black art ". . . must expose the enemy, praise the people, and support the revolution."

"In the event of widespread and continuing racial disturbances in the United States, King Alfred at the discretion of the President is to be put into action immediately." Thus begins the first paragraph of the King Alfred Plan, the American version of *"Alliance Blanc,"* a plan formulated by European powers in order to maintain political and social hegemony over newly independent African States; "It was quite clear that the Europeans had Africa well under control—and that was all they cared about. America, sitting on a bubbling black cauldron, felt that it had to map its own contingency plan for handling 22 million black Americans in case they wanted everything freedom fighters got by stepping off the boat." Although the most important episodes of *The Man Who Cried I Am* center around the King Alfred Plan, from beginning to end the novel is the story of its central character, Max Reddick. King Alfred serves as a unifying device, bringing a host of disparate characters together in intrigue, mystery, and death: Harry Ames; his wife, Charlotte; his mistress, Michelle Bouilloux; Alfonso Edwards and Roger Wilkins, agents of the CIA; Minister Q; Paul Durell; and Jaja Enkzwu, the African minister who discovered the secret of Alliance Blanc. Enkzwu passes the secret to Ames, who, in turn, passes it to Michelle with instructions to pass it on to Max. Ultimately, the secret plan reaches Minister Q via a long-distance telephone call from Max.

Reddick, the protagonist, a reporter on the Harlem *Democrat,* has one novel under his belt before he meets Ames, an established black novelist. Incidents throughout his life have led him to accept the authenticity of Alliance Blanc. The death of his fiancée, Lillian, from an unsuccessful abortion can be attributed, in part, to his inability to secure meaningful employment. There is the disillusioning experience of working as a speech writer for the President of the United States and attempting, unsuccessfully, to convince him of the necessity for proposing meaningful civil rights legislation. There is marriage to a white woman, with all that such an act entails in racist America, and his friendship with Minister Q, leader of a Black Nationalist organization. Each experience convinces Reddick of the fallacy of the American creed, renders the democratic myth a little more untenable.

"I'm the way I am, the kind of writer I am, and you may be too," Ames tells Reddick, "because I'm a black man; therefore, we're in rebellion; we've got to be. We have no function as valid as that one." To be a black writer is to challenge the validity of creeds and myths, to accept the militant program of Minister Q over the more moderate one of Paul Durell, who typifies the "old and comforting image of the Negro preacher as leader." To accept the minister is to embrace Black Nationalism, to think in terms of newer, more powerful images. The premise—that America is a free society—is revealed as erroneous. No one understands this fact better than does Moses Boatwright. "To answer your question of some months ago," Boatwright informs Max from prison, "I took the heart and genitals; for isn't that what life is all about, clawing the heart and balls out of the other guy?" Boatwright is a *cause célèbre*. He has performed the act of cannibalism, eaten human flesh. His act coupled with Max's affliction—terminal cancer of the rectum—stand as symbols of the corruption and deterioration of the American ideal.

Although slowly dying, Max continues to hurl the fact of his existence into the face of a world morally inferior to himself, one which dares not confront its own truth, which cannot accept the inevitability of *its* death. Boatwright is a symbol of this death and decay; his act, an appropriate metaphor for a society in which, daily, Blacks and whites devour one another, "heart and balls." In so brutal and destructive a climate, the execution of the final stage of the King Alfred Plan is a matter of course, "When that emergency (racial warfare) comes, we must accept the total involvement of all 22 million members of the minority, men, women, and children, for once this project is launched, its goal is to terminate, once and for all, the minority threat to the whole of the American society, and, indeed, the free world."

Like the earlier novel, *Sissie,* analysis is the major feature of *The Man Who Cried I Am.* In the former novel, Williams isolates the black family in order to scrutinize it in detail, while in the latter, the entire Western world comes under scrutiny. Thus the novel is as much a historical and political document as it is a literary one. As history, the book is peopled by characters based upon real-life models: "Harry Ames (Richard Wright), Marion Dawes (James Baldwin), the President of the United States (John F. Kennedy), Minister Q (Malcolm X), and Paul Durell (Martin Luther King). Historical conflicts between Blacks and whites, Europeans and Africans, as well as ideological ones between Baldwin and Wright, and Malcolm X and Martin Luther King are also related. The conflict between Malcolm X and King, dramatized in that between Minister Q and Paul Durell, is waged on the plane of high politics; "Durell's people came from the churchgoing middle class; Minister Q's from the backwashes of Negro life. The white man was going to have some choice to make between them, but he would, Max knew, choose to deal with the remembered image, and that would be Durell."

The choice is between illusion and reality. When Max cables Minister Q on the eve of his own assassination at the hands of two black members of the CIA, he chooses reality over illusion, accepts the American society for what it is—a place in which freedom consists, in the words of Boatwright, of "clawing the heart and balls out of the other guy." Furthermore, in accepting reality, Max has attained manhood, has validated his own self-worth. He has made clear to a world, which daily hunts him down for daring to transgress against its definitions, that he will not acquiesce in its attempt to castrate him, that he has no intention of remaining passive while the juggernaut rolls over him. Like Lumumba, he is the new black protagonist, one who refuses to accede to the role of willing victim, will not be robbed of his manhood without resistance. But he is, too, a man with few illusions about America and white Americans. His survival, as he so well knows, depends as much upon awareness as it does upon his ability to outmaneuver his hired assassins, and he knows that the telling mark of his manhood is not that he win his battle against overwhelming odds, but only that he wage the struggle against the evil seeking to engulf him, valiantly and diligently.

Like Solly Saunders before him, Reddick must realize that individualism for Blacks is impossible in modern-day America. Alliance Blanc is designed, not only against Blacks in America, but against those from Mississippi to Africa. The King Alfred Plan, which unites American and European oppressors, symbolizes the evil confronting Blacks throughout the world, the attempt, to paraphrase Du Bois, of the Western world to maintain in subjugation men of darker complexion. Thus, the acknowledgment must be made that the act of Moses Boatwright holds meaning not for individual Blacks, but for Blacks everywhere. When Max informs Minister Q of the King Alfred Plan at the end of the novel, he displays his oneness with black mankind and makes the necessary commitment owed one black man to another.

Such a commitment precedes obligation to mankind as a whole and serves to enunciate a doctrine of universality which goes beyond that held by the Euro-American writers. The assumption has been widely held that the metaphor of man is to be found in the literature of Western man, that the prototype of man in the twentieth century is depicted in the angst-ridden literature of such novelists as Jerzy Kozenski and Norman Mailer. In opposition to this assumption, however, Williams' thesis holds that the prototype of man is to be found in the literature of the outsiders, those writers who not only concern themselves with the problems of tyranny and subjugation confronting two thirds of the earth's people, but make the one-to-one connection between their condition and that of others. Understandably, therefore, the archetypal hero of the twentieth century is the black man evidencing, in his daily struggles, the most universal of characteristics—hope, love, determination, and courage. Yet, this doctrine, not new with Williams, was impossible to arrive at before black men moved to reclaim their history. For if images and symbols of positive import were to be created, if the black man was to be seen as representative of the best in mankind, if the definitions were to be redefined, the terminology reexamined, the black writer would have to wage warfare against the white man's interpretation of history.

Such a war is the major concern of Williams' most recent novel, *Captain Blackman*. Two major conflicts form the plot structure of this five-part novel. The major conflict involves Abraham Blackman, captain in the United States Army, and his superior, Major Ishmael Whittman. The other pits Blackman against history. The first is that of old, the unifying structure of the plots of too many black novels; it details the struggle between Blacks and whites, symbolized in the characters of Blackman and Whittman. Only the characters are different. Blackman is cognizant of the fact that his position vis-à-vis that of the major's— an inferior one—is due, not to any defects in his intelligence or his worth as a human being, but, instead, to the mechanics of a white society which does not allow equal competition between Blacks and whites: "Listen, Ish," Blackman establishes the parameter of the conflict, "don't pull that rank shit with me. . . . Now you know . . . well that the only reason you're sitting there and I'm sitting here is that you're white and I'm not. Right?"

Both men begin their military careers simultaneously, and each moves slowly through the ranks. Whittman, early evidencing hatred for Blacks and Jews, serves with the occupation forces in Europe after

World War Two before being connected with an all-black unit in Japan. A pretentious man, with a desire for power, expensive cigars, and fashionable mistresses, he has little intellect, is a failure as man and soldier. Nevertheless, in Korea, he is assigned the command of two squads of Blacks. From this assignment he begins the ascent which will lead him to the rank of general. Blackman, southern born and educated, one of six children, reaches Korea by way of Japan. Here he meets Whittman for the first time, and the conflict ensues. Blackman, who commands one of the rifle units, under the over-all command of Whittman, discovers that the major is incompetent and informs him of it: ". . . Whittman couldn't read the map, although he kept pretending he could." Each time Blackman pointed out an error, Whittman crumpled up the map. "This cat don't care," Blackman thought. "He's got two squads of niggers and he don't care. . . ."

The two go separate ways after the armistice is declared in Korea. Whittman remains in the service, moves up in the ranks; Blackman returns to civilian life, attends college, marries, divorces, and finally returns to the Army. Tours of duty in Europe, a commission as a second lieutenant, and a first stint in Vietnam, where he learns, firsthand, the true history of the Vietnam war during a battle involving Blacks and whites against Asians; the Blacks and whites were more interested in killing each other and were prevented from doing so only because the Vietnamese represented their "each other." "Today was one of the days their Vietnamese were their each other. Today . . . black men became like white men; they, too, raped, murdered, and castrated; murdered in the heat of hysteria. . . . No, Blackman told himself . . . No! We're not joining them in this. . . . We ain't payin *that* price for belonging. . . ."[15]

After the revelation at My Suc, Blackman decides to initiate a seminar in Black History for the education of his regiment. He re-enlists, is promoted to captain, and comes once again under the command of Whittman. The hostility between the two is resumed in a changed army, integrated with more assertive black recruits. Whittman would like to prevent the seminar on Black History—fearing the animosity of his men—but he is unable to do so. The inability to prevent Blackman from pursuing his objective ranks, in Whittman's mind, second only to past maltreatment he received at the hands of the black major: a beating in Korea and derision at the major's inability to read military maps. As a result, Whittman sends Blackman into ambush and, hopefully, death against the North Vietnamese. Though Blackman loses a leg and a kidney, death is avoided. Nevertheless, Whittman gloats over the injury he has caused his old antagonist: "This was white power; this is what he'd done, finally, to the nigger who whipped his ass in Korea. . . . I did this. . . . I sent him in when intelligence as usual didn't know shit from Shinola about what was out there."

The final confrontation, however, is yet to come. Years later, Blackman, out of the service, works to put a secret plan into operation. The plan, which revolves around the concept of cultural warfare, if successful, would result in crippling the American war machine. Blackman formulates the plan: Select thousands of mulattoes, quadroons, octoroons, etc.; take them to secluded places in Africa; debrainwash them of white values and sentiments; infiltrate them into the American Army in strategic positions: "Take thirty years, about. Set them in Norad, the Skylab probes, Sac, the Pentagon; to the tracking stations at Kennedy. . . . And sit there lookin white, but be black. . . ."[16] As the American military machine collapses, as a result of the usurpation of control by bogus whites, Whittman, now general, realizes defeat when a jeering voice informs him over the telephone that "nothing will work, Ishmael. It's ours. All of it. I've kicked your ass again."

The conflict between Blackman and Whittman, however, is overshadowed by the conflict between Blackman and history. His decision, after My Suc, to initiate a seminar in Black History is based upon a desire to educate his men to the truth of history. Such an education is designed to form a link between present and past, to inform black soldiers that they were not the first to "do what they were doing." In preparation for his seminar, "He'd gone back to the American Revolution, to Prince Eastbrook, Peter Salem, Crispus Attucks and all the unnamed rest; from there to the War of 1812, the Civil War, the Plains war, the Spanish-American War—all the wars. . . ." This lesson, given shortly before Blackman's injury, serves to foreshadow his own journey through history. Badly wounded by the Vietnamese, as he is spun completely around by one of the shells which hit him, he loses consciousness, descends into the dream world, is transported from the nineteen sixties to the sixteen hundreds. He awakes during the time of the Revolutionary War, and the odyssey of Captain Blackman has begun.

Parts One through Four of this ambitious novel deal with Blackman, cast adrift in history. Suspended somewhere between consciousness and semiconsciousness, the incapacitated Blackman, wounded in Vietnam, is overshadowed by the robust, fighting Blackman who moves through each of America's wars. Parts One and Two of the novel are devoted to the Revolutionary War, the Civil War, the Indian wars, and the war against Spain. Part Three is devoted almost exclusively to the First World War, Part Four, to the Second. Blackman, in each, is not only participant, but observer and commentator as well. In the Revolutionary War, he is privy to untold history, learns from the words of an official the true reason for rebellion against British rule: ". . . once the common man is made to realize that the Crown cares nothing about him— no representation and all that—he will come . . . to know that the only path left to him is to revolt to freedom. In the meantime we can extend our range from the Atlantic to Balboa's Pacific, increase the slave trade and America will see another, larger Greece."

Blackman's knowledge of history gives him an advantage over his fellow soldiers, the black heroes of the Revolutionary War. He knows that those who follow Peter Salem, Cato, Salem Poor, and Crispus Attucks will not receive land and freedom after the war, will instead be returned to slavery. He knows that George Washington, having been told to free his own slaves, will do so only upon his deathbed, that the promises made to black men by Andrew Jackson will come down through the ages as metaphors of America's deception against Blacks in and out of the Army: "To every noble-hearted, generous freeman of color volunteering . . . to serve during the present contest with Great Britain, and no longer, there will be paid the same bounty in money and lands, now received by the white soldiers of the United States. . . ."[17] The pattern of deception established in this first war continues unchanged throughout history. There are the secret maneuverings of the war planners, the heroic efforts in defense of democracy by Blacks, and the promises made, and broken, to them and their progeny. Here too is the irony of history, one pointed up by an Indian who informs Blackman, during the Indian-American war, that black people, who allowed themselves to be dragged to America in chains, would survive the Indians only because they refused to fight whites; yet, one day, he avowed, they would have to fight, would be forced to die in order to prevent the genocide which they and the whites perpetrated upon the Indians.

The murder of black soldiers by whites runs like a leitmotif through history. There are the indiscriminate murders during the Revolutionary War; the execution and castration of black soldiers by southern troops during the Civil War; the maiming and murder of Blacks in New York during the draft riots; thirteen men hanged, and one hundred imprisoned for life after the Houston riot, preceding World War I.

The symbol of mass murder, however, remains Tombolo, the setting of an incident which occurs during the Second World War. Reacting against unjust treatment, two hundred black soldiers retreat into the Italian swamps with their girlfriends and rifles. Here a commune of sorts is formed, including escapees from Nazi terror. Tombolo is besieged eventually by the American armed forces, however, and all its residents murdered. The massacre is passed off as one of the minor battles against the enemy: "We left them where they fell. There'll be a Graves Registration detachment sent up from our end today. They'll be buried in the military cemetery south of Florence. Killed in action. Ten thousand bucks for their wives, sisters, or mothers. . . ."

The past is almost indistinguishable from the present, the dream world no different for Blackman than the real. He regains consciousness in a hospital in Vietnam; stream of consciousness takes the place of dream sequence; the reader is filled in on the exploits of black soldiers in Korea and Vietnam. The old pattern is repeated, broken only by the new black soldiers coming into the army in the fifties and sixties. The new recruits, informed of their own history, with Blackman will move with greater awareness to take collective action to reverse the historical pattern: "It was a mistake, I mean to expect my enemy, which he was, always has been, to reward my services with equality. A serious misjudgment. Worse, tragic . . . there were things I was catching from him, just being in his company. I could feel it deep in my soul; I could see it happening, if not to me completely, to others." The revelation leads him from Vietnam to Africa, where other black men, having digested the true facts of history, make preparations for the final war.

To trace Williams' progress from *The Angry Ones* to *Captain Blackman* is to recognize not only a change in perception but in form and structure as well. The earlier novels were heavily imbued with protest, were straight narratives, and designed to catalogue the wrongs perpetrated against Blacks by whites. The shift from protest to analysis began with *Sissie* and demanded a form and structure allowing for freer interplay between history and ideas. New characters were needed—men and women, cosmopolitan and sophisticated, whose experiences were national and international as well. Killens had created such a character in Lumumba, Kelley in Chig Dunsford. Both are world travelers, have learned to view racism from a universal perspective. Though antecedents are to be found as far back as *Clotel,* it is Williams who develops the character to the greatest degree of sophistication. Reddick and Blackman are cosmopolitan men; each has discovered through empirical observation and personal experience, how this world goes. The odyssey undertaken by each, therefore, is not for self-awareness or self-revelation, but to bring about revelation and awareness for the reader. Each seeks to reveal, for a predominantly black reading public, the magnitude of Western racism. Such an objective demanded not only change in character but change in the format of the novel itself.

The agent of change was time. After *Nightsong*, Williams discovered that the writer was master of time in the novel; that time was never static but an ever-changing reality. To merge history and fiction, therefore, necessitated that the writer exercise great control over time; that he prepare to break it up—change endings into beginnings and vice versa. Flashbacks are used to accomplish this feat in *The Man Who Cried I Am* and, as a result, Reddick moves quickly and easily across three continents. In *Captain Blackman,* the manipulation of time occurs through dream sequences and stream of consciousness. Blackman, therefore, appears simultaneously as a wanderer through history and a patient on an operating table in Vietnam. Williams, however, has not completely mastered the usage of time in either novel, and, thus, both are flawed by confusion. Past and present incidents are thrust upon the reader so quickly that sometimes it is difficult to distinguish between the two. When the technique works well, however, more often in the latter than the former novel, Williams comes close to mastering the form of the historical novel.

This is no small achievement. More important is Williams' determination to explore black life realistically, to search for paradigms of the distant past, to search out images, symbols, and metaphors relevant to the present. Thus the close parallel between past and present, shown specifically in *Captain Blackman,* between characters and incidents is neither artificial nor contrived. Those who appear in Blackman's Odyssey in the sixteen hundreds, eighteen hundreds, nineteen hundreds have their mirror images in those who appear in the nineteen sixties. In other words, the men who struggled in the distant past, who met the test of manhood, differ little from those who act accordingly in the twentieth century; in the lives and experiences of Peter Salem, Salem Poor, Crispus Attucks, and Paul Belmont are the examples followed by black men of today. Blackman is their modern representative; he is Nat Turner, Denmark Vesey, Martin King, and Malcolm X; he is the unnamed, unheralded black slave fighting for freedom and dignity; he is the rebellious Black in the urban black community of the nineteen seventies.

He is, finally, every black man who struggles to retain his manhood in a world determined to rob him of it. He is Max Reddick who, though dying of cancer, struggles to make some sense out of life, to impose his meaning upon the world; he is Blackman who, though incapacitated, refuses to surrender in his conflict between man and history. Williams' obsession with struggle—the hallmark of each of his characters—reveals his evaluation of its importance. For one's manhood depends, not so much upon success, but upon how tenaciously one wages the fight in behalf of that manhood. This is the chief characteristic of his heroes, the test each must pass in order to claim existence. Those who succeed, and many do not, struggle against history as well as against other men—a fact which, for Williams, constitutes history itself. For it is to history that one must look for those values which address the best in men, which speak to his sense of humanity. It is to history, also, that one looks for the best example of modern black men; there, that the falsity of the old images, stereotypes, and metaphors can be seen. History then, rewritten and corrected, holds the key to success in the war against the modern imagists, and the black novelist's venture into this area meant that the war was near completion. Along with *And Then We Heard the Thunder* and *The Cotillion, The Man Who Cried I Am* and *Captain Blackman* were valuable assets in the final culmination of this war.

XIII

———◆◆◆———

THE WAY OF THE NEW WORLD, PART II

"People and time," argues Miss Jane Pittman, "bring forth leaders."

Whether this combination holds true in the political realm is conjectural. There is evidence, however, in the works of black novelists in the sixties and early seventies that the formula holds true for black literature. A combination of time and people helped to turn the black novel inward and forced the novelist to deal with artifacts of the racial heritage heretofore all but neglected. The people who marched from Montgomery to New York, who rebelled in the streets from Newark to Los Angeles, were sending messages to Blacks as well as whites, to artists as well as politicians. They were demanding a new interpretation of the black experience; new ideas from the politician, the formulation of a new contract between whites and Blacks. They demanded from the artist truer images, symbols, and metaphors—those that reflected the actuality of their lives. That to meet such demands required a new look at, and approach to, history, they knew from the works of Baraka, Killens, and Williams, from the proponents of the new Black Art.

The new approach to history was necessary for the education of young Blacks growing up in twentieth-century America, a fact recognized not only by such prominent black historians as John H. Clarke and Lerone Bennett, but by black novelists as well. A product himself of time and the people, the novelist was concerned, more so than his predecessors had been, with racial hegemony; he was committed to reinterpreting history in line with the black historians, adding to it those nuances peculiar to the writer of fiction—dramatizing facts, recreating situations, and ennobling men and events. He was more likely, however, than the historian, to be interested in specifics, to seize upon singular examples and exploit these, rather than generalize and suggest all-inclusive metaphors. "The protagonists in Mr. Gaines's . . . novels," writes Hoyt Fuller, ". . . share a fiber and strength that, though always present in black men of their backgrounds, have rarely been portrayed in fiction."[1] This is true in another sense of William Melvin Kelley and the young black writers of the seventies, whose works have come to the attention of a black reading public. Most are concerned with the strength and courage that produced the Mary Lou Hammers and the Angela Davises, with the culture that produced a creative people, with rebellion and endurance. In their own way, each deals with aspects of the racial past and suggests, in so doing, that time and circumstances demand that black people look inward, for paradigms of positive import. The people, in the nineteen sixties and seventies, caught up with time and began to travel the byways and highways of the new world, and the best of their novelists—those who believed in history as revelation—followed suit.

Among such novelists, write the name of Ernest J. Gaines (1933–   ). A product of the South of which he writes so eloquently, Gaines has won numerous awards and received a number of grants and fellowships, not alone for his work in long fiction, but also for his collection of short stories, *Bloodline* (1968). From his first novel, *Catherine Carmier* (1964), to his latest, *The Autobiography of Miss Jane Pittman* (1971), he is concerned with specific elements of the racial past. Love, tragedy, interracial antagonisms, and rebellion are aspects of the themes comprising his works. That which takes precedence, however, is that men are circumscribed by historical patterns and that those who step outside such patterns are paradigms for future generations. The idea is not new. Attaway was one of the first to suggest that after the desertion of man by God, man was left to construct patterns of living and dying. Wright, accepting this premise, added a further dimension: The patterns were constructed by a white society and, therefore, not binding upon black men. Rebellion against such patterns was mandatory, even though the result of rebellion produced not the historical example, but the nihilist, not a paradigm for Blacks, but a warning for whites. Accepting some aspect of both ideas, Gaines avers, however, that those who break white-man-made patterns serve not as warnings, but as examples; they are the historical counterparts, the paradigms, of men and women today. *Of Love and Dust* (1967) and *The Autobiography of Miss Jane Pittman* are fine examples of the explication of this theme.

Gaines's second novel, *Of Love and Dust,* ostensibly a story of love, hate, and rebellion, is an accounting of the historical rebellion by Blacks against predetermined folkways and mores. The overt outlines of the plot structure are quickly discernible. Marcus Payne, Black, orphan, kills another Black during a fight over a girl. Through the influence of an aged aunt—onetime employer and confidant of plantation owner, Herbert Marshall—Payne is sent, not to the county jail, but to Marshall's plantation to work while awaiting trial. To work as a black man on the plantation means to come into conflict with the Cajun overseer, Sidney Bonbon: ". . . he got to try you," Aunt Julie avers. "He got to break you." In other words, one must accept the authority of the overseer over one's life; to refuse to do so means rebellion and conflict. The conflict is historical not personal; it is rooted in the mores of the region, and the roles of Bonbon and Marcus are prescribed in legend and folklore, "We is nothing but little people." Bonbon remarks in the course of the novel. "They make us do what they want us to do. . . ."[2]

They are the aristocrats, the large landowners, like Marshall, who symbolize power and arrogance. Ruthless and unprincipled, Marshall has held on to his plantation, acquired greater wealth and land by lying, cheating, manipulating poor whites and Blacks, and by murder. The act of murder has placed him at the mercy of his overseer. Pressed by a gambler to pay a debt owed by his brother, the gambler is later murdered. Rumor has it that Bonbon, on the scene the night the gambler was killed, murdered the second man after having paid him to kill Marshall's adversary. Thus Marshall is open to blackmail from those with evidence of his part in the murder. Miss Julie uses her knowledge to blackmail the plantation owner into accepting her nephew on the plantation, thus saving him from jail; Bonbon uses his knowledge to protect himself, while stealing and selling Marshall's produce. Wanting to see Bonbon killed, but unwilling to do so himself, Marshall settles upon Marcus as his agent ". . . he makes Bonbon work Marcus like a slave so Marcus can get mad enough to kill him."

The conflict between Marcus and Bonbon, however, has other dimensions. Bonbon, following custom and pattern established by the folkways and mores of his region, has taken Pauline, a black worker, as his mistress. For the people on the plantation, his association with Pauline is not surprising, is part of the order of things, for everyone "expected the white overseer to have a black woman—even his wife expected that." Neither, however, expected the overseer to neglect his wife for the black mistress, to care more for his mulatto twins than for his own white daughter. Louise, his young wife, did not expect it and accumulated anger takes the form, first, of wanting revenge and, later, complete liberation. After Marcus is humiliated and rebuffed in an attempt to date Pauline, he seeks revenge upon Bonbon through Louise. The dejected wife broadens her plan. If she can entice Marcus into seducing her, Bonbon, given the unwritten rule of the region, would be forced to kill Marcus, and Marshall, in turn, to get rid of Bondon. In addition to the humiliation she would have inflicted upon her husband—sexual relationship with a black man—she would also be free.

The plan goes awry, however, when the two transgressors fall in love with each other. After the first seduction, each surrenders his plan of revenge, becomes genuinely interested in the other. Their eventual decision to run away together receives condemnation from Blacks and draws the following retort from Louise, "You and your kind don't want us to go. It's the end for you and your kind if we get away. . . . It's all right for Sidney and that—that Pauline down there. But it's not all right for me and Marcus. Well, I say we go, and we will go."[3]

The lovers enlist the aid of Marshall. Marcus is familiar with the mores of the South and Marshall's predicament in relationship to Bonbon as well. He knows that if he runs away with Louise, Bonbon must come after him. This would free Marshall of his burden. In payment, Marshall must fix the trial so that Marcus goes free, place money and a car at the couple's disposal, and maneuver Bonbon away from the plantation on the day the event occurs. The conflict facing the plantation owner is apparent. He is asked to aid in the transgression of patterns established by him and his ancestors, asked to sanction the relationship between a black man and a white woman. He is incapable of going so far, though he agrees to the plan; he arranges to have Marcus declared innocent; he places money and a car at the couple's disposal. In addition, he places a gun in the glove compartment of the car. He does not, however, maneuver the overseer away. Bonbon discovers the runaway attempt and a bloody battle between himself and the black man ensues. Marcus, oblivious of the gun placed in the glove compartment for his use, is killed, reluctantly, by Bonbon, who had hoped that the black man would not fight him, would, instead, run away so that the overseer would not have to obey the unwritten law: ". . . when Marcus didn't run, he had to fight him. Not just fight him, but he had to kill him. If he hadn't killed Marcus, he would have been killed himself. The Cajuns on the river would have done that." Pauline and Bonbon go off together at the end of the novel; Louise is remanded to an insane asylum, and the narrator, Kelley, is forced to leave the plantation because of his knowledge of the true circumstances surrounding the incident.

Of Love and Dust, upon first reading, appears to be a novel in the naturalist tradition. The same emphasis on the predominance of patterns discernible in works by Hardy, Attaway, and Wright is prevalent here. The note of angst and human despair at the forces outside man's control is sounded early in the narrative: "I spoke to the old man [God]" the narrator, Kelley, remarks, "but I'm sure he didn't hear a word I said. He had quit listening to me a million years ago. Now all he does is play chess by Himself or sit around playing solitaire with old cards. So man has to do it for himself now. No, he's not going to win, but if he struggles hard and long enough, he can ease his pains a little." The abdication of God is pronounced and has created a vacuum which southern aristocrats have moved to fill. Though defeated in the Civil War, they have regained power and prestige, have become God's vice-regents on earth, the creators of patterns for poor whites and Blacks alike. Some of these patterns, in the form of laws and rules, prescribe legal modes of living; others, in the form of mores and folkways, prescribe moral modes, based upon definitions of the past, and are enforced by intimidation, threats, and naked force. Together, unwritten and written, the laws comprise a mosaic of intricate design in which men validate or surrender their manhood through blind obedience, compliance, or naked rebellion.

Exactly when the new order came into being—the reign of God's vice-regents in his stead—is not known; in *The Autobiography of Miss Jane Pittman,* Gaines sets the time at the point of slavery. However, at some point of time, men established the patterns of discipline and order, which led to the symbol of the plantation as the agency of authority, and the plantation owner as the new Lycurgus. To maintain the new order, Blacks were played off against poor whites: "The plantation . . . had all its crops far back in the field. The front land was for the sharecroppers. The Cajuns (poor whites) had the frontest and best land, and the colored people . . . had the middle and worst land." The abdication of God, however, which allowed some men to assume dictatorial authority over others, also freed man from responsibility and dependence, freed him, also, from history. He was no longer forced to obey the biblical statutes and, if bold enough and daring enough, he was free to accept or reject the patterns described by the vice-regents, free to rebel against arbitrary rules imposed by other men, free to step outside of history and to create new patterns for living.

Such attributes are common to the historical rebel, and Marcus Payne shares them all. From the beginning of the novel, it is plain that he intends to rebel against arbitrary authority. He has no intention of remaining on Marshall's plantation nor of being broken by Bonbon. He is as disdainful of the new form of slavery as his ancestors were of the real model: "Things can't get harder for me, Jim. I'm a slave here now. And things can't get harder than slavery." The central episode of the novel—the seduction of the white overseer's wife—is of minimal importance in establishing the nature of Marcus' rebellion. For he rebels, not so much against the social restrictions, but against the superior—inferior patterns, handed down from the past, upon which the social fabric of the South has rested. Far more indicative of his role as the rebel against historical patterns is the retort made by the house servant of Marshall, who had refused Marcus admission to enter the front door of the plantation house: "He just pushed his foot in there. . . . The house his great-grandparents built. The house slavery built. He pushed his foot in that door. . . . any black person who would stick his foot in a door that slavery built would do almost anything."

However, such a person serves, also, as a model for others. The life of James Kelley, tractor driver on the plantation, and the narrator of the story, is changed most by the example of Marcus. Kelley is a hard-drinking, serious-minded man of principle, a confidant of Bonbon; he remains on the plantation, due to inertia, after his Billy Jean runs off in search of material things. Part idealist, part homespun philosopher, he is wise beyond his years, knows the workings of the mores and folkways of the region. A tractor driver—a skilled trade, of sorts—he is inured against much of the hardship occasioned by working in the fields; as a non-sharecropper, he is more in charge of his own fate than are other Blacks in charge of theirs. He maintains a quiet dignity and does not deserve the epithet—Uncle Tom—used to describe him by the younger Marcus. He has, however, accepted the jurisdiction of the new law-givers, refuses to challenge rules and laws he abhors: entering back doors for service, fronting for Pauline and Bonbon—since he wants her himself—when they arrange trysting episodes in the town, are a few of the indignities he suffers without outward rebellion.

The change in Kelley occurs when he accepts Marcus as a bona fide rebel, when he believes that the young man had demanded from the aristocrat certain favors in return for favors to be rendered on his behalf: "I leaned back against the window to look at Marcus. Now I did believe him. I believed him because I remembered he had fooled that dog and jumped through that window to get to Bonbon's wife. I believed him because I remembered he had stuck his foot in that door—

that slavery had built. I believed everything Marcus said. . . ." Kelley moves from belief to admiration and, on the day of Marcus' death, accepts him as an example of courage and determination, a paradigm by which he might now order his own life: "No, I didn't blame Marcus any more. I admired Marcus. I admired his great courage. . . . I wanted to tell him how brave I thought he was. He was the bravest man I knew. . . . I wanted to tell him that. And I wanted to tell Louise how I admired her bravery. I wanted to tell them that they were starting something—yes; that's what I would tell them; they were starting something that others would hear about and understand and would follow."

Of Love and Dust gains its dramatic power from Gaines's ability to magnify the specifics of history and to use the novel for explorations into the past and present. If others used history as a vehicle for instruction, drew comparison between men like Douglass and the young Blacks of the fifties and sixties, Gaines moves to new ground. History to be sure is a vehicle to be used in enhancing knowledge and understanding; but it is to be used, also, to present, in microcosm, man's age-old struggle against authoritarianism by focusing upon singular examples of black rebellion. In this analysis, the meaning of the lives of Douglass, Malcolm, Nat Turner and Sojourner Truth, H. Rap Brown and Stokely Carmichael might be known by examining the many-faceted character of Marcus Payne. For to be Black in America is to rebel against age-old patterns of injustice, to throw oneself into conflict with mores and folkways designed to rob man of dignity and freedom, to carve manhood, independence, and freedom out of the act of rebellion itself.

Marcus refuses to be bounded by the scriptures of the new gods. From the moment he enters the novel, struggle and rebellion are the important elements in his character. He lives as he dies, in combat with those who seek to restrict his freedom; he dies in nobility and grandeur, fighting against man-imposed laws and customs. Yet, he is not a character without flaws; he is, after all, a murderer, having killed another Black. He appears oftentimes to be more concerned with Marcus Payne than with black people in general. "Me, I don't care for nobody but me . . ." he remarks in a statement, which tars his image as a historical rebel of importance for Blacks and diminishes his grandeur and his achievement. Here, the salient distinction between Bonbon and Marcus is the latter's unwillingness to conform to prescribed patterns. As a devotee of the philosophy of individualism, like Bonbon, in the area of collective responsibility, he is unresponsive, opts not for the unity of all black men, but for the independence of a chosen few. As such, the only real similarity between him and black heroes, past and present, is his act of rebellion, his defiance of patterns which limit freedom, his ability to help, in the words of Kelley, to start something "that others would hear about and understand and would follow."

He is, to be sure, a crusader against injustice; yet, he is not a crusader in the interests of black men; he is unwilling to abide by arbitrary rules and authority, yet he offers no moral and ethical counterparts; he is not concerned with bringing to birth the new man, but only in gaining greater freedom for the old. In all of this, Marcus Payne remains an image well within the definition of Western history. One may still admire him as a rebel, as one who sought a higher meaning in life, who, to attain this, transgressed against the codes of old. He is, however, only part of black history, and *Of Love and Dust,* though brilliant in execution, only a reminder of how many examples of specific instances of courage and bravery lay buried in the earth vault of the black past. To accept the rebel as true to black history mandates that such as Marcus undergo transformation, display the predominant characteristics found in rebels of the past as well as in those of the present time. This meant, for Ernest Gaines, the creation of a different kind of novel and a new vision of the protagonist. In *The Autobiography of Miss Jane Pittman* (1971), he accomplishes both feats.

The Autobiography of Miss Jane Pittman is history rewritten and sifted through the mind of a talented novelist. It has been likened to Faulkner's novel, *The Sound and the Fury*—though such comparison has relevance only in terms of themes. The themes of guilt and redemption, enmity and hatred, of men trapped in old patterns are as much a part of this novel as they are of that of the white Southerner. To these themes, however, Gaines has brought a black sensibility, which transforms them and makes them less important than his major character. Faulkner knew that such themes were an intricate part of the dust and blood of the South and thus attributed great importance to them. Gaines, on the other hand, sees such themes as only part of the historical record; he deems people more important in the over-all historical picture. To endure in Faulkner's universe is to accept predominance of guilt and redemption and, thus, to accept, too, the inevitability of fate. To endure in Gaines's universe is to minimize such themes, concentrate upon people, and, thus, to struggle endlessly against fate.

The Autobiography of Miss Jane Pittman is about struggle, fate, and people. To travel with Miss Pittman from adolescence to old age is to embark upon a historic journey, one staked out in the format of the novel. Divided into four books—"The War Years," "Reconstruction," "The Plantation," and "The Quarters"—Miss Pittman's life is scrutinized and explored, her struggle to maintain dignity and self-esteem recorded, and her eventual victory over fate, declared. She emerges at the end of the novel, much as she appears at the beginning—a symbol of strength and endurance. Endurance is a telling characteristic of Miss Pittman. When she agrees, after some reluctance, to tell her story to a history teacher, she is over one hundred years old. The story, to be shared in by her living contemporaries, is her own—the teacher little more than her amanuensis: "I could not possibly put down on paper everything that Miss Jane and the others said on tape during those eight or nine months. Much of it was too repetitious and did not follow a single direction." He has tried, therefore, only to retain Miss Jane's words, speech rhythms, language, and meaning, and to allow her free reign in her commentary upon her life, the people who shared in it, and the events which magnified it. The stage is set for the narrative of Miss Jane Pittman.

History begins for Jane after she acquires a readily discernible identity of her own. A young slave girl, she was called Ticey by the master and mistress of the plantation upon which she was born. She is rescued from namelessness by Corporal Brown, whose forces invade the South, and who encounters her on the plantation. The corporal from Ohio bestows the name of Jane Brown on the young child; moreover, he invites her to visit him in Ohio after freedom occurs. The Emancipation Proclamation is signed a few days after the soldiers depart, and Jane undertakes her odyssey in search of the corporal who gave her an identity. This odyssey, begun with those few Blacks who refuse to remain on the plantation, forms the narrative of her life. Big Laura is one of the Blacks who desert the plantation. The leader of the little band of ex-slaves, she is "as tough as any man" and equally as efficient.

Laura has two children—a little girl, and a boy, Ned. Together, men, women, and children, spend their days dealing with internal strife and hiding from the Patrollers—bands of whites prowling the countryside for ex-slaves who have left their plantations—and the Secesh—soldiers from the rebel army who select white sympathizers, as well as Blacks, as targets of revenge. The Patrollers accost the little band a short distance from the plantation. In the ensuing massacre, only Ned and Jane survive. The child, with one younger still at her side, continues the journey toward Ohio.

Remaining close to the bushes, in order to escape the Secesh and the Patrollers, the two encounter various people along the way. Jane puts the same question to each: How far to Ohio? The answer is that they have not traveled far from the plantation, remain in the state of Louisiana. After more circuitous traveling and a chance meeting with a white farmer, Jane and Ned are taken to a plantation, run by a Northerner, near the Texas-Louisiana border. In bartering with the plantation owner for work, Jane displays the spunk and courage that enables her to survive the trek from slavery to freedom: "I might be little and spare, but I can do any work them others can do. . . ." She is fated never to reach Ohio. She remains on the plantation, supervises the growth of Ned, bears witness to the rise of the Klu Klux Klan and other terrorist groups, and becomes a firsthand observer of the new "slavery instituted after the end of Reconstruction." She knows the fate of those who wrote letters to Washington protesting their treatment; she has witnessed the exodus begun by Blacks, moving from south to north, as well as the successful attempt of whites to halt it, once the value of black labor was recognized.

With the approach of manhood, Ned, a thoughtful, serious young man, remembering still the murder of his mother, decides to leave the plantation. The first step in this direction is to assume a new identity: "He had changed his name now—Ned Douglass. Before he was Ned Brown, after me. Then he changed it to Douglass, after Mr. Frederick Douglass. He was gon be a great leader like Mr. Douglass was. . . ."[4]

A group of black soldiers organize a committee to investigate the treatment accorded Blacks in the South, and Ned leaves to work with the committee. Twenty years later, college educated, he returns with the intention of building a school and contributing toward the education of his people. He returns, in truth, however, to die. Not yet "The One," but only the forerunner, he is more moderate than revolutionary, cautioning thrift, hard work, and respect, without hostility, toward whites. He is ever cognizant, nevertheless, of the inevitability of his own death: "I myself probably'll be killed by a white man. . . . I'll blame ignorance. Ignorance on the part of the black man and the white man. . . . Our own black people had put us up in pens like hogs, waiting to sell us into slavery."[5] Moderation avails nothing and prophecy is fulfilled: The attempt to build a school for Blacks in Louisiana brings death at the hand of a hired assassin.

Between the time of Ned's leaving and returning, Jane leaves the plantation with a husband, Joe Pittman, and settles down to life as a housewife. Joe Pittman, a man possessed of wit and homespun philosophy, is a breaker of horses. Nagged by Jane, who fears for his life because of his occupation, and a dream foretelling his coming death, Joe answers his wife in words bordering upon egalitarianism: Man was put upon the earth to die, and all that he can accomplish while alive is to do something well: "When the time comes for them to lay you down in that long hole, they can say one thing: 'He did it good as he could.' That's the best thing you can say for a man. Horsebreaker or yard sweeper, let them say the poor boy did it good as he could." Joe meets his death, as foretold in Jane's dream, from attempting to break in a new horse. Afterward, Jane marries a fisherman, who soon deserts her, and she resumes her odyssey, traveling to an unidentified area of the state, finally settling, after Ned's death, in Sampson, Louisiana—a locale bearing the name of the owner of the county's largest plantation. She moves from the position of field hand to that of houseworker and is able to comment upon the structure of the plantation system, those who run it, and those who work upon it. Among those who work upon it are a succession of black teachers, including the creole, Mary Agnes Lefarbe.

The entrance of Mary into the narrative allows Jane to comment upon the overlords of the plantation, the Sampson family—father, mother, and son—and upon the unwritten codes passed from one generation of whites to another. Sampson, descendant of a long line of aristocrats, has fathered two sons—one by a black woman, the other by a white. His wife is reminded daily of the sins of her husband: Everyone on the plantation knew that Tee Bob, white, and Timmy, Black, were brothers. White father-black son relationships in the South, however, must give way to custom and mores: Tee Bob is thrown from a horse and injured; Timmy is blamed and assaulted by a white man. Though Timmy suffers the worst of the altercation, he had raised his hand in defense against a white man. Parentage, notwithstanding, Sampson banishes him from the planation: "You pinned medals on a white man when he beat a nigger for drawing back his hand."

But the unwritten codes spell disaster for Blacks and whites alike. Tee Bob falls in love with the young creole teacher and pursues her relentlessly. She offers no encouragement, rejects his proposal that the two run away. Out of frustration he assaults her. He had been told the rules, learned from everyone, teacher and father alike, that if a white man wanted a "nigger" he took her; ". . . she's there for that and nothing else." Tee Bob, however, cannot abide by the rules and, failing in his attempt to win the creole, he takes his own life. The key statement of the novel is sounded after his death: "Somewhere in the past . . . way, way back, men like Robert could love Mary Agnes. But somewhere along the way, somebody wrote a new set of rules condemning all that. I had to live by them. . . . Clarence Caya told Jimmy to live by them, and Jimmy obeyed. But Tee Bob couldn't obey. That's why we got rid of him. All of us . . ."[6]

As in *Of Love and Dust,* Blacks initiate the major rebellion against the old mores and folkways. The final segment of Jane's narrative concerns Blacks who transgress against the rules of old—written and un-

written. More specifically, however, the narrative deals with the coming
of "The One," whose function is to lead the people to freedom and liberation. "Peoples always looking for somebody to come lead them. . . .
Go to the Old Testament; go to the New. They did it in slavery; after the
war, they did it; they did it in the hard times that people want call Reconstruction; they did it in the depression. . . . They have always done
it. . . . and the Lord has always obliged in some way." Jimmy, "The
One," is discovered by Jane after she leaves the big house to return to
the quarters. Descendant of a long line of black heroes from Douglass
to King, Jimmy is the messiah, reborn in the modern age. To his birth
and the events of the twentieth century, the novel has been heading; to
this point in time it has moved swiftly, carrying along people and events;
to this moment in the narration, when the adventures of Miss Jane
Pittman reach culmination amidst the most determined assault to date
upon the old patterns. Through myth and legend, Gaines reveals the
meaning of Jane's life—a meaning highlighted and illuminated by the
example of "The One."

Being "The One," however, involves obligation. Jimmy must prove his
worth, demonstrate qualities of concern, care, and consideration for the
people. Once it is decided that he is the chosen one, moral strictures are
imposed upon him: no marble playing, no fighting with others in the
quarters—"he was supposed to stand up for them"—no sexual relationships. Steady attendance at school is demanded, along with involvement in church affairs: The people want their leader to be a man of
the cloth. Jimmy chooses a different route. He leaves the quarters in the
year the first civil rights bill is passed in order to attend college. During
the three years of his absence, the civil rights revolution erupts throughout the country and even threatens the established order in Sampson.
Remarks Jane: "These white people had been living like this for hundreds of years and they wasn't about to give up without a fight." Blacks
who either participated in or had relatives who participated in demonstrations were dispossessed, forced to leave the plantation. A tradition
of fear, however, keeps Blacks from engaging in the movement. For
this reason, Jimmy is rebuked on his return to the plantation to fulfill his
destiny, to bring the modern age to Sampson. The rebuff takes place
during a church meeting, where he asks the people to join himself and
his comrades in bringing the first demonstration to Sampson—picketing
the segregated water fountain in the town. He answers rebuffs by
enunciating the doctrine of the youth movement, one designed to destroy old patterns, whether sanctioned by Blacks or whites; ". . . you
want me to see your way of life. . . . I want you to see our way of life.

And that's the kind of life the young will feel from now on. Not your way, not no more."

The denial of the old way does not mean denial of the people, themselves. Jimmy continues to plead for help and assistance, though the people turn deaf ears toward him. They refuse to take part in what he calls "their fight," refuse to engage in the quest for liberation; yet the refusals have little to do with their love for him, as Jane points out. It is, however, that freedom is a word of abstraction, defined in Sampson as being able to work and receive compliments from whites. Sure enough they want to be relieved of their pain, yet they do not want to confront the truth that they are as good as whites ". . . they been told from they cradle that they wasn't much better than the mule. You keep telling them this over and over, for hundreds of years, they start thinking that way."

Jane is not altogether correct. At the age of one hundred, she prepares to join Jimmy and his colleagues in the demonstration. She is moved by the activity in the quarter: ". . . the number of people I saw coming toward me was something I never would a dreamed of. . . . I stood there watching them, thinking: Jimmy . . . Look what you've done. . . ." The people, having been moved by the example of the young man and the old woman, are not to be stopped, no, not even after they are informed that Jimmy has been murdered, not after the white man orders them to return to the quarters. They continue to move toward the town, old and young, moving outside of history, moving to the slow, determined cadence of Miss Jane Pittman.

The Autobiography of Miss Jane Pittman, centered not around a solitary hero but around a people whose collective deeds border upon the heroic, is a novel of epic proportions. Though Jane is the dominant personality of the narrative—observer and commentator upon history, as well as participant—in her odyssey is symbolized the odyssey of a race of people; through her eyes is revealed the grandeur of a people's journey through history. The central metaphor of the novel concerns this journey: Jane and her people, as they come together in the historic march toward dignity and freedom in Sampson, symbolize a people's march through history, breaking old patterns, though sometimes slowly, as they do so. The novel, therefore, is the autobiography of a people: it recounts the life and death struggles of slaves and freedmen alike, and, always, such dramatic incidents as emancipation, the exodus, and civil rights demonstrations are clarified and illuminated by the keen mind of Jane Pittman.

The novel, as history rewritten, must move beyond mundane facts, beyond mere reportage. The facts of history—places, dates, sketches of individuals, specific statements concerning historical events—can never depict the anguish, pain, joy, hope, heartbreaking defeats, and stimulating victories of men and women who are its participants.

Neither can such factual data reveal the ethical significance of a people's struggle against patterns of old, nor the moral quest involved in the search for self-identity and racial identity. Instead, the historical novel must illuminate the importance of men and events, tell the untold story of those, like the people around Jane, who have no amanuensis: those whose history has been written by others and consists of little that is valuable outside of dates and cold statistics.

The schoolteacher who records Miss Pittman's words and thoughts serves as her amanuensis, and she, in turn, serves a similar function for slaves and ex-slaves as well. She describes their heroism in deeds and actions: look to Big Laura fighting to protect her wards; reread again the description of Jane's march from bondage to semifreedom; witness the efforts of Ned to bring education to his people; walk with those who follow "The One" in an assault upon segregation; when such deeds are recorded, struggle and defiance are highlighted and meaning is derived from the events occasioned by those who lived them. The black novel, more so than any other, is concerned with the meaning implicit in the sojourn of a people in a strange land. The format is that of the slave narrative of old, history, yet not history, departing from history in its dramatic portrayal of people and events, conforming to it in its close attention to shifting, changing reality.

The greatest difference between the historian and the novelist is this: The historian simply demands a recognition of history; seldom does he encourage men to alter it; the novelist demands recognition of history only as a prelude toward changing it. The Jane Pittmans, Ned Douglasses, and Jimmy Arrons are able to assault the patterns of the past, only when they understand the matrix of the society in which they live; only through such understanding can they move to alter reality. Gaines demands such understanding from his people as evidenced in his novels from *Catherine Carmier* to *The Autobiography of Miss Jane Pittman,* and the formula for his historical novels is easy to discern: Realization precedes action; recognition of the truth of history is a prelude for rebellion and revolution.

This is the final theme, arrived at by the author, after three novels. If *Catherine Carmier* suffered from an intricate, not well-developed plot structure, and if *Of Love and Dust loses* strength and power through flaws in the makeup of the major protagonist, *The Autobiography of Miss Jane Pittman* reaches near perfection because of the unity of form and content, because the themes are interwoven into the fabric of the novel in such a way as to complement the form. The autobiographical novel which takes history as its material must be so well structured that events proceed in chronological order—if not on the printed page, then in the eyes of the reader. If clarity is to prevail, smooth transition from episode to episode is demanded. Through limiting the use of flashbacks and stream of consciousness, and depending upon the central narrator to move the story along, Gaines avoids a chaotic novel.

The result is a people's novel, one revealing unwritten history and depicting the examples of those who, in refusing to accept reality without question, rebelled against it. Thus Jane Pittman is a more well-developed character, a better model, than either Marcus, Jimmy, or Ned. Her development from child to adult, her odyssey from one town to another, from one century to another, reveal the brash, sassy child and woman at odds with arbitrary authority. In the quiet dignity of her later years, she gains a maturity that enables her to view her people in ways that sometimes escape the century's uneducated rebels: "I have a scar on my back I got when I was a slave. I'll carry it to my grave. You got people out there with this scar on their brains, and they will carry that scar to their graves. The mark of fear. . . is not easily removed. . . ."[7]

Jane Pittman, too, is "The One." She is symbolic of an African people in America whose odyssey through history has been marked by heroism and grandeur. Like Saunders, Blackman, Youngblood, and Lumumba, the example of her life provides encouragement to those who wage constant warfare against man-made laws and rules, who unceasingly rebel against oppression and tyranny. The narrative of her life is not hers alone; the novel depicting her experiences belongs not only to this committed generation of Blacks. Jane and the novel are products of a people's culture and history, their most cherished artifacts of the racial past and present: *The Autobiography of Miss Jane Pittman* belongs to black people of all ages, in all places—everywhere.

Gaines's achievement in effectuating the perfect unity between form and content parallels a similar achievement in the works of his contemporaries and has freed the black novelist, at long last, from undue concern with the academic conundrum of the supremacy of form over content. For all too long, the academics prohibited an all-out war by black novelists upon the imagists, by dragging out the red herring, form, arguing that is, with Ellison, that form must take precedence over content, that, somehow, the style of living is more important than life itself. The new black critics moved to influence the content of the novel, to make it an effective vehicle for the most important war in the history of black people—to control the symbols, images, and metaphors of black life; in so doing, they sought to turn the novel inward, force it to deal with aspects of the black condition that reveal positive examples of black courage and heroism, and to correct a distorted historical perspective. Their critical works say very little about form, for they know that it is merely the vehicle with which ideas are delivered, and that in this area, the novelist is on his own, governed by the skill and talent he possesses.

Thus form has varied in the works of African-American novelists from author to author, sometimes even among the works of particular artists, and been mastered by the best of them. The novels of Ishmael Reed, George Davis, and Barry Becham border upon the surrealistic; those of Paule Marshall, Charles Wright, and Louise Merriwether upon the historic, and those of George Cain, Sam Greenlee, and Nathan Heard upon the naturalism of Richard Wright. None, however, has deserted the racial artifacts; each has used the novel to war against symbols, images, and metaphors of Blacks handed down from the Euro-American past, and each has enhanced an understanding of the black condition. These, and more, deserve complete analysis in any literary work concerning the black novel; however, the present study cannot hope to encompass them all, can hope only to select from among the many novelists of the present time. Experimental works that point out the successes and problems confronting them in the area of experimentation with form and continual preoccupation with a historical perspective.

William Melvin Kelley is such a novelist, and two of his novels, *A Different Drummer* (1962) and *Dunsfords Travels Everywheres* (1970), reveal the variety of forms available to the talented black novelist. In the first novel, Kelley is both mythologist and historian, and the search for the historical importance of the black migration has taken him back to the latter half of the nineteenth century, to the exploits of old Pap Singleton, the slave's Moses, leading men, women, and children from south to west. The fictional migration begins in a small central southern state. Without warning, simultaneously, Blacks throughout the region begin to desert their homes; they use all available means of transportation—cars, buses, wagons, "their own two legs." The exodus causes consternation among the state's white inhabitants; yet many, initially, react like the governor: "There ain't nothing to worry about. We never needed them, and we'll get along fine without them. . . ."[8]

As the exodus continues, however, it becomes the central concern of the people of Sutton. Townspeople arise early to congregate around the porch of the town store in order to observe the Blacks in flight. Some even travel along the exit routes. The lives of some citizens are directly affected, among these, members of the Wilson family, descendants of the state's first governor, and the Lelands, a father-son team. All have been intimate with the prime mover of the migration, Tucker Caliban, who early one morning, arose, shot his horse and cattle, poured salt over his fields, destroyed an old relic—a grandfather's clock left from the days of slavery—and set fire to his house. Consequently, he packed his belongings, gathered up his wife and child, and left the town.

As if following on signal, other Blacks duplicated his actions, causing whites to focus upon Caliban, to search for motives in the personality of this seeming black Moses. Explanations take the form of genealogy, history, and myth. The genealogical motivation is presented by the town's wise man: ". . . it's pure genetics; something special in the blood . . . if anybody . . . got something special in his blood, his name is Tucker Caliban. It's got to be the African's blood. That's simple." The argument based upon legend and history complements that based upon genealogy. Tucker is said to have inherited the rebellious spirit of the first Caliban, an African, captured and sold to the first Dewey Wilson, who broke away on the day he was landed in Sutton, returned and "freed every last one of Dewitt's Negroes and led them off into the woods." Subsequently the African is caught and killed with his baby— the first Caliban—in his arms. His rebellious spirit, goes the legend, has been inherited by the last of the Calibans. Those, unwilling to settle for such rationales, search for others. In the eyes of Harry Leland, proprietor of the town store, Vietnam veteran and white liberal, the Blacks are merely making a strategic retreat, grouping to reunite their forces. Those who knew Caliban best, the Wilson family, David, Camille, Dewey, and Dymphna, father, mother, son, and daughter respectively, are less perceptive concerning the man who has been their employee for years. The Wilson family is a troubled one. Inner conflicts abound. The father lives under the shadow and legend of his grandfather, the first governor; his inability to measure up to the image of old causes frustration and doubt, which infects the entire family, and accounts, in part, for the inability of David, in particular, and the other members of the family, in general, to understand Tucker Caliban. Reverend Bradshaw, black, former college friend of David's come south, drawn by the spectacle of the exodus, suggests that Caliban's motivations might be attributable to years of suppressed anger. The answer of David is immediate: "No, that's wrong. You're wrong. There's no anger in Tucker. He accepted everything almost as if he knew it was going to happen and there was no way he could stop it."

The motivation for Caliban's actions are apparent. From the moment he discovers his father, dead of a heart attack on a town bus, lying beneath a sign labeled colored, the exodus is formed in his mind. The death of the old man draws different responses from white and Black. Dewey Wilson sees irony in the fact that the last thing the old man sees is "the colored sign on a segregated bus," whereas for Caliban, the death of his father is the signal for action. "Not another time," he remarks after the funeral. "This is the end of it."[9]

Though the exodus of Blacks from the southern state and white reaction against it form the central conflict of the novel, there is another—that between Bradshaw and Caliban, two men who never meet in the novel. College educated, onetime socialist, Bradshaw is representative of a media-created black leader: "As the torch glinted off his six-inch watchfob crucifix, and cries of 'Jesus is black' died in the packed hall, the Rev. Bennett T. Bradshaw, founder of the Resurrected Church of the Black Jesus Christ of America, Inc. . . . harangued his flock in a not quite legitimate English accent: We have declared war on the white man: to the white world and all it stands for, we vow death."[10] Bradshaw is an opportunist; his organization, the Black Jesuits, is anti-Semitic, anti-white, and ruled by Bradshaw who claims divine inspiration. The chief export of the Jesuits is rhetoric; its major accomplishment, frightening liberal whites. Bradshaw, in contrast to Caliban, remains devoted to material things, concerned not with racial unity, but with individual aspirations. In a moment of truth, he acknowledges the difference existing between himself and Caliban: "The day is fast coming . . . when people will realize there isn't any need for me and people like me. . . . your Tuckers will . . . say I can do anything I want. I don't need to wait for someone to give me freedom. I can take it myself. . . ." Caliban is the true revolutionary who, in his own dignified way, has said "enough" to oppression and vaulted outside of history. In this period of mass demonstrations and leader-led rebellions, he is one who, because of his intuitive understanding of a people's history, steps to history's center stage. To be sure, he is a man of myth and legend; to those, however, who know of the exploits of old Pap Singleton, he is history rewritten and updated.

A first novel by a twenty-three-year-old author will contain its share of flaws, and *A Different Drummer* is no exception. The major flaw, however, lay in Kelley's unwillingness to experiment with the form of the novel, to fashion a distinct vehicle. He has gone to Faulkner's *As I Lay Dying* for a model, and, as a result, *A Different Drummer* borders on structural chaos. Kelley's characters, like those of Faulkner, comment upon the action of the novel and each other through a series of autobiographical portraits. Kelley attempts innovations, however, within this format. Some chapters are straight narrative; in others, stream of consciousness is used to delineate character; in addition, the experiences of David Wilson are told through use of a diary format. In attempting to merge these disparate elements into a complete unit, the novel is rendered fragmentary. Like Baldwin in *Another Country,* Kelley, too, has been influenced by Henry James's *The Ambassadors,* finding here a central consciousness whose personality and actions will cement the novel together in terms of form and content. Rufus Scott, killed off early in Baldwin's novel, performs this function; Caliban does likewise in Kelley's novel. In both cases, however, the result is that other characters appear to have no life of their own, are robots, manipulated by superior egos.

The flaws notwithstanding, *A Different Drummer* is a novel evoking in its immediacy and relevancy. The attempt to merge form and content is not unsuccessful, and the major protagonist is a counterfoil to the images of the past, as are those of Killens, Williams, and Gaines. Also Kelley evidences a willingness to experiment with form—a willingness that pays dividends in a later novel, *Dunsfords Travels Everywheres.*

The adventures of Charles Chig Dunsford begin in a village in a small European town, in a cafe, The Cafe of One Hand, which, like everything else in the town, is divided into two compartments by ". . . a bell-bedecked white wire supported at one end by a ring in the outside wall of the cafe. . . ." The division in the cafe and town reflects division among the populace: ". . . none of the natives on either side of the wire owned wardrobes composed entirely of one side's colors. In the morning, each native in the country would pick an outfit for that day. He might choose blue-red, making himself, for the day, Atzuoreurso or a Jualoreurso."[11]

Dunsford and his friends—mostly white—Frank, Lane, Wendy, Ira, and Martin, are outsiders in the village, and Dunsford is an outsider among his middle-class white friends. He knows, on one level, that his role is to serve as his friends' black ambassador; on another level, however, the problem of his own racial identity persists.

Before he can return home to Harlem, he must become cognizant of his true identity. He takes the first step in this direction during a colloquy between himself and a white friend, centering around the singing of patriotic songs. Dunsford's refusal to join in the singing brings this comment:

"Well, didn't you feel like singing?"

He [Chig] could only smile; his mind still buzzed, louder now.

"Chigboy, did you hear me? Didn't you feel—"

"No, motherfucker! Wow."[12]

". . . Where on earth," Dunsford asks himself, "had those words come from?" He was the son of middle-class parents, and though he had lived in Harlem, his upbringing shielded him from the language of the street. After the dialogue with the white man, however, "he smiled, laughed behind closed lips at the street-words that had waited inside him all these years to jump out at Lane's face." The first step on the voyage toward racial identity involved language; the other involved a journey through the dream world of the racial consciousness, highlighted by a Joycean manipulation of words. The manipulation of words serve a twofold purpose: It reproduces elements of the racial heritage for Dunsford, while expanding the novel form to include a story within a story, one highlighting the exploits of two African detectives. The acknowledgment of the street language as part of his subconscious unlocks the vault of racial memory for Dunsford: "Witches oneway tspike Mr. Chigyles Languish, n, currying him back treality, recoremince wi humisereaducation. Maya we now go on wit yReconstruction Mr. Chuggle?"[13] Certain revelations occur in Mr. Chigstyles' "dreamage." Arguments are advanced in favor of integration, as well as those which support the system of slavery, ranging from riots to poisoning of masters: "Do you know the weapon of the week? Let those with whippins more with pore, wile you, on bented skis llserve up arson eek! in scribbled eggs and puncakes, humberly miser, and put a possum pin in the collar that mass wars."[14]

For this Ivy League Negro, reconstruction of the racial past through dream sequence is paralleled by the real-life drama concurrently unfolding on the streets of Harlem. The dream world and the real world meet at the fulcrum point of heightened imagination. Dunsford, at one time Chigyle, at another, Charcycle, and at still another, Chirlyle, is a product of both: "Have you learned your caughtomkidsm? Can we send you out on your hownor? . . . Passable. But proveable not yetso tokentinue the cansolidation of the initiatory natsure of your helotinary sexpereince, let we smiuve for illustration of your chiltural rackaige on the cause of a Hardlim denteeth who had stopped loving his wife."[15]

The dream-not-so-dream episode involves two colorful Harlem characters, in addition to the dentist. Carlyle Bedlow is hired by the dentist to seduce his wife and make photos of the act in order that the dentist might secure a divorce the wife refuses to grant. Carlyle brings his friend Hondo into the enterprise, and, after much confusion, the photographs are taken. Carlyle, uneducated man of the street, knowledgeable in the ways of the black life-style, serves as a foil for Dunsford in much the same way that Caliban served a similar function in relationship to Bradshaw. Carlyle has never needed to embark upon a journey to discover his racial identity, has long possessed racial awareness, has learned from his education in the streets that the adversary with whom he deals daily, the devil, comes in many guises. Informed by his friend Hondo that the latter has sold his soul to the devil, Carlyle moves to break the contract and save his friend's life. The ordeal, thus undergone by Dunsford in both the dream and waking worlds, is unknown to such men as Carlyle, whose lives are governed most often by action, seldom by introspection. As in the earlier novel, Kelley contrasts the man of reflection with the man of action, and *Dunsfords Travels Everywheres* moves upon two levels of conflict: one involving the man of reflection; the other, the man of action.

Dunsford, pushing steadily toward recognition of a greater reality, continues his travels. An affair with the girl, Wendy, which ends abruptly, brings him to the realization that he has spent too much time abroad, attempting to discover his identity in the capitals of Europe. After booking passage and boarding the ship home, he encounters Wendy again, proposes marriage, and is again rejected. He discovers, in addition, that a hundred African slaves are secreted in the hold of the ship. When he attempts to discover how they came there, he comes into conflict with the Tiwaz Youth Organization (TYO). Thus intrigue and mystery add to the completion of Dunsford's education.

Hostilities and rivalries between TYO and a rival organization, Family Westnorthwest, center around the human cargo aboard ship. Wendy—in reality, Mary-Joan Dinley—counteragent, was previously a representative of Family Westnorthwest, assigned at one time to the Cameroons. Discovered aboard ship by TYO, she is staked out and killed. Her death produces further awareness for Dunsford. Not only was the woman he had met among white friends in Europe involved in the slave trade, but she was not white but Black. "Back in his cabin, he . . . shook his head. He tried to picture Wendy's parents, light-skinned Virginians of African descent, passing perhaps. But probably not; more than likely they just lived ordinary light-skinned lives. His own parents had acquaintances with at least three such couples. Chig had met their children at parties."

Dunsford returns to Harlem in the company of Harriet, a "soul sister," a wiser, more aware man. The travels which began in the Cafe of One Hand ends in the Golden Grouse Bar and Restaurant in Harlem. As Dunsford listens in on Hondo's narrative of his bout with the devil, illusion, dream, and reality merge. . . . "trying to tell you something about the time I sold my soul to the damn Devil, then took that soul right straight back again." Allegorically, Dunsford too has undergone the Mephistophelean experience; like his Harlem counterparts, he has confronted the illusionary world, abrogated the contract which surrendered his culture, history, and racial identity centuries ago. At the end of his travels, he has rescued his soul from the demon of the absurd and returned home.

Dunsfords Travels Everywheres is almost the complete novel. So well has the consolidation between form and content been executed that the novel resembles a well-constructed dream. Language is the key to unraveling the dream, and Kelley utilizes three language systems in order to tell his narrative. There is the standard English used by the narrator, setting the tone of the novel and describing various incidents. There is the language of experimentation, found in the works of such writers as James Joyce and Melvin Tolson, which characterizes the dreamlike surrealistic world and contrasts reality and illusion. There is, finally, the rich language of the Harlem community, spoken by Carlyle and Hondo, pointing to racial homogeneity even within diversity: "Carlyle sat back, smiled at Ma Buster. 'Just steadying the ship, Ma. . . . We'll have us a good time, Ma. We'll get some fried clams and fries and have a little party, just the three of us, and him too, if he wants. . . . We'll drop off Hondo and send your man home, and have a little party, just us. . . .' "[16]

All three language systems contain their own legends and myths, hold their own allegorical content; each is reflective of cultural plurality.

Cultural plurality is the key phrase necessary in any attempt to understand the over-all meaning of *Dunsfords Travels Everywheres*. In the Cafe of One Hand, in the city of Atzuoreurso and Jualoreurso, exists a cultural system bearing analogy to that of the Americans. Each segment of the society is defined by the clothes it wears, and each opts for sameness over diversity, for cultural hegemony instead of cultural plurality. Therefore, each surrenders his identity, chooses similar lifestyles to those of each other. The same holds true for Dunsford and Wendy. For Wendy, the end result is self-hatred—a Black involved in the slave trade—and finally, death. For Dunsford, salvation is possible because he has not forgotten elements of a language system which speaks to the question of diversity and non-conformity, is capable of retaining contact with his cultural past. Thus his travels, which take him through the cultural capitals of the Western world, lead inevitably back to Harlem, where cultural democracy, not cultural hegemony, is the prevailing factor.

In *A Different Drummer* and in *Dunsfords Travels Everywheres*, Kelley is cognizant of a black cultural history which his characters either know or must discover. Caliban, intuitively, has always known that the cultural system which defined him was not that of the Euro-

American imagists. Dunsford, on the other hand, must discover his cultural heritage anew, and in so doing undertake the journey to a black identity. Eventually the journey will lead outside the definition of the West, away from images and symbols that represent Western man, and toward those, rich and enduring, in the African/Black heritage. At the end of the novel he has come to partial awareness, has made his break, tenuous though it may be, with the paraphernalia of imagistic language handed down from the West and gained a new perception of himself.

Both novels, however, flounder on the precipice of the same dilemma. Having opted for cultural plurality and manifested awareness of a distinctive African-American cultural system, how can such plurality and such distinction be contained within the European art form, the novel? Are the literary models of Joyce, Faulkner, and Zola able to sustain the black reality? "A novel," writes Ishmael Reed, "can be anything it wants to be." If this is true, however, can it become a viable form for articulating the new-found sense of cultural awareness of its author and readers as well? There is an argument to be made in the affirmative for *A Different Drummer.* Legend and myth are part of the African cultural, historical matrix; the narrative format itself—different characters relating their individual experiences—has its origins in the "Animal Tales" and antedates William Faulkner. There are, however, few models in black literature for *Dunsfords Travels Everywheres.*

One thinks of *Cane,* but Toomer is too indebted to Waldo Frank and the Russian mystics; one thinks of *Invisible Man,* yet Ellison, too, is indebted to the Europeans. Thus the dilemma persists and will continue to do so until, after years of experimentation, trial, and error, a new form is created to contain the nuances of black thought, speech rhythms, life-styles, and storehouse of images and symbols which have helped to validate a people's humanity. Kelley has begun the experimental novel in *Dunsfords,* an exceptional novel in which form and content combine to offer a well-told story.

Add to this the presentation in both novels of new symbols and images, a preoccupation with racial mythology and legend, and the ground toward a new tradition has been broken. The pact signed with the Mephistophelean imagists by too many black writers in the past has now been abrogated, and the imagists assured that the word is no longer their special prerogative. Kelley, like many of his contemporaries, has opted for the thought of Imamu Baraka and Maulana Karenga, opted, that is, for literature which deals with the historical and cultural ramifications of the long journey of black men through the Western nightmare and the recognition that, despite diversity, Blacks everywhere are an African people. The novels of Killens, Williams, Gaines, Kelley, and others offer fine examples of what critic Hoyt Fuller has called a "new Renaissance."

London, 1974

AFTERWORD

Despite a decline in the interest of black literature and attacks aimed at Black Aestheticians by whites and Blacks, the Renaissance continues. To label Killens, Williams, and Gaines as Black Aestheticians would be erroneous; to suggest, however, that they and their contemporaries have been influenced by, and have influenced, the writings and ideas generated by the Black Aesthetic movement would not. It is due largely to the efforts of such men that after a century of adhering to the dictates of white propagandists, the novelist has been freed from the tendency to follow those who would lead him either down the road of protest literature or into the elitist sanctuary of literature for art's sake. Both directions represented dead ends and neither led to a realistic confrontation with the problems facing black people in the American society.

This is not to accept Baldwin's argument, in his celebrated attack upon Richard Wright, that the protest novel was a useless vehicle in producing societal change. Though a direct cause-and-effect relationship between work and situation is impossible to discern, the influence of the protest novel upon changes in the social order, and in the actions of men and women, can be proven in the impact of such novels as *Uncle Tom's Cabin, The Leopard's Spots, Germinale,* and *The Jungle.* Baldwin's criticism holds, however, in the case of protest novels written by Blacks. Conceived as an appeal to the conscience of whites, the dismal failure of the novel to bring about substantial changes has been registered by works from *Clotel* to *Native Son.* The fault lies not in the genre itself, but upon the flimsy premise upon which the writer based his protest— that Americans wanted and desired an egalitarian society in which man opted for truth and beauty over narrow interests, material gain, and selfish pursuits. Most whites, themselves victims of imagists from the cotton barons to the men of Richard Nixon's crime-ridden administration, were incapable of empathizing with the problems of Blacks, could not accept that collective guilt of a nation which to ensure its own survival relegated a race of people to the status of subhumans.

Despite its failure in this regard, however, the black protest novel was necessary; it was a genre which had to be offered and surpassed; for at its best it revealed the absurdity of the American creed, pinpointed the oneness between white liberal and white bigot alike, succeeded in proving the futility of addressing appeals to white conscience in demonstrating how far distant in vision and expectations whites were from Blacks and how narrow and parochial American thought which conceived of the world as little more than the creation of Anglo-Saxon civilization. Most important, in so educating Blacks, the protest novel vouchsafed the most important of all truths: that change in the black condition is possible only through the efforts of black people themselves. Such changes demand the commitment of all Blacks and, most specifically, the black writer; they demand a commitment not to literature for art's sake, but to literature for the sake of black people.

Literature for art's sake, which has its genesis in the Harlem Renaissance, might have died a natural death had the black novelist and poet been free of the need for recognition from a white literary world and the paternalism and condescension which accompany such recognition. Nothing could be more ludicrous than the attempt on the part of an oppressed people to validate the existence of *ars poetica* in America. Such a golden age, where art flourished for the sake of art has never been—not even in that ancient Greece which Matthew Arnold and Archibald MacLeish forwarded as their example. That men have at all times desired such a millennium is irrefutable. Who among us is not overawed by the beauty of which Plato spoke; what human being not aesthetically stimulated by the elegance of style, the proportion and symmetry of line, the pageantry and mixture of color in a superb painting? Who cannot derive compassion and feeling from a deeply felt chord, from the purity of sound, the perfection of rhythm and movement of a well-orchestrated musical rendition, and who does not feel inwardly fulfilled at a lyrical verse, at the staccato movement of words and lines in a Baldwin essay, or the solemn dignity of a Proustian passage? What human being cannot be, does not desire to be, moved by that which is beautiful, that aesthetic sense which distinguishes man from other animals?

To argue the affirmative is not to make the case for literature for art's sake. Man's capacity to appreciate the beautiful, to cultivate a wholesome, healthy aesthetic sensibility, depends upon the security of the environment in which he lives, in the belief in his own self-worth, in an inner peace engendered by his freedom to develop to the extent of his abilities. In a sharecropper's shack in Mississippi, a rat-infested ghetto in

Harlem, or a mud hut in Vietnam, a portrait of the Mona Lisa, the strains of a Brahms concerto, the soothing lines of a Keats or a Countee Cullen are ludicrous at best, cruel at worst. In order to cultivate an aesthetic sensibility, given an oppressive society, the first prerequisite is that the oppression must end; to pave the way for the possibility of an ars poetica, the oppression must end; in more concrete terms, before beauty can be seen, felt, heard, and appreciated by a majority of the earth's people, a new world must be brought into being; the earth must be made habitable and free for all men. This is the core of the Black Aesthetic ideology and forms the major criterion for the evaluation of art: How much better has the work of art made the life of a single human being upon this planet, and how functional has been the work of art in moving us toward that moment when an ars poetica is possible for all?

This thesis is not shared by all black writers. Many continue to exhibit a spirit of elitism, to see literature only in terms of belles-lettres; such writers are ofttimes more zealous than their white colleagues in calling upon the black writer to create literature which adheres to often non-existent criterion governing form and structure, to attempt to create a "universal art," and to write novels which eschew social commentary. Such black writers and critics there are; yet sane men shun their pretensions and look back to the time of Brown and Delany in an attempt to fashion ideas of what the work of art must mean for a people whose liberation has not yet come.

In so doing, the flaws of black writers of the past are revealed: These have little to do with the argument that their art was not universal or was marred by social commentary; their major flaw was that the literature they produced failed to deal adequately with the central problem confronting any oppressed people—that the symbols, images, and metaphors which substantiate a sense of self-worth and achievement were controlled, manipulated, and defined by outsiders, by those who continued that oppression of the mind begun by their ancestors. Here lay the great battlefield for the black writer, and it is in waging war upon this battlefield that the black novelist of the present time has brought the literary artifact to its greatest height of maturity. By refusing to accept the images and stereotypes of white liberals and white bigots alike, like Killens, Gaines, and Williams he attempts to recreate and create those paradigms which have been the major defining characteristics of a courageous and heroic people. He has, like Dunsfords, come back to the Harlem of the mind to discover those images of a people which testify to the greatness and inviolability of humanity everywhere.

Yes, the Renaissance continues, thanks mainly to the Black Aestheticians of the sixties and seventies who moved to gain control over the history and culture of black people. Not only did they explode the myth that whites were more capable than Blacks of evaluating black literature, but the establishment of publishing institutions like Third World Press, Jihad, Broadsides, and Emerson Hall; the success of such magazines as *Black World, The Black Scholar, Liberator,* and *Black News;* and the founding of such educational institutions as The Institute of the Black World and Malcolmn X University were attempts to maintain hegemony over the cultural artifacts of a people.

Nothing would be more desirable than to end this study on such a positive note, to herald the arrival of the black writer in the persons of Killens, Gaines, and Kelley as constituting a final victory over white nationalism, to pronounce once and for all the death knell of the old stereotypes, images, and metaphors which enslaved the minds of generations of Blacks. Yet to do so would be to engender false optimism. For white nationalism is not dead, the attempt to control the images, metaphors, and symbols of black life as much a part of the present as of the past. The stereotypes of Harris, Page, and Dixon, of Van Vechten, Mailer, and Styron live again in movies and television fantasies written by Blacks, performed in by Blacks, and supported and sustained by Blacks. The list is almost too numerous to mention: *Superfly, Melinda, Shaft, Coffy,* "The Flip Wilson Show," "Sanford and Son," and "The Red Ball Express" represent only the most flagrant examples.

These, the new imagists, because for the most part they are Blacks, are more immune from criticism than the imagists of old. They ignore criticism from the black community and are content to exist as the ventriloquist dummies of their more sophisticated masters irrespective of the damage wrought by their actions. One thinks of the novelists, of Charles Chesnutt and Sutton Griggs, of Richard Wright and William Smith, of Ann Petry and Zora Hurston; they were men and women who, despite flaws in perception which often limited their vision, believed in the sanctity of the black spirit, who sought, through their art, to elevate a race of people. These were no scavengers, ignoring the worth and dignity of a people; they were not brainless narcissists unable to realize that their own dignity and sense of achievement were tied in, inseparably, with that of their people. They would have held no truck with those who created and performed in the *Superflys* and the *Melindas,* would not have joined with those who, here, in this period of the twentieth century, attempt to recreate the stereotypes of old—the darky entertainer, docile child, or brute Negro. Like John Killens, they were dedicated to preserving the historical artifacts of a people and would have demanded films based upon the lives of Frederick Douglass, Malcolm X, Sojourner Truth, and

Harriet Tubman, films that reveal the dignity of a people whose travels have extended from the middle passage to twentieth-century America.

There is no correlation to be made, however, between the black syco-phants of the present time and the novelists, past and present, and thus, the renaissance wrought by the Black Aestheticians, the new sense of historical vision in the works of black poets and novelists, the progress made in gaining control over the images, symbols, and metaphors of black life are threatened by men and women of little talent and far less intelligence, whose objective is not to inform but to disparage, not to create positive images, but to recreate negative ones of the past, to glamorize the hustler and the hipster, to elevate ignorance and down-grade intelligence in a world in which intelligence, knowledge, and understanding are paramount for a people who must yet break the bonds of oppression.

And thus there is little cause for optimism. One is gratified, of course, at the progress of the black novel from 1853 to the present, and the maturity of the novelists support Fuller's assertion of a new Black Renaissance; one knows, however, that the final battle against the imagists continues, and that the new propagandists are more often Black than white; one watches their "artistic" offerings, listens to their infantile rationalizations, is dismayed at their inability to dedicate themselves to what is noble and beautiful in a race of people and one, despairingly, re-calls the lines from a Baraka poem, "Will the machine gunner please step forward?"

NOTES

INTRODUCTION

1. Allen Tate, "Introduction" to Libretto for the Republic of Liberia.
2. Robert Bone, *The Negro Novel in America* (New York, Yale University Press, 1959), p. 153.
3. Lawrence Clark Powell, "Who Is B. Traven?" in *New Masses: An Anthology of the Rebel Thirties,* ed. by Joseph North (New York, International Pub., 1969), p. 304.
4. Langston Hughes, "The Negro Artist and the Racial Mountain," in *The Black Aesthetic* (Garden City, N.Y., Doubleday & Co., 1971), p. 177.

CHAPTER I

1. Milton Cantor, "The Image of the Negro in Colonial Literature," in *Images of the Negro in American Literature,* ed. by Seymour L. Gross and John Edward Hardy (Chicago, Univ. of Chicago Press, 1966), p. 39.
2. Samuel Sewall, *The Selling of Joseph,* quoted in *Images of American Literature,* p. 40.
3. Cantor, op. cit., p. 34.
4. J. Saunders Redding, *To Make a Poet Black* (Chapel Hill, North Carolina, Univ. of North Carolina Press, 1939), p. 55.
5. Ibid, p. 54.
6. Booker T. Washington, *The Future of the American Negro* (Boston, Small, Maynard, 1899), p. 194.
7. Frank J. Webb, *The Garies and Their Friends* (New York, Arno & Boni and the New York *Times,* 1969), p. 275.
8. Ibid, p. 276.
9. Martin Robison Delany, *The Condition, Elevation, Emigration and Destiny of the Colored People of the United States* (New York, Arno Press and the New York *Times*), p. 14.
10. Ibid, p. 10.
11. Dorothy Sterling, *The Making of an Afro-American: Martin Robison Delany 1812–1885* (Garden City, N.Y., Doubleday & Co., 1971), p. 95.
12. Martin R. Delany, *Blake; or the Huts of America* (Boston, Beacon Press, 1970), p. 194.
13. Ibid, p. 39.
14. Ibid, p. 155.
15. Ibid, p. 31.

CHAPTER II

1. Sterling A. Brown, Arthur P. Davis, and Ulysses Lee, *The Negro Caravan* (New York, Arno Press and the New York *Times,* 1969), p. 139.
2. Sterling Brown, *Negro Poetry and Drama and the Negro in American Fiction* (New York, Atheneum, 1969), p. 50.
3. Ibid, p. 54.
4. Sterling Brown, "Negro Character as Seen by White Authors," in *Dark Symphony: Negro Literature in America,* ed. by James H. Emanuel and Theodore L. Gross (New York, Macmillan, 1968), p. 152.
5. Redding, *To Make a Poet Black,* p. 50.
6. Emanuel and Gross, op. cit., p. 142.
7. Ibid, p. 148.
8. Brown, *Negro Poetry and Drama and the Negro in American Fiction,* p. 51.
9. Hugh M. Gloster, *Negro Voices in American Fiction* (Chapel Hill, Univ. of North Carolina Press, 1948), pp. 9–10.
10. John Hope Franklin, *From Slavery to Freedom: A History of Negro Americans* (New York, Knopf, 1967), p. 342.
11. Brown, "Negro Character as Seen by White Authors," p. 150.
12. Gloster, op. cit., p. 11.
13. Booker T. Washington, *Up from Slavery* (New York, Al Burt, 1901), p. 52.
14. Ibid, pp. 311–13.
15. Ibid, p. 207.
16. Washington, *The Future of the American Negro,* pp. 23–25.
17. Gloster, op. cit., p. 10.
18. Redding, op. cit., pp. 77–78.
19. Francis L. Broderick, "The Fight Against Booker T. Washington," in *Booker T. Washington and His Critics: The Problem of Negro Leadership,* ed. by Hugh Hawkins (Boston, Heath, 1962), p. 45.
20. W. E. B. Du Bois, *The Souls of Black Folk* (Greenwich, Conn., Fawcett, 1961), p. 190.
21. Ibid, pp. 16–17.
22. Ibid, p. 74.
23. Ibid, p. 75.
24. Paul Laurence Dunbar, *The Uncalled* (New York, International Assoc. of Newspapers and Artists, 1901), p. 23.
25. Ibid, p. 244.
26. Redding, op. cit., pp. 61–62.
27. Paul Laurence Dunbar, *The Sport of the Gods* (New York, Macmillan, 1970), p. 20.
28. Ibid, p. 32.
29. Ibid, pp. 116–17.
30. Helen Chesnutt, *Charles Waddell Chesnutt* (Chapel Hill, Univ. of North Carolina Press, 1952), p. 150.

31. Ibid, p. 58.

32. Charles W. Chesnutt, *The House Behind the Cedars* (New York, Macmillan, 1969), p. 110.

33. Ibid, pp. 116–17.

34. Charles W. Chesnutt, *The Marrow of Tradition* (Michigan, Univ. of Michigan Press), p. 211.

35. Ibid, p. 291.

36. Ibid, p. 281.

37. Ibid, p. 283.

CHAPTER III

1. Sutton E. Griggs, *Imperium in Imperio* (Miami, Mnemosyne, 1969), p. 245.

2. Ibid, p. 175.

3. Ibid, p. 252.

4. Gloster, *Negro Voices in American Fiction*, p. 71.

5. Ibid, p. 71.

6. W. E. B. Du Bois, *The Quest of the Silver Fleece* (Florida, Mnemosyne, 1969), p. 111.

7. Ibid, p. 295.

8. Ibid, p. 126.

9. Ibid, p. 240.

10. Van Wyck Brooks, "The Critical Movement in America," in *Literary Opinion in America*, Vol. I, ed. by Morton Dauwen Zabel (New York, Harper & Row, 1962), p. 80.

11. Ibid, p. 80.

CHAPTER IV

1. Alain Locke, ed. *The New Negro: An Interpretation* (New York, Albert & Charles Boni, 1925), p. 5.

2. Edward David Cronon, *Black Moses: The Story of Marcus Garvey and the Universal Negro Improvement Association* (Milwaukee, Univ. of Wisconsin Press, 1969), p. 26.

3. J. Saunders Redding, *They Came in Chains* (Philadelphia, Lippincott, 1950), p. 261.

4. Claude McKay, *Harlem: Negro Metropolis* (New York, Dutton, 1940), p. 158.

5. Shawna Maglangbayan, *Garvey, Lumumba, Malcolm: Black Nationalist-Separatists* (Chicago, Third World Press, 1972), p. 31.

6. McKay, op. cit., pp. 177–78.

7. Benjamin Brawley, *The Negro Genius* (New York, Dodd, Mead, 1937), pp. 232–33.

8. James Weldon Johnson, *Along This Way* (New York, Viking Press, 1945), p. 304.

9. Brawley, op. cit., pp. 233–34.

10. Vachel Lindsay, "The Congo," in *The Black Experience,* ed. by Francis Kearns (New York, Viking Press, 1970), pp. 326–27.

11. Carl Van Vechten, *Nigger Heaven* (New York, Harper & Row, 1971), pp. 12–13.

12. Ibid, p. 5.

13. Ibid, pp. 89–90.

14. Ibid, pp. 252–53.

15. Ibid, p. 28.

16. James Weldon Johnson, *The Autobiography of an Ex-Coloured Man* (New York, Hill & Wang, 1960), p. 42.

17. Ibid, p. 210.

18. Ibid, p. 155.

19. Ibid, p. 156.

20. Ibid, pp. 80–81.

21. Ibid, p. 87.

22. Ibid, p. 42.

23. Ibid, p. 68.

CHAPTER V

1. Jean Toomer, *Cane* (New York, University Place Press, 1967), p. 23.

2. Ibid, p. 21.

3. Ibid, p. 191.

4. Ibid, p. 215.

5. Langston Hughes, *The Big Sea* (New York, Hill & Wang, 1968), p. 228.

6. Nella Larsen, *Quicksand* (Macmillan, 1971), pp. 173–74.

7. Ibid, p. 124.

8. Ibid, pp. 189–90.

9. Nella Larsen, *Passing* (New York, Macmillan, 1971), p. 184.

10. Ibid, p. 57.

11. Larsen, *Quicksand,* p. 173.

12. Ibid, p. 15.

13. Jesse Redmond Fauset, *There Is Confusion* (New York, Boni & Liveright, 1926), p. 19.

14. Ibid, p. 157.

15. Ibid, p. 292.

16. Jesse Redmond Fauset, *Plum Bun* (Frederick A. Stokes, 1928), p. 73.

17. Ibid, p. 77.

18. Ibid, p. 182.

19. Ibid, p. 326.

20. Wallace Thurman, *The Blacker the Berry* (New York, Macmillan, 1970), p. 12.

21. Ibid, p. 147.

22. Ibid, p. 144.

CHAPTER VI

1. Claude McKay, *Home to Harlem* (New York, Harper & Bros., 1928), p. 243.
2. Ibid, p. 234.
3. Ibid, pp. 157–58.
4. Ibid, p. 328.
5. Claude McKay, *Banjo* (New York, Harcourt, 1970), p. 31.
6. Claude McKay, *Banana Bottom* (New Jersey, Chatham, 1970), p. 31.
7. Ibid, p. 125.
8. Ibid, p. 212.
9. Rudolph Fisher, *The Walls of Jericho* (New York, Arno Press and the New York *Times,* 1969), p. 42.
10. Ibid, p. 29.
11. Zora Neal Hurston, *Jonah's Gourd Vine* (New York, Lippincott, 1971), p. 15.
12. Ibid, p. 200.
13. Ibid, p. 309.
14. Zora Neal Hurston, *Their Eyes Were Watching God* (New York, Fawcett, 1969), p. 16.
15. Ibid, p. 25.

CHAPTER VII

1. Richard Wright, "Blueprint for Negro Writing" in *The Black Aesthetic,* ed. by Addison Gayle (Garden City, N.Y., Doubleday, 1971), p. 339.
2. Wilson Record, *The Negro and the Communist Party* (New York, Atheneum, 1971), p. 110.
3. Daniel Aaron, "Richard Wright and the Communist Party," in *New Letters,* Vol. 38, ed. by David Ray and Robert M. Farnsworth (Kansas City, Univ. of Missouri, 1971), p. 176.
4. Wright, op. cit., p. 337.
5. E. Franklin Frazier, *The Negro in the United States* (New York, Macmillan, 1957), p. 599.
6. Record, op. cit., p. 69.
7. Gloster, *Negro Voices in American Fiction,* p. 197.
8. Richard Wright, *12 Million Black Voices: A Folk History of the Negro in the United States,* photo direction by Edwin Rosskam (New York, Viking, 1941), p. 145.
9. Ibid, p. 86.
10. William Attaway, *Blood on the Forge* (New York, Macmillan, 1970), p. 15.
11. Ibid, p. 212.
12. Ibid, p. 233.

CHAPTER VIII

1. Constance Webb, *Richard Wright: A Biography* (New York, Putnam's, 1968), p. 363.
2. Richard Wright, *The Long Dream* (New York, Ace, 1958), p. 133.
3. Ibid, p. 132.
4. Ibid, p. 326.
5. Blyden Jackson, "The Blithe Newcomers" in *Phylon*, Vol. XIV (Atlanta, Atlanta University, 1955), p. 10.
6. Chester B. Himes, *If He Hollers Let Him Go* (Garden City, N.Y., Doubleday & Co., 1946), pp. 181–82.
7. Ibid, p. 179.
8. Ibid, pp. 62–63.
9. Chester B. Himes, *Lonely Crusade* (New York, Knopf, 1947), p. 4.
10. Ibid, p. 238.
11. Ibid, p. 303.
12. Ibid, p. 88.
13. Ibid, p. 197.
14. Ibid, p. 362.
15. Ann Petry, *The Street* (New York, Pyramid, 1966), p. 59.
16. Ibid, p. 165.
17. Ibid, p. 266.
18. William Gardner Smith, *The Stone Face* (New York, Farrar, Straus, 1963), p. 27.
19. Ibid, p. 129.
20. Ibid, p. 206.

CHAPTER IX

1. Herbert Hill, ed., *Soon, One Morning* (New York, Knopf, 1966), p. 452.
2. Du Bois, pp. 16–17.
3. Ralph Ellison, *Invisible Man* (New York, Random House, 1952), p. 13.
4. Ibid, p. 107.
5. Ibid, p. 118.
6. Ibid, p. 180.
7. Ibid, p. 189.
8. James Baldwin, *Notes of a Native Son* (New York, Dial Press, 1963), p. 10.
9. Ibid, pp. 10–11.
10. James Baldwin, *Another Country* (New York, Dial Press, 1962), p. 4.
11. Ibid, p. 67.
12. Ibid, p. 105.
13. Ibid, p. 417.
14. Ibid, p. 414.
15. Ibid, pp. 212–13.

CHAPTER X

1. Robert Bone, *The Negro Novel in America* (New Haven, Yale University Press, 1958), p. 246.
2. Baldwin, *Notes of a Native Son,* p. 148.
3. Ronald Berman, *America in the Sixties: An Intellectual History* (New York, Harper & Row, 1970), p. 73.
4. William Robert Miller, *Martin Luther King, Jr.: His Life, Martyrdom and Meaning for the World* (New York, Weybright & Talley, 1968), p. 56.
5. Ibid, p. 154.
6. Ibid, pp. 73–74.
7. Stokely Carmichael and Charles V. Hamilton, *Black Power: The Politics of Liberation in America* (New York, Random House, 1967), pp. 34–35.
8. Norman Mailer, "The White Negro: Superficial Reflections on the Hipster" (*The Cosmos Reader,* ed. by Leslie Fiedler et al., New York, Harcourt Brace Jovanovich, 1971), p. 943.
9. Ibid, p. 938.
10. Ibid, pp. 943–44.
11. Irving Howe, "Black Boys and Native Sons" in *Richard Wright's Native Son: A Critical Handbook,* ed. by Richard Abcarian (California, Wadsworth, 1970), p. 141.
12. Ibid, p. 137.
13. Ralph Ellison, "The World and the Jug," in Abcarian, p. 148.
14. Imamu Amiri Baraka (Leroi Jones), *Home* (New York, Morrow, 1966), p. 164.
15. William Styron, *The Confessions of Nat Turner* (New York, New American Library, 1968), p. 46.
16. Ibid, p. 249.
17. Ibid, p. 318.
18. Ibid, p. 354.
19. Ibid, p. 99.

CHAPTER XI

1. Martin Luther King, Jr., *Where Do We Go from Here: Chaos or Community* (New York, Harper & Row, 1967), p. 59.
2. William Robert Miller, *Martin Luther King, Jr: His Life, Martyrdom and Meaning for the World* (New York, Weybright & Talley, 1968), p. 269.
3. Ibid, p. 231.
4. Ibid, p. 263.
5. Ibid, p. 275.
6. Alex Haley and Malcolm X, *The Autobiography of Malcolm X* (New York, Grove Press, 1965).
7. Ibid, p. 151.
8. Ibid, p. 288.

9. Imamu Amiri Baraka (Leroi Jones), *Raise Race Rays Raze: Essays since 1965* (New York, Random House, 1971), p. 28.

10. Haley, op. cit., p. 345.

11. Maglangbayan, *Garvey, Lumumba, Malcolm* (Chicago, Third World Press, 1972), p. 73.

12. Ibid, p. 76.

13. Baraka, *Home*, p. 10.

14. Imamu Amiri Baraka, "Black Art," in *Understanding the New Black Poetry* by Stephen Henderson (New York, Morrow, 1973), p. 213.

15. Baraka, *Home,* p. 235.

16. Ibid, p. 85.

17. Ibid, pp. 85–86.

18. Ibid, p. 165.

19. Ibid, p. 248.

20. Baraka, *Raise Race Rays Raze,* p. 24.

21. Ibid, pp. 79–80.

22. Ibid, p. 118.

23. Ibid, p. 129.

CHAPTER XII

1. Gayle, *The Black Aesthetic,* p. 9.

2. Ibid, pp. 33–34.

3. John Oliver Killens, *And Then We Heard the Thunder* (New York, Knopf, 1964), p. 362.

4. Ibid, p. 84.

5. Ibid, p. 86.

6. Ibid, p. 459.

7. Ibid, p. 71.

8. Ibid, p. 407.

9. John Oliver Killens, *The Cotillion; or, One Good Bull Is Half the Herd* (New York, Simon & Schuster, 1971), p. 6.

10. Ibid, p. 195.

11. Ibid, p. 219.

12. Ibid, p. 255.

13. Ibid, p. 256.

14. Louis-Ferdinand Celine, *Journey to the End of Night, passim.*

15. John A. Williams, *Captain Blackman* (Garden City, N.Y., Doubleday & Co., 1972), p. 315.

16. Ibid, p. 333.

17. Ibid, p. 49.

CHAPTER XIII

1. Gayle, *The Black Aesthetic,* p. 346.

2. Ernest J. Gaines, *Of Love and Dust* (New York, The Dial Press, 1967), p. 270.

3. Ibid, p. 240.

4. Ernest J. Gaines, *The Autobiography of Miss Jane Pittman* (New York, Dial, 1971), p. 73.

5. Ibid, p. 108.

6. Ibid, p. 191.

7. Ibid, p. 227.

8. William Melvin Kelley, *A Different Drummer* (Garden City, N.Y., Doubleday & Co., 1962), p. 4.

9. Ibid, p. 134.

10. Ibid, p. 193.

11. William Melvin Kelley, *Dunsfords Travels Everywheres* (Garden City, N.Y., Doubleday & Co., 1970), p. 3.

12. Ibid, p. 46.

13. Ibid, p. 49.

14. Ibid, p. 57.

15. Ibid, p. 61.

16. Ibid, p. 129.

BIBLIOGRAPHY

Abcarian, Richard, *Richard Wright's Native Son: A Critical Handbook*. Belmont, California, Wadsworth Publishing Co., 1970.

Aptheker, Herbert, *American Negro Slave Revolts*. New York, International Publishers Co., Inc., 1952.

Attaway, William, *Blood on the Forge*. New York, The Macmillan Co., 1970.

———, *Let Me Breathe Thunder*. Chatham, New Jersey, The Chatham Bookseller, 1969.

Baldwin, James, *Another Country*. New York, The Dial Press, 1962.

———, *The Fire Next Time*. New York, Dell Pub. Co., Inc., 1962.

———, *Go Tell It on the Mountain*. New York, Dell Pub. Co., Inc., 1965.

———, *Nobody Knows My Name*. New York, Dell Pub. Co., Inc., 1961.

———, *Notes of a Native Son*. New York, The Dial Press, 1963.

Baraka, Imamu, *Its Nation Time*. Chicago, Third World Press, 1970.

Bennett, Lerone, Jr., *Before the Mayflower: A History of the Negro in America, 1619–1964*. Baltimore, Maryland, Penguin Books, 1968.

Berman, Ronald, *America in the Sixties: An Intellectual History*. New York, Harper & Row, 1970.

Bone, Robert, *The Negro Novel in America*. New Haven, Yale University Press, 1965.

Bontemps, Arna, ed., *American Negro Poetry*. New York, Hill & Wang, 1963.

———, *One Hundred Years of Negro Freedom*. New York, Dodd, Mead & Co., 1961.

———, and Conroy, Jack, *Anyplace But Here*. New York, Hill & Wang, 1966.

Botkin, B. A., ed., *Lay My Burden Down*. Chicago, Chicago Press, 1945.

Bracey, John H., Jr., Meier, August, and Rudwick, Elliott, eds., *Black Nationalism in America*. Indianapolis, Indiana, The Bobbs-Merrill Co., 1970.

Brawley, Benjamin, *Early Negro American Writers*. New York, Dover Publications Inc., 1970.

———, *Paul Laurence Dunbar: Poet of His People*. Port Washington, N.Y., Kennikat Press, Inc., 1967.

———, *A Social History of the American Negro*. New York, The Macmillan Co., 1970.

Brignano, Russell Carl, *Richard Wright: An Introduction to the Man and His Work*. Pittsburgh, Univ. of Pittsburgh Press, 1970.

Brown, Sterling, *Negro Poetry and Drama and the Negro in American Fiction*. New York, Atheneum Pubs., 1969.

————, Davis, Arthur P., and Lee, Ulysses, *The Negro Caravan*. New York, Arno Press and the New York *Times*, 1969.

Butcher, Margaret Just, *The Negro in American Culture*. New York, Knopf, 1957.

Carmichael, Stokely, and Hamilton, Charles V., *Black Power: The Politics of Liberation in America*. New York, Random House, 1967.

Chesnutt, Charles W., *The Colonel's Dream*. New York, Doubleday, Page & Co., 1905.

————, *The Conjure Woman*. Boston, Houghton Mifflin Co., 1899.

————, *The House Behind the Cedars*. New York, The Macmillan Co., 1969.

————, *The Marrow of Tradition*. Ann Arbor, Michigan, Univ. of Michigan Press, 1969.

————, *The Wife of His Youth and Other Stories*, Ann Arbor, Michigan, Univ. of Michigan Press, 1968.

Chesnutt, Helen M., *Charles Waddell Chesnutt*. Chapel Hill, Univ. of North Carolina Press, 1952.

Clarke, John Henrik, ed., *William Styron's Nat Turner: Ten Black Writers Respond*. Boston, Beacon Press, 1969.

Cleaver, Eldridge, *Soul on Ice*. New York, McGraw-Hill, 1968.

Cook, Fred J., *The Muckrakers*. New York, Doubleday & Co., Inc., 1972.

Conrad, Earl, *The Invention of the Negro*. New York, Paul S. Eriksson, Inc., 1966.

Cothran, Tilman C., ed., *A Collection of Annual Critiques* (1948–1965). University Microfilms, 1968.

Cronon, Edmund David, *Black Moses: The Story of Marcus Garvey and the Universal Negro Improvement Association*. Madison, Wisconsin, Univ. of Wisconsin Press, 1955 (also revised ed., 1966).

Crossman, Richard, ed., *The God that Failed*. New York, Harper & Row, 1949.

Cruse, Harold, *The Crisis of the Negro Intellectual*. New York, William Morrow & Co., Inc., 1967.

Davis, Arthur P., and Redding, Saunders, eds., *Cavalcade: Negro American Writing from 1760 to the Present Time*. Boston, Houghton Mifflin Co., 1971.

Degler, Carl N., *Out of Our Past: The Forces That Shaped Modern America*. New York, Harper & Row, 1959.

Delany, Martin Robison, *Blake; or the Huts of America*. Boston, Beacon Press, 1970.

————, *The Condition, Elevation, Emigration and Destiny of the Colored People of the United States*. New York, Arno Press and the New York *Times*, 1969.

Demby, William, *Beetlecreek*. New York, Avon Books, 1967.

———, *The Catacombs*. New York, Random House, 1965.

Dixon, Thomas, Jr., *The Leopard's Spots*. New York, Doubleday, Page & Co., 1902.

Dunbar, Paul Laurence, *The Love of Landru*. New York, Dodd, Mead & Co., 1900.

———, *The Uncalled*. Miami, Florida, Mnemosyne Publishing Co., Inc., 1969, New York, Dodd, Mead & Co., 1898.

Du Bois, William E. B., *The Autobiography of W. E. B. Du Bois*. New York, International Publishers Co., Inc., 1968.

———, *Dusk of Dawn: An Essay Toward an Autobiography of a Race Concept*. New York, Schocken Books, 1968.

———, *The Quest of the Silver Fleece*. Miami, Florida, Mnemosyne Publishing Co., Inc., 1969.

———, *The Souls of Black Folk*. Greenwich, Conn., Fawcett Publications, Inc., 1961.

Eckman, Fern, Marja, *The Furious Passage of James Baldwin*. New York, M. Evans & Co., 1966.

Edwards, Adolph, *Marcus Garvey: 1887–1940*. London and Port of Spain, New Beacon Publications, 1967.

Ellison, Ralph, *Invisible Man*. New York, Random House, 1952.

———, *Shadow and Act*. New York, The New American Library, Inc., 1966.

Emanuel, James A., *Langston Hughes*. New York, Twayne Pub., 1967.

Fanon, Frantz, *The Wretched of the Earth*. New York, Grove Press, Inc., 1963.

Fauset, Jessie Redmond, *Comedy: American Style*. New York, Frederick A. Stokes Co., 1933.

———, *Plum Bun: A Novel Without a Moral*. New York, Frederick A. Stokes Co., 1928.

Fauset, Jessie Redmond. *There Is Confusion*. New York, Boni & Liveright, 1924.

Fisher, Rudolph, *The Conjure-Man Dies*. New York, Arno Press and the New York *Times,* 1971.

———, *The Walls of Jericho*. New York, Arno Press and the New York *Times,* 1969.

Farrison, William Edward, *William Wells Brown: Author and Reformer*. Chicago and London, Univ. of Chicago Press, 1969.

Foner, Phillip S., ed., *The Life and Writings of Frederick Douglass: Early Years*. New York, International Publishers Co., Inc., 1950.

———, *The Life and Writings of Frederick Douglass: Pre-Civil War Decade, 1850–1860*. New York, International Publishers Co., Inc., 1950.

———, *The Life and Writings of Frederick Douglass: The Civil War*. New York, International Publishers Co., Inc., 1952.

———, *The Life and Writings of Frederick Douglass: Reconstruction and After*. New York, International Publishers Co., Inc., 1955.

Fox, Stephen R., *The Guardian of Boston: William Monroe Trotter*. New York, Atheneum Pubs., 1970.

Franklin, John Hope, and Starr, Isidore, eds., *The Negro in Twentieth Century America*. New York, Random House, 1967.

Frazier, E. Franklin, *Black Bourgeoisie*. New York, The Macmillan Co., 1969.

Friedenberg, Edgar Z., et al., eds., *The Cosmos Reader*. New York, Harcourt Brace Jovanovich, Inc., 1971.

Gaines, Ernest J., *The Autobiography of Miss Jane Pittman*. New York, The Dial Press, 1971.

————, *Catherine Carmier*. Chatham, New Jersey, The Chatham Bookseller, 1964.

————, *Of Love and Dust*. New York, The Dial Press, 1967.

Gayle, Addison, Jr., *The Black Aesthetic*. New York, Doubleday & Co., Inc., 1971.

————, ed., *Black Expression*. New York, Weybright and Talley, 1969.

Garvey, A. Jacques, *Garvey and Garveyism*. Kingston, Jamaica, A. Jacques Garvey, 1963.

Gloster, Hugh M., *Negro Voices in American Fiction*. Chapel Hill, Univ. of North Carolina Press, 1948.

Griggs, Sutton E., *The Hindered Hand: or the Region of the Repressionist*. Nashville, Tennessee, Orion Publishing Co., 1905.

————, *Imperium in Imperio*. Miami, Florida, Mnemosyne Publishing Inc., 1969.

————, *Overshadowed*. Nashville, Tennessee, Orion Publishing Co., 1901.

————, *Pointing the Way*. Nashville, Tennessee, Orion Publishing Co., 1908.

————, *The Unfettered*. Nashville, Tennessee, Orion Publishing Co., 1902.

————, *Wisdom Calls*. Miami, Florida, Mnemosyne Publishing Co., 1969.

Gross, Seymour L., and Hardy, John Edward, eds., *Images of the Negro in American Literature*. Chicago, The Univ. of Chicago Press, 1966.

Herskovits, Melville J., *The Myth of the Negro Past*. Boston, Beacon Press, 1941.

Hill, Herbert, ed., *Anger and Beyond*. New York, Harper & Row, 1966.

————, *Soon One Morning: New Writing by American Negroes, 1940–1962*. New York, Alfred A. Knopf, 1966.

Himes, Chester, *If He Hollers, Let Him Go*. New York, Doubleday & Co., Inc., 1946.

————, *Lonely Crusade*. New York, Knopf, 1947.

————, *The Primitive*. New York, The New American Library, Inc., 1955.

————, *The Quality of Hurt: The Autobiography of Chester Himes*. New York, Doubleday & Co., Inc., 1972.

Huggins, Nathan Irvin, *Harlem Renaissance*. New York, Oxford University Press, 1971.

Hughes, Carl Milton, *The Negro Novelist, 1940–1950*. New York, Negro Citadel Press, 1970.

Hughes, Langston, *The Big Sea*. New York, Hill & Wang, 1949.

———, *I Wonder As I Wander*. New York, Hill & Wang, 1956.

Hurston, Zora Neal, *Their Eyes Were Watching God*. New York, Negro Univ. Press, 1969.

Jahn, Jameheinz, *Neo-African Literature: A History of Black Writing*. New York, Grove Press, 1969.

Johnson, James Weldon, *Along The Way*. New York, The Viking Press, 1933.

———, *The Autobiography of an Ex-Coloured Man*. New York, Hill & Wang, 1960.

———, *Black Manhattan*. New York, Atheneum Pubs., 1968.

———, *The Book of American Negro Poetry*. New York, Harcourt, Brace, World, Inc., 1922.

Jones, Leroi, and Neal, Larry, eds., *Black Fire*. New York, William Morrow Co., 1968.

Kelley, William Melvin, *A Different Drummer*. New York, Doubleday & Co., Inc., 1962.

———, *Dunsfords Travels Everywheres*. New York, Doubleday & Co., Inc., 1969.

Kent, George, *Blackness and the Adventure of Western Culture*. Chicago, Third World Press, 1972.

Killens, John Oliver, *And Then We Heard the Thunder*. New York, Knopf, 1962.

———, *The Cotillion; or, One Good Bull Is Half the Herd*. New York, Simon & Schuster, 1971.

———, *Youngblood*. New York, Dial Press, 1954.

King, Martin Luther, Jr., *Where Do We Go from Here: Chaos or Community*. New York, Harper & Row, 1967.

Larsen, Nella, *Quicksand*. New York, Collier-Macmillan, 1971.

Lee, Don L., *We Walk the Way of the New World*. Detroit, Broadside Press, 1970.

Locke, Alain, ed., *The New Negro: An Interpretation*. New York, Albert & Charles Boni, 1925.

McKay, Claude, *Banana Bottom*. Chatham, New Jersey, The Chatham Bookseller, 1970.

———, *Banjo*. New York, Harcourt & Brace, 1929.

———, *Harlem: Negro Metropolis*. New York, Dutton & Co., 1949.

———, *Home to Harlem*. New York, Harper & Bros., 1928.

———, *A Long Way from Home*. New York, Lee Furman, Inc., 1937.

McPherson, James M., Holland, Laurence B., Banner, James M., Weiss, Nancy J., and Bell, Michael D., eds., *Blacks in America: Bibliographical Essays*. New York, Doubleday & Co., Inc., 1971.

Maglangbayan, Shawna, *Garvey, Lumumba, Malcolm: National-Separatists*. Chicago, Third World Press, 1972.

Margolies, Edward, *Native Sons; A Critical Study of Twentieth Century Negro American Authors*. Philadelphia, J. B. Lippincott Co., 1968.

Marshall, Paule, *Brown Girl, Brownstones*. New York, Avon Books, 1970.

Meier, August, Rudwick, Elliott, and Broderick, Francis L., *Black Protest Thought in the Twentieth Century*. New York, The Bobbs-Merrill Co., 1971.

North, Joseph, ed., *New Masses: An Anthology of the Rebel Thirties*. New York, International Publishers, 1969.

Nye, Russell Blaine, *The Cultural Life of the New Nation, 1776–1800*. New York, Harper & Row, 1960.

Ottley, Roi, *New World A-Coming: Inside Black America*. Boston, Houghton Mifflin Co., 1943.

Parrington, Vernon Louis, *Main Currents in American Thought: Beginnings of Critical Realism in America, 1860–1920*. New York, Harcourt, Brace, World, Inc., 1930.

Petry, Ann, *The Narrows*. New York, Pyramid Publications, Inc., 1971.

———, *The Street*. New York, Pyramid Publications, Inc., 1966.

Ransom, John Crowe, et al., *I'll Take My Stand*. New York, Harpers Brothers, 1962.

Ray, David, and Farnsworth, Robert M., eds., *Richard Wright: Impressions and Perspectives*. Michigan, Univ. of Michigan Press, 1973.

Record, Wilson, *The Negro and the Communist Party*. New York, Atheneum Pubs., 1971.

———, *Race and Radicalism: The NAACP and the Communist Party in Conflict*. Ithaca, New York, Cornell University Press, 1964.

Redding, J. Saunders, *On Being Negro in America*. Indianapolis, The Bobbs-Merrill Co., 1951.

———, *They Came in Chains*. Philadelphia, J. B. Lippincott Co., 1950.

———, *To Make a Poet Black*. Chapel Hill, Univ. of North Carolina Press, 1939.

Rudwick, Elliot M., *W. E. B. Du Bois: Propagandist of the Negro Protest*. New York, Atheneum Pubs., 1968.

Schwartz, Barry N., and Disch, Robert, eds., *White Racism*. New York, Dell Pub. Co., Inc., 1970.

Smith, William Gardner, *The Stone Face*. New York, Farrar, Straus, Giroux, 1963.

Spiller, Robert E. *The Cycle of American Literature*. New York, The Macmillan Co., 1955.

Stern, Milton R., and Gross, Seymour L., *American Literature Survey: The Twentieth Century*. New York, The Viking Press, 1962.

Sterling, Dorothy, *The Making of an Afro-American: Martin Robison Delany: 1812–1885*. New York, Doubleday & Co., Inc., 1971.

Schuyler, George, *Black No More*. New York, The New American Library, 1969.

Stanton, William, *The Leopard's Spots: Scientific Attitudes Toward Race in America, 1815–1859*. Chicago, Univ. of Chicago Press, 1960.

Styron, William, *The Confessions of Nat Turner*. New York, The New American Library, 1968.

Thurman, Wallace, *The Blacker the Berry,* New York, The Macmillan Co., 1970.

Toomer, Jean, *Cane.* New York, University Place Press, 1967.

Turner, Arlin, ed., *The Negro Question: A Selection of Writings on Civil Rights in the South by George W. Cable.* New York, W. W. Norton & Co., 1958.

Van Vechten, Carl, *Nigger Heaven.* New York, Harper & Row, 1971.

Vinson, James, ed., *Contemporary Novelists.* New York, St. Martin's Press, 1972.

Walker, David, *David Walker's Appeals in Four Articles.* New York, Hill & Wang, 1965.

Washington, Booker T., *The Future of the American Negro.* Boston, Small, Maynard & Co., 1899.

————, *Up from Slavery.* New York, A. L. Burt Co., 1900.

Warren, Robert Penn, *Who Speaks for the Negro?* New York, Random House, 1965.

Webb, Constance, *Richard Wright: A Biography.* New York, G. P. Putnam Sons, 1968.

Webb, Frank S., *The Garies and Their Friends.* New York, Arno Press and the New York *Times,* 1969.

Weitz, Morris, *Problems in Aesthetics.* New York, The Macmillan Co., 1959.

Wellek, René, and Warren, Austin, *Theory of Literature.* New York, Harcourt, Brace & World, Inc., 1956.

Wiggins, Lida Keck, *The Life and Works of Paul Laurence Dunbar.* Naperville, Ill., J. L. Nichols & Co., 1907.

Wilson, Edmund, *Classics and Commercials.* New York, Random House, 1962.

————, *Eight Essays.* New York, Doubleday & Co., Inc., 1954.

————, *Patriotic Gore: Studies in the Literature of the American Civil War.* New York, Oxford University Press, 1966.

————, ed., *The Shock of Recognition.* New York, Grosset & Dunlap, 1943.

Williams, John A., *Captain Blackman.* New York, Doubleday & Co., Inc., 1972.

————, *The King God Didn't Save.* New York, Coward-McCann, Inc., 1970.

————, *The Man Who Cried I Am.* Boston and Toronto, Little, Brown & Co., 1967.

————, *Sissie.* New York, Farrar, Straus, Cudahy, 1963.

————, *Sons of Darkness, Sons of Light.* Boston and Toronto, Little, Brown & Co., 1969.

Williams, Sherley Anne, *Give Birth to Brightness.* New York, The Dial Press, 1972.

Wright, Richard, *Lawd Today.* New York, Walker & Co., 1963.

————, *Native Son.* New York, Harper & Row, 1940.

————, *Uncle Tom's Children*. Cleveland, Ohio, The World Publishing Co., 1936.

————, *The Outsider*. New York, Harper & Row, 1953.

————, and Rosskam, Edwin, *12 Million Black Voices*. New York, The Viking Press, 1941.

Young, Thomas Daniel, Watkins, Floyd C., and Beatty, Richard Croom, *The Literature of the South*. Glenview, Illinois, Scott, Foresman & Co., 1968.

Zabel, Morton Dauwen, *Literary Opinion in America*. Vol. 1. New York, Harper & Row, 1962.

————, *Literary Opinion in America*. Vol II. New York, Harper & Row, 1962.

Zinn, Howard, *The New Abolitionists*. Boston, Beacon Press, Inc., 1964.

INDEX